Beginning Psychology

Fifth Edition

Malcolm Hardy
Steve Heyes

OXFORD

UNIVERSITY PRESS

OXFORD
UNIVERSITY PRESS

Great Clarendon Street, Oxford OX2 6DP

Oxford University Press is a department of the University of Oxford.
It furthers the University's objective of excellence in research, scholarship, and
education by publishing worldwide in

Oxford New York

Auckland Bangkok Buenos Aires Cape Town Chennai
Dar es Salaam Delhi Hong Kong Istanbul Karachi Kolkata
Kuala Lumpur Madrid Melbourne Mexico City Mumbai Nairobi
São Paulo Shanghai Taipei Tokyo Toronto

Oxford is a registered trade mark of Oxford University Press
in the UK and in certain other countries

First published 1979
Second edition 1985
Third edition 1987
Fourth edition published by Oxford University Press 1994
Fifth edition 1999
10 9 8 7 6 5 4 3

British Library Cataloguing in publication Data

Data available

ISBN 0 19 832 821 4

Typeset in Ehrhardt by Advance Typesetting Ltd, Long Hanborough, Oxon
Printed in Hong Kong

*To Pam, Trish, Emma, Agnes, Sam, Eileen, Len, Tim, Peter
and Matthew, and to our students – pass, Present and future*

Contents

Preface to the Fifth Edition

At a party given by an astronaut and her husband it was discovered that the household's electric kettle had broken. The woman asked each guest in turn to mend it (they were all expert engineers). None of them would attempt it, and all gave the same reply: 'Sorry, ma'am, I'm not that kind of engineer.'

Often the response of people who are asked to take part in a psychology experiment is: 'What will it tell me about my personality?' even when it has been explained to them that the experiment is designed to measure something as unromantic as speed of reaction. Psychology is becoming more and more specialized. Few psychologists spend their time sitting next to patients lying on couches; these days a psychologist is likely to be an expert in a particular field – learning, memory, or perception, for example – and not in psychology as a whole: 'Sorry, ma'am, I'm not that kind of psychologist.' However, psychologists have one thing in common: they all study *behaviour*. Behaviour is a very broad term: anything an organism does is behaviour. This explains why nobody is an expert on psychology as a whole: there is simply too much behaviour for one person to understand.

The aim of this book is to show how different psychologists approach the study of behaviour, and to describe the kinds of things which they have found. No book could hope to show all the findings gained over the last ninety years or so in which scientific psychology has largely developed. We have therefore taken a cross-section of the subject to try and demonstrate its range.

In recent years there has been a growth in the awareness of the responsibilities that psychologists have when studying human or animal behaviour. For this reason we have started this edition by looking at the ethics of research. Other early chapters of the book deal with the basics of how we receive information from the world, understand it, learn from it and remember it. When discussing topics such as perception, learning and memory, psychologists often concentrate on the individual acting on their own, and so to redress the balance later chapters look at the way that we understand other people, the effects of others on our behaviour and how we learn to fit in with society through the process of socialization. Towards the end of the book is a chapter on the basics of the nervous system – after all without the 'nuts and bolts' we would not be able to understand, learn and mix with others.

Above all, psychology is a practical subject and so the final chapter is intended to help you design your own pieces of research, analyze them and report your work to other people.

We have planned the order of the chapters logically but each chapter can be read on its own – so the book can be read through like a novel or the reader can be selective and dip into it wherever they like. No matter which approach is chosen, it is well worth bearing in mind two things:

1 Any psychology book will be split into chapters, dealing with different aspects of behaviour, but in a human being several kinds of behaviour can be going on at the same time.
2 Individuals' experiences, needs and hopes differ; no book would be able to tell everybody what they want to know. So the reader should constantly ask himself the question, 'How could this apply to me?' or 'How could I apply this?'

The Fourth Edition of this book was based on the Northern Examining Association's GCSE syllabus, and the Fifth Edition now incorporates material for the Midland Examining Group's syllabus. However, some chapters go beyond the strict requirements of GCSE so that the book can serve as an introduction to psychology for students on other courses up to undergraduate level.

The book is the result of a joint experience in the teaching of psychology at varied levels in Further Education over several years. Our students have acted as guinea pigs for most of the work in the book; we have been encouraged by their reactions to it, and by the enthusiasm which they seem to have developed for psychology generally. We hope, therefore, that this book will prove to be equally interesting to the general reader, whether or not it is used for an examination.

Our thanks are due to Eileen Heyes and Pamela Hardy for typing the manuscript, correcting our spelling mistakes and proofreading. In addition, we are most grateful to Paul Humphreys for his generous contribution to the section on writing reports on practical work and to Tim Heyes for his help with the section on study tips. Our thanks also go to Jenny Crews for all her help and support.

We were tremendously pleased to see the success of the first four editions of this book, and are most grateful to those people who wrote to us with corrections, comments and suggestions. We hope to hear from you about this one too.

Cheshire, January 1999   MALCOLM HARDY
                                                         STEVE HEYES

Chapter 1

The Ethics of Research

Psychology is the scientific study of behaviour and experience. The use of the word 'scientific' in that definition implies that we do more than simply think about behaviour and its causes. Psychologists observe behaviour and make hypotheses (or guesses) about what causes or affects it; they then test those hypotheses by making further observations, asking questions or performing experiments.

When we first became involved in psychology we were very attracted by this practical research bias to the subject and that as students we could make hypotheses and test them and did not simply have to accept facts given from on high. The best research, of course, usually results from a thorough knowledge of the subject, but sometimes the fresh mind can make a breakthrough that others have missed by going along with accepted wisdom.

While encouraging you to get involved in the practical side of psychology as early as possible it is important to draw your attention to the ethical constraints within which we must all work.

There is a story that a king in the Middle Ages imprisoned a child and deprived him of all human contact in order to settle an argument about whether Latin or Greek was the most natural language. He expected that without the normal exposure to English the child would grow up speaking one or other of the classical languages. In fact the boy died before any language development had taken place. There is always a danger when we are dreaming up new research projects that we are seduced by the attractions of new knowledge into using methods which, although rarely as extreme as the king's, are ethically questionable. When discussing the ethics of research we are talking about the morality of our methods and what is acceptable behaviour on the part of researchers.

Nobody these days would find the king's research acceptable, but where exactly do we draw the line between what is ethical and what is not? In the 1960s Milgram performed a well-known study of obedience. We will look more closely at the details in a later chapter but participants were told that they were helping a study of the effects of punishment on memory and were instructed to give an electric shock to a learner each time they made a mistake in a memory task. The size of the electric shock was raised with every mistake and when participants questioned the advisability of going on with the study they were told to continue. A remarkable number of people went on to administer shocks of up to 450 volts under these conditions despite the screams and apparent collapse of the recipient. Milgram was able to vary the study to tease out the major variables affecting obedience to authority. In reality the participant was not giving electric shocks, though they believed that they were at the time. Milgram and others believe that the study taught us much about human nature. The study could not have been done without deceiving the participants as to the nature of the investigation. Many participants found the study very stressful and probably discovered things about themselves that they might rather not have known. Is this acceptable? What do you think?

Research in psychology and other disciplines has produced many benefits which range from providing new insights into why we behave as we do to techniques that help those suffering from a variety of different behavioural problems. There is a tendency for researchers to emphasize the benefits of the results of their research but to minimize the costs, particularly those of the participants. Ethical decisions often involve weighing the balance between costs (in the widest sense) and benefits; the bias of researchers means that it is important to have clear guidelines to ensure that their enthusiasm doesn't carry them away.

One of the roles of professional bodies is to draw up codes of ethics that all members of the profession must adhere to. The British Psychological Society (BPS) produces the ethical guidelines for psychological research.

The main ethical guidelines for conducting psychological research are:

- The researcher has an obligation to consider the ethical implications and consequences of the study being contemplated.
- Whenever possible participants should be volunteers with full knowledge of what the study is about and they should be aware that they can withdraw from the study at any stage. If the participants are children then consent should be gained from their parents or an adult *in loco parentis*. There is an obligation to debrief the participant giving information about the findings of the study.
- Researchers must not reveal details of individuals and their behaviour. Participants are never referred to by name in any report of the study.
- Researchers have a responsibility to ensure the safety of participants.
- There may be times when the researcher feels that it would be impossible to perform a study without contravening one of the above ethical guidelines. It is not enough for the researcher to believe that the benefits of the study outweigh the costs of breaking the guideline; he or she should convince an ethical committee made up of experienced people who have no personal interest in the proposed study.

- An ethical committee should definitely be involved if the study involves deception of participants, exposing them to stress or invading their privacy.

Ethical considerations have always been important in research but there has been a cultural change in the social sciences over the last twenty years which has given them greater prominence. A number of well-known and, some would argue, important studies such as those of Milgram which were performed in the 1960s and 1970s would probably be turned down if proposed to one of today's ethical committees. Until very recently the people we studied in our research, especially in experiments, were known as 'subjects'. This change reflects the change of culture with regard to the way the social scientists view the people involved in their studies; the word 'subject' is associated with somebody who is passive, who has the experiment *done* to them under the control of the experimenter. The title 'participant' attempts to reflect the view that these are individuals who voluntarily join us in our research and are entitled to be treated in a manner which reflects their equal status.

There are laws to restrict animal research which involves deprivation and pain though many people feel that the legal system should offer far more protection. Many readers will feel that some of the studies reported in chapter 15 on the development of perception and chapter 17 on the functions of parts of the brain are extremely questionable on ethical grounds. It is noticeable that most of this research dates from a few decades ago and that more recent studies in these areas focus on human beings and are much easier to accept as ethical as well as being more relevant.

Further Reading

'Ethical principles for conducting research with human participants,' *Psychologist*, Vol. 6, No. 1, January 1993.

Chapter 2

Perception

Seeing, hearing, tasting, smelling and feeling are so easy for most of us that we often overlook the fact that the brain has to do a lot of work to build up the detailed model of the world that we carry around in our heads. Surely, you would think, all that has to be done is point the eyes at something and a picture appears in the brain. The reality is far more complicated than that and the information coming in from the sense organs is only one part of it.

One of the problems is the sheer amount of information being fed into the brain at any one time. If you paid conscious attention to all this information you could never get on with anything. As you are reading this your brain is also receiving information about how hot or cold it is in the room, how comfortable your seating position is, what your clothes and shoes feel like and a thousand and one other things.

Psychologists call anything which stimulates any of our senses a *stimulus* (plural, *stimuli*). The images which are formed in your eye are therefore stimuli. Brunswik calls stimuli such as these *proximal stimuli*, meaning that they occur at the proximity, or boundaries, of the individual. Look at figure 2.1 below. What does it say? Did you notice the repetition of the word 'the'? The proximal stimulus (the image of the figure on your retina) contained two 'the's' but most people do not perceive both of them. We do not expect to see two 'the's' together.

Figure 2.1

4

The proximal stimulus at the eye is only the start of the perceptual process.

The Physiology of Perception

The brain cannot deal directly with light. It can deal only with information in the form of electrical impulses. It is therefore the function of all sense organs to translate physical information – light or sound waves, for example – into electrical impulses. This translation, or *transduction*, means that for each type of external stimulus there must be an electrical impulse code. This section looks at how transduction occurs, and what routes the coded information takes to the brain. Only the major system vision will be described here, but the same general procedures occur for all sensory information.

However, before the research in these areas is described a very important point must be made. The physiology of vision shows how coded electrical 'pictures' of the outside world reach the brain; but we know that once there, this information is reorganized and interpreted by the brain. The pictures entering the eye are usually not exactly the same as the finished perception. As a result of previous learning, motivation and emotion, the same individual may interpret the same retinal image in different ways at different times.

As an example, imagine taking a walk in the country with a biologist and a geologist. The biologist might see many kinds of plants and flowers, while you might just see a mass of greenery; the geologist might see escarpments and moraines where you can only see hills. Their previous learning and different interests will have enabled them to extract much more information from their retinal images than you could. But because their interests are different – biological events versus geological – they will each have extracted different information from their retinal images.

The Visual System

Light passes through the cornea and lens of the eye and is focused onto the retina, causing nerve impulses which describe the image (see figure 2.2). The nerve impulses are passed to the brain via the optic nerve.

The retina contains two types of light sensitive cells called *rods* and *cones*.

RODS

These cells are mainly responsible for vision in low levels of light, and at the edges of the retina. They do not signal colours, and give only black-and-white vision.

Figure 2.2 Cross-sectional Diagram of the Human Eye

CONES

These are responsible for colour vision and fine-detail vision. The small region of the retina which gives the most detailed vision, the centre of the *fovea*, consists entirely of cones. However, cones only work well in good illumination; at night, or in low levels of illumination, the cones are not effective and the rods take over. This is why one does not see much colour at night.

The 'picture' which is passed up to the brain must be of very poor quality because the neurons which take the nerve impulses from the rods and cones are actually in front of the light-sensitive cells (see figure 2.3).

Figure 2.3 A Simplified Diagram of the Inverted Retina showing the Three Main Layers of Cells

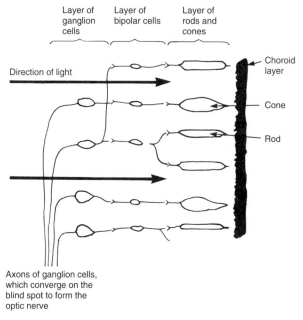

The axons of the ganglion cells leave the eye via the *blind spot* to form the optic nerve. The blind spot is so called because it has no rods or cones, so that an image falling on this part of the retina is not sent to the brain. The brain normally compensates for this small area of lack of information but its effects can be shown in special circumstances.

Close your right eye and view the spot with your left eye directly in front of the spot. Move the page slowly towards and away from you and keep your gaze fixed on the spot. At some point (when the image hits the blind spot) the cross will disappear. The nerves from each eye cross at the optic chiasma in such a way that information from the left of each eye goes to the left hemisphere and that from the right half goes to the right hemisphere; this ensures that each hemisphere receives two slightly different pictures of the same part of the visual field, helping to produce a three-dimensional mental picture from the two-dimensional retinal images (see figure 2.4). The nerve impulses pass up to part of the thalamus known as the *lateral geniculate body* (LGB), which contains many synapses. The function of the LGB is unknown but it has a large number of connections with the reticular activating system (see page 306), and may therefore be involved in the process of attention. From the LGB the nerve impulses pass on to the visual cortex for an analysis which results eventually in the 'mental picture' which most of us take for granted. The mental picture is built up not only from information from the eyes but also by reference to previous experience,

Figure 2.4 Diagrammatic View of Human Visual Pathways

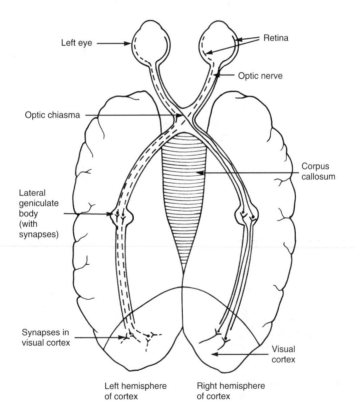

motivations and emotions, so many parts of the brain have an indirect involvement in perception.

Some nerve fibres branch off before the LGB and travel to the *superior colliculus* which has a role in the control of eye movements and in the perception of where objects are. Animals with damage in this area of the brain have no difficulty recognising objects but seem to have difficulty deciding exactly where they are; perhaps the experience is similar to that of a drunk trying to find the hole in which to put his key!

Perception of Shape

Many cells in the visual cortex change their activity when light is shone on to a particular area of the retina; this area is called the *receptive field* of the cortical cell. In 1963 D. Hubel and T. Wiesel discovered these receptive fields by shining spots and bars of light onto a screen in front of a cat, and at the same time monitoring the activity of single cells using microelectrodes which were implanted into the cortex of the anaesthetized animal (one eye was used and the other was blindfolded). They found two main types of cortical cell.

SIMPLE CELLS

These are cells near the surface of the cortex. Hubel and Wiesel found that these cells fired when a bar of light was shone on to the retina. An individual simple cell would fire if the line produced by the bar of light was on a particular part of the retina and in a specific orientation. Some cells only responded to vertical lines; others to horizontal or diagonal lines (see figure 2.5). Under normal circumstances the lines stimulating the receptive fields of these simple cells would be produced by the edges and contours of objects being viewed.

*Figure 2.5 The Receptive Field of a Simple Cortical Cell. The only stimulus which will make this simple cortical cell fire is an edge or line at this angle \ . Therefore, this simple cortical cell represents \ – if it was artificially stimulated (for example by a micro-electrode) you would actually see *

Rods and cones on retina

Part of optic nerve

L.G.B. cells

Simple cortical cell in visual cortex

Image of boat on retina

COMPLEX CELLS

These cells are found when the microelectrodes are pushed deeper into the cortex. Like simple cells they are responsive to lines in specific orientations, but they are not as particular about the part of the retina on which the light falls.

The way in which cells of the visual cortex are particularly responsive to lines which form the edges of objects may explain the very clear mental pictures that we produce. Television pictures from space probes are 'tidied up' by computer in a similar way. The shape of an object will be coded by the overall activity of the cortical cells with receptive fields in the area of the retina which receives its image. In 1972 Gross *et al.* found a cell in the temporal lobe of a monkey which responded only to a picture of a monkey's hand. Cells which respond to complicated shapes like this are known as *hypercomplex cells*, and some people have argued that every shape that we recognize is coded by these cells.

Movement

When the eye is stationary the image of a moving object passes across the receptive fields of many cortical cells. Movement can then be coded by the passage of excitation from one cell to another, and also by some cortical cells which only fire when an object passes in a particular direction across its receptive field. The detection of movement is, however, more complicated than this, since images pass across the retina when the eye is moved even though movement of the eye does not cause the world to appear to move in front of the observer. The reason for this appears to be that as nerve impulses pass from the brain to the eye muscles they also act on the movement-perception system, so that when the command is made to move the eyes, this also counteracts the effect of images passing across the receptive fields; these are perceived as static if they move in the opposite direction to the eye at a speed similar to that of the eye. An image that remains on the same spot of the retina while the eye moves is perceived as moving, which is why we can follow an object with our eyes and perceive it as moving in relation to its background.

The brain can compensate for the fact that the whole body is moving in the analysis of images moving across the retina so that a driver perceives the road as still while he moves along. Confusion sometimes occurs when inadequate information is available. For example, when you are looking out of a carriage window at a station, it can be difficult to decide whether it is your train or the one adjacent that has started to move.

The perceptual system uses more than the information concerning movement of the eyes and passage of images across the retina in deciding what is moving. As K. Duncker showed, the brain takes account of the size of objects in deciding on relative movement. He shone a spot of light on to a large screen and moved the screen to the right. Most observers reported that they saw the screen as stationary and the spot of light moving to the left: the perceptual system assumes that smaller objects are more likely to move. In this example the perception of movement contradicts the information from the eye and image-movement systems.

The Psychology of Perception

Look up from the book for a moment at the scene in front of you. You will see a world that has three dimensions – height, width and depth. No great surprise in that but think about the job that the perceptual system has to do in order to built the three-dimensional model of the world that you experience. Light from the scene in front of you was focused on the retina at the back of the eye to form an image which caused nerve impulses which were passed back to the brain to be interpreted. The image on the retina is very much like that formed on a film at the back of a camera; it is two-dimensional. The image has height and width but it has no depth. The brain has to put depth back into the picture by analyzing the retinal image and looking for clues to decide which objects are close to you and which are further away. Any artist who has mastered the technique of putting depth into their landscapes could describe to you what the brain is looking for; the difference is that the artist spent years mastering the technique using deliberate strategies but the brain does it all unconsciously in what seems like no time at all. Some of the clues that the brain uses go beyond the techniques used by artists and take advantage of the fact that we have two eyes; these are known as *binocular depth cues*. Clues which only require the examination of one retinal image are known as *monocular depth cues*.

Monocular Depth Cues

1 Linear perspective. If there are lines in the image which appear to converge this may be because the object we are looking at stretches away into the distance (as when looking along a straight road, for example).
2 Interposition. An object which partially blocks our view of another object must be in front of it (see figure 2.6.).
3 Texture gradient. If, for example, you stood on a pebble beach, you would be able to see pebbles of difference sizes close to you. The further away you look, the more even the texture appears to be.
4 Relative size. Objects which are further away will produce a smaller image on the retina than the same object nearby.
5 Height in the visual plane. As a general rule, the higher up your field of view something is, the further away it is.
6 Motion parallax. This is a cue that a painter cannot use. It comes to us because the head and eyes are usually moving and when they do the

Figure 2.6

The car is nearer

image on the retina moves. Objects close to the eye will move more quickly across the field of vision than those which are further away. This effect is particularly noticeable if you look out of a train; an object on the side of the track seems to fly by but a tree in the distance passes slowly across the window.

Binocular Depth Cues

RETINAL DISPARITY

Because your two eyes are separated by about 7 cm, each eye receives a slightly different image of the world. You can show this yourself if you hold one finger in front of your face, about 25 cm in front of your nose, then look at it with your right eye (close your left eye), then use the left eye, closing your right eye this time. If you do this several times quite quickly you will see your finger apparently 'jump' from side to side as each eye sees it from a different angle. The brain seems to 'overlap' these two images, and it uses the differences in the position of objects, to give an impression of depth. The general rule seems to be that the greater the difference in the position of an object, the nearer it is. The brain's treatment of retinal disparity gives us an impression of depth, but we also have a second process which acts like a range finder to tell us the distance of objects.

CONVERGENCE

Hold a finger at arm's length directly in front of you, and fix your gaze on it. Gradually bring your finger towards your nose and keep focusing on it with both eyes. As your finger nears your nose, you can feel your eyes turning towards each other and somebody watching you would see you go cross-eyed. This turning of the eyes towards each other is called *convergence* and it is the second binocular depth cue which the brain uses. The brain uses information about how much the eyes are pointing towards each other as a distance cue. The rule seems to be that the more the eyes have to point towards each other, the nearer the object.

Size Constancy

Another perceptual process which occurs, called constancy scaling, gives an effect called size constancy. You may have noticed that if someone is walking away from you, they seem to get smaller, but not apparently by very much. This relatively small shrinking in perceptual size occurs despite the fact that the image on the retina shrinks by half when they move from 5 to 10 feet away from you. Some perceptual process must keep the size of things fairly constant (that is, it gives us size constancy), even though the size of the retinal image changes greatly. R. L. Gregory calls this process *constancy scaling*. It may help if you think of constancy scaling as being like an automatic perceptual computer program which increases the size of distant objects to keep them looking the same size. Constancy scaling, says Gregory, is switched on by depth cues and the further away the object appears to be, the greater the amount of constancy scaling is applied.

Constancy and Illusions

Constancy scaling seems to happen automatically; it doesn't require us to think about it. Therefore, it can be tricked. Look at the Ponzo illusion (figure 2.7). The top horizontal line looks longer than the line below it despite the fact that they are actually the same size.

Gregory has a general theory to explain this and other illusions of size such as the Muller-Lyer illusion (figure 15.7) and the Orbison illusion (figure 2.8). He argues that these illusions contain false depth cues which trigger the size constancy mechanism inappropriately. In the case of the Ponzo illusion

Figure 2.7 The Ponzo Illusion

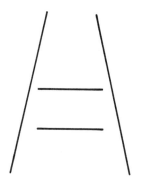

Figure 2.8 The Orbison Illusion

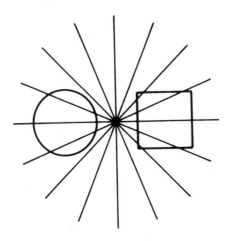

the converging lines are the false depth which suggests that the top line is further away than the other. The size constancy mechanism therefore expands the perceived size of the top line. In most cases automatic triggering of the size constancy mechanism by a simple depth cue would result in an accurate perception – illusions are the price we pay for a system which works so quickly and which produces accurate results 99.5 per cent of the time.

You will have noticed that although the depth cue is strong enough to trigger size constancy it does not fool the system into perceiving the Ponzo figure in three dimensions. The conscious perception of the figure is two-dimensional as a result of the analysis of all the depth cues including those which show that the lines are drawn on a flat piece of paper.

Illusions are relatively rare in the natural world and so there has been no evolutionary pressure to produce a perceptual system which overcomes them.

One illusion which does occur in the natural world is the *moon illusion*. The moon (and sun) appear larger when low down on the horizon than when high in the sky (see figure 2.9). The size of the retinal image of the moon does not change – you can 'black out' the moon by holding a $\frac{1}{4}$-inch disc at arm's length, whether the moon is high or low in the sky. Why, then, does it appear to be much larger when it is near the horizon? One reason sometimes given is that the image of the moon when low down is travelling at a shallow angle through the earth's atmosphere, and the dust and water vapour in the atmosphere somehow 'blur' the moon's edges, making it look larger. However, if you look at the moon high in the sky through smoked glass (which should affect the moon's image rather like dust in the atmosphere is supposed to do), the moon changes little in size, so the 'dust' theory is unlikely to be the best explanation for the moon illusion.

Figure 2.9 The Moon Illusion

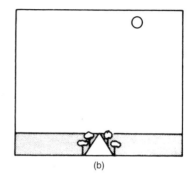

(a)   (b)

A better explanation is constancy scaling. When the moon is high in the sky, there is no depth/distance information visible, so you see the moon as its correct (i.e. retinal image) size. However, when the moon is low down, near the horizon, depth cues come into play. The horizon is as far away as it is possible to see, so anything which is near the horizon (as the moon appears to be) is assumed to be a long way away. Therefore, just as in the Muller-Lyer and Orbison illusions, constancy scaling automatically increases the size.

Shape Constancy

Just as the size of objects doesn't seem to change much when they move towards or away from us, so the shape of objects seems to stay the same, even when the retinal image changes shape drastically. For example, if you look at a door as it is opening it remains door shaped (rectangular) even though the image on the retina changes from rectangular to trapezoid as shown in figure 2.10.

In the same way, we see car wheels as round even though the retinal image is oval when viewed from an angle other than directly side on. These are two examples of shape constancy which suggests that our perceptual systems are keeping the shape of things constant, even though the shape of the retinal image varies.

An experiment by Thouless was an early attempt to demonstrate shape constancy. People were allowed to look through a viewing slit at, for example, a plate on a table. A photograph was also taken through the viewing slit, to show what the retinal image was like. These people were then asked to point out from a series of cardboard shapes, the shape they actually saw (see figure 2.11(b)).

People did not pick out the retinal shape but a shape (called the 'phenomenal shape') part-way between the retinal shape and the real shape

Figure 2.10 Shape Constancy

Figure 2.11 Thouless's Experiment

(a)	(b)
The viewing arrangements	Cardboard shapes from which subject chooses the one originally viewed

of the plate. Thouless called this 'phenomenal regression to the real object' (which means that the perceived shape moved towards the real shape). The perceptual system seems to have 'rounded' the retinal shape to try to keep it more like a plate actually is, rather than like its retinal image.

Bower devised an experiment to see whether young babies had shape constancy. He presented the babies first with a shape like that of the top of figure 2.12 – in fact a triangle with a bar laid over it. The babies were conditioned (see p. 46) to turn their heads whenever the shape was put in front of them. Next, other shapes (A, B, C and D) were shown to the

Figure 2.12 Bower's Shape Constancy Experiment

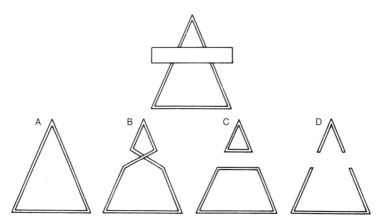

babies, and the amount of head-turning acted as a measurement of how similar they saw the shapes to the original. The results showed quite clearly that the babies, who were only eight weeks old, had shape constancy, because they saw shape A as being most similar to the original; in other words, they could perceive that the original figure was a triangle with something on top, not for example a small triangle with a trapezoid shape underneath as in C.

Brightness and Colour Constancy

The perceptual system has a tendency to keep the brightness and colour of objects fairly constant even when lighting conditions cause changes in pictures taken by a camera. The page you are reading now appears to be printed on white paper whether or not it is in shadow – even though paper in shadow gives a retinal image which is grey. Similarly, a piece of coal looks black, whether under very low or very high levels of illumination.

It seems obvious from this that our perception of the brightness of an object cannot depend solely on the amount of light which it reflects. What seems to happen is that the perceived brightness of an object depends on the percentage of light which it reflects compared with the percentage reflected by its surroundings.

Familiar objects tend to retain their colour under lights of different colours, provided there is enough contrast between the objects and their backgrounds. The perceptual system seems to be asking two questions: 'How does this object reflect light compared with its background?' and 'What colour is the light illuminating the scene?' For example, if the object is reflecting turquoise light, and the overall illumination is blue, the brain computes that the object's real colour is green.

Colour memory can also play a part – if you know something is blue, you tend to perceive it as blue whatever the colour of the light illuminating it.

Colour constancy is probably the least effective of the constancies and it is easily 'fooled'. It disappears, for example, if the background is masked (so there is nothing to compare the object's colour with), and by masking part of the object's shape so that memory colour processes cannot work.

Hypothesis Testing

THE AMES ROOM

Figure 2.13(a) shows what you would see if you looked into an Ames room. Figure 2.13(b) shows how the Ames room is actually constructed – the ceiling slopes down to the right, and the floor slopes down to the left. The room is not rectangular, nor are the 'windows', or 'door'. The person on the left looks small because she is twice as far away from the person on the right.

This illusion shows that the visual retinal impression of a person's size depends on how far away from us they are. The Ames room is constructed to make the back left-hand corner appear to be as near to us as is the back

Figure 2.13(a) The Ames Room

Phil Schermeister

Figure 2.13(b) The Actual Shape of the Ames Room

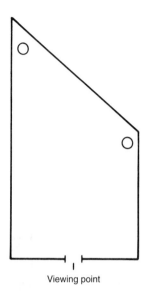

Viewing point

right-hand corner, though in fact it is twice as far away. So strong is this distance and size link that it leads to your perceiving one person as being twice the size of another – even though this is a most unlikely state of affairs. Your perceptual system has to choose between two possibilities (R.L. Gregory calls these *perceptual hypotheses*). Hypothesis 1 is that two people are very different in size, and Hypothesis 2 is that the room is not rectangular, and that the two people are at different distances. The room is constructed so that it is more likely that your perceptual system will accept Hypothesis 1, even though Hypothesis 2 is the correct one.

AMBIGUOUS FIGURES

The Ames room was constructed so that you would believe the false hypothesis. It is possible to construct other figures which also give us two hypotheses to choose between, but this time there isn't enough information in the figure to allow us to choose our hypothesis with certainty. Figure 2.14, the Necker cube, is one such figure – the small circle may be at the bottom left of one face (Hypothesis 1) or the middle of the other face (Hypothesis 2). Both hypotheses are correct, so your perceptual system cannot reject either, and it keeps flip-flopping between them.

Figure 2.14 The Necker Cube

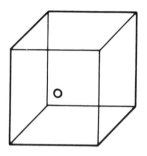

Figure 2.15 The Figure-Ground Illusion

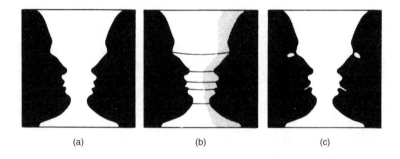

(a)	(b)	(c)

Now try figure 2.15(a). The two hypotheses here are that there are two faces pointing towards each other, or one vase or candlestick. Again, your perceptual system will flip-flop between them, because there is not enough information to enable it to clearly choose one hypothesis only. If, however, the vase were shaded (figure 2.15(b)), or if the faces were given other features (figure 2.15(c)), the ambiguity disappears.

Another famous ambiguous figure is the young woman/old woman picture shown in figure 2.16(a). This figure, too, allows our perceptual systems to make up two hypotheses – one that the picture is of an old woman (like figure 2.16(b)) and the other that it is a young woman (like figure 2.16(c)). There is not enough information in the figure to allow either hypothesis to be accepted as 'real', so we constantly 'flip-flop' between them. It is possible, however, to get people to accept only one of these hypotheses without changing the figure itself. Leeper, who designed the original figures, showed some people figure 2.16(b) first, and to other people he showed figure 2.16(c). Both sets of people were then shown the ambiguous figure (figure 2.16(a)) and the hypothesis which people accepted was the one which they had originally been shown. So, for example, the people shown figure 2.16(b) first would be much more likely to see the old woman.

Figure 2.16(a)   The Ambiguous 'Young/Old Woman' Figure

(a)

Figure 2.16(b) and (c)   Unambiguous Figures Showing Old Woman (b) and Young Woman (c)

(b)   (c)

This is an important study, because it shows how our perceptual hypotheses can be affected by what we expect to see. In addition to expectations, several other factors affect the ways in which we organize and translate the information from our sense organs.

Gregory's theory, then, is that in perception we act like scientists – the perceptual system makes hypotheses (guesses) about what is 'out there' and tries to match the information coming from our senses with those hypotheses. The model of the world that we experience is continually being updated as a result of the matching.

The Gestalt Theory of Perception

Gestalt psychologists working in Germany in the 1920s developed several laws of perceptual organization. 'Gestalt' can be translated as 'shape' or 'form', and Gestalt psychologists believed that the laws of perceptual organization are innate and cause us to perceive things as a whole rather than as a series of separate items. For example, if a series of still pictures is shown one after the other (as in a film) we tend to see the situation not as a series of separate pictures but as a scene involving movement.

The main Gestalt laws of perceptual organization are:

FIGURE/GROUND

We are innately programmed to perceive things standing out from a background (see figure 2.15). We can't perceive the vase and the face simultaneously because our perceptual systems automatically choose something to be the object and this appears to stand out from the background.

SIMILARITY AND PROXIMITY

We perceive this figure as a rectangle made up of circles, surrounded by a square of crosses, because our perceptual systems tend to group similar things together.

Similarly, we see the figure below as a group of lines rather than eight single lines, because the single lines are grouped in pairs in proximity to one another.

CLOSURE

Our perceptual systems try to fill in any missing information. So, for example, in the figure below, we tend to see a triangle and circle, even though they are not complete:

The Gestalt laws of perceptual organization are interesting descriptions of what our perceptual systems do and they suggest some of the sorts of hypotheses which may be used in perception. However, they are simply descriptions, and the Gestalt psychologists were unable to show the mechanisms by which these laws operated. Modern work on computer recognition of objects has taken up the laws, but there is little acceptance these days that the laws themselves are innate.

Factors Affecting Perception

We are constantly being bombarded with a wide range of stimuli (a stimulus is anything which affects any of our senses). One of the problems of perception is the decision about which stimuli to attend to. Try shutting your eyes and pay attention to your touch senses – concentrate on the feel of your clothes on your body, of your weight pressing down on the chair, the slight pressure on your skin of any jewellery or spectacles you might be wearing.

You were probably able to do that quite easily, but normally you are not aware of those touch stimuli – only when you are told to pay attention to them. Indeed, it would make life difficult if you were constantly aware of them, preventing you from concentrating on more important matters. 'Attention' involves selecting some of the many stimuli which reach you and concentrating on them.

Some stimuli almost force their way into our attention – for example, a sudden loud noise as you sit in a quiet room will certainly be noticed. Teachers sometimes gain the attention of their classes by stopping talking; students who had been chatting to each other suddenly notice the silence even though they had not been listening to the voice that had been lecturing. Repetition gains our attention too; some television advertisements make use of this device when, for example, they repeat the name of the firm or product several times. It is sometimes difficult not to notice moving objects; advertising signs which involve movement tend to stand out from those which are static.

Size, change, repetition and movement (SCRAM, for short) of stimuli are all very strong *external factors* which cause us to notice things, but much of the control of attention lies within us. I sometimes decide to watch or listen to one thing rather than another but most control of attention is unconscious; I don't need to *think* about it.

Perceptual Set

Some things are more easily noticeable than others even if they don't fit the SCRAM categories. Have you ever been at a crowded party chatting with friends when someone a little way off mentions your name? You usually hear it even though you weren't listening to the other conversation. People on diets often report that they can't help noticing cream cakes or chocolate. It seems that we unconsciously *set* our attention mechanisms to pick out certain things and we notice these even when we only have a brief glance or hear the vaguest whisper.

This Perceptual Set means that we will notice some things rather than others and is the way that the brain copes with the fact that we can't pay conscious attention to everything. In some cases, Perceptual Set for a stimulus is more or less permanent (e.g. your own name), but in other cases it is temporary (e.g. the set for food when you are hungry). Because we all have different perceptual sets we have slightly different perceptions. Go for a walk along a country road with a botanist and they will point out to you tiny plants that you never even noticed; the same road will be full of different coloured stones for a geologist but you and I may have noticed nothing of these because we were busy perceiving the green grass, blue sky and birdsong.

The technical definition of a Perceptual Set is the temporary or permanent lowering of the threshold for perceiving a certain type of stimulus. Threshold means the intensity of stimulus which is required for it to be perceived. Intensity may refer to its loudness, brightness, length of time it is shown, clarity or the amount of the total object necessary for you to recognize it correctly. The threshold at which items can be correctly identified can be studied using a machine called a *tachistoscope* which presents stimuli for controlled brief periods of time at controlled brightness levels.

Perceptual Sets may be produced by previous experience leading to familiarity and expectation, and also by motivational or emotional states.

THE EFFECTS OF EXPERIENCE ON PERCEPTION

When we meet people we make perceptual judgements about the sort of person they are. Our actual perception of them is not only affected by their appearance and behaviour on the day but also by what we have heard about them before the meeting and our previous experience of similar people.

Reputation has a great effect on our perception of people. Ernie Wise, half of the great comedy team Morecambe and Wise, used to say that once you are established as a comedian people laugh at everything you say whether you meant it to be funny or not. As soon as people meet a well-known comedian they have a perceptual set for comedy and notice it much more quickly than they would had someone else said exactly the same thing.

Kelley performed an experiment which demonstrated the effect that previous information can have on the perception of a newcomer. Students in a college class were each given brief descriptions of a guest speaker's personality before his arrival. The descriptions given were identical except that half described his personality as warm, the other half as cold. After hearing the lecture the students were asked to rate the speaker on a series of personality characteristics. The students given the 'warm' description rated him as more considerate of others, more informed, more sociable, more popular, better-natured, more humorous and kinder than those given the 'cold' description. There were no differences between the groups on the assessment of such characteristics as his intelligence. The earlier descriptions given to the students seemed to affect the likelihood of perception of certain characteristics in the lecturer. The descriptions had given the students different perceptual sets.

Kelly noticed that a greater percentage (56%) of the students with the 'warm' description participated in the class discussion than did those with the 'cold' description (32%). This shouldn't surprise us because behaviour usually varies as a result of our perceptions. If you meet someone who appears approachable you are much more likely to respond to them in a friendly manner; this causes them to perceive you as a warm person and their resulting behaviour will reinforce your original opinion.

Could it be, then, that the students were seeing what they expected or were told to see? Bruner (1955) conducted an experiment which suggests that this might be the case. Two groups of people were chosen, one of which was shown pictures of capital letters, while the other was shown pictures of numbers. They were both then shown a figure similar to this:

and asked to report what they saw. The 'number' group reported seeing the number 13, and the 'letter' group the letter B. Their previous experiences had obviously developed in them an expectancy (perceptual set) that the stimulus figure would be of a similar type to the stimuli they had already been shown.

An experiment by Siipola (1935) showed this effect with briefly presented strings of letters. One group of people was told that they would be shown words relating to boats, and another that their words would be related to animals. The type of stimulus words used were

sael   wharl

The 'boat' group saw these as 'sail' and 'wharf' while the 'animal' group saw 'seal' and 'whale'.

These studies demonstrate how perceptual sets can be built up in the laboratory. Outside the laboratory each of us builds up our personal perceptual sets as a result of life experiences.

PERCEPTUAL SETS AS A RESULT OF MOTIVATION AND EMOTION

The appearance of objects may be changed in the final perception, according to their relevance to a person's wishes or needs. G. Murphy saw babies' perceptions as being, to an extent, autistic – when a baby is hungry it actually perceives food, even if there isn't any food there. For example, babies often make sucking movements with their mouths when they are hungry – as if they are eating.

Hunger can affect the perception of food making it more noticeable. Lazarus (1953) presented blurred pictures of food and non-food objects. The number of food-related objects identified increased up to about six hours food-deprivation, but decreased after this. As hunger increases, therefore, the perceptual system seemed to become more sensitive to food-objects, but after six hours or so this effect decreased. In evolutionary terms it is useful for animals to have a perceptual set for food when they are hungry because this makes it more likely that they will find some; once they have eaten it is useful to focus attention elsewhere.

Longer-term motivations also cause perceptual sets. Studies show that aggressive people have lower thresholds to stimuli related to aggression. For example, Erikson (1951) showed that they recognized aggressive words more quickly and Forest (1962) that they correctly identified aggression in pictures sooner than people with low aggressive tendencies. Given equal presentation times, then, it seems that words and concepts related to strong personality traits in a participant are more liable to be perceived quickly and accurately than those not related to such personality traits.

Similar effects were shown in experiments studying the effects of values and interests on perception. Postman, Bruner and McGinnies (1948) found that participants perceived most easily those words which fitted their values and interests (aesthetic, religious, social, charitable, philosophical, etc.). When they guessed at what a word might be, they tended to give words which related to their own values, even if the word shown originally was not so related. But here a problem arises: do the participants perceive the valued words quicker because of some kind of 'motivational perceptual set' or simply because, due to their particular interests and values, those words are more familiar? When the valued and non-valued words were carefully chosen on the basis of equal frequency in literature, the preference for 'valued' words disappeared. It would appear, therefore, that the perceptual sets demonstrated in this study were a result of what people were experienced at seeing rather than what they wanted to see.

Figure 2.17 The Effect of Reward and Punishment on Perception of Juxtaposed Faces

Murphy and Schafer (1943) showed each side of the double face in figure 2.17 separately to children who were rewarded when one was shown and punished when the other was presented. Although they had equal familiarity with both faces, when the full drawing (both faces juxtaposed) was shown, only the rewarded face was perceived suggesting that motivation can have an effect upon and beyond familiarity. However, Jackson (1954) found that adults showed large individual differences in susceptibility to this effect. Murphy and Schafer's study demonstrates another difficulty of studying perception because, of course, the only way that we can know what the children perceived is by asking them; there is no way of knowing whether the children actually perceived the rewarded face first or whether they simply decided to say that was the face they saw.

Freud suggested that perception can be affected by unconscious motivations (see p. 193 for a discussion of Freud's theory of personality). According to Freud an individual may have strong urges of a sexual or violent nature hidden deep in the unconscious; the personality system protects the individual from consciously realizing that they have these urges especially if they consider themselves to be of a high moral standing. It is not possible, however, to totally suppress these urges, they constantly try to emerge and the process of pushing them back down into the unconscious is a bit like trying to stop the steam coming out of a boiling kettle. Pressures build up and the urges need to express themselves in some way. One way of relieving the pressure is the process that Freud calls *projection* where the feelings are 'thrown out' on to the world which is then perceived as full of sex and violence. The individual goes around noticing all the sex and violence that there is in the world; we might call this a set for sex and violence. At a conscious level the individual is disgusted and only spends time with such things as pornographic videos so that they can say how awful they are and argue for censorship, but at an unconscious level their hidden motives are being satisfied.

The Effects of Success and Failure on Perception

A number of studies have shown that the ability to make difficult perceptual judgements is affected by how well the individual thinks they are doing. One group of participants was shown pictures of objects at low intensity and short exposure time, and was asked to name them. Few, of course, got any correct, but half of the participants were given reassurance ('Don't worry, most people have difficulty with this task'), while the other half were reproached ('Most people do better on this task than you'). In subsequent tasks, the 'reproached' group (who were told, in effect, that they had failed) were slower to perceive the material than the 'reassured' group. They also tended to make wild, irrelevant guesses, and began guessing even when the pictures were flashed so quickly that there was little chance of getting it right. The 'reassured' group, however, waited until they had a reasonable idea of what the picture was, before they began guessing (Postman and Bruner, 1948).

In 1952 Postman asked participants to predict how well they thought they would do in a similar experiment. After the first trial, half the group was told that they had exceeded their own expectations, while the other half was told that they had performed worse than they had expected. Both groups were then briefly shown words related to

success: excellent, succeed, perfection, winner
failure: unable, failure, obstacle, defeat
striving: improve, achieve, strive, compete

The 'success' group was markedly better at picking out 'success' words, and the 'failure' group better at picking out 'failure' words. There was no difference in the two groups' abilities to perceive the 'striving' words. The groups had been given a perceptual set for success or failure.

The Effect of Value on Perception and Memory

Studies have shown that objects that have value for the observer may not only be perceived at a lower threshold but may also be seen or remembered as larger or brighter than they really are.

Bruner and Goodman (1952) asked ten-year-old children to adjust lights until they looked the same size as either coins or cardboard discs. There was little misjudgement when estimating the size of cardboard discs, but with the coins the children tended to overestimate the size and this effect was greater for poor than for wealthy children. They argued that this was due to the greater value of the coins for the poor children, although others have suggested that the difference between the judgements of poor and wealthy children was due to difference in familiarity with the coins. Other experiments have shown that this effect only occurs when the children judge from memory, suggesting that perception is not affected but that value or familiarity has an effect on the memory.

Lambert and Solomon looked at the effect of value in a study which controlled for the effect of familiarity. They asked two groups of children to crank a handle for which they were rewarded with either sweets (Group A) or discs which could later be exchanged for sweets (Group B). The children were asked to judge the size of the discs in the same way as in the Bruner and Goodman experiment. Group A tended to overestimate, but only by about 6 per cent, whereas Group B overestimated by 13 per cent, showing the effect of value. To show that this difference was not just due to familiarity, they demonstrated that the difference between the groups' perceptions disappeared when the discs were no longer exchanged for sweets. Again, this effect may be on memory rather than perception.

Gilchrist (1952) showed a perceptual effect of value. He deprived participants of water and asked them to rate the brightness of pictures of drink-related and non-drink-related objects. They consistently rated the drink-related pictures as brighter – the difference disappeared as soon as they were given water.

Perception and Emotion – Subliminal Perception and Perceptual Defence

Freud felt that the perceptual process contains systems which protect us from consciously perceiving information that might cause us extreme upset. The parent who refuses to see their delinquent child as dishonest or the cheated spouse who fails to see that their partner is unfaithful may be demonstrating perceptual defence. Like many Freudian ideas it is difficult to test this experimentally because it would hardly be ethically correct to submit participants to the sort of traumatic experiences that would be expected to lead to perceptual defence. Some studies have, however, been made of the perception of mildly emotional words.

McGinnies (1949) showed a higher threshold on the tachistoscope for 'taboo' words than for those without emotional meanings. Taboo words are words which may cause anxiety because they are rude or frightening. He argued that this was due to perceptual defence, which prevented the words reaching the conscious level (this seems to be almost the opposite of perceptual set).

The idea of perceptual defence is an odd one, in that to put up a defence surely you must first perceive the stimulus. There is a temptation to equate 'attention' with 'consciousness', but there appears to be a possibility that we are not conscious of at least some of the information to which we attend and on which we act. Earlier in this chapter we referred to the way in which you might be chatting at a party and hear your name being used by someone on the other side of the room despite the fact that you had not been consciously attending to their conversation. This is known as the *cocktail party phenomenon* and clearly demonstrates that some analysis of incoming information is done at an unconscious level. If information for which we have a perceptual set is detected then the material is brought to conscious attention.

Freudian psychologists believe that unconscious mechanisms analyse the emotional content of messages. Eriksen calls this the theory of the 'super-discriminating unconscious' which states that the stimulus is first perceived by a non-conscious mechanism, and that this mechanism blocks the conscious if it is likely to be unpleasant.

There is some evidence which might back up the idea of the super-discriminating unconscious. This is shown in an experiment by Lazarus and McCleary (1951) who presented a random series of ten nonsense syllables (e.g. NYJ, XIC, MOC). Electric shocks were paired with five of them, and eventually a galvanic skin response (an increase in the skin's sweat production, often taken to be a measurement of anxiety) occurred to the shocked, but not the non-shocked syllables. Then they presented the syllables at below threshold level in the tachistoscope and found that the GSR response occurred to the previously shocked syllables and not to the neutral syllables, even though the participants couldn't consciously read the syllables.

This phenomenon of perception at sub-threshold levels is termed *subliminal perception*, and caused some outcry a few years ago when a New York advertising agency claimed to have shown the effect of subliminal advertising by flashing a three-millisecond message every five seconds during a film. The audience did not notice the message at a conscious level but the firm claimed a 56 per cent increase in the amount of Coca-Cola bought in the intermission (the message was 'BUY COCA-COLA'). Studies trying to replicate this experiment have, perhaps fortunately, failed. The Lazarus and McCleary study is, however, reproducible, and Dixon (1958) showed a GSR response to taboo words shown at sub-threshold levels. Edwards (1960) presented stimuli subliminally and found that, when participants were allowed to choose from a list of five words the word they thought was shown, the success rate was high. This suggested that although subliminal information cannot usually be recalled, it nevertheless seems to have 'gone in'.

DO PERCEPTUAL DEFENCE AND SUBLIMINAL PERCEPTION REALLY EXIST?

The experiments quoted above support the Freudian idea of perceptual defence but many psychologists are not convinced of the existence of perceptual defence as an unconscious process. Some argue that in experiments like those above the participants simply don't report everything that they see, particularly if they think they might be mistaken. Barthel found that people with a strong desire for approval were most likely to show high thresholds to taboo words, perhaps because they fear disapproval.

Howes and Solomon (1952) suggested that at near-threshold level, fragments of the stimulus are consciously perceived. This fragment may be enough to trigger an emotional reaction and would explain why the participants have a degree of success in recognizing rather than reporting the word in the usual way. Because participants pick up only a fragment of the stimulus they have to guess what was actually shown. There are two reasons why participants are less likely to suggest a taboo word than a neutral one:

1 Expectancy: they don't expect to be sworn at during an experiment.
2 Frequency: taboo words are less frequent than normal words.

Dixon (1958) attempted to control for expectancy and frequency by warning his participants to expect some taboo words and by using taboo and neutral words that were of the same frequency of occurrence (from the Thorndike-Lorge word-count tables). He showed that even under these circumstances the participants did not report the taboo words, although they showed the GSR response, which suggests that frequency and expectancy are not the cause of perceptual defence.

Bruner and Postman (1947) showed that some people exhibited lower thresholds for taboo words than for neutral words, i.e. they show sensitization to these words. Carpenter (1956) used questionnaires to measure his participants' reactions to sex and aggression under normal circumstances, and found that those who showed an interest in these topics under normal circumstances showed no perceptual defence, whereas those who normally repressed sex and aggression showed perceptual defence. This does not tell us whether the sensitization or defence is at the perceptual or the response level, but it does show differences between people in the phenomenon.

The evidence for perceptual defence and for subliminal perception of such complicated stimuli as words is highly questionable. It is likely that they are due to conscious perception of fragments of the stimuli and to analysis of the general shape and size of the words which may occur at a non-conscious level. We know that such processes as size and shape constancy do go on without our conscious awareness. A very reliable experiment by Dunlap shows that subliminal analysis of size can occur. Dunlap asked his participants to judge the relative size of two lines while presenting 'barbs' subliminally, to produce the Muller-Lyer illusion. Although the participants did not report the barbs, they reported the line associated with the ingoing barbs as shorter.

Conclusions to Visual Perception

The organization and interpretation of information from the sense organs to provide a conscious perception are processes which require a great deal of computation. An actual perception results from an analysis of the information bombarding the sense organs which is affected by the individual's wants, needs, emotions and previous experiences. Studies that have tried to tease out the effect of all these factors have had varying degrees of success. Most of them have relied on the use of stimuli which are unclear, open to a variety of interpretations and presented for very short periods of time and are, therefore, open to the criticism that they do not reflect perception in the real world. On the other hand it is only when perception is performed in these exacting conditions that it is possible to tease out some of the important factors because usually the perceptual processes are extremely good. Like metallurgists who find out a lot about metals by stressing them to breaking point, we learn a lot about perception by pushing it to its limits of effectiveness. Many studies can be criticized because they failed to separate perception from memory or what the participants say about their perception. This should not surprise us because those processes are totally intertwined and interdependent. When we try to separate them artificially for the sake of study we will never be 100 per cent successful.

Summary

1 Perception is an active process involving the organization, translation and reconstruction of information (proximal stimuli) from the senses.

2 The rods and cones of the retina produce nerve impulses when stimulated by light. In normal light the cones are most active and allow colour vision; the rods are responsible for twilight vision.

3 A visual image causes nerve impulses to pass to the visual cortex via the optic nerve, optic chiasma, and lateral geniculate body.

4 Cells in the visual cortex fire when groups of retinal cells known as *receptive fields* are stimulated, giving the perceptual system information about shape.

5 Movement of an image across the retina causes sequential firing of cortical cells with adjacent receptive fields and this may cause the perception of movement but is interpreted in the light of eye movement. Even when this system signals movement of one object rather than another, the perceptual system may accept a different interpretation based on expectations.

6 Binocular and monocular depth cues are used by the perceptual system to turn the two-dimensional proximal stimulus on the retina into the three-dimensional perception of depth.

7 Size, shape, brightness and colour constancies are all processes in the visual systems which alter the proximal stimulus (or sensation) to help produce the final perception.

8 The Gestalt psychologists suggested laws of perceptual organization, to describe some of the (innate) hypotheses which our perceptual systems use.

9 Some external stimuli force us to pay attention to them – size contrast repetition and movement (SCRAM).

10 Internal factors can cause us to be tuned (set) towards particular types of stimuli, to create perceptual sets.

11 Previous experiences and instructions, motivation and emotion can all create perceptual sets.

12 There is not yet clear agreement among psychologists about the importance (or even the existence) of perceptual defence or sensitisation. There is better evidence that some information-processing does take place at an unconscious level.

Further Reading

Gregory, R.L., *Eye and Brain* (5th edn, 1997, Oxford University Press).
Gordon, I.E., *Theories of Visual Perception.* (1989, New York: J. Wiley).

Chapter 3

Basic Forms of Learning

Some of the lower animals appear to be like machines whose behaviour is determined totally from the way that they are built. Many insects are born, feed, build shelter, mate and die in such a short time that it would be inefficient to have to learn things. Insect species survive because there are so many of them and they reproduce so quickly that if the environment changes those that can't cope die and those that can cope with the change pass on their abilities to the next generation as a genetic inheritance. In humans, each individual has a much more flexible repertoire of behaviour; if things change we can *learn* to adapt.

What is Learning?
If you consider the many different kinds of behaviour which are commonly termed learning, you will see that if any definition of learning is to include them all it must be fairly vague. Compare 'learning to walk' and 'learning psychology for an exam'; the latter involves concentration, application, dedication and frustration, but with the former it is quite unnecessary and inappropriate to sit down and study from books the principles of loco-motion. However, we use the word 'learning' in both cases.

In psychology the most frequently used definition is:

Learning is a relatively permanent change in behaviour, attitude or percep-tion as a result of experience; this does not include changes in behaviour brought about by physical damage, disease, drugs or maturation processes.

Learning causes changes in the nervous system so that it reacts differently. The changes probably take place at the *synapses* which are the connection between cells (see p. 297).

Conditioning

In this section we shall begin by describing some of the simpler forms of learning, and then go on to more complex kinds. One of the earliest forms of learning to be studied was called *classical conditioning*, which is now linked with the name of Ivan Pavlov. In fact, he was not the first to devise the technique; an American named Twitmeyer published the results of classical conditioning-type experiments several years before Pavlov. Nevertheless, it is Pavlov's name which has become so associated with classical conditioning that it is sometimes known as *Pavlovian conditioning*.

Classical Conditioning

Pavlov was a physiologist, working on the salivary reflex in dogs. As part of his experiments he devised an apparatus for measuring the amount of saliva secreted by a dog. Then he noticed that whenever the dog caught sight of the laboratory assistant carrying the bucket which contained its food the rate of salivation increased, even when the dog could not actually see the food. Dogs normally salivate only at the sight, smell, or taste of food, yet the dog was definitely salivating at the sight of the bucket. Pavlov wanted to know why this dog should show such a change from its normal behaviour. He wondered whether, if the dog could associate the bucket with its food, it could also associate some completely different object or event with the food and begin to salivate in response to that.

For the next few feedings, each time the dog received its food a bell was sounded for a few seconds, and the amount of saliva secreted was measured. After several such trials Pavlov sounded the bell without accompaniment of food and the dog still salivated, nearly as much as it normally did when food was presented.

Pavlov gave scientific names to the parts of this procedure. The food is termed the *unconditional stimulus* or UCS: it is the stimulus which normally elicits the salivary reflex response. It is 'unconditional' because it works by itself; it needs no other help, or 'conditions', to allow it to work. The bell is a *Conditional Stimulus* or CS because it will only activate the reflex on condition that it is presented at the same time as the food. Salivation to the food is therefore the *unconditional response* or UCR; it is a response to an Unconditional Stimulus; and salivation to the bell is a *conditional response* or CR – a response to a conditional stimulus.

We can summarize Pavlov's procedure in this formula:

Food		Salivation	(Basic
UCS	$\longrightarrow$	UCR	reflex)
Bell + Food		Salivation	
CS UCS	$\longrightarrow$	UCR	
Bell		Salivation	(Sometimes called
CS	$\longrightarrow$	CR	a Conditional reflex)

Dogs learn to salivate when they hear the sound of a bell alone, after hearing the bell rung at the same time as they have received food, which does make them salivate. Thus the salivation of the dog to the sound of a bell is conditional upon the bell having been associated with food. Please note that we have used the terms 'unconditional' and 'conditional' here. In some books, you may see the terms 'unconditioned' or 'conditioned' used instead. However, both sets of terms mean the same thing. The use of both endings – 'al' and 'ed' – arose from an error when Pavlov's work was first translated from the original Russian into English. Pavlov actually wrote 'conditional', but this was mistranslated as 'conditioned'.

Pavlov found that the conditioning technique was most effective when the conditional stimulus was presented very slightly before the unconditional stimulus.

EXTINCTION OF THE CR

The UCS *reinforces* the response to the CS: it strengthens it. Without the UCS the CR would not develop. If we now continue to sound the bell but never reinforce the response of the animal with food, the UCS, the CR – salivation – will gradually die out, a process known as *extinction*. If the CS is again rung after a time-lapse to give the animal time to rest, the CR may reappear, although it will be much weaker in form. This is known as *spontaneous recovery*.

GENERALIZATION

The basic conditioning process does not only affect the original connection between the conditioned stimulus and the conditioned response. Other stimuli, if they are fairly similar to the original CS, will also be found to elicit the response; a bell with a slightly higher or lower tone than the original, for example, or a tapping noise, will probably elicit the salivary response in the experiment just outlined. The response gets weaker as the new stimulus gets more and more different from the original CS. The way in which other stimuli can elicit the CR is known as *generalization*.

DISCRIMINATION

The animal can be taught to 'choose' between stimuli, to *discriminate*; for example, we can condition animals to respond only to specific shapes. If we pair a circular shape with the presentation of food, the animal becomes conditioned to salivate at the appearance of the circle. However, it may, and usually does, generalize the response so that, although a white circle may have been presented originally, the animal will also respond to circles of other colours. In this case we can get the animal to discriminate between these circles by reinforcing only the presentation of the white-circle stimulus; because the appearance of differently coloured circles is not reinforced, salivation at their presentation soon stops.

Discrimination is often used for experiments assessing perception in animals. If we want to see whether an animal has colour vision we may condition it to salivate when it sees (say) a red square. If other coloured squares are presented the animal will probably generalize, but if only the red square is paired with food the animal with colour vision should learn to discriminate, whereas one that has only black-and-white vision will not learn the discrimination (it would be necessary to make sure that all the squares were exactly the same, except for colour, so that discrimination could not be made simply on the grounds of brightness or other qualities). If we want to see whether an animal can perceive a triangle among several other shapes, we condition the animal to salivate at the presentation of a triangle and eliminate any tendency towards generalization so that the animal responds to triangles only. Then the triangle, together with other shapes, is presented to the animal. If it salivates only on the presentation of the triangle we can conclude that the animal can actually perceive that the shapes are different; some animals have great difficulty discriminating between shapes such as triangles and squares which are obviously different to human observers.

The Use of Classical Conditioning

One way in which classical conditioning is being used today is in the area of the treatment of behaviour problems termed 'behaviour therapy'. Behaviour therapists are usually psychiatrists who believe that so-called 'abnormal' behaviour is really a learning problem: the patient may either have failed to learn a particular kind of 'normal' behaviour, or have learnt some kind of 'abnormal' behaviour. Such problems can therefore be treated by conditioning techniques.

One such technique, which is really a standard classical conditioning procedure, has been applied to behaviour problems such as alcoholism and drug addiction, and is called *Aversion Therapy*. The aim of this is to get the patient to develop an adverse reaction to alcohol or drugs by using the vomiting reflex; this can be activated by giving the patient an injection of a vomiting-inducing drug such as apomorphine. Once the patient is injected with apomorphine he or she will vomit as soon as they drink alcohol. Drugs which bring on vomiting are called *emetics*.

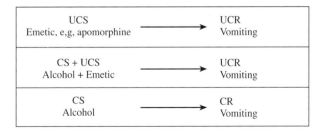

The vomiting is deliberately associated with drinking alcohol. However, note that it is always a reflex that we condition: the patient cannot stop himself vomiting. He may realize that it is the emetic which is causing the vomiting, but the association between the CS and the UCS happens automatically; thinking about it cannot stop it.

Aversion therapy thus assumes that the individual has not sufficiently learnt to avoid alcohol or drugs; the conditioning process enables him to learn this avoidance response. Most therapists feel that aversion therapy on its own is unlikely to have a lasting effect and it must be combined with other action. If the patients are released into exactly the same situation in which they started drinking, it is likely that the same pressure will lead to renewed drinking; even though at first this will cause vomiting, this response will extinguish because the patient keeps coming into contact with alcohol.

Other behavioural problems may be caused by an individual having learnt some kind of 'abnormal' behaviour. Behaviour therapies believe that phobias, for example, are a result of learning and can originate through a process very similar to classical conditioning. Phobias are strong irrational fears of things like dogs, cats, open spaces, crowds or many other stimuli that most of us take for granted. Lesser fears and other emotions may develop in a similar way. A terrifying experience obviously causes fear and anxiety; according to classical conditioning anything which becomes associated with that terrifying experience may thus become a CS and may itself induce fear and anxiety. The table below shows how a behaviour therapist might interpret the way in which a person's cat phobia could develop.

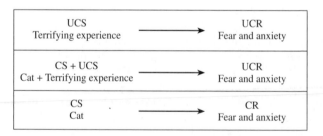

UCS Terrifying experience	⟶	UCR Fear and anxiety
CS + UCS Cat + Terrifying experience	⟶	UCR Fear and anxiety
CS Cat	⟶	CR Fear and anxiety

Such a phobia can last for years, and yet in Pavlov's experiment when the CS was presented several times without the UCS, the CR was extinguished. Why does this not happen with a phobia? The answer seems to be that the phobic individual never allows himself to get anywhere near the CS – a cat in this case – and will even go to the extreme of refusing to go out of doors, watch television or read a newspaper, in case he sees or hears mention of a cat. In this case of course the CS is not being presented over and over again, either with or without the UCS, so the CR is not extinguished. A behaviour therapist would therefore set up a situation in which extinction can occur and he could do this in two ways:

(1) *Flooding and implosion therapy.* Using this technique the patient is presented directly with the object of fear. In the unlikely event that anyone would use this technique for our cat phobia described above, it would mean locking the patient in a room with the cat until the CS–CR bond is extinguished. This can of course be a fairly dangerous procedure, especially when the phobia is very strong, so in general the second method (below) would be preferred for the cat phobic. The technique is more appropriate to an individual who has had a bad car accident or fallen from a horse; under these conditions it is a good idea to get back in a car or on to the horse as quickly as possible to extinguish possible phobic reactions. This may be easier to do immediately after the accident because there is some evidence that phobias may increase in intensity over the first few days or weeks following the incident.

(2) *Systematic desensitization.* Instead of being directly exposed to the feared object the patient is only gradually exposed to it. The first part of the procedure involves discussing the patient's fears and building up an *anxiety hierarchy*; that is a list of the things that the person is afraid of running from extreme fear to slight anxiety. The cat phobic might be terrified of a real cat in the same room, disturbed by a photograph of a cat but only slightly anxious about a cartoon figure of a cat (anxiety hierarchies are usually a lot longer than that). The patient is then introduced to objects low down on the anxiety hierarchy. As the anxiety response to each object is extinguished, so the next item on the hierarchy is presented. In addition, as each object is shown, the patient is trained in various relaxation methods so that he can learn to associate relaxation with each of them in turn. By the time the object of the phobia is presented the level of anxiety will be much less than it was originally due to the effect of extinguishing the anxiety responses all the way up the hierarchy (a sort of generalization of extinction).

Notice that with this system it is not really necessary to know what the original terrifying experience was; all the behaviour therapist must find out is the type of stimulus that triggers off the fear response, and then he can set about extinguishing the bond between then.

Freudian psychologists and psychiatrists, however, feel that it is important to find out the underlying cause of a phobia. This is because they believe that phobias are a result of deep unconscious conflicts. If they are right, curing the phobia won't help and the conflict will find another way of showing itself, it would be a bit like trying to cure measles by simply removing the spots. Eysenck argues that there is very little evidence of this *symptom substitution* (the production of a new problem once the phobic response has been removed).

Classical conditioning is a very simple form of learning; it may not seem very clever learning to us, but its importance is that it acts as a model of learning. It was, for example, about the earliest description and explanation of how learning can take place, through the association of stimuli and responses.

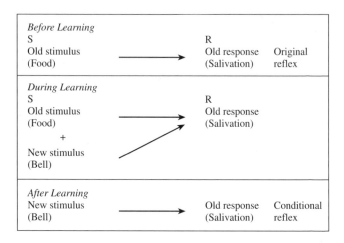

Classical conditioning cannot, however, explain the whole process of learning. When early psychologists tried to use it to explain all learning and behaviour they utterly confused themselves. In order to explain even fairly simple behaviour, such as getting up and opening the door when the doorbell rings, they have to invent such strange terms as 'door-opening reflexes' in order to follow the classical conditioning formula. It thus became clear fairly quickly that the model of classical conditioning was too inflexible; humans obviously do not require the presentation of stimuli together tens or even hundreds of times before they can associate them, nor is their behaviour restricted to involuntary reflex actions. A quicker and more flexible model of learning is therefore required.

One-Trial Learning
Before we leave classical conditioning to look at the more flexible operant conditioning we will look at a special case of classical conditioning which questions many of the rules. It used to be thought that one of the most important factors governing the association of stimuli was time; the closer together in time two stimuli are presented the more likely they are to be associated. In Pavlov's research he showed that a delay of only a second was enough to make conditioning more difficult. It was also thought that conditioning could be understood without taking into account the particular

animal that was being conditioned; it didn't matter much whether it was a dog or a rat, the principles were the same. Finally, nearly all classical conditioning, unless the conditions are very traumatic, requires a number of pairings.

The special case is known as the *Garcia effect*. If rats are given a new food they will only take a small amount and if they feel sick within an hour they will not touch the new food again. The food and the sickness are associated even though there is a long time-gap between them. This only happens with food. Garcia and Koelling (1966) made rats sick one hour after drinking saccharine. Although there were bright lights flashing at the same time as they drank the saccharine, the rats later avoided saccharine but did not avoid bright lights.

With another group Garcia and Koelling showed that rats could learn to avoid flashing bright lights, but only when they were given electric shocks at the same time as the lights were flashing. If, however, the rats happened to be drinking saccharine at the same time, the electric shocks wouldn't stop them drinking in the future. It seems that rats have a built-in bias to associate certain types of stimuli and not others, and for certain stimuli only one pairing is necessary, even though the CS and CR are separated in time.

Operant Conditioning

The basis of *Operant Conditioning* was discovered by E.L. Thorndike in 1911, shortly after Pavlov's work on classical conditioning. Thorndike was studying problem-solving in animals, and had devised a 'puzzle box' in which cats had to solve the problem of how to escape (see figure 3.1). When the cat pulled the loop of string with either its paw or its mouth the catch was released and the door sprung open. Thorndike would put a cat into the

Figure 3.1 Thorndike's Puzzle Box

box and time how long it took the animal to escape. When it had escaped it was put in again, and once more the time it took to escape was noted. When these times were plotted on a graph (see figure 3.2), Thorndike noted that in general, as one might expect, the animal spent less time in the box with each trial. After about 20 trials the cat was able to escape as soon as it was placed in the box.

Figure 3.2 Simplified Graph of Results of Puzzle Box Experiment

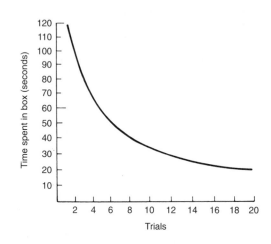

Thorndike put forward the following hypothesis: if a certain response has pleasant consequences, it is more likely than other responses to occur again in the same circumstances. This became known as the *Law of Effect*. Pulling the loop permitted escape, and therefore had 'pleasant consequences' for the cat; it was thus more likely to be repeated than other behaviour which did not lead to escape.

B.F. Skinner is regarded as the father of operant conditioning, but his work was based on Thorndike's Law of Effect. Skinner, however, introduced a new term into the Law of Effect – *reinforcement*. Behaviour which is reinforced tends to be repeated; behaviour which is not reinforced tends to die out, or to be extinguished. To reinforce is to strengthen, so behaviour which is strengthened tends to be repeated – obvious enough perhaps, but Skinner's contribution was to show what sort of things or events could act as reinforcers. In the first type of experiment, described below, a reinforcer is used in very much the same way as a reward, but it should be remembered that rewards are not the only possible type of reinforcers (see positive and negative reinforcement on p. 48).

The term 'operant conditioning' was coined by Skinner; it means roughly the changing of behaviour by use of a reinforcement which is given after the desired response. An 'operant' is an operation which the organism performs on or in its environment – motor behaviour, usually voluntarily performed.

Skinner developed machines for operant conditioning which have been named 'Skinner boxes', and in which rats and pigeons are the animals most often used.

When placed in a Skinner box the animal has to press a lever to open a food tray and thus obtain reinforcement in the form of food. In any situation an animal has a certain repertoire of behaviour; a rat, for example, will show exploratory behaviour when first placed in the Skinner box, such as scratching at the walls, sniffing and looking around. By accident, in the course of its exploration, it will press the lever and food will be presented. Every time the rat does so it is given food; thus its pressing of the lever is reinforced by the presentation of food and the animal comes to associate this particular action with receiving this reward. Any other responses such as those mentioned above are not reinforced, and so tend to die out. After several presentations of the reinforcement, the rat will press the lever far more often than it did previously. When the animal has been conditioned in this way, the lever pressing, which began as an accidental response, has become a conditional response.

Figure 3.3 A Skinner Box

Food dispenser

To experimenter's switch

Lever

Food tray

Although the experimenter may wait for the rat to press the lever accidentally a much quicker way of ensuring the response is to use the process of *shaping*. When shaping is used, the animal is first reinforced for moving closer to the lever and then for being close to the lever. When this has been done the rat is far more likely to accidentally press the lever which is then the only response that is reinforced.

In classical conditioning the unconditional stimulus itself provides the reinforcement; this is presented before the conditional stimulus. In operant conditioning, however, the reinforcement is presented after the response. operant conditioning, then, uses reinforcement to single out one specific action from the animal's normal behaviour and to ensure that it is repeated more often than the rest. The reinforcement in classical conditioning causes the response to be made in the first place. (For other differences between classical and operant conditioning, see p. 54.)

Figure 3.4 The 'Formula' for Operant Conditioning

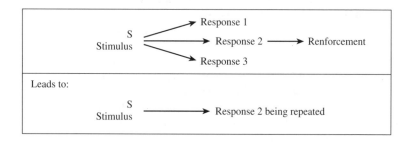

Schedules of Reinforcement

So far we have described how an animal in the Skinner box receives a pellet of food each time it presses the lever. If we stopped giving this reinforcement the lever-pressing behaviour would gradually be extinguished, usually after only a few minutes. What makes operant conditioning important as an explanation of learning, however, is Skinner's development of schedules of reinforcement – different ways of providing reinforcement, which can have different effects on both the rate at which the animal presses the lever, the *response rate*, and the rate at which the lever-pressing behaviour is extinguished, the *extinction rate*. It is these schedules of reinforcement which make operant conditioning a very flexible form of learning. Any response, once it has been conditioned, can be made to last as long as it is required. The various schedules of reinforcement and their effects on response and extinction rate are described below.

CONTINUOUS REINFORCEMENT
This is the method used when setting up the conditioning procedure. Each response is reinforced, but if reinforcement is ceased extinction occurs fairly quickly.

FIXED RATIO REINFORCEMENT (FR)
The subject's behaviour is reinforced only after a fixed number of responses. Pigeons in a Skinner box have been known to respond to an FR of 1:1,000, or one reinforcement for 1,000 responses – commonly written as FR 1,000. This gives a fast rate of response and fairly rapid extinction.

FIXED INTERVAL REINFORCEMENT (FI)
The subject's behaviour is reinforced only after a fixed period of time, following the previous reinforcement. This method provides a slow rate of response, often only one response per period; for example in an FI 2 schedule, reinforcement is provided after the animal's first response after two minutes. If the animal makes a response during the two-minute period, it is not reinforced. This has a fairly rapid rate of extinction.

VARIABLE RATIO REINFORCEMENT (VR)
Reinforcement is given after an average number of responses; for example, a VR 10 schedule is one on which on average, ten responses gain a reinforcement. The actual reinforcement does not arrive on every tenth response, but there will be three reinforcements given for 30 responses (as in figure 3.5).

This method provides a steady rate of response which is resistant to extinction: the animal makes many responses before extinction occurs.

Figure 3.5 Responses

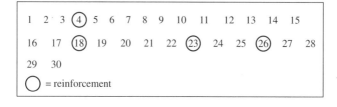

VARIABLE INTERVAL REINFORCEMENT (VI)

Reinforcement is given, say, every five minutes on average, but not on every fifth minute. A VI 5 reinforcement schedule would look like this, with three reinforcements per 15 minutes:

Figure 3.6 Minutes

This provides a steady rate of response, but not as high as with the VR schedule. The response becomes very resistant to extinction: the animal continues to respond for a long time after the reinforcement ceases.

It is obvious that we cannot switch suddenly from a continuous reinforcement schedule to, say, an FR 1,000 schedule; the process has to be a gradual one. For example, to obtain an FR 1,000 schedule the intermediate stages might be FR 5, FR 10, FR 20, FR 50, FR 100, FR 200, FR 300, FR 500, and so on up to FR 1,000.

Table 3.1. Effects on Response and Extinction Rates

Schedule		Effect per minute on Response Rate	Effect on Extinction Rate
	Continuous	Steady – 5 per min.	Fast
FR	Fixed ratio	Fast – FR 5 gives 20 per min.	Fast
FI	Fixed interval	Slow – FI 1 gives 2 per min.	Fast
VR	Variable ratio	Fast – VR 5 gives 15 per min.	Slow – many responses
VI	Variable interval	Steady – VI 5 gives 10 per min.	Very slow – long time

Successive Approximation or Behaviour-Shaping

All the schedules of reinforcement detailed above are generally used, and are only applicable to a single response. This response, however, can be far more complex than a single lever-pressing reaction. Skinner, for example, taught – or more properly, conditioned – pigeons to play ping-pong, and to act as pilots in rockets.

Such feats are achieved by *successive approximation*. Operant conditioning selects particular actions and by reinforcing them ensures that they are repeated. Once an animal has been conditioned to perform a particular action it tends to use this as the basis of its behaviour and elaborates on it. If, for example, we want a pigeon to turn round and to walk in a left-hand circle, we first reinforce any movement the pigeon makes to the left. It repeats this and elaborates on it, maybe by pecking at the floor, fluttering its wings, and moving its head further to the left. We reinforce only this last response, so that we now have two conditioned acts of behaviour – one the pigeon's turning perhaps 15 degrees to the left, the second a turn of another 20 degrees or so. With two reinforcements we have therefore conditioned the pigeon to turn 35 degrees to the left. If we continue to reinforce only movements that take the pigeon further to the left, eventually the pigeon will turn full circle. The whole process may take as little as five minutes or so. Each successive behavioural action *approximates* – becomes closer – to the final type of behaviour required.

Extinction, Generalization and Discrimination in Operant Conditioning

In classical conditioning, extinction could be produced by removing the UCS, which was the reinforcer. The same procedure applies in operant conditioning but takes time; removing reinforcement completely after, say, a VR 5 schedule will not extinguish the response as quickly as removing the reinforcer after an FR 5 schedule.

Generalization can also occur: a response to stimuli similar to, but not identical with, the original can be made. The rat in the Skinner box, for example, may have been conditioned to press the left-hand lever but may occasionally generalize the lever-pressing response to the right-hand lever.

Discrimination in a subject can be achieved, and can overcome generalization if desired, using the same principles as those employed in classical conditioning. We could, for example, teach the animal to discriminate between a situation in which it will be reinforced for pressing the lever, and one in which it will not; for example, we could condition the animal to press the lever only when the light above the lever is on, by giving reinforcement only if the animal presses the lever when the light is on.

Positive and Negative Reinforcement

You will remember that the formula for operant conditioning is:

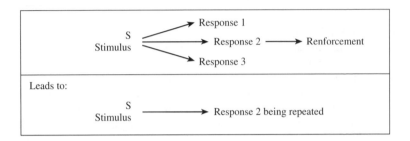

By giving the animal something it wants, such as food, we reinforce response 2. Giving the animal something it wants, needs or likes is called *positive reinforcement*.

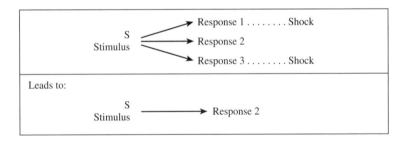

The negative-reinforcement formula, however, looks slightly different: Here, the reinforcement occurs when we stop something which the animal does not like. Thus the presentation of something which the animal wants or needs and the removal of an unpleasant stimulus are both reinforcers, because they both strengthen the required response.

Escape and Avoidance Learning

Learning which is brought about by *negative reinforcement* is termed *escape learning*. For example, an animal is made to stand on an electrified floor grid and is given a mild electric shock; if it jumps or runs away from the grid, the shock stops. Escape behaviour is thus reinforced by the cessation of the painful stimulation. The problem with this type of learning, however, is that it can deal only with very simple types of behaviour: because the shock produces large emotional responses in the animal it is unlikely to try to do anything more complex or unusual than escape.

However, if we give the animal in the Skinner box a warning buzzer a few seconds before the shock starts we can develop more sophisticated behaviour. If the animal accidentally moves closer to the lever between the sound of the buzzer and the occurrence of the shock, we stop the shock. The action of approaching the lever is then reinforced by the non-appearance of the shock – it is negatively reinforced – and we can thus shape lever-pressing behaviour.

Once this behaviour has been established, it is very resistant to extinction – more so even than VI schedules. This form of learning is called *avoidance learning*. The animal makes a particular response in order to avoid the shock; the particular response is negatively reinforced.

Secondary Reinforcement

In the examples of operant conditioning discussed above, food is involved as a reinforcer; it is the main or *primary reinforcer*. However, if we pair another stimulus with the primary reinforcer, the second stimulus also acquires reinforcing properties. For example, when the animal makes a correct response in the Skinner box, a food tray may click into position with an audible sound. This clicking noise can thus become associated with food because every time the animal hears the click, food appears. In time the animal will perform the required responses while accepting the clicking noise alone as a reinforcer: the sound becomes a *secondary reinforcer*. Something which has been associated with a primary reinforcer, such as food, can thus become a reinforcer too.

You will remember this idea of pairing or associating from the earlier description of classical conditioning; the above case is also an example of this. Consider how much more flexible secondary reinforcers can make operant conditioning: the reinforcer need not always be a primary one so that the range of possible reinforcers can be greatly extended; more or less anything that has been paired with a primary reinforcer can become a secondary reinforcer. Perhaps the most obvious case with humans is that of money, which in the past was associated mainly with primary reinforcers: you can use money to buy food and drink. Thus it is now possible to re-inforce and induce repetition of behaviour with money. Although money can be a motivator or reinforcer for people at work, it is by no means the only possible one; social reinforcement such as attention and praise from other people is also a very powerful reinforcer (see chapter 9). Yet some social reinforcers may also be an entirely separate kind of reinforcement and perhaps innate; Harlow's experiment concerning love in infant monkeys (see p. 154) suggests that this might in fact be the case.

Is Reinforcement Necessary for Learning?

We have seen the powerful effect that reinforcement can have on behaviour, and how its removal may result in extinction of responses; but can learning occur without reinforcement? Conditioning theorists sometimes fall into the trap of assuming that if a piece of behaviour is repeated it *must* have been reinforced, but the danger of this is that it stops us looking any further. If reinforcement is used as the explanation for everything without looking any deeper, then it will no longer remain a useful concept.

Tolman (1930) showed that learning does occur without reinforcement but the learning does not always show itself. He put rats into a maze and left them to explore it, there was no food available in the maze and so the rats simply wandered around and gave no outward sign of having learned anything from the experience. Later he put the rats into the same maze, but this time put food into the *goal box* at the centre. These rats learned to run to the goal box much more quickly than a control group that had not been in the maze before. The rats had obviously learned something while in the box on the first occasion but were not able to show that they had learned. This is known as *latent learning* because it only shows itself sometime later when reinforcement is present. It is important to distinguish between *learning* and *performance*. Learning can occur without a noticeable change in observable behaviour as in the latent learning study above; performance involves the actual production of the behaviour. In most conditions learning and performance go together, but Tolman's work shows that this is not always the case. It appears that reinforcement may be more important for performance than learning.

The work of Bandura on imitation learning shows that reinforcement is not always necessary and backs up the distinction between learning and performance. In studies where children have seen somebody being punished for their actions they tend not to imitate, but when later told that they will be rewarded for reproducing the punished behaviour they show that they have, in fact, learned it (see p. 172).

The fact that it is possible to learn without demonstrating it causes problems for our definition of learning as a relatively permanent change in *behaviour* (see p. 34 for the full definition). This definition combines learning and performance, but we will stick with it because although latent learning *can* occur, we cannot be sure that it *has* occurred until it is demonstrated in a change in behaviour.

The Use of Operant Conditioning

Operant conditioning, like classical conditioning, is used in the treatment of behaviour disorders. One fairly recent innovation is the use of operant conditioning to develop speech in schizophrenics and autistic patients. Nobody really yet knows what the cause of autism is, but it is characterized by a withdrawal from the environment, and seems to affect the individual in childhood. An autistic child does not respond when somebody talks to him, rarely makes an effort to interact with anybody else and could be said to live in a world of his own.

Operant conditioning can be used to induce autistic children to begin to speak. The basic principle of reinforcing the required behaviour is used to shape into speech patterns what few verbal responses the child does make. Often food is used as a reinforcer, or the opportunity to perform some activity which the child obviously likes. It is difficult to use cuddles or praise with autistic children because they do not often respond to such attention, and do not seem even to hear when they are addressed. From time to time even an autistic child makes some kind of noise with his vocal organs, usually grunts, groans or squeals. By using successive approximation, behaviour-shaping, the therapist first reinforces those sounds which come closest to words and then uses them as a basis to condition the child actually to utter proper words.

The next task is to condition the child to link words together into sentence form, in the hope that once the child begins to do so he will also begin to interact more with his environment and cease to be isolated.

Apparently it is not too difficult to condition an autistic child to utter some words. It is usually possible to persuade him to say one or two in an intensive two-hour session of conditioning, but the therapist often finds difficulty in getting him to string words together into sentence form. Some therapists are now training the parents of autistic children in the techniques of operant conditioning, so that the treatment continues outside the clinic.

It is important not to overestimate what can be achieved with this technique; it is most unlikely that this treatment alone will result in the child achieving 'normal' fluent conversation. The stresses on family life that can be caused by continually having to consider the reinforcement contingencies of an autistic child are often so great that the treatment is ended and the autistic's behaviour is accepted as it is.

BIOFEEDBACK

Until the mid-1960s it was assumed that classical and operant conditioning were absolutely separate types of learning, the major difference between them being that classical conditioning could work only with reflexes and operant conditioning could work only with voluntary – non-reflex – behaviour. However, some intriguing experiments in 1969 by N.E. Miller and L.V. DiCara at Rockefeller University in the USA suggested that the differences between classical and operant conditioning are much less great than had been thought. Miller and DiCara used operant conditioning to control the activity of parts of the autonomic nervous system in rats. By using behaviour-shaping techniques they were able to alter such involuntary responses as heart-rate, blood-pressure and intestinal contraction – responses it had been assumed it was not possible to control with anything other than classical conditioning, and then only with difficulty. Miller and DiCara administered a curare-derived drug which paralysed all the voluntary muscles in their subject in order to ensure that any changes in the autonomic responses were not caused by the conditioning of motor responses such as the animal relaxing or contracting its muscles. (Experienced practitioners of yoga can alter their heart-rate and blood-pressure, for example, with conscious muscular and breath control.) Because the rats were paralysed, food and water could not be used as reinforcers, so, following work by J. Olds, electrodes were implanted in a part of the rat's brain known as the 'pleasure centre'. Artificial stimulation of this part of the brain is apparently pleasurable, and can be used as a reinforcer. By making a correct response – lowering its heart-rate for example – the animal would be given a brief, mild electrical stimulation to the pleasure centre and this stimulation acted as the reinforcement.

Biofeedback techniques have now become very popular with the general public and the medical profession, and machines are commercially available which, when used to study humans, display EEG traces or galvanic skin-response changes (see pp. 301–3). An individual can condition himself, for example, to lower his arousal level, by using the knowledge that he is succeeding in doing so as a reinforcement. Research on biofeedback continues at an intense rate. There are indications that small groups of as few as three or four neurons can be controlled by an individual using biofeedback techniques, and some doctors are now becoming interested in using biofeedback on their patients as a method of controlling high blood-pressure, for example, without the use of drugs.

Even though biofeedback techniques have been shown to work as a therapy for reducing stress, blood-pressure and many other disorders, the original work of Miller and DiCara has not been successfully replicated, and so we cannot be sure that the effect really is produced simply by conditioning of the autonomic nervous system.

PROGRAMMED LEARNING

The shaping of human behaviour is similar to, but more complex than, the shaping of animal behaviour, because human beings can, of course, understand quite complicated instructions, and their initial repertoire of behaviour – from which certain responses will be selected – may already be much nearer the required goal. In addition, the range of reinforcers of humans is much wider. In a learning situation, for example, the knowledge that a correct response has been made, and therefore that the problem has been understood, is reinforcement in itself: a sense of satisfaction is derived from achievement. Acknowledgement of the correctness of a response may be given by a teacher or parent; alternatively a student or child may assess his own performance.

Learning, as we have said, involves a change in behaviour. What makes learning 'better' or more useful is the range of behaviour that can be produced by the new knowledge – the wider the range of behaviour, the better the learning. Operant conditioning in the form known as *programmed learning* seeks to improve student learning.

Programmed learning material may be presented in book form or on a computer. Skinner pointed out that when reading textbooks or listening to lectures, students are usually relatively inactive, making no responses that can be reinforced. In a lecture everybody is forced to progress at the same pace which may be too fast for some and too slow for others. Skinner devised programmed learning to get over these problems.

In the planning of a learning programme it is essential to predict behaviour; it must be known at which points a student may go wrong. This problem is greatly reduced by breaking down the information into very small steps called *frames*. After the student has read the information in a frame he is immediately given a question to answer. Once he has answered a question he is shown the correct answer. If his response was right he can move on to the next frame. Skinner argues that the programmes should be constructed in such a way that students will be correct at least 95 per cent of the time. The satisfaction of being right is supposed to be a reinforcer and so makes the student more likely to remember the material.

We can interpret the basis of this type of programmed learning, using the operant conditioning formula (if the student makes an incorrect answer he is not reinforced and has to repeat the frame that he got wrong):

Programmed learning techniques can be very useful in the teaching of material that can be broken into an orderly logical sequence. Some forms of programmed learning use frames with more information than those used by Skinner. In these forms, which are usually known as *branching programmes*, students choose their response to the question from a series of alternatives. If the answer is correct they move on to the next frame, just as in Skinner's *linear programmes*, but if they are wrong they are sent to another frame which gives an explanation of what they have done wrong and gives more information so that they can move forward at a slower pace than the student who gets all the answers right. The branching programmes do not fit so neatly into the operant conditioning framework, since they assume that students can learn a lot from their mistakes and are less concerned with immediate reinforcement. Many people prefer the branching programmes because they are usually more challenging than the other type, and although being right is pleasant, the frames of a linear programme tend to be so simple to ensure 95 per cent correct answers that they can become boring.

The Differences Between Classical and Operant Conditioning

In some ways classical and operant conditioning are quite distinct. Table 3.2 sets out the differences.

Table 3.2. Classical and Operant Conditioning

Classical conditioning	Operant conditioning
Deals only with voluntary behaviour	Deals with voluntary behaviour and involuntary (biofeedback) as well
Reinforcement strengthens the conditional response but is neutral: it works whether or not the organism likes it	Reinforcement strengthens the conditional response and is either positive (something the organism likes) or negative (the removal of an unpleasant stimulus)
The response is elicited by the reinforcer which has to be given before the response is made	Reinforcement is given after the response is voluntarily made, and strengthens it
Little or no weakening of the reinforcement is possible otherwise the response is extinguished. Schedules cannot be used to alter the response and extinction rate	The reinforcer may be greatly diffused, using schedules of reinforcement, to alter the response and extinction rates
A reinforcer can only trigger one type of response, for example, a puff of air across the eye always gives an eye-blink	A reinforcer can be used to strengthen many different responses using shaping techniques
Shows generalization, discrimination, extinction, spontaneous recovery	As classical conditioning
Relies on the linking or association of stimuli and responses, S–R	As classical conditioning

Insight and Learning Sets

Remember that one of the criticisms of classical conditioning is that it cannot explain all learning; and particularly, that it takes a long time. It must be admitted, however, that under certain conditions – usually when the unconditional stimulus is very strong – the conditioning procedure may take place in a single presentation of the CS and UCS. This is sometimes called *single-trial learning*.

Despite the possibilities afforded by one-trial classical conditioning it is not flexible or quick enough to explain all the learning processes which humans can show. operant conditioning, including the reinforcement schedules, gives us a better explanation; it shows how reinforcement is not necessary on every trial, and also how new forms of behaviour can develop gradually. But to some extent, operant conditioning is open to the same criticism as classical conditioning – that the process of learning takes such a long time.

A list of all the different forms of behaviour which humans can show would be massive. At a hazardous guess, adult humans may each have a repertoire of several thousand different kinds of response; yet from this vast repertoire they are able with remarkable speed to select those responses which help them to adapt to, or control their environment. Theoretically, operant conditioning can explain how we develop these large numbers of responses in the first place, but it does not seem to be so good at explaining how we are able to select the most efficient and appropriate response from our repertoire.

Thorndike's experiment with the cat's puzzle box (see p. 41) showed that learning came gradually as the correct response was reinforced and in-correct or non-reinforced responses were extinguished, but this took time – about 20 trials in the Thorndike experiment. The gradual development of new behaviour by the reinforcement of correct responses and the extinction of incorrect ones is termed *trial-and-error learning*, because with each successive trial the number of errors is reduced, until eventually the cor-rect response is the only one left. From your own experience it will seem that you do not have to spend such a long time working out the answer to a problem, but nothing we have looked at so far gives a really convincing explanation of how we can process so much information so quickly.

Certainly trial and error does play a part in our learning, particularly when we are developing entirely new types of response; but if we really do have several thousand different types of response, trial-and-error learning would surely involve our scanning the whole repertoire of our responses and trying them one by one. This would take a very long time to do. Psychologists studying the development of language in humans, for example, have said that if a child had to learn all the words and different sentence formations in English by trial and error he would reach adult fluency only at the age of a hundred. Because we know children do not take this long, some other process in addition to trial and error must be involved.

Kohler (1925) performed a range of studies with chimpanzees which demonstrated a different kind of learning known as *insight*. In most of the studies the chimps were presented with food that was out of reach and in order to get it they had to produce a novel piece of behaviour such as stacking up a set of boxes so that they could climb on to them and reach a piece of fruit, or using a stick to extend their reach and so draw a piece of food into their cage. Kohler claimed that the chimps solved these problems in a very different way to the trial-and-error methods that Thorndike and others had described. In the stick study, Sultan, Kohler's best-known chimp, tried first to reach the fruit by hand. Seeing that this was impossible, Sultan sat down and gazed around him. Suddenly he went over to the stick, picked it up and completed the task of retrieving the fruit as though he had thought out the solution and required no trial and error. The main stages of insight are:

1 A period of initial helplessness.
2 A pause in activity.
3 A sudden and smooth performance of problem solution.

Kohler argued that insight depends on the arrangement of the problem; all the tools and processes necessary for the solution of the problem must be available within the vision of the animal (for humans it can occur if they are all 'available' mentally). The solution comes as a process of what Kohler called *perceptual reorganization*, that is, the problem is suddenly seen differently and all the parts fall into place.

When this happens, for humans, we get a sudden 'Aha' experience, as the light dawns and a problem we have been thinking about for ages suddenly becomes crystal clear. This is very different to the gradual process of eliminating errors that occurs in trial-and-error learning. Once a solution has been produced by insight it can be transferred to other situations much more readily than one that has been produced by trial and error, because it is not so closely tied to *specific* stimuli and responses. What has been learnt is a general approach.

IS INSIGHT A SPECIAL FORM OF LEARNING OR CAN IT BE EXPLAINED USING THE PRINCIPLES OF TRIAL AND ERROR?

The special characteristics of insight seem to be that it is a form of learning which doesn't depend on previously existing responses or training, and that the insightful solutions occur suddenly after a period of apparent inactivity.

A number of studies suggest that insight can be explained by the same principles as the trial-and-error learning of operant conditioning.

Schiller (1952) showed that the responses used by Kohler's chimpanzees are already present in chimps that have not been in a situation where the responses were necessary to solve a problem. He left chimps with boxes in the cage and found that they would stack them in exactly the same way as Kohler's animals – even though they had been set no problem of reaching the food. If this sort of behaviour is already in the animal's repertoire, then Kohler's chimps were not producing a totally new insightful response, they were simply using an existing response in the same way as Thorndike's cats in his original work on trial-and-error learning.

Birch (1945) demonstrated that previous experience of using sticks was necessary to produce the 'insightful' solutions that Kohler described. He pointed out that Kohler had used apes which had grown up in the wild before being caught and brought to the experimental enclosure. Birch used chimpanzees that had been born in captivity and separated from their mother within two weeks of birth. The chimps were raised in a group, and diaries of their behaviour had been kept. Only one of the chimps had been seen to play with sticks before Birch put them into the experimental situation where, in order to gain food, they had to use a stick. Under these conditions Birch found that only two of the chimps solved the problem; one was the individual who had played with sticks before, and this animal acted very much like Kohler's apes. The other chimp solved the problem after accidentally knocking the sticks against the food and observing it move (this fits in well with the Thorndike interpretation of learning). The other chimps were perfectly capable of solving the problem but only managed to do it after Birch allowed them to play with sticks for a few days before retesting them.

At the Primate Laboratory of the University of Wisconsin in 1949, Professor Harry S. Harlow performed some brilliant investigations into how 'short cuts' allied to trial-and-error learning may enable us to apply previous learning to the learning of new things. Both monkeys and children were used in these experiments. The first type of experiment was a simple discrimination test. Two objects of different size, shape and colour were presented and by the use of straightforward operant conditioning they were conditioned to choose one of the objects. A peanut or raisin, or brightly coloured macaroni beads, were placed under the 'correct' object. They learnt to choose the correct object by trial and error, and as soon as they were able to choose the correct object immediately, two new objects were substituted and the same process repeated. After many trials involving several hundred different pairs of objects, Harlow reported that each new problem was solved more quickly than the one before, until the new problem solving shapes that had never been seen before would be solved in one trial. Harlow found that the children learnt more rapidly than the monkeys but still made the same kinds of error: in fact the fastest monkeys learnt more quickly than the slowest children.

But what was happening here? This was certainly not pure trial-and-error learning, especially not in the later trials. Trial-and-error learning certainly took place in the earlier trials, but after possibly two hundred such trials the participants were able to pick out the objects after only one trial, and thereafter continued to pick them, even though they might never have seen the particular pair of objects before. The later responses look very like those in the insight experiments.

Consider the behaviour of a monkey after two hundred such trials. It is presented with two shapes it has never seen before, one of which is the 'correct' one. By chance it may pick up the correct object first and if it does so will pick up the same object every time. If, however, it picks up the incorrect object on the first trial it will immediately pick up the correct object on the next trial and continue to do so from then on. Although pure trial and error was necessary in the earlier problems, it is clearly now no longer necessary. The animal seems to have performed quite a sophisticated piece of learning: as a result of having experienced the trial-and-error learning of the earlier tests, the monkey seems by this time to have developed some kind of ability to understand the type of problem, or to have understood the principles involved in solving this type of problem.

This was Harlow's belief. The rule (or rules) which enables the learner to solve problems similar in principle to those already solved, but which do not use the same objects or elements is called a *learning set*. A Learning Set is therefore a way of solving a particular type of problem, and this is why Harlow's experiments and the concept of learning sets are important: they provide an explanation of how, by trial and error, we can develop structures which enable us to learn quickly and efficiently.

An experiment in 1941 by Hendrikson and Schroeder showed that Learning Sets may be developed more quickly by the combination of a verbal explanation of the principles behind a problem, and practice. They gave two groups of boys the task of shooting pellets with an air-groups. The task facing both groups was to shoot pellets with an air-rifle at a target which was submerged in water, but before their target practice one group was given an explanation of the way in which water bends the light by refraction, so that the target is not actually in the position in which it appears. The other group received no explanation about refraction. Both groups were then allowed to shoot at the target and their performances were compared. There was very little difference in the number of trials which both groups needed to learn to hit the target, but once both groups were able to hit it, the depth of water covering the target was increased, which in turn increased the refraction. Under these circumstances the group who had had refraction explained to them performed much better than the other group, learning to hit the deeper target in fewer attempts. This was because the group who knew the principle of refraction were able to use this information to guide their trial and error. On its own the lecture of refraction was not enough to produce a strong learning set, and this is why the group did no better on the first trial, but the explanation *combined with the practice* did produce a learning set that would become even stronger with additional practice. From Harlow's work we would expect the group who had no explanation to develop a learning set if they had lots of practice with lots of different depths of water. Our language gives us a short cut to the development of learning sets.

There doesn't seem to be any need to think of insight as a special *explanation* for a particular type of learning, though the term may be useful as a description of particular pieces of behaviour where problem solutions are reached very quickly without *obvious* trial and error. The experience of insight can be very rewarding to human subjects – indeed many successful games have an insightful solution as their end point. When students solve problems in an insightful way they tend to remember more than if they are given the answer or put in a position where the solution is very easy. The teacher's task in this situation is to set a problem to which the student's previous experience is likely to allow an insightful response.

Conditioning theories can explain a lot of behaviour and have been used together with concepts such as imitation learning (see pp. 171–3) by the social learning theorists to explain much of human development. With their stress on external events, however, these theories often overlook the individual who is doing the actual learning. The work on imprinting (see pp. 150–3) shows us that learning may be easier at some times in the lifespan than others. Piaget's work (see pp. 89–93) stresses the importance of the development of the individual's capacity to learn.

Summary

1 Learning is a relatively permanent change in behaviour as a result of experience.
2 Classical conditioning (Pavlov) is probably the simplest form of learning, and is best on reflexes. The organism can be conditioned to make a reflex response to a different stimulus by repeated presentation of this new (conditional) Stimulus with the original (unconditional) stimulus. If the conditional stimulus is continually presented alone, the conditional response will gradually become weaker and stop; this is known as extinction. The organism will generalize the response to stimuli similar to the conditional stimulus, generalize the response to stimuli similar to the conditional stimulus, but generalization can be overcome by discrimination conditioning.

3 Classical conditioning may provide an explanation of how fears and anxieties can develop, and has been used by behaviour therapists to remove phobias, or to develop aversions to undesirable behaviour.

4 Operant conditioning (Skinner) is based on Thorndike's law of effect, and shows that responses which are reinforced by something an animal wants, needs or likes are repeated. Negative reinforcement involves the removal of unpleasant stimulation when the correct response has been made. It can deal with voluntary behaviour and with involuntary behaviour, using biofeedback techniques. Schedules of reinforcement and successive approximation or behaviour-shaping make it a very flexible technique.

5 Operant conditioning can be used, for example, in the shaping of speech in autistics; it is the basis of programmed learning.

6 Learning can occur without reinforcement, as shown in the latent learning experiments of Tolman.

7 Kohler suggested that insight learning was a distinct form of learning which required no trial and error. Insightful solutions occur suddenly after a period of apparent inactivity.

8 Harlow's work on trial-and-error learning and learning sets suggests how operant conditioning can enable an individual to learn not only single facts or responses but rules and principles.

Further Reading

Martin, G. and Pear, J., *Behaviour Modification: What it is and How to do it* (1998, Prentice Hall Int.).

Chapter 4

Memory

The term *memory* is used in a few different ways. We talk about memorizing something so that it can be remembered later, in the meantime the material is held in our memory. These parts of memory are known as:

ENCODING   This involves putting material into memory and is part of the learning process. People who complain that they have a poor memory often fail to pay attention at this stage and so it is not surprising that they cannot remember later. If, for example, you know that you have a bad memory for people's names then listen carefully when you are introduced, and use the name a few times while in conversation, you are much more likely to recall the name later.

STORAGE   When something has been learnt there is a change in the connections between cells in the brain. In the first few minutes or hours of storage the information may be easily lost, but if this does not happen the material may be stored for a lifetime.

RETRIEVAL   Memories are not stored in a form like video or tape recordings which can be simply played back later. Retrieving information involves reconstructing an event from clues available in the present situation as well as in the memory stores.

The first systematic studies of memory were performed over a hundred years ago by Ebbinghaus who used long lists of nonsense syllables. Nonsense syllables are three-letter 'words' like *cag* or *zos*. They are often used in memory experiments because they are meaningless; they do not have any special associations that would make some more easy to learn than others. Much of the work on memory follows the Ebbinghaus tradition of learning lists and remembering after a period of time. There are lots of possible variations that can be studied, such as the effect of different learning methods, what happens during the time interval and under what conditions the remembering occurs.

Rate of Forgetting

In 1885 Ebbinghaus learnt lists of nonsense syllables, and then tested himself at different intervals. For one list he would test himself after ten minutes, for another he would wait an hour, and so on until he had made tests for intervals up to 30 days. He found that by far the greatest amount of forgetting occurred during the day after learning, and that most of this was lost during the first hour. The amount that could be remembered after a week was almost the same as that after one day.

Many students test themselves immediately after revising a topic and then go on to study something else. When the exam occurs they may not remember much. To avoid this it is worth tackling the problem of forgetting during the first day or so; remember that this is when most forgetting occurs. After a revision session of about an hour, Tony Buzan recommends reviewing what you have learnt about ten minutes later. This review should only last a few minutes, and might take the form of going through the major points in your head and checking this against your notes. He argues that this slows down the early forgetting. Review again after one day, and perhaps again after a week, then after a month.

The amount of forgetting that is shown in an experiment depends partly on the method of measuring memory. If a participant is simply asked to write down the words or nonsense syllables that he or she has learnt in any order, this is known as free recall, but there are a number of other methods.

Sometimes people are asked to learn lists of word pairs such as tree–moat, dog–shoe, etc. This is known as *paired associate learning*. The participant is then given the first word of the pair and asked to recall the second, this is known as cued recall since the first word is the cue for what is to be recalled.

The *recognition method* requires people to pick out from a new list those words which they originally learnt; this method often results in greater amounts being remembered. You have probably had the experience of being unable to answer a question and yet, when the answer is given, realizing that you knew it all along. The recognition method is sometimes said to be an extreme form of cued recall, because all of the originally learned material is presented.

Another technique that can be used in the laboratory is the *relearning* or *savings method*. When this is used participants are timed when they first learn the list (usually until they can repeat the list once with no errors). After a time interval they are asked to learn the list again to the same proficiency. If anything is stored in memory, the relearning should take less time; the *savings score* is then worked out by the following formula:

$$\text{savings score} = \frac{T_a - T_b}{T_a} \times 100$$

where T_a is the time taken to learn the list the first time and T_b is the time taken to relearn. If a list takes ten minutes to learn on Monday, and five minutes to relearn on Tuesday, the savings score is 50 per cent.

It was the relearning method that Ebbinghaus used on his study of the rate of forgetting mentioned earlier. Similar results can be found with recall and recognition, except that it is more difficult to remember as much using the recall method.

Ebbinghaus showed that the amount forgotten could be reduced by *over-learning*, that is, continuing to study the list of nonsense syllables even after the whole list could be recited without error.

Serial Position Effect

When people hear a reasonable long list of unrelated words and are asked immediately to recall them in any order, there is a strikingly similar pattern in the words that they remember. Words at the end of the list tend to be remembered well (*the recency effect*), as do those at the beginning (*the primacy effect*), but the middle of the list is far less likely to be recalled. This pattern of recall is known as the *serial position effect* and is thought to occur because we have two sorts of memory, *short-term memory* (STM) and *long-term memory* (LTM). The effect also occurs if people read the list; as long as they are presented with each word separately, one after the other. The important thing is that the list is long enough to prevent people repeating all the words to themselves while they are receiving them, and that they are asking for a free recall *immediately* afterwards.

Figure 4.1 The Serial Position Effect

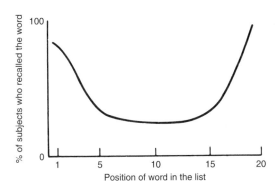

Let us examine the three parts of the serial position curve separately.

The recency effect. The words presented toward the end of the list are remembered well as long as the recall is done immediately after presentation. If people are not allowed to recall immediately, the recency effect disappears. Glanzer and Cunitz (1966) delayed participants' recall by asking them to count backwards for 30 seconds after presentation of the list. This removed the recency effect. Their participants recalled as few words from the end of the list as they did from the middle. Normally the words at the end of the list are in short-term memory which can only hold a small amount of information for a short period of time; unless they are retrieved almost immediately or put into long-term memory, the words will be lost.

The primacy effect. Glanzer's participants had little difficulty with recalling the words from the beginning of the list because these were in the long-term memory store which is not as affected by delay in recall. When they listen to the list, most people try to repeat the words to themselves; this is quite easy for the first few items on the list, but after that it gets more difficult because new words are being continually presented and there is not enough time to repeat the old one before a new one arrives. It is this *rehearsal* of the first few words that puts them into LTM and thus causes the primacy effect. Anything which prevents the rehearsal of the first few words will damage the primacy effect because fewer words will be put into LTM. Murdock (1962) did this by presenting the words more quickly and found that the primacy effect was reduced without damaging the recency effect. It is the fact that the primacy and recency effects are affected by different things that lends weight to the idea that there are two different memory stores.

The middle of the list. By the time we get to the middle of the list there are already too many words to allow much rehearsal of the new ones. The middle words go into STM, but without rehearsal they don't reach LTM, and are replaced from the short-term store by later items.

If a word in the middle of the list is outstanding in some way, it tends to be remembered despite its position. This is known as the *Von Restorff Effect.* The item might be the name of a famous person or it could be shouted while the others were all spoken. The fact that it is outstanding may make it more likely that people pick it out for rehearsal, or it may simply be easier to put this sort of item into LTM and retrieve it later. People have lots of existing connections for the words *Margaret* and *Thatcher* and so if these were put into the middle of a list they would probably be recalled. Simply remembering that there was a politician in the list or a well-known woman or an ex-prime minister might be enough to bring the precise words back.

Short-term and Long-term Memory

The Length of Time that Information can be Stored in STM and LTM

If you have ever dialled a new telephone number and, after hearing the engaged tone, realized that you can't remember the number to dial again, you have experienced the nature of short-term memory. Information is held in this store for a matter of only a few seconds and can only be kept there by rehearsal, repeating the information over and over. Peterson and Peterson (1959) showed that material can be kept in STM for only about 18–30 seconds; they found that people were unable to recall a nonsense syllable if they had counted backwards for more than this length of time after hearing it. (The idea of counting backwards was to prevent rehearsal of the nonsense syllable.)

Figure 4.2 The relationship between Short- and Long-term Memory (as outlined by Atkinson and Shiffrin, 1971)

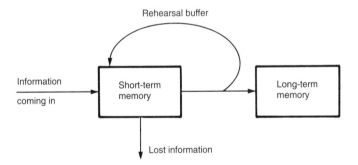

Once information is passed into LTM it may stay there for a lifetime, although it may not be easy to retrieve. The difficulty with LTM may be finding the right retrieval cues to get the information out again. We have already mentioned that people can often recognize things that they were unable to recall.

The Capacity of STM and LTM

Lots of studies have been performed to show how much information can be stored in STM. Participants are asked to repeat lists of words, letters or numbers immediately after they have heard or read them. The list may contain three, four, five or more items. People can usually do this successfully for lists of four or five items but are rarely able to repeat ten or more reliably. The short-term memory span is the amount of information that can be held in STM, and these studies show it to be between five and nine pieces of information with an average of seven for most people. With lists of random numbers or letters people are reliably successful on those containing seven items, but if the item can be *chunked* into units more can be retained. For example, most people would have difficulty repeating the following list of 13 randomly assorted letters:

w t l b o u r s e i a h c

but if the letters are rearranged, they can be chunked as three bits of information rather than 13:

two blue chairs

A 'chunk' is a unit of information but what is one chunk for some people may be a few chunks for others. For a mathematician the phrase 'the square on the hypotenuse is equal to the sum of the squares on the other two sides' may be one chunk. A student coming across the phrase for the first time might find that it comes very close to memory span.

It would be almost impossible to communicate if *all* we could do was receive each word separately and then pass on to the next. That is what would happen if short-term memory span was as small as one item with no possibility of chunking. Because short-term memory span is greater than that, we are able to hold a group of words as we receive them. This allows us to understand the idea being communicated by inspecting not only the individual words but also the relationship between them.

Because they have a lot of experience in a particular field, 'experts' are able to chunk into seven units of information ideas that the rest of us have no chance of fitting into STM. When this happens the 'expert' appears to be talking 'double Dutch'.

Broadbent has shown that memory span varies with age: young children and old people tend to have smaller spans. The difficulties that some older people report in learning new tasks may be related to this. E. and R.M. Belbin have shown that these learning difficulties may be reduced by the use of training techniques which involve learning through doing, rather than learning by listening to instructions.

Although the capacity of STM is limited the amount of information to be stored in LTM is not a problem. For all practical purposes there is no limit to the amount of information that can be stored.

Storage in STM and LTM

When people are asked to repeat lists of letters such as R, K, L, B, S, T, I not many mistakes are made, but those that do occur usually involve mixups between letters such as B, C, D, T and V which have a similar sound. Conrad (1964) showed that this occurs even when the letters are read rather than heard. This suggests that information is stored in STM as a sound pattern, rather like a tape of the original. This is known as *phonetic storage*, and is thought to be the main type of short-term storage, though non-verbal material such as pictures may be stored in a visual form. Confusions in LTM recall are much more likely to involve mixing up words with similar meanings; the word CAR may be recalled instead of VAN, for example. The form of storage which retains the general meaning rather than the specific sounds of the original message is known as *semantic storage* and is thought to be the main mode in the LTM.

Levels of Processing

A number of psychologists question the idea that we have two different memory stores. Craik and Lockhart (1972) prefer to think of memory as a by-product of what is done with the information rather than as a series of stores. When we read or hear something they argue that it is usually analyzed in a series of stages as shown below:

The first stages of analysis involve inspection of what the message looks or sounds like, and only after the material has been inspected in that way does the brain look at the meaning of the information (*semantic analysis*).

Each stage or level of analysis contributes to the memory store; the strongest memories are produced by the later (deeper) levels of analysis. They argue that the characteristics of memory that we have discussed so far should be explained in this way rather than taken as evidence for two separate storage systems. They say that when people are asked simply to repeat a list, the items are only analysed at the first (shallow) levels and not at the deeper, semantic level. Information that is not deeply analysed will not be stored so well and this looks like an STM store; deeply processed information is well stored and has the characteristics of LTM.

Craik and Tulving (1975) showed people words for a short time and asked them a question about each word as it was shown. There were three kinds of question, each of which needed a different level of analysis of the word. At the shallowest level the question asked whether the word was written in capital letters. Another type of question asked if it rhymed with the word 'weight'; this needed slightly deeper analysis. The deepest level of analysis was encouraged by asking if the word could sensibly be fitted into the sentence like 'He met a — in the street'; to answer this question the word had to be analysed at the semantic level. People were not told before they looked at the words that they were later going to be asked to remember them. When given another list of words and asked which ones they had previously been shown, people recognized 15 per cent of the words associated with the first type of question, 50 per cent of those which had had the question about rhyming and 80 per cent of those which had required semantic analysis.

Atkinson and Shiffrin's theory of long-term and short-term memory states that rehearsal helps the transfer of information from one to the other, but Craik and Watkins (1973) showed that rehearsal does not necessarily put things into LTM. They read lists to participants after asking them to remember only critical words (e.g. those starting with C). If the words were early in the list it was assumed that they would be rehearsed a lot; if later, then only a few times. They found that the amount of rehearsal made no difference to whether the word was remembered.

Craik and Watkins distinguish *maintenance rehearsal* and *elaborative rehearsal*. Maintenance rehearsal involves only simple repetition of words and does not help long-term retention. Elaborative rehearsal occurs when you think about the meanings of the words that you are trying to remember and this makes the information more likely to be stored for a long period.

In general, we can say that searching for meaning, rather than simply repeating things over and over again, is important for learning, and this will be shown in later sections of this chapter.

Although the levels of processing theory is attractive and can explain many of the things we know about memory it has a big problem when it comes to defining the level at which you process any particular piece of information; the tendency is to wait until it is remembered well, and then to say that it must have been processed at a deep level. This is a bit like the guy in the pub who can always tell you why a particular horse won the race yesterday but can never give reliable tips before the event.

Working Memory

Rather than thinking of STM as a simple storage space Baddeley proposed an active process concerned with the reception of material from the senses, holding words we are about to speak and keeping information in conscious thought. The limitations on the system are not a matter of storage space but of limited capacity to process information. Baddeley uses the term *working memory* to distinguish it from Atkinson and Shiffrin's model of STM. The short-term memory of Atkinson and Shiffrin can be compared to a cupboard with limited space but Baddeley's working memory is more like somebody sorting out pieces of information with a limit to the amount that they can do at any one time. STM is a single store but working memory is a number of memory processes as shown below:

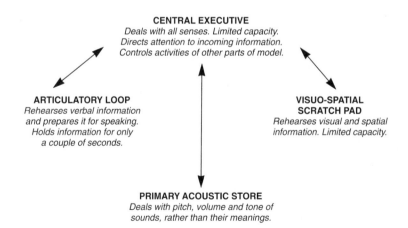

CENTRAL EXECUTIVE
Deals with all senses. Limited capacity. Directs attention to incoming information. Controls activities of other parts of model.

ARTICULATORY LOOP
Rehearses verbal information and prepares it for speaking. Holds information for only a couple of seconds.

VISUO-SPATIAL SCRATCH PAD
Rehearses visual and spatial information. Limited capacity.

PRIMARY ACOUSTIC STORE
Deals with pitch, volume and tone of sounds, rather than their meanings.

The central executive is the controller of this system. It can deal with information from any of the senses and allows us to switch attention between different senses. It also directs the operations of the other three parts of the system, and can store a small amount of information itself.

The articulatory loop is similar in function to Atkinson and Shiffrin's STM. When hearing something it allows the rehearsal of verbal information in order to prevent it being lost and when we are speaking it holds ready the next few words which we are about to say. You may be conscious of the activities of the articulatory loops as an 'inner voice'.

The visuo-spatial scratch pad deals with visual and with spatial (where things are) information. Like the articulatory loop, it allows us to rehearse both incoming and outgoing information; if you close your eyes and try to remember what objects are presently in the room you will be using this scratch pad. The output part of the visuo-spatial scratch pad comes into play when, for example, you are travelling down a familiar route and you can see in your mind's eye what to expect round the next bend.

The primary acoustic store deals with the volume, tone and pitch of sounds; it does not deal with the meanings of words (that is the function of the articulatory loop). In chapter 2 we briefly remarked that if someone across the room mentions your name you quite often hear it, even though you may be involved in another conversation at the time; this is known as the *cocktail party phenomenon*. The acoustic store is responsible for this because, even though it doesn't recognize your name as a word, it is highly sensitive to this particular pattern of sound, and alerts the central executive which causes us to turn our full attention to the direction from which the sound came.

The Constructive Nature of Memory

Although much work on memory has been in the Ebbinghaus tradition, which allows tight control of experimental conditions and easily measured results, there is also another strand in the history of memory research. These studies don't always provide such clear-cut numerical evidence, but they have the advantage of dealing with material which is more realistic than lists of nonsense syllables. Early work using this approach was conducted by Bartlett (1932) using the method of *serial reproduction*. He read an Eskimo folk tale called 'The War of the Ghosts' to someone, who then had to repeat as much of it as they could to a second person, who then repeated it to a third, and so on. After six or seven reproductions the story had become much shortened from its original 330 words to approximately 180 words. What was interesting, however, was the way in which the story changed. The overall meaning of the folk tale was not easily understood by British listeners, and the first people in each experiment tended to distort the story in a way which produced a theme that made sense in our culture. This constructed theme usually remained undistorted through all further repetitions of the story. In one unpublished experiment performed with our own students, the supernatural theme of the original story became transformed into a short tale of gang warfare, and a part of the original story, which ran '"Arrows are in the canoe," they said', became distorted into 'We've got some guns in our car', and 'Kalama', one of the place names in the original study, was changed to 'Colombo'.

Bartlett believed that the information which fitted into an individual's existing *schemas* (mental frameworks) was likely to be retained. Information which did not fit was liable to be either forgotten or distorted, so that it did fit. This distortion Bartlett believed, occurred as a result of people's 'efforts after meaning': that is people's attempts to get the story to fit their schemas by changing the sentence structure from its original, rather stilted form into a more flowing style; by interpreting the story so as to provide a more understandable theme or moral; and by rationalization: that is, the introduction of the people's own reasons for unexplained occurrences in the original story.

Bartlett pointed out that people drew inferences from the information to be retained. For example, in later reproductions of 'The War of the Ghosts' if people are given the information that 'Indians' were involved, they might well infer that 'Indians' stood for 'Red Indians', and bias their story accordingly. However, when people leave out information about canoes and arrows, those following them might well infer that 'Indians' stood for 'Indians from India' (which perhaps explains where 'Colombo' came from). It is therefore apparent that we do not receive information passively and store it just as a tape recorder might: we process the information in an active attempt to understand it. If a nuclear physicist and a lawyer were given passages of material involving nuclear physics concepts of study, and were later given recall tests, it is a reasonable supposition that, other things being equal, the nuclear physicist's recall score would be higher than the lawyer's. In Bartlett's terms, more of the material would fit into the nuclear physicist's schemas than it would into the lawyer's, who, if they were to attempt to obtain an equally high score, would have to show a great deal of 'effort after meaning'. This idea is, of course, not new: Ebbinghaus was aware of it in the nineteenth century and used nonsense syllables specifically to control for the fact that words may have different levels of familiarity and meaning from one person to another.

The work of Loftus and others in the section on eye-witness testimony (later in the chapter) follows the Bartlett tradition and sheds further light on the constructive and inferential nature of memory.

The Effect of Organization on Memory

If memory were simply a matter of playing back the original event, like a video recording, it would be very easy to remember the exact words used earlier in this chapter to describe long- and short-term memory. It is unlikely that you could do that, but you could probably give a general summary of what we wrote. The summary would probably reflect the general organization of the information in the book, but the way in which your answer was organized would also tell us something about your own schema for the topic. Even when people are shown lists of words presented in a random order, their later recall usually has some order imposed on it. Bousfield (1953) took lists of animals, cities, weapons and other categories, and mixed them into a random order. He then asked participants to memorize the lists. When they remembered the words later, the typical participant recalled the words in related groups, for example they recalled some cities, then some animals, followed by a group of weapons, and so on.

Later studies have looked at how memory can be affected by a variety of methods of organizing the original material before or during learning.

Bower et al. (1969) showed that organization of the material to be learnt could greatly improve future recall. He asked people to learn the words on four cards, a total of 112 words in all. The words were arranged in the form of branching diagrams, one of which is outlined in table 4.3. The learners were allowed to study each card for a minute, and as soon as they had seen all four they were asked to recall as many of the words as possible. Half the learners had cards where the words were presented in logical branching diagrams as in the table; the other half were shown the words but they were presented randomly on the branches. Once people had recalled the words, they were allowed to study the cards again. This was repeated until they had recalled the words four times. The group who studied the logically organized cards averaged 73 correct words on the first recall, 106 on the second, and remembered all 112 words on the subsequent recalls. The other group learned more slowly, recalling first 21, then 39, followed by 53 words on the third recall and 70 words on the fourth.

Table 4.3. The Sort of Hierarchical Organization of Material Used by Bower et al. (1969)

Minerals				
Metals			Stones	
Rare	Common	Alloys	Precious	Masonry
Platinum	Aluminium	Bronze	Sapphire	Limestone
Silver	Copper	Steel	Emerald	Granite
Gold	Lead	Brass	Diamond	Marble
	Iron		Ruby	Slate

Wittrock and Carter (1975) showed that memory was even better when learners organize the material themselves. They produced tables in the form of hierarchies like the ones used by Bower, except that some of their 'hierarchies' were scrambled so that they did not make sense (e.g. the word 'brass' might appear at the top and 'minerals' appear somewhere else, together with many other changes). Half the people were asked simply to copy the lists out and the other half were asked to look for connections between the words and to rearrange them into a sensible order before writing them down. Everyone was asked to recall the words. The results are shown in table 4.4.

The results show that the effect of organization of material on later recall is greatest when the learner does at least some of the organizing. The improvement may be interpreted as a result of a deeper level of processing of the material, or it may simply be that the new organization links better with the learner's existing schema.

Table 4.4. The Mean Number of Words Remembered in Wittrock and Carter's Study

	Scrambled hierarchy	Real hierarchy
Subjects asked to copy list	11	17
Subjects asked to search for connections before writing the list	21	22

The amount of detail put into the organization of material while studying it affects later recall. Mandler (1967) used a set of cards each of which had a word on it. He asked people to sort the words into categories; they had to produce at least two but no more than seven categories, the exact number was up to them. People were not told to learn the words but were later tested for recall. He found that the number of words recalled increased with the number of categories that they had sorted the cards into. There is a tendency for more intelligent individuals to divide the words into more categories and this may partly explain the results, but it does appear that the detail of organization itself is an important factor.

Active organization to pick out the distinctive properties of the material seems to be more important than the intention to learn, as far as later recall is concerned. Mandler found that people who had been told to learn the words while sorting them did no better than those who were not told this. Those who were instructed to learn the words, but not told to sort them into categories, did not recall as many words as others who were simply asked to sort the cards into categories without knowing they would be tested later.

The most efficient learners actively search for organization in the material to be learned, but most people don't do this unless it is pointed out to them. Learning is partly a process of fitting new information into our existing mental framework; if the new information doesn't fit in with our existing schemas it will be much more difficult to remember, and is likely to be forgotten or distorted, as Bartlett showed. Organization of material may help identify the appropriate existing schema in which to store the material or may contribute to the production of new schemas.

The importance of helping the learner identify the appropriate schema can be shown by reading the passage below:

> The procedure is actually quite simple. First you arrange items into different groups. Of course one pile may be sufficient depending on how much there is to do. If you have to go somewhere else due to lack of facilities that is the next step; otherwise, you are pretty well set. It is important not to overdo things. In the short run this may not seem important but complications can easily arise. A mistake can be expensive as well. At first the whole procedure will seem complicated. Soon, however, it will become just another facet of life. It is difficult to foresee any end to the necessity for this task in the immediate future, but then one never can tell. After the procedure is complete one arranges the materials into their appropriate places. Eventually, they will be used once more and the whole cycle will then have to be repeated. However, that is part of life (Bransford and Johnson 1972).

The passage appears very badly written and you probably had great difficulty following it; it is unlikely that you would remember it for long even if you tried. The passage is about washing clothes: look back at it now and you will find it much easier to read and remember. Telling you that it was about washing clothes enables you to understand it using your existing schema for this subject; subsequent recall will be relatively easy because you already know quite a lot about this and you will use this existing knowledge when reconstructing the passage.

Bransford and Johnson (1972) found that giving the title to participants before they encountered the 'washing clothes' passage was far more effective for understanding and later recall than presenting the title after the passage.

When given before the passage the title acts as an *advance organizer*. Advance organizers provide a framework in which new material can be understood by selecting the appropriate schema to analyze and store the information. Ausubel argues that teachers should provide advance organizers to help in the learning of new material. At the beginning of the lesson, teachers might give a general summary of what was going to be learnt before proceeding with specific points of information, or they may ask the students to look out for particular points while watching a film.

Most material that we read makes more sense than did the Bransford and Johnson passage, but simply reading through a chapter is not the most effective way of studying. A study by Boker (1974) shows that asking questions can help later recall. He gave students questions before or after reading a passage of about 2,500 words and tested them a week later. The test contained the same questions that had been given during the study period plus some that had not been seen before. The results are shown in table 4.5.

Table 4.5. Boker's Results

	Score on the test a week later	
	For questions presented in the study period	For other questions
Control group (no questions)	12.5	11.5
Questions seen before reading	13.8	10.9
Questions seen after reading	15.2	13.9

For the test as a whole, questions asked after the students had read the material were most effective. Perhaps this was because those who had seen the questions first tended to concentrate on those parts of the passage that were relevant to the question, and paid less attention to the rest. Those who looked at the questions after reading the passage could use them to review what they had read. Boker asked simple factual questions, but others have shown that questions that require reflection have even greater effect.

Other researchers have shown that questions asked in advance of study can help later recall, but the nature of the questions is important. Specific questions such as 'Who was Henry VIII's fourth wife?' don't work well as advance organizers and are best asked after study. General questions such as 'What factors affected the relationship between Henry VIII and the pope?' work well as either advance organizers or for reflection after study.

Mnemonics

Mnemonics are techniques used to aid memory. They provide a framework which can be used during memorization and later when the material is recalled. These devices may be used to perform memory stunts where large numbers of unrelated words are learnt on one presentation and recalled very accurately, but they can also be put to more serious use. There are a number of different systems.

One type is the *method of loci*. With this method it is necessary to imagine yourself in a place that you know very well. If the place you choose is your own front room and the words to be remembered are BUS, HORSE, SHIP, etc., you should imagine walking around your house, and when the word BUS is presented visualize a BUS on the mantelpiece, the HORSE possibly sitting in your favourite chair and the SHIP could be floating through the door. The more unusual the image, the better. When asked to recall the list, you should simply make another mental walk around the house and notice the images.

This is an example of a *peg system* where the new material is hung on to a series of 'pegs' that have been previously well learnt. Another well-known example involves first of all learning a set of peg words that rhyme with the numbers one to ten as follows:

one	bun
two	shoe
three	tree
four	door
five	hive
six	sticks
seven	heaven
eight	gate
nine	vine
ten	hen

The first word of any new list to be learnt is now combined in an image with a bun, the second with a shoe and so on. Again the more unusual the image the better; so that if you had to learn BUS, HORSE, SHOP, etc., you might imagine a huge cream bun with a bus sticking out of the middle, a horse with a shoe on its head and a tree with ships hanging from its branches. Using this system, it is quite easy to answer questions such as 'What is the seventh word in the list?', or to recall the list in reverse order by simply using the peg words to recall the words of the list.

Many people remember the colours of the rainbow in the correct order by recalling the phrase Richard Of York Gave Battle In Vain. The first letter of each word stands for the colours, red, orange, yellow, green, blue, indigo, violet. Using this method avoids forgetting any of the colours, and ensures that they are recalled in the right order.

Most people know rhymes to help remember things such as the number of days in each month, or when to put an 'i' before an 'e' in spelling.

Mnemonics are useful for learning lists of words which have no obvious logical order, and some people consider them to be nothing more than interesting party tricks, useful only to primary school children, or for a few instances where a student may have to learn a list such as the names of the ten cranial nerves (there is a wonderfully rude mnemonic for that!). It is true that mnemonics will not aid understanding and reasoning, but they can be used to ensure that basic facts are remembered, allowing a student to concentrate more on the high-level intellectual skills. We once had a group of students who were very keen on the use of mnemonics; when asked to write an essay on conformity and obedience (see pp. 113–23) they first of all recalled the mnemonic SMACK which reminded them that the work of Sherif, Milgram, Asch, Crutchfield and Kelman *might* be relevant to the essay. It was then up to them to decide whether to include all this work or not. The mnemonic did not tell them exactly what each psychologist had contributed to the area, but it did ensure that an important part of the essay was not missed simply because it slipped from memory.

The very act of making up a mnemonic can be useful because to do it, you have to look through your notes and decide what is worth remembering; the research into levels of processing (see p. 67) tells us that activities like this make information more likely to be recalled at a later date.

State-dependent Memory

A number of studies have shown that we are more likely to remember things if the conditions at the time of recall are similar to when we first experienced them; this is known as *state dependency*. I'm sure you have at one time or another gone to fetch something from another room – only to find when you get there you have forgotten what it was you came for. The most effective way to solve this is to go back to the original room where the memory often immediately comes back. The reason for this is probably that the original room contains many cues which help you reconstruct the original thought.

The similarities between the first experience and later remembering may be external conditions (such as the room you are in), or personal conditions (such as the mood you are in).

Baddeley has done a lot of work with deep-sea divers to try to improve their performance and safety at work. In one experiment he asked them to learn a list of words and recall them later. The divers learnt the words underwater and then returned to the surface. Later half of them were asked to recall the list underwater, and the other half to recall on shore. He found that those who learned and recalled under the same conditions did far better than the others. Later research showed that this effect only worked for recall and not for recognition; this is presumably because the extra cues that are available when in the same conditions as learning are relatively weak compared with the extra retrieval cues available in a recognition task.

Eich and others have done a number of studies which show that people who have taken drugs such as marijuana before learning remember best if they are under the influence of the drug during recall. Those who had no drug at the time of learning do best if they have no drugs at the time of recall. The words that Eich used came from a number of categories. If participants are given these category names when trying to remember, they remember far more than when the recall is not cued in this way, and it no longer makes any difference whether there is a match between their drug state when learning or remembering.

Bower (1981) showed that individuals are more likely to remember things if they are in the same emotional state as when they first experienced them. His participants kept diaries for a week, recording anything that they found pleasant or unpleasant. They were later tested for recall after being hypnotized and put into a pleasant or unpleasant mood. Participants recalled more of the experiences that matched their hypnotically induced mood. This study has great implications for people who suffer from depression, since when they are in this state they are far more likely to remember un-pleasant than pleasant things, thus making it even more difficult to recover; treatment should involve trying to overcome this effect by strengthening the recall of pleasant things.

Eye-witness Testimony

At one time, the most effective form of evidence that could be given in a court was that someone had seen the defendant actually committing the crime. This eye-witness testimony is no longer regarded in such high esteem as a result of several notorious cases in the 1970s, where eye-witnesses were shown to be inaccurate, and also as a result of a mass of psychological evidence which shows that our memories of events cannot be considered as a simple rerun of the event itself.

A study by Loftus and Palmer (1974) demonstrates the problems with this form of testimony. They showed a film of a car accident and later asked viewers to estimate the speed of the car that was moving. There were, of course, variations in the answers, but Loftus and Palmer showed that much of the variation depended upon the way that the question was asked. They asked the same basic question each time, but varied one or two words. The basic question was 'About how fast were the cars going when they — each other?' and the words used at the point marked — could be 'hit', 'contacted', 'smashed into', or others. The average estimate of speed was greater when the question used the words 'smashed into' than when it included the word 'contacted' (see table 4.6).

Courts have always tried to avoid the use of the *leading question* such as 'When did you stop beating your wife?', which contains within it the assumption that you did at one time beat your wife, and could lead people into saying things that they did not mean. Loftus and Palmer's study shows that the precise words used have an effect on the replies to questions that are not so obviously leading.

The effect shown by Loftus and Palmer fits in well with the view of memory as a constructive process involving the rebuilding of events from information, feelings and beliefs held within a schema (see p. 71). The actual words used in questioning have an effect on the schema and the reconstruction of the event.

If the question does have an effect on the schema, it is a lasting one and does it alter the general memory of the event? The answer appears to be yes. In a similar study to their original Loftus and Palmer quizzed their participants again a week after viewing the film. This time they asked a new question: 'Did you see any broken glass?', and found that although most people correctly answered 'No' some said 'Yes'. The likelihood of their reporting broken glass was affected by the question that they had been asked a week earlier. Of those asked about the speed the cars were going when they 'smashed into' each other, 32 per cent reported broken glass, but only 14 per cent of those whose questions included the word 'hit'. Of viewers who had not been questioned at all after the film, only 12 per cent reported broken glass when asked a week later.

Table 4.6. Showing the Word Used Within the Question 'About How Fast Were the Cars Going When They — Each Other', and the Resulting Speeds Estimated by Witnesses

Words used within the question	Average estimated speed in miles/hour
Contacted	31.8
Hit	34.0
Bumped into	38.1
Collided with	39.3
Smashed into	40.8

Schemas are mental models involving the attitudes, beliefs and experiences related to particular areas of our psychological world; they help us to understand events as well as remember them, and so someone's memory of an event can be affected by their experiences before they ever witness it. (See chapter 2 for a discussion of the factors that affect the perception of an event.)

Loftus has done a number of studies to discover common mis-conceptions about eye-witness testimony. She found that people generally believe that the more confident a witness is, the more you can rely on their evidence, though in fact research suggests that there is little or no relation-ship between confidence and accuracy. Most people felt that violent crimes were more likely to be remembered accurately though, in fact, the opposite is true.

Early in the investigation of a crime the most important information that the police need may be a good description of the criminal. This may be acquired in a number of ways but our ability to produce accurate infor-mation is questionable.

In laboratory studies, when people are asked to pick out photographs that they have been shown earlier from the larger group of photos, the success rate is often 90 per cent or more, but when witnessing a real crime or accident the situation is often one which makes accurate perception and memory less likely. The event itself may be over very quickly and occur in the dark or at a distance from the observer. The witness may be paying attention to something else, not realizing that a crime is being committed. If the accident or the crime is violent the observer may be frightened, causing problems with perception and memory. Loftus argues that when a weapon is used the observer's attention may be focused on this rather than upon the person holding it.

Buckhout (1974) staged a 'crime', in which a professor was attacked in front of 141 students: he then asked each witness to say what had happened and to give a description of the assailant. As with most studies of this type, he found that the witnesses overestimated the length of time the incident lasted. He also found that the accuracy of description of dress and appear-ance was only about 25 per cent. The estimations of height and weight were fairly accurate, but his 'criminal' was average in both these respects and this might have helped. In classroom studies with our own students we have found that estimates of height and weight vary considerably when describ-ing such 'criminals' from memory. This effect is not solely due to memory problems, however, since many errors were made when estimating the height and weight of a stranger when the students were seated and he was actually standing in front of them; the most common error we found was the underestimation of the weight of 'well-built' males by light, female students.

The identikit system was designed to help produce a reasonable likeness of suspects by building up a face bit-by-bit, but the system assumes that we notice all the pieces of a face, although we may, in fact, simply have a general impression. Studies show that only about one-third of people are able to build up an accurate identikit picture immediately after seeing a photograph of the person to be described, even when helped by experienced photokit operators. The new computer-based systems may give a more lifelike end product, but will still be limited by the perception and memory of the witness.

Most of the discussion so far has been about *recall* of events, and we know that *recognition* is usually a more powerful method of remembering things (see p. 62). In criminal investigations recognition is involved when a witness is asked to look through a series of photographs of known criminals, and also in the identity parade. A witness may recognize the photograph of a suspect whom they were not able to describe fully, providing useful leads for the police to work on. They may, however, pick out the wrong person altogether, due to a few basic similarities. Loftus talks about the way that the original memory of an event becomes blended with later information, and there is some evidence that searching through these 'mugshots' may affect selection in later identity parades.

The identity parade itself has a number of inbuilt problems which can have an effect on accurate identifications. Dent and Gray point out that witnesses are often very nervous during an identity parade, because they have to inspect people closely in a way which is unusual in normal social relationships; at the same time they have to make important decisions and confront someone they believe to be a criminal. As a result of this nervousness, the process of comparing the parade members with the original memory may suffer: witnesses may actually make their judgement too quickly in order to escape from the ordeal. The fact that it is known in advance that the police suspect somebody in the parade makes it more likely that an identification will be made, even if the real criminal is not present.

The rules governing the conduct of identity parades try to ensure that the suspect does not stick out like a sore thumb, but the 'criminal' may draw attention to himself by his own nervousness. Care needs to be taken so that the other members of the parade don't stand further away from the suspect than they do from each other; there are many other non-verbal signs which could be given out without any conscious intention, and which might point to the person whom the police suspect.

Dent and Gray (1975) showed that people were more likely to make a correct identification of a suspect seen earlier in a filmed 'crime' if they looked at pictures of the people on the identity parade than if they were involved in a live identity parade. When the photographs were used, 29 per cent of people made a correct positive identification (i.e. when making the identification they were sure that they had chosen the right person and they were in fact correct); in the live condition only 17 per cent made a correct positive identification. In both conditions 17 per cent of witnesses identified the wrong person, but felt sure that they were right. In a later study Dent showed that viewing the identity parade through a one-way screen also increased the number of correct positive identifications, and she argues that this is because the witnesses are less emotional and spend more time making their judgement.

The evidence about the unreliability of eye-witness testimony shows how important it is that it is not used as the sole criterion for convicting someone. Judges in their summing-up before a jury retires to consider its verdict are now required to comment upon the nature of the identification evidence.

A number of claims have been made for the use of hypnosis to improve witnesses' memories, but the fact that people are very suggestible when under hypnosis makes it very difficult to be sure that an undistorted recollection of the event is produced. A more promising technique involves taking the witnesses through the event step by step, asking them how they felt, what they were doing just before the event, and making them relive the event mentally. This technique fits in with the work on state-dependent memory (see p. 77).

Forgetting

We have already seen that if information is not passed into LTM, it is forgotten within about half a minute, unless it is repeated. This short-term forgetting may simply be due to the passage of time, the memory may fade like a tablet dissolving in water. Since STM has such a small capacity, it is more likely the contents are displaced by new material coming in.

In LTM much is 'forgotten' within the first few hours, as shown by Ebbinghaus, but material which can still be recalled after a few days is likely to be remembered for a long time. The problem of forgetting in LTM is not that the memory is lost altogether, but that it may be difficult to retrieve the information, or that it has been distorted as shown in the work of Bartlett and Loftus discussed earlier.

Forgetting is the other side of the coin to remembering, and so most of the preceding part of this chapter can be seen to relate to forgetting just as much as it does to memory. In this section we shall look at just three factors affecting forgetting. They are *interference, physical damage* and *emotion*.

Interference
Activity before or after learning a piece of information may cause forgetting. The effect of old experiences on new learning is known as *proactive interference*. Ebbinghaus experienced this when he found that his memory for new lists of nonsense syllables was being affected by those he had learnt before; sometimes a syllable that he thought was from one list turned out to be from a list he had studied earlier in the day.

Dallenbach (1924) showed that forgetting is not just a matter of time: it depends more on what happens during the time interval between learning and remembering. He trained two groups of cockroaches to walk through a maze without making any errors and then tested them again after eight hours. One group of cockroaches was wrapped in cotton wool during the time interval; when this is done the insect becomes very inactive. The others were left to do whatever cockroaches do. When tested on the maze eight hours later, the active group made three times as many errors as the inactive animals. This effect is known as *retroactive interference*.

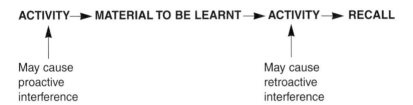

ACTIVITY➤ MATERIAL TO BE LEARNT➤ ACTIVITY➤ RECALL

May cause
proactive
interference

May cause
retroactive
interference

Interference damages more than the recall of lists of nonsense syllables or maze-learning by cockroaches; it can also affect learning of meaningful information. The study of Anderson and Myrow (1971) is an example. They asked high school students to study a passage about a tribe known as the primitive Himootians. Two days later they were asked to study a second passage. For half the students (the experimental group) the second passage was about another tribe whose behaviour had both similarities and differences to that of the Himootians. The rest of the students (the control group) studied a passage on drug addiction.

A week later both groups were tested on their knowledge of the primitive Himootians. The experimental group did better than the controls when recalling information that was the same for both tribes, such as the fact that they both brewed their own beer. When, however, they were tested on information which appeared only in the Himootian passage, the experimental group fared worse than the controls, and worse still when the information in the Himootian passage was directly contradictory to that in the passage for the other tribe. An example of this contradictory information was that the Himootian male had to remain single until they had mastered their work, but men in the other tribe had to perform a feat of daring before marriage was allowed. When the information in the two passages was contradictory, students often mixed up the two.

The most important factors affecting interference are *similarity* and *time*. New information is most likely to interfere with existing memories if it is of a similar type, and comes soon after the first material is learnt.

When doing your own studying you can avoid the worse effects of interference by following the guidelines below:

1 Identify topics that may interfere with each other. An example in psychology is the work on operant and classical conditioning. The topics are often confused because they are both concerned with such concepts as stimulus, response, reinforcement, generalization, etc. There are similarities between the two areas, but also differences.

2 Learn or revise one of the topics, and leave the second for a few days or weeks. Although operant and classical conditioning appear in the same chapter of this and other textbooks, you do not have to revise them both at once.

3 When studying the second topic, highlight the differences between the two topics and try to think about the reasons for those differences. One of the basic differences between operant and classical conditioning is whether the reinforcement comes before or after. The response in classical conditioning deals with reflex reactions, something is necessary to get the animal to respond in the first place. It doesn't really matter that your reason for linking one piece of information with one topic is the 'right' one; as long as it makes sense to you, interference is likely to be avoided.

4 Interference does not necessarily occur immediately; getting 100 per cent when you test yourself at the end of a revision period does not necessarily mean that you will have no difficulties a few days later. It is good practice to return to the material the next day and spend just a few minutes reviewing it.

Physical Damage

A severe physical shock, such as a drug overdose or a bang on the head, can cause amnesia. It is very rare that amnesia involves total forgetting, and in cases where someone has no memory at all it is much more likely that a severe emotional crisis is involved. Material in STM is most affected by physical shock, and it is not unusual for people who have had bad car accidents to be unable to remember the crash itself. In the early stages memory may be more affected, but it usually returns; and Russel and Nathan (1946) in a survey of accident victims suffering from amnesia showed that memory is usually affected for no more than a half-hour before the event.

Studies in which animals are taught to run mazes and then given a severe electric shock either immediately or a while later also show that forgetting occurs if the shock is given within half an hour or so of the maze learning.

It seems that when memories are first encoded there is a period of *consolidation* during which time they are easily disturbed and after which they are relatively safe from damage.

Physical damage to some parts of the brain can make it impossible to remember anything for more than a few moments. Milner (1966) had a patient with damage to the part of the brain known as the *hippocampus*. This patient could remember details of his life before the accident, but was unable to put new information into LTM; he could hold brief conversations but lost the thread quickly – a few minutes after reading a comic, he could re-read it as though it were completely new to him. This is an example of *anterograde amnesia*, which is the inability to store things in memory after a trauma such as illness or brain damage. *Retrograde amnesia* occurs when some trauma prevents the patient from recalling information stored before the trauma. For example, the Russel and Nathan study described above shows the effects of retrograde amnesia.

In general terms, physical damage is a rare form of forgetting. Memory is much more often disturbed by psychological factors.

Emotion

We have already seen in the section on state-dependent memory that if we are unhappy this increases the likelihood that we will find it difficult to recall pleasant events. Freud, however, saw emotion as a very important factor in a form of forgetting known as *repression*. He thought that if an event was so traumatic that its memory would disturb the conscious personality, the record of the event would be hidden from consciousness and held in the unconscious to protect the individual. Although the person concerned cannot consciously remember something that has been repressed, it can still have an effect on behaviour. For example, a woman who was sexually assaulted at the age of two or three may have no conscious recollection of the event, but may find that as an adult she has great difficulties in her relationships with men as a result of the repression.

Psychoanalysis is claimed to work by bringing repressed memories to a conscious level in a way that avoids too much stress. Once the memory is at a conscious level, it can be seen for what it is and should stop having its negative effects.

One problem with the concept of repression is that it is very difficult to test experimentally: a researcher can hardly induce the level of emotional trauma necessary to cause the event to be repressed.

Meltzer (1930) performed a study which can be related to repression. On arrival at college after Christmas, he asked students to record all the pleasant and unpleasant things that had happened to them during the holiday. Six weeks later he asked them to do the same thing, and found that they had forgotten only 47 per cent of the pleasant events, but 60 per cent of the unpleasant ones. This could be interpreted as a very mild form of repression but, if the students were in a good mood on the second recall, it could simply be a matter of state-dependent memory.

There is some evidence that some emotional events are better remembered than others, even if they are unpleasant. This usually occurs because we tend to talk about these things and therefore strengthen the memory.

Those of you who suffer from exam nerves known that anxiety can make it very difficult to recall complicated material. The information may come flooding back as soon as the exam is over and the anxiety has abated. On the other hand, a little anxiety may help memory under exam conditions (see Yerkes–Dodson Law, p. 234).

Study Tips

As a student you may need to learn and remember material from this and other chapters. Use what psychologists have discovered about memory to help you study. Here are a few tips:

- Find a working pattern which suits you – a number of shorter study periods are usually better than one long one.
- Before starting the study period decide how long it is going to be and what you will do at the end of the period.
- Try to organize your study area so that you won't have to break off to go and find books, pencils or other bits and pieces.
- Try to make your study area comfortable so that you can concentrate.
- Use short periods in the day that would otherwise be wasted – that way you will be able to watch your favourite TV programme.
- Set yourself targets – what you will learn by when. If you don't achieve the target think about why (perhaps the target was unrealistic) and what you are going to do about it.
- Test yourself at the end of a study session.
- Be an *active* learner – ask questions, decide which bits are most important, think about how you can apply what you are learning to real life.
- When reading new material scan it before reading in detail – look at headings, diagrams, summaries. Then think up questions that you hope the text will answer.
- Use a highlighter pen to pick out the main points of a text or the bits that you didn't already know. If you are working from a library book take a photocopy first.
- When going about your everyday life try and pick out things which could relate to your studies, e.g. if you are on a diet and keep noticing cream cakes think about perceptual sets; if you have a friend who has a fear of spiders think about the theory of phobias and how you could help them (pp. 37–9).

- Talk about what you are studying – pair up with another student.
- Teach someone – if you and your study partner look at different topics you can teach each other (some say the best way to learn something is to teach it).
- Reduce your notes to keywords and phrases – this activity makes you read your notes and puts them into memory; when reading the keywords afterwards you have to actively think what they mean and therefore practice the reconstruction of memories which will be required in the exam.
- Work out mnemonics – especially useful for lists which contain some items you may forget or for making sure you don't leave a major area out of an essay because you simply forgot it (see SMACK example, p. 77).
- Return to a topic soon after you have learnt it – most forgetting occurs in the first 24 hours; if you can spend a few minutes reducing the amount of forgetting during this period it will ensure more is retained in the long term.
- If you can't recall something don't give up – it is probably in storage, the problem is a retrieval one. Try to think of related things. Think about when you first came across the material, what were you doing?
- Relearning is nearly always quicker than learning for the first time so even if you don't remember material that you studied at the beginning of the course you are still better placed than the student who didn't bother with it at the time.
- At the start of a revision period try brainstorming – write down anything at all to do with the topic you are revising. It might be slow to start off with but one idea will trigger another and you will be amazed how much you can produce. Don't worry if you can't get a lot of detail, that can be filled in later.
- If you find that you get confused between two topics look at one in detail and leave the other for the moment. After a few days check that you really know the first topic and then look at the second. Make a conscious effort to pick out the differences – note these down (see p. 84).
- If something doesn't make sense, query it – ask another student or your teacher. Maybe there is something wrong with your notes or the hand-out; perhaps you are missing the point.

Summary

1 There are three parts to memory: encoding, storage and retrieval.

2 Most material that is forgotten is lost in the first few hours after learning. If something is still remembered after a few days, it is unlikely to be forgotten.

3 STM has a very small capacity, but the amount in storage can be increased by chunking. Material in STM will be lost within 30 seconds if it is not rehearsed.

4 LTM has a more or less unlimited capacity, but the problem is how to retrieve the information.

5 Memory is not like a video-recording. When we remember we reconstruct the event on the basis of information available in schemas. Bartlett, Loftus and Palmer, and others, have demonstrated the way that material can be distorted in memory.

6 Memory is most efficient when there are lots of recall cues. When there are few recall cues it may help to be in the same physical or mental state as you were when you first came across the material.

7 What we do before and after learning something may interfere with later recall. This is especially true if the interfering material is of a similar nature to the learnt material and is presented just before or just after it.

8 Physical shock can disturb memory, especially for events that occurred up to half an hour before the shock. Anterograde amnesia affects the storage of new material after a trauma, whereas retrograde amnesia affects recall of information stored before the trauma.

9 Freud argued that highly emotionally charged material might be repressed. This does not involve total loss, since the information is in the unconscious and may still have an indirect effect on behaviour.

10 Use the research findings on memory to help improve your study habits.

Further Reading

Baddeley, A.D., *Your Memory (A User's Guide)* (1996, Erlbaum).

Cohen, G., Kiss, G. and Le Voi, M., *Memory: Current Issues* (2nd edn., 1993, Oxford University Press).

Chapter 5

The Development of Intellect and Morality

Jean Piaget's Theories

The chapter on learning discussed some of the ways in which experience shapes behaviour. We saw how the development of Learning Sets allows the understanding of new situations. The impression may have been given that development is simply a matter of trial and error, the order of which is at the mercy of the particular environment in which individuals find themselves. This is not the case, however, and in this chapter we will consider some of the regular patterns of child development.

Piaget was interested in how children understand the world. He observed behaviour and produced a theory which stressed that children think in a different way to adults. He argued that children go through a series of stages in their cognitive development (the development of thinking, memory, perception, etc.). The order to these stages does not vary, and each one brings with it a different way of thinking. The theory is not simply maturational, because although children move from one stage to the next as they get older, development depends upon interaction with the environment. In a stimulating environment an active child will progress from stage to stage more quickly than in a deprived environment.

The child's intellectual development takes place through the development of what Piaget calls *schemata*. He says nothing about the form that they take in the brain, but that they are the internal representation of a series of physical or mental actions; they can be likened to a set of rules about how to interact with the environment.

Once a child has a particular schema he is motivated to use it. Piaget stresses that it is the activity of the child bringing him into contact with his environment which results in cognitive development. The way in which the child interacts with his environment depends upon his existing schemata. The motivation to repeat the actions related to a schema can be seen particularly in children a few months old who kick their legs, causing objects to move in the pram, and will repeat this indefinitely; at about ten months the child may drop a toy out of the cot as often as an adult will retrieve it.

The child understands his world through his schemata, so that the three-year-old's toy car is simply an object that is pleasant to suck and rattle to a four-month-old infant. This process of understanding the world through an existing schema is known as assimilation. The assimilation of things into existing schemata allows the child to remember more and more information about the world, even though in some cases fitting things into the existing mental frameworks makes the child act in a way that adults consider odd. Four-year-old children, for example, have a series of schemata about numbers which are not the same as those for adults; these schemata are such that when asked which of the rows below has more dots in it, they say the top row has more dots.

$$\begin{array}{cccc} \bullet & \bullet & \bullet & \bullet \\ \bullet & \bullet & \bullet & \bullet \end{array}$$

The child gains feedback from the environment as to how accurate his perceptions are; when his experiences are mismatched between his schema and this feedback he is said to be in a state of *disequilibrium*. For example, as a baby in the first few months exercises the grasping and sucking schema, some objects will make a noise when grasped. The existing mental structure cannot deal with this, and disequilibrium exists, causing alteration of the schema so that it can cope with the new stimulation. A new schema, which will allow the child to use rattles, has now been formed and equilibrium exists once more. The child can now assimilate objects into this new schema and starts to decide which are good rattles and which are not. The equilibrium is, of course, only temporary, since continued action will bring new forms of stimulation to the child and the process of changing his mental structures, known as *accommodation*, will occur again. If a child is only exposed to information and experiences that can be easily assimilated, no accommodation will occur and development will be retarded. On the other hand, accommodation cannot occur if experiences are too far removed from those with which the child is familiar.

The assimilation of information into schemata and the accommodation of schemata to cater for the demands of new experiences occurs throughout the stages of development. At each stage the organization of schemata becomes more complex.

The Sensorimotor Stage

The sensorimotor stage runs roughly from birth to two years of age. The newborn has a few very limited in-built schemata which allow him to grasp, suck and look at objects. The child is only concerned with what is going on at the present time; as soon as an object disappears from sight, the baby seems to forget it altogether. It is not until about eight months that the child seems to become aware that objects still exist when out of sight and will reach for a toy hidden behind something. Piaget called this the development of *object permanence*. Between eight and twelve months the child will search for an object only in the place where it is usually hidden; when a toy is hidden behind a pillow they have no difficulty in retrieving it but, after playing this game for a while, if the toy is first hidden in the usual place and then moved to another hiding place while the child watches, they will search behind the original pillow and may show surprise that he cannot find the toy. By the end of the sensorimotor stage infants have developed some understanding of the relationships between their muscle movements and effects on the environment. They have developed mental structures which allow them to symbolize the world and think about objects that are out of sight. Children begin to produce words in the latter half of this stage, and use these as well as physical actions to represent and act upon their environment.

The Pre-operational Stage

This stage generally runs from two to seven years of age. With the develop-ment of language and memory the child can remember more about the environment and is able to predict it better. These predictions are still simple ones, and the child tends to over-generalize – calling all men 'daddy' for example. The child's intellect is limited by *egocentricity*: he is unaware that other people may have a different view of the world. Piaget and Inhelder (1956) placed a model landscape on a table, and seated a doll on one side and a child on the other. The child was then asked to draw what the doll could 'see'. Children in the pre-operational stage drew a picture of what they could themselves see, showing egocentricity.

The intellect is also limited by the way in which only one aspect of a problem can be considered at a time. This causes the child to show lack of *conservation*. Lack of conservation of volume can be demonstrated by pour-ing water into two wide glasses until the child agrees that there is the same amount in each. If the water from one of the glasses is then poured into a tall, thin glass, pre-occupational children will report that there is more water in the tall glass than in the short one. The child appears to concentrate only on the height of the liquid; he cannot focus on its width at the same time. When judging a quantity of sweets the same children may say that there are more when they are spread out that when they are bunched together, thereby showing lack of conservation of number. It is not surprising that children of four or five squabble about shares of orange juice or sweets even when an adult has been scrupulously fair in making sure that everyone has the same amount.

As the pre-operational stage comes to an end the child starts to conserve number and then volume.

The Concrete Operational Stage

In the *concrete operational* period, from seven to eleven years, the child is still dependent on the appearance of objects but is becoming able to learn the rules of conservation and can use simple logic to solve problems, provided that they involve real objects. They can, for example, put a number of different-sized dolls into order of size, but cannot solve the same type of problem when it is presented verbally; for example Gladys is taller than Freda; Freda is taller than Mary. Who is the shortest?

The Formal Operational Stage

The *formal operational* phase covers the period from eleven years to adulthood. The child learns the more sophisticated rules in this time. They can now develop general laws and scientific reasoning. Their thoughts are no longer always tied to the concrete; they can form hypotheses and make rules about abstract things. The learning of new rules does not end with the ending of childhood, but continues throughout life.

Some Reservations about Piaget's Theories

A number of researchers have argued that Piaget under-estimated the ability of young children. Marvin *et al.* (1976) asked children to choose an object from a table while their mother had her eyes closed; when asked if Mum knew what object had been chosen, two-year-olds said yes – the egocentric response – but four-year-olds realized that their mothers could not know. It appears that the extent to which pre-operational children show egocentricity depends on the type of task, rather than being an overall characteristic of the stage.

N. Freeman, S. Lloyd and C. Sinha (1980) investigated the situation where a toy is hidden first behind object A for a series of trials and then moved, while the child is watching, from behind A to behind B. Children between about eight and twelve months of age generally continue to search for the toy behind object A. Freeman and his colleagues discovered that twelve-month-old children have little difficulty with the task when the toy was hidden in an upright cup, but were much less successful if the cups were inverted. Children seem to know how a cup is normally used and are distracted from the task when the cup is inverted. When the cup is used in its normal fashion the child can concentrate on finding the toy. It seems that the child may be concerned with more aspects of the task than the Piagetian psychologist is!

Some people have argued that children's problems with conservation tasks simply reflect the way in which they understand the words used; the words 'more than' or 'less than' do not have the same links with number and volume that they do for adults. Piaget believed that failure in the conservation tasks reflected something much more central to the whole of the child's understanding of the world.

J. McGarrigle and M. Donaldson suggested that the child uses a *social logic* when he fails to conserve on a Piagetian task. They argued that under normal circumstances if an adult asks a child about something such as a set of counters, then rearranges the counters and asks the same question again, it is a safe bet that the child's answer should now be different. They backed this up by devising a task where the social logic did not force the child into an incorrect answer. Instead of having an adult both asking the questions and changing the length of a row of counters, they introduced a 'naughty teddy' which made the rearrangement. The researcher asked whether there were more in one row than the other, or whether there were the same number in each. The 'naughty teddy' puppet then joined in and disturbed the rows, making one researcher ask the question again. Out of 80 children tested, 54 conserved in the test compared with only 33 of them when tested in the traditional way.

Piaget pointed out that the order of the stages is invariable, but that some children pass through them more quickly than others. The stages themselves are not so rigidly separated as appears from summaries such as the one that we have made in this chapter; it is often quite difficult to decide whether a child is in one stage or another since in reality the stage boundaries are blurred.

Piaget's early studies were based on a very small sample of subjects, often his own children, but follow-up studies have shown that his results have much wider applicability. His work has stimulated a great deal of research designed to support, expand or contradict his theories, and as a result has been one of the most valuable contributions made to psychology.

Jerome Bruner's Theories

Bruner's theories towards intellectual development broadly resemble those of Piaget, but there are also some important and fairly fundamental differences. Piaget's work is largely concerned with the description of what happens; he discusses the mechanisms by which intellect develops mainly in order to clarify the descriptions themselves. Bruner, on the other hand, concerns himself much more with questions about how and why intellectual development occurs. While Piaget regards maturational processes as being probably the most important factors, and culture and education as modifying factors, Bruner places much more emphasis on these last two. He disagrees with Piaget's view that the major motivator or influence in intellectual growth is biological and argues that, if biological development 'pushes' the individual towards more adaptable behaviour, the environment 'pulls' him in the same direction. Here Bruner is stressing that simply to study the child without also examining his experience and environment is bound to give an incomplete picture. Where Piaget simply states that intellectual development involves an interaction between individual and environment, Bruner stresses the point, and regards the child's environment as being rather like a loudspeaker, amplifying the child's abilities.

However, like Piaget, Bruner believes that the developing child plays an active part in its own development; although the family, the educational system and the child's friends, for example, obviously have an influence on development, the child makes his own sense of the world. Remember from chapter 2 that perception is an active, constructive process; from the raw sensory information, we make inferences and draw conclusions about what is really 'out there'. Just as we process stimuli and put our own interpretations on them, so, Bruner argues, do we develop our cognitive abilities in order to understand and interact more successfully with our environment.

To be able to control our environment we have to learn to predict it, and in order to be able to do that we have to be able to pick out reliable patterns – of which the earliest are the constancies – in the events which affect us. So we have to learn to represent and internally organize our experiences. Bruner has been very interested in how we develop the ability to represent our environment internally and use this information to predict what will happen next. He has identified three types of representation which he believes are the basis of cognitive development. They will be described in the order in which they appear in humans. They should be compared with Piaget's developmental stages: Piaget's proposed stages describe what the child himself is biologically capable of doing, whereas Bruner's types of representation are more concerned with the changes in the individual's interpretation or prediction of his environment.

Enactive Representation

The first type of representation to appear in the child is termed by Bruner *enactive representation*. A useful way to think of this type is to regard it as 'motor' or 'muscle memory'. Past experiences cannot yet be stored in symbolic form: a baby can represent past experiences only in the form of motor patterns. It might, for example, at one time have a string of rattling beads strung across its cot, and be able to make them rattle by hitting them with its hands. You might notice that when they are taken away it continues to move its hands as if to hit them. It seems to show that it has some form of internal representation of its experience with the beads, and indicates this in motor form, by repeating the motor patterns associated with them. No images of the beads need to be involved; this earliest form of internal representation does not seem to require the use of visual images. Similarly most people say that they do not have to pay attention to every motor movement they make. They have, in effect, a 'muscle memory' which they can use to guide their limb movements. An old party game requires people to describe a helter-skelter without using their hands, and most people find it very difficult to do so. Even adults store helter-skelter information using enactive representation. So it must be with babies' earliest representations of their environments.

Iconic Representation

The second type of representation to appear is termed *iconic representation* – 'icon' meaning 'likeness'. The child now develops the ability to retain images – visual, auditory or tactile – as a faithful representation of the stimuli that reach its sense organs. This method is a very good way of storing information about the environment, but it can have its drawbacks. In the following hypothetical experiment, suppose we used a group of children who relied mainly on iconic representation, and another group who did not; the former group would be expected to do better at learning to attach the artificial names to the pictures in figure 5.1.

Figure 5.1. Type of Figure used by Kuhlman (I)

In 1960 Kuhlman indeed found this result. Children who used iconic imaging are able to make a fairly faithful representation of the picture plus the label, and to recall it when required. Non-imaging children, on the other hand, and those who are not very good at imaging, seem to find it difficult to remember the label and to fit it to the correct picture because the words themselves do not indicate at all which pictures they fit. This ability to make faithful representations – although it may seem to be a heaven-sent gift if you have to learn psychology notes for an examination – can in fact create problems for children who possess it. These arise because iconic imaging is too inflexible: it usually allows a child to learn only specific images of parts of the environment and makes it difficult for him to extract from them the underlying similarities between objects. Thus children who use iconic imaging seem to find it more difficult than non-imagers to categorize things. Kuhlman showed this in another part of the experiment already described. The imagers and non-imagers were each given a series of pictures and all were asked to determine what each of the pictures had in common (see figure 5.2). The answer is, of course, that they are all dwelling-places. Non-imaging children had little difficulty in picking out this common factor, but imaging children, just because they were so tied to the pictorial images, found it harder to think beyond the pictures and to extract the significance from them.

Figure 5.2. Type of Figure used by Kuhlman (II)

Symbolic Representation

The problem with both enactive and iconic representation is that they are relatively inflexible: enactive representation enables the child to interpret the environment only in the form of motor patterns, while iconic representation enables him to represent his environment only in the form of photograph-like images. Because the environment is constantly changing, these two forms, with their usefulness only for individual movements or fixed images, cannot effectively code enough information about the environment to enable predictions to be made.

Symbolic representation, however, overcomes this problem by using symbols, as the name suggests. A symbol is something which represents something else; for example, the handshake we exchange with somebody we meet originally symbolized the idea that we would not attack him (we usually shake hands with the right hand, which would normally hold a weapon in a situation of hostility). Bruner thus believes that human language provides a series of symbols in the form of words and sentences with which we can represent and store information about the ever-changing environment: the word 'vegetable' may be just a series of letters printed on a piece of paper, but if you can read and interpret their meaning they contain, and remind you of, a large amount of information – lists of different vegetables and their description; memories of how they taste; how to grow and cook them, and so on. The single word 'vegetable' therefore enables you to store a large amount of information about your environment. Words in themselves are only squiggly marks on paper, or breath expelled from the mouth, but they symbolize information very effectively.

When we develop language, therefore, we develop a collection of efficient, information-storing symbols. Moreover these symbols, because they are not applicable only to the simple characteristics of single objects, can contain information about whole classes of objects. Thus in symbolic representation two major information-storage systems are used – *categorization* and the formation of *hierarchies*.

CATEGORIZATION AND THE FORMATION OF HIERARCHIES

The vegetable example is a case of categorization: 'vegetable' refers not to a specific potato which we once ate, but to a whole realm of edible objects. As another example, consider the category 'cat'. All the figures in figure 5.3

Figure 5.3. All Different, but all Cats

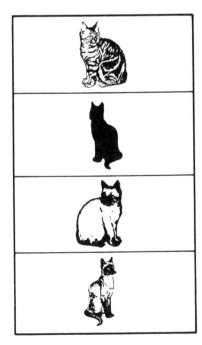

are recognizable as members of the cat category, yet they are all different: one has no tail; one has a leg missing; they have different types of coat, colour, and so on. If you were shown each picture in turn and asked to say what it was, you would have no difficulty in deciding that it was a cat even though the pictures you saw were of markedly different sizes, shades and posture. Your possession of the ability to categorize, however, has enabled you to look behind the differences in the sensory information and pick out the common factors belonging to the category.

In addition, however, symbolization enables us to construct hierarchies in order to store information; a list of words organized into a hierarchy – for example 'room', 'flat', 'house', 'street', 'hamlet', 'village', 'town', 'city', 'metropolis', 'country', 'country', 'continent', and so on – is much easier to recall than words which are randomly organized. The work of Bower *et al.* (1969), discussed on p. 72, demonstrated the strength of the effect of this type of organization on memory.

An experiment in 1966 by J.S. Bruner and H. Kenney confirms how effective symbolic representation is in helping us to store and use information about our environment (see figure 5.4). The subjects were children whose ages ranged from five to seven years, the younger ones using mainly iconic representation while the older ones could use symbolic representation. The glasses used in the task were graded and placed in order according to both height and diameter; the experimenter first removed a few glasses and then asked the children to replace them, which all managed to do. Similarly when the glasses were mixed up and replaced out of position, all the children could put them back in their original places. Next, however, all the glasses were removed, and only one glass was placed in a different square. The children were then asked to replace the rest of the glasses so as to complete the new pattern. The older children – those capable of symbolic representation – could perform the task satisfactorily but the

Figure 5.4. Bruner and Kenney's Experiment

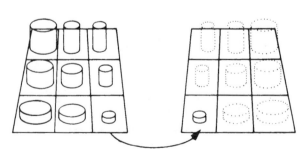

iconic representers could not. Their iconic representation helped them when asked to remake the original pattern, but because their images were of the original order, they were of little use to them in helping to solve the problem when the new arrangement did not match their images; they were not able to go beyond the bare image of the problem and to deduce that the relationship between the sizes of the glasses were important, and consequently they could not solve the problem when looking at it from a different viewpoint.

Bruner regards language as an important aid in developing symbolic representation because language enables us to form categories and hierarchies. Although much of Bruner's work parallels that of Piaget, it is partly on the importance of language that their views differ. Piaget originally regarded language as relatively unimportant in the formation of intellectual abilities; however, he more recently moved towards the view that thought and language develop as separate systems but that the existence of language helps the child's intellect to develop faster, and with greater breadth.

Piaget	Bruner
Sensorimotor	Enactive representation
Pre-operational	Iconic representation
Concrete operational	
Formal operational	Symbolic representation

Moral Development

Piaget's Theory

Moral development is about the way that children come to learn about right and wrong, concepts of punishment and justice and rules about how to behave 'correctly'. In chapter 9 on Socialization we will see how imitation and reinforcement can have an effect on this behaviour, but in this chapter we will concentrate on the theories which stress the *order* in which moral development occurs.

As in his theory of cognitive development, Piaget argues that maturation, experience and social interaction are all vital factors in social and moral development. Processes such as assimilation and accommodation of schema are as relevant to ideas about right and wrong as they are to decisions about the physical world. The stages of moral development are not as clearly defined as the stages of cognitive development, but obviously the child's moral reasoning will be different in the concrete operational stage than in the pre-operational stage, when the child is unable to take into account the views of others (being egocentric).

Much of the theory comes from the observation of a relatively small number of children during normal behaviour or in question-and-answer sessions. Despite the few children observed in the initial work, many other researchers have found similar patterns in the development of social and moral behaviour.

Piaget was interested in three areas of social development:

1 The child's ideas about rules.
2 How a child decides what is right and what is wrong.
3 The child's ideas about punishment and justice.

THE CHILD'S IDEAS ABOUT RULES

Piaget studied how children learnt and internalized rules by studying their understanding of the game of marbles (the rules of which, incidentally, show wide variations from culture to culture). To do this, he used a questioning technique: When I was little, I used to play a lot, but now I've quite forgotten how. I'd like to play again. Let's play together. Can you teach me the rules? Then I'll play with you. Other questions were: Have the rules always been the same? Where do the rules come from? Could new rules be made up, and would they be fair?

Piaget noticed that there seemed to be a sequence of development in children in the understanding of these rules; that is, the children's answers changed as they got older. Piaget believed that the main causes of this development were maturation of the child's schemata, and assimilation and accommodation of information from the child's environment.

Very young children (aged under 3) have no rules - each child devises and plays their own version of the game.

Three-to-six-year-olds (still at the pre-operational stage) notice new rules but still play egocentrically. Even when two children are playing together, they do not interlink their behaviour or cooperate. Although both know the rules, they often ignore them and, in effect, play as individuals. Such children (even though they ignore the rules) regard them as being absolutes. They cannot be changed, and have the same force as physical laws – they have always existed, but were probably invented by God. Piaget called this the stage of heteronomous morality, or the stage of *moral realism*.

There is a gradual development from age 6 up to about 11 or 12 (late concrete operational), at which point the rules have become fully internalized and understood. Whereas the younger child believes that the rules have always existed (possibly given by older children, parents, or God), the concrete operational child realizes that the rules are developed by children themselves and can be changed by the agreement of all the players. Piaget called this the stage of *autonomous morality* or *moral reciprocity*.

HOW THE CHILD DECIDES WHAT IS RIGHT AND WHAT IS WRONG

In this research, Piaget was interested in how the child comes to assess the seriousness of a crime. The research technique used here was to put hypothetical situations before the child and ask them to assess how wrong the action was, and why it was wrong. For example, children would be told a story about a boy called John, and one about a boy called Henry:

> 'A little boy who is called John is in his room. He is called to dinner. He goes into the dining room. But behind the door there was a chair, and on the chair there was a tray with fifteen cups on it. John couldn't have known that there was all this behind the door. He goes in, the door knocks against the tray, bang go the fifteen cups and they all get broken!'

> 'Once there was a little boy whose name was Henry. One day when his mother was out he tried to get some jam out of the cupboard even though he knew he was not allowed to do this. He climbed on a chair and stretched out his arm. But the jam was too high up and he couldn't reach it and have any. While he was trying to get the jam he knocked over a cup. The cup fell down and broke.'

The child would then be asked 'who was the naughtier: John or Henry?' Young children in the stage of moral realism usually say that John was naughtier because he broke so many cups. For them, a crime's seriousness depended upon its visible effects rather than the intention behind the act. This reflects pre-operational and concrete operational thinking.

The adult type of morality (the stage of moral reciprocity) which involves judging by intention, begins to develop about age 7, and is usually well developed by about 10 years of age. For the under-7 (pre-operational) child, however, an adult's punishments for misdeeds must seem very odd – a large punishment for Henry but a small or negligible one for John, because the adult's judgement is based on intention, not damage, and the child cannot yet understand this.

In adult moral standards, intention and seriousness are often separated. For example, a driver whose car kills somebody walking right into its path is not held to blame – in fact, is often given comfort (but still feels remorse and guilt) – whereas a near-identically serious act (killing someone with a car) when committed by a drunken driver, or committed intentionally, is severely condemned and penalized. The ways in which children judge lies follow a similar pattern too, but with an intermediate third stage:

Stage 1, Moral Realism. A lie to a 6-year-old can be an actual untruth, or an oath. Both are punished by parents, and the child cannot tell the difference between them. Some 6-year-olds believe that any behaviour which leads to a punishment is a lie.

Stage 2, Intermediate Stage. 8–9-year-olds' lies are statements which are not factual – the bigger the unreality of the statement, the bigger the lie to them. For example, 'Today, I saw a dog as big as a cow' would be judged as a much bigger lie than a child saying he did well at school when he really did poorly. Because the former is a bigger departure from fact, and is less believable, it is a bigger lie.

Stage 3, Moral Reciprocity. 10–11-year-olds would call the former statement a joke – it is so obviously untrue that it is not a lie. The second statement, however, was made with intent to deceive and is therefore considered the bigger lie. At this stage intention again becomes the criterion for judgement.

THE CHILD'S IDEAS ABOUT PUNISHMENT AND JUSTICE
Children in the stage of moral realism believe that the size of the punishment should fit the crime (although their ideas of what is a crime are different from ours, as shown above), but Piaget found no evidence that a child below 7 years wanted to match the type of punishment to the type of crime. Piaget found that, by the age of 11 or 12, 80 per cent of children favoured letting the punishment fit the crime, so that they favoured being made to sleep in a cold room as a punishment for breaking a window or being smacked for hitting a smaller child. Unlike the younger child, the 12-year-old felt that restitution (making good for the damage caused) was also important (the stage of moral reciprocity).

Piaget argued that the child moves from a stage of moral realism – when he is largely swayed by physical, observable effects of action and thinks of rules as 'tablets of stone' which cannot be changed – to a stage of moral reciprocity (some researchers call this stage *moral insight*) when he takes intention into account, is able to fit the punishment to the crime, and sees rules as things which allow groups to function and can be changed by agreement.

The movement between moral realism and moral insight is gradual, and people of any age may show characteristics of both types of moral thinking.

Although maturation is important, social interaction is vital to the change from one stage to the other. For example, the pre-school child may have experienced only one set of rules about how to play a game (so his schema for the game at this stage would consist only of this one set of rules). In order to assimilate the behaviour of another child who plays by different rules, he regards the other child as cheating. However, when he comes across many children with many different rules, it becomes more difficult to simply assimilate these differences into his schema by saying that they are all cheating, so the child has to change his schema (i.e. he has to accommodate these different rules). The child's schema for rules now includes a recognition that there are rules other than his own. Further social experience enables the child to accommodate the idea that the rules of a game may be changed if all the players agree.

Kohlberg's Theory

Kohlberg's method and theory is a direct follow-on from Piaget. However, Kohlberg believed that these stages were much more clearly defined than did Piaget. Like Piaget, Kohlberg posed questions to people about what was right and what was wrong. For example:

> 'In Europe, a woman was dying from cancer. One drug might save her, a form of radium that the druggist in the same town had recently discovered. The druggist was charging 2,000 dollars, ten times what the drug cost him to make. The sick woman's husband, Heinz, went to everyone he knew to borrow the money, but he could only get together about half of what it cost. He told the druggist that his wife was dying and asked him to sell it cheaper or let him pay later. But the druggist said "No". The husband got desperate and broke into the man's store to steal the drug for his wife. 'Should the husband have done that? Why?'

By using stories like this, and by asking people to explain the reason for their answers, Kohlberg, like Piaget, produced a 'stage' theory of moral development – but as you will see, the stages are more clearly defined than Piaget's; he also asked a wider range of age-groups than did Piaget.

Kohlberg believed that there were three levels of morality, each level being divided into two stages, giving six stages in all.

We set out below the levels and stages of Kohlberg's theory, together with some of the sorts of decisions which people at each stage might make about Heinz's dilemma. (Note, though, that whilst most of these decisions say that Heinz was right, it is perfectly possible at each stage to get answers which say that Heinz was wrong.)

LEVEL 1, PRE-CONVENTIONAL MORALITY
Stage 1, called 'Punishment and obedience orientation' by Kohlberg. People in this stage believe that something is wrong if it is punished or punishable. If

the behaviour is not punished, then it is right. Heinz would therefore be wrong to steal the drug, because stealing is punishable.

Stage 2, Instrumental Hedonism. In this stage, people conform to rules and laws to gain rewards, or to have a favour they have done to somebody returned. Heinz would not gain by obeying the law, and he doesn't owe the 'druggist' any favours, so he is probably right to steal.

LEVEL 2, CONVENTIONAL MORALITY
Stage 3, 'Good child' morality. What is good is that which pleases others (particularly the family), and the intention behind an action begins to be taken into account. Heinz's behaviour would not have pleased the 'druggist', and perhaps also not pleased his friends and family. However, the intention behind the theft was to save a life, so he was probably right to steal the drug.

Stage 4, Law and order orientation. What is right and wrong is not so much determined by family and friends, but by society. Society's laws are designed to maintain social order, and should only be disobeyed in extreme circumstances. Heinz was wrong to break society's laws, but the possible death of his wife is an extreme circumstance, so stealing the drug is not entirely wrong.

LEVEL 3, POST-CONVENTIONAL MORALITY
Stage 5, Social contract orientation. While laws should be upheld, they can be changed by agreement. Anyway, one should behave so as to bring the greatest good to the greatest number of people. Despite the law, some things are more important – a person's right to life and freedom. Therefore, Heinz was right to take the drug.

Stage 6, Universal ethical principles. People in this stage have developed their own moral principles, based on the sacredness of life and respect for the individual. Most laws conform with these principles, but where they do not, it is better to uphold the principles. Heinz was right to steal the drug – the universal ethical principle of the sacredness of life is more important than any law.

Figure 5.5. Summary of Kohlberg's levels of moral development

Level 1
Pre-conventional morality
Stage 1 Right or wrong determined by punishment
Stage 2 Something is right if it results in pleasure

Level 2
Conventional morality
Stage 3 It is right if it pleases other people. Intentions become important
Stage 4 Society makes the rules and they should be obeyed

Level 3
Post-conventional morality
Stage 5 Rules can be changed by agreement
Stage 6 Personal moral principles have been developed based on respect
for others

EVIDENCE FOR AND AGAINST PIAGET'S AND KOHLBERG'S THEORIES

There are really two questions to answer in connection with Piaget and Kohlberg's theories. First, what evidence is there that people's moral development occurs in stages? Second, Kohlberg's and Piaget's theories are about the development of moral thinking; what evidence is there that what a person actually does (i.e. his moral behaviour) develops in the same way as his moral thinking?

Are there stages in moral development?

Since Kohlberg's stages are more clearly defined than Piaget's, we will concentrate on the evidence for or against Kohlberg's stages.

The best way to study this question is to perform a longitudinal study by testing the same people's moral development over a number of years. Kohlberg performed a six-year longitudinal study on Turkish city and village boys and American middle and working-class boys aged between 10 and 16 years at the start of the study. He found, when he tested the boys at three-year intervals, that 50 per cent of them stayed at the same stage and the other 50 per cent had moved up or down a stage.

A 20-year study by Rest supported the idea that moral development occurs in stages, but Rest also found that the amount of development through the stages was not as great as Kohlberg's theory predicted, in fact on average, Rest's subjects only increased by two stages. Kohlberg himself found very few subjects who showed stage 6 morality and fewer than predicted at stage 5. (Kohlberg is now in doubt as to whether there is in fact a separate stage 6 at all.)

Although there seems to be some evidence for the existence of stages in the development of moral thinking, it is not exactly strong evidence. (Some of Kohlberg's subjects dropped a stage, and Rest's subjects did not seem to make much moral progress in 20 years!) Kohlberg believed (like Piaget) that the stages in moral thinking are due to maturation, but an alternative explanation may be that parents reward or punish different kinds of moral thinking in their children at different ages. For example, children in Kohlberg's stage 1 obey to avoid punishment. This may be due (as Kohlberg believed) to their level of maturation, or it may be because with young children, reasoning with the child by the parents doesn't work as well as punishment does.

Are moral thinking and moral development the same thing?
Piaget and Kohlberg both believed that a person with a higher level of moral thinking would also behave more morally than a person at a lower stage. Kohlberg set up situations where children were able to cheat, and looked at whether the child's stage of moral thinking (as measured by Heinz-type questions) predicted their moral behaviour (i.e. whether or not they actually cheated). He found that 70 per cent of stage 1 and 2 children cheated, 55 per cent of stages 3 and 4 children cheated, and only 15 per cent of stage 5 children cheated. This result, however, is very much an exception. Other studies show a much weaker relationship between moral thinking and behaviour.

Damon found that some children who thought that there ought to be an equal division of sweets among a group of children who had worked to-gether behaved differently in a real situation - they demanded more sweets than other children. Similarly, children who thought that the hardest worker should get most sweets changed their view in the real situation when that child was someone else!

The general trend of research evidence suggests that, while there might be some evidence for the existence of stages in the development of moral thinking, there is not much evidence for a strong link between moral thinking and moral behaviour. What people say they would do in a situation and what they actually do in that situation are often different.

Piaget's and Kohlberg's theories have been very influential in directing other psychologists' research towards the development of moral thinking in children. Both theories, however, are weak at predicting how children actually behave when faced with moral decisions.

Gilligan's Theory

Gilligan (1977) criticized Kohlberg for having a male bias in his study of morality. Most of the people that Kohlberg studied were male, and following a few studies with women he classified their level of morality no higher than stage 3. Gilligan argued that male and female morality is based on different principles and that it was the sex bias in Kohlberg's classification which led to women gaining a lower general level of development.

Gilligan went on to produce her own stages of moral development with a particular focus on the development of female morality, which she claimed was based on the *morality of care*, as against the male morality described by Kohlberg and based on the *morality of justice* which puts moral principles and law above caring for others.

Gilligan's three stages of development in the morality of care are:

1 Stage of self-interest, where decisions are made on purely selfish grounds.
2 Stage of self-sacrifice, where other people are most important and their interests are put first.
3 Stage of the principal of non-violence, the mature stage where the woman tries to be fair to all involved.

Other researchers have not demonstrated consistent differences between the morality of men and women even using Kohlberg's classification.

Summary

1 Piaget proposed that the ability to learn matures in four main stages – sensorimotor, pre-operational, concrete operational and formal operational – through the formation and enlargement of cognitive structures called *schemata*. As the child develops stage by stage his behaviour becomes more complex, and this enables the individual to adapt to the environment more successfully.

2 Bruner's views parallel those of Piaget, but he describes the three major ways in which the individual stores and uses or represents information about the environment – *enactive*, *iconic* and *symbolic representation*. Symbolic representation is the most flexible, but requires the use of

language to enable the categorization of information. Consequently, Bruner stresses the importance of language much more than does Piaget.

3 Moral development is about the way that children come to learn about right and wrong, concepts of punishment and justice, and rules about how to behave 'correctly'.

4 Piaget suggested that children go from the stage of moral realism where things are wrong if they are punished, through an intermediate stage, to a stage of moral reciprocity where judgements of right and wrong are based on the intention behind the act and there is an understanding that rules are matters of agreement between individuals to help control social action.

5 Kohlberg suggested that there are more stages to moral development though not everybody gets to the highest level where people have developed their own moral principles based on the respect for the individual.

6 Gilligan argued that female morality is based upon care for others but male morality puts moral principles and law above caring for others.

Further Reading

Donaldson, M., *Children's Minds* (1978, Fontana).

Hardy, M., Heyes, S., Crews, J., Rookes, P. and Wren, K., *Studying Child Psychology* (1990, Oxford University Press).

Smith, P.K. and Cowie, H., *Understanding Children's Development* (1988, Basil Blackwell).

Chapter 6

Social Influence

Social Facilitation and Bystander Intervention

When psychologists talk about perception, learning, memory and other aspects of experience or behaviour it is often possible to get the idea that people act in isolation from others and that we can explain everything by concentrating on the individual or even on parts of the individual's intellect. This, of course, is far from the truth; all behaviour and experience take place within a social context. Even if the individual is alone at the time, their behaviour is affected by previous and future interactions with others; even the hermit's behaviour is affected by other people, if only to the extent that he is avoiding them.

The social context of behaviour does not necessarily get prime consideration in studies of topics such as memory and perception because there are many other factors that need to be teased out, but that does not mean that it should be ignored. Indeed, if a teacher is interested in students, he or she will lose a lot of the flavour of classroom learning if the social level of analysis is ignored.

In this chapter we are going to concentrate on the effect that other people have on our behaviour, whether they are part of our group, are in authority over us or simply in the same room at the same time.

The mere presence of other people, whether they are watching us or working alongside us, has an effect on the speed and skill of our performance on many tasks. Allport did a number of studies in the 1920s showing that a majority of people performed faster on tasks such as simple arithmetic problems when others were working alongside them. He tried to reduce any rivalry by telling them that their results would not be compared, but the effect remained. Although the quantity of work increased in these studies, quality often declined; many participants were more accurate when performing alone. Allport used the term *social facilitation* to refer to the energizing effect of the presence of other people. In the following half-century numerous studies of the effects of audiences or co-workers were carried out. Many studies showed improvement of performance when others were present, but just as many showed the opposite.

Zajonc (1965) put forward an explanation of these contradictory results. He pointed out that the presence of others tends to increase the general level of arousal of the nervous system. (At low levels of arousal we are sleepy and as arousal increases we become alert. At the highest levels of arousal we display extreme emotions such as ecstasy or rage.) It is well known that level of arousal affects performance on a wide range of tasks (see p. 234). The amount of arousal caused by the presence of others varies depending on the individual, their past experience and the present situation. Zajonc looked at studies where the presence of others had produced a decline in performance and found that they tended to be ones where arousal was high and the task complicated. High arousal tends to increase the likelihood of well-learned, common responses and Zajonc found that if the study had required the people to produce this sort of response the presence of others improved performance.

A number of studies support Zajonc's theory that an audience facilitates well-learned responses but inhibits the tasks that we are not so good at. In one study by Michaels *et al.* (1982) the researchers first watched pool players from a distance to classify them as above or below average; at this stage the players did not know they were being observed. They then placed four observers around the table as the players were competing. As expected, the best players improved their accuracy (by 9 per cent) and the poor players got worse (shot accuracy reduced by 11 per cent).

Zajonc sees the arousing qualities of other people as an automatic innate response, and points to the fact that audience effects occur widely across the animal kingdom; even cockroaches run mazes faster when other cockroaches are watching! This gives the impression that cognitive processes (perceptions, thoughts, memories) are not important. Others argue that the thought of competition, in the case of co-workers, and thoughts that they are being judged, in the case of audiences, are important.

The energizing effect of other people that Allport talked about can lead to the performance of feats that would not be possible alone. An Olympic athlete needs the crowds and other competitors if the record is to be broken. On the other hand, crowd effects are not all so beneficial; when panic breaks out in a crowd it becomes contagious, and the mass energizing can cause individuals to be severely injured in the crush. There is evidence, however, that early in an emergency groups of people are slower to react than are individuals on their own. Crimes are sometimes committed in broad daylight without any of the onlookers lifting a finger to help; this is partly due to fear, but there is more to it than that. Someone who faints in a crowded street cannot rely on getting immediate help from passers-by.

The early part of an emergency or incident is often ambiguous; it is hard to be sure exactly what is happening and exactly what action should be taken. It is under these circumstances that bystanders are likely to look to others to help decide what is going on and what to do about it. If there is someone present who has responsibility to act, such as a policeman in the street or a teacher in a school, then the situation becomes clear and the bystander can stay and watch or move on. If, however, there is no clear 'rule' about who steps in and provides help, individuals often feel inhibited from standing out from the crowd.

Latané and Darley have performed a number of experiments to investigate the inhibiting effect of other people on our actions in situations where we might be expected to report danger or help others. The first experiments looked at the effects of the presence of others in situations that might lead to personal danger or those where another person was in trouble. In both experiments, the participants (who were all male) had been invited to an interview about life in a university, and on arrival were asked to sit in a waiting room and fill in a questionnaire. Some people were alone in the waiting room, others were not. In one experiment smoke was passed into the room through a ventilator; this could obviously lead to personal danger. In a second, the lady who had shown them into the waiting room and had then gone next door was heard to have an accident followed by a scream and moans. The researchers wanted to know how many people would report the incidents.

Results of the 'smoke' incident (Latané and Darley, 1968). When participants were alone 75 per cent of them reported the smoke, but when accompanied by two stooges who showed no great concern about the smoke only 10 per cent reported, even though the room was full of smoke by the end of the six-minute period of the study. One of the ways that we interpret a situation as dangerous is to see how other people react; the stooges had been instructed to be calm and this obviously had an effect. Latané and Darley also tried the experiment using groups of three real subjects with no stooges, but still found that the smoke was reported by only 38 per cent of the groups. Latané and Darley point out that in most western cultures there is a tendency for individuals to put on a calm exterior even if they are worried; this is especially true of young males. This 'macho' image makes it difficult to interpret the situation as dangerous, but also inhibits each individual from 'making a fool of himself' by overreacting to the smoke.

Results of the 'accident' incident (Latané and Rodin, 1969). In this situation another person was in distress, and so we might expect more people to report the incident or help, because there shouldn't be the problem of losing face by appearing afraid of personal danger. The results show, however, that the presence of others inhibits action even under these conditions. When alone 70 per cent of participants offered help but when a stooge was also present in the room only 7 per cent assisted the lady in distress. When the other person in the room was another real participant 40 per cent offered help. Latané and Darley tried having two friends in the room when the accident occurred; under this condition at least one person reported the incident in 70 per cent of the pairs. Obviously, friendship reduced the inhibition to act, but not totally, as this 70 per cent figure was lower than expected since there were twice as many people available to report compared with the 'alone' condition.

Latané and Darley argue that in situations like this an individual has a responsibility to act, but when there are other people around this responsibility is shared. At the same time there is a tendency not to want to make a fool of yourself by acting incorrectly; it is much easier to give in to this tendency if the responsibility for action is shared. A conscious decision to let others take responsibility is not necessarily involved in this inaction – indeed most people who failed to report the accident or the smoke said that they hadn't taken any notice of the other people in the room.

In another experiment by Darley and Latané (1968), people were seated in an experimental booth connected to others by microphones and speakers. The microphones were set up so that only one person could speak at a time, and the subjects were asked to talk about their problems as college students. It was explained that they were in booths to reduce embarrassment. Each person was allowed two minutes to comment on what the others had said and to present their own problems. In fact there was only one real participant; all the other contributions were tape-recorded. The first 'participant' talked about his adjustment to living in the city and how he coped with his studies. He showed obvious embarrassment when he mentioned that he was prone to seizures especially when he was studying hard or taking exams. The other participants, including the real one, all took their turn. Some were in a group of six, others in a group of three, while others had only the first 'participant' with them.

When it was the first 'participant's' turn again he began talking, but started to raise his voice and slur his speech; he asked for help, said that he was having one of his seizures and made choking sounds before going quiet. When people believed that they were the only other participant every one of them went for assistance, but when they believed that there were four others only 62 per cent did this. In addition, the subjects who thought they were alone acted more quickly than those in groups.

Darley and Latané looked at the effect of varying the characteristics of the other supposed subjects. In the groups of three they used either males or females together with the female real subjects and the victim. This made no difference to the amount of help received. In one variation the other participant was supposed to have some medical expertise; this neither reduced nor increased the likelihood of the real subjects going for help. The important factor was simply the *number* of other people present. The researchers did, however, find two other factors that affected helping. If the participant had met the seizure victim before the experiment started they offered help much more quickly, even though they had only met for one minute and had not discussed health problems. When two friends were in the discussion with the victim, help was given as quickly as if the real participant was alone; it seems that friendship with other observers can reduce the inhibiting effect on action.

At the end of the experiment the researchers opened the booths and told the subjects that they could go. Those who had done nothing when the seizure had occurred nearly all asked how the subject was, and they showed all the signs of inner conflict, such as sweating and rubbing hands, suggesting that their inaction was as a result of being unable to solve their conflict rather than an actual decision not to act. This inaction by bystanders is sometimes known as bystander apathy, but the stress shown by the participants in the 'seizure' experiment suggests that they are far more apathetic.

In the 'smoke' and 'accident' experiments participants who made no report of the incident often said that they didn't think the incident was very serious or that they thought other people would be dealing with it. Their perception of the situation had been affected by the other people present. These participants behaved as the others in the group did. The way in which groups seem to exert a pressure on individuals to behave all in the same way has been examined in a number of conformity studies.

Conformity

Why do people conform? Do they have to be forced to do what other people want them to do, or do they do it willingly? It is tempting to equate conformity with uniformity or conventionality; but the definition of conformity by R.S. Crutchfield (1962) is 'Yielding to group pressures'. This does not mean that a group actually forces the individual to behave in a particular way; the mere existence of a group belief may make some individuals conform to it, without overt force of any kind.

The major experiments in this area are M. Sherif, S. Asch, R.S. Crutchfield and S. Milgram, who are all social psychologists. We shall look first at various demonstrations of conformity, and then at attempts to define levels of conformity and the situations in which it can be increased or decreased.

MUZTAFER SHERIF (1935)

When a stationary spot of light is seen in a dark room it appears to move; this phenomenon is known as the autokinetic effect. Sherif used this effect, telling people that he was going to move the light and asking them to report the extent of the movement. In a series of tests he found that each individual was very consistent in their estimates but that there were wide differences between the estimates of different people. However, when two or more were tested together, their estimates converged and became similar (see table 6.1). Sherif had not told the people that they had to agree on the 'correct' figure, but each one could hear the other's estimate.

One shortcoming of this experiment was that it provided no absolute correct answer against which the participants' degrees of conformity could be measured. It would be better to conduct an experiment in which people had to answer questions for which there was a correct solution, so that their degrees of conformity relative to this could be gauged.

Table 6.1. An illustration of the Type of results found in Sherif's Study

Subject	Reported movement when tested: (a) Individually	(b) In the group
A	4 in.	4.5 in.
B	1 in.	4 in.
C	7 in.	7 in.

SOLOMON ASCH (1951)

Asch realized that this was so. He therefore tested people on simple perceptual tasks, such as deciding which of three lines was the same length as a standard line (see figure 6.2). Each participant was first tested separately. Only three mistakes were made when 36 people did about 20 trials each; therefore the task was an easy one. Participants were then tested with a number of stooges who were actually confederates of the experimenter. These people had been instructed to give incorrect answers on some of the trials. Under these conditions, if the stooges said that line A in the figure was the same as the standard line, some of the participants conformed and changed their response from the correct answer, B, to A. Seventy-four per

Figure 6.2. An Asch-type Figure

Standard line   Comparison line

cent of participants conformed at least some of the time and the mean average conformity rate for participants was 32 per cent.

FACTORS AFFECTING CONFORMITY IN THE ASCH STUDY

1 The actual number of stooges is important in such experiments. If there is only one participant and one stooge, conformity is very low indeed: 'It's my word against yours.' The breaking point comes when there are three stooges. Having more than three does not increase the conformity much further. If, however, in a group of perhaps thirteen stooges there are two real participants the conformity level drops from 32 per cent to 6 per cent. The presence of another 'deviant' seems to help the participant to abide by his answer.

2 The status of stooges also affects the likelihood of a participant conforming – the higher the stooge's status, the higher the conformity. Thus, a student is more likely to conform if the stooges are teachers than if they are fellow students.

3 The difficulty of the task affects the conformity rate – the more difficult the task (for example, if the comparison lines are all similar to the standard line), the greater the conformity.

An interesting effect has been noted over the years since the original Asch study. The early Asch studies were carried out in the USA at a time (the McCarthy anti-Communist era) when conformity was viewed, if not as a good thing, then at least as a sensible thing. During the 1960s and 1970s other experimenters have repeated Asch's study, but found gradually decreasing levels of conformity – reflecting perhaps the reduction in conformity in the USA since the 1950s (for example, the civil disobedience over the USA's involvement in the Vietnam war). Perrin and Spencer (1980) reproduced the Asch experiment with groups of six stooges and one genuine participant; they found conformity on only one trial out of 396. The Asch study is so well known these days that it is difficult to find naive participants. Perrin and Spencer used engineering, mathematics and chemistry students because they were less likely to have come across the study before. After the experiment they asked the students whether they had come across the study before and discarded the results of anyone who had. The fact that they used this type of participant makes it less easy to make a direct comparison with the Asch study since engineers and mathematicians may have a different approach to the judgement of line length and may see it as more important to be correct than other types of student. Perrin and Spencer report that they have in fact gained results which begin to approach those of Asch when using participants such as young offenders on probation, with people who normally were in authority over them acting as the experimenters. The change in results over time and between different groups emphasizes the need to be careful about over-generalizing the results of any experiment and to see social experiments within their historical context.

Asch's studies have been criticized on two main grounds: first, that his average conformity figure (32 per cent total conformity) is a misuse of statistics. It is usual to use the *median* as the measure of average when there is a large number of participants who have either a very high score or a very low score. Twenty-four per cent of Asch's participants made no conforming responses at all. Asch's figure of 32 per cent average conformity is a mean average; the median gives an average conformity figure of 25 per cent.

Secondly, social psychologists have criticized Asch's use of such abstract tasks as line-judging, which bear little or no relevance to real life. However, Asch chose the task quite intentionally to ensure that there was little chance of attitudes changing, because he wanted to measure pure conformity to group pressure. He did not want his subjects conforming because there was an element of doubt about the correct answer.

RICHARD CRUTCHFIELD (1954)

The type of experiment undertaken by Asch is very time-consuming, as only one person can be tested at a time. Crutchfield altered the experimental situation so that several people, usually five, could be tested simultaneously. Each participant sat in a booth with an array of lights and switches in front of him. Participants had to give answers to problems of the Asch type; each was told that he was the last to guess, and the guesses of the others were indicated by the lights on his panel. Of course each individual was actually given the same display, which gave incorrect answers on approximately half the trials.

Similar though generally lower conformity was found: 23 out of 50 (46 per cent) of the military men tested agreed that the star in figure 6.3 had a larger area than the circle. Similar conformity was found when the participants were tested on opinions. When tested privately, none of the 50 military men agreed with the statement 'I doubt whether I would make a good leader', but when given bogus agreements in their booths, 37 per cent did agree.

Figure 6.3. Type of Figure used by Crutchfield

Like Asch, Crutchfield found that conformity increased with the difficulty of the judgement being made.

Crutchfield's work shows us that the group doesn't have to be visible to have an effect on behaviour; it is enough to believe that you know what everyone else is doing. Some people have argued that opinion poll results may have an effect on people's voting in elections in the same sort of way; other factors such as deliberate tactical voting are also affected by such 'knowledge' of other people's intentions.

STANLEY MILGRAM (1961)

Milgram showed that people from different cultures display different amounts of conformity. He compared Norwegian and French people on a task which required them to judge which of two sounds lasted longer. The people wore headphones and heard the two tones followed by the judgements of five other people, and then they had to give their own judgement. The other five judgements were simply the recorded statements of stooges who were always unanimously agreed but on just over half the trials gave the incorrect answer. The conformity rate of the Norwegians was higher (62 per cent) than that of the French (50 per cent), and Milgram argued that this reflected basic differences in the two cultures.

The importance of the task also affects conformity rate. Milgram repeated his study but this time told people that their results would be used in the design of aircraft safety signals. Under this condition conformity fell for both the Norwegian (56 per cent) and French (48 per cent) groups. Note that the cultural difference was still shown.

When Milgram's participants were allowed to record their results privately rather than call them out, conformity dropped again but was still 50 per cent for the Norwegians and 34 per cent for the French.

Types of Conformity – Compliance and Internalization

H. Kelman (1958) proposed that there are really two types of conformity: the first is *compliance*, when the participant outwardly agrees with the group to save argument, but inwardly disagrees. The second is *internalization*, when the participant conforms because they believe or trust the answers given by the rest of the group.

Sherif's experiment with the autokinetic phenomenon seems to be a clear case of internalization. Because there is no right answer, participants' replies converge; they may be unaware that this is happening and believe that their own answers are correct. They may not be aware that they have deviated from their individual pattern of response towards that of the other participants.

Asch's study showed mainly the compliance type of conformity. Nearly all the participants reverted to their original answers when removed from the group's pressure. However, Asch performed an experiment similar to that involving line-judgement, in which he asked his participants to state their strength of agreement or disagreement with statements such as 'I feel that the unions are allowed too much power in this country.' He found that most people conformed just as they had in the perceptual tasks, but in this case some subjects showed internalization: when asked, individually, the same question two weeks later, 50 per cent of the participants gave them the same answer as the group had given. The reason that many subjects internalized in the second Asch experiment was that there was no obviously right answer to the problem, as there was with the perceptual task.

The conformity experiments stress the important influence that others have on an individual's behaviour. Much of the behaviour and many of the opinions of a person are the result of these outside forces. This means that there is a much greater uniformity within groups of people than we might expect if we considered them as single individuals.

Obedience

STANLEY MILGRAM (1963)

Unlike those in the conformity studies, participants in obedience studies are given orders or instructions to carry out by some figure of authority. Usually, the measurement of obedience is the extent to which they are prepared to carry out orders which go against their values and beliefs.

In Milgram's experiment, which was conducted at Yale University, a real participant and a stooge drew lots to decide who would be teacher and learner in a 'memory experiment'. The stooge became the learner. The 'teacher' then watched while the stooge was strapped in a chair with his arms attached to electrodes which could give a shock. The subject was shown the shock generator and was given a mild shock himself to prove that it was real. The stooge warned the experimenter that he had a heart condition, but he was told that the procedure could do 'little physical damage'. The 'teacher' then sat in a separate room with the shock generator, and asked the stooge memory questions. If the stooge responded wrongly – via a light system – the 'teacher' pressed a 15-volt button, and thereafter increased the shock by 15 volts each time an incorrect response was made. At about 150 volts the 'learner' started to complain; at about 250 he yelled 'Let me out! My heart's starting to bother me now!'; at 300 volts he kicked the wall and after this there was silence.

The experimenter supervised the arrangement, and followed a script of responses if the 'teacher' was unwilling to continue. The responses to the 'teacher's' protest increased in strength from: 'Please continue' or 'Please go on', 'The experiment requires that you continue' and 'It is absolutely essential that you continue', to 'You have no other choice: you must go on.' In addition there were some 'special prods which could be used to answer the 'teacher's' questions: for example, if the 'teacher' became worried about hurting the 'learner' the experimenter could say, 'Although the shocks may be painful, there is no permanent tissue damage, so please go on', and if the 'teacher' felt that the 'learner' did not want to continue, 'Whether the learner likes it or not, you must go on until he has learned all the word pairs correctly. So please go on.'

Milgram described the experimental situation beforehand to psychiatrists, and asked them to predict how many people would give shocks as high as 450 volts. The reply was that less than 1 per cent would continue to this extreme level. However, in the actual experiment, 62.5 per cent of the participants went as far as 450 volts; all who began giving shocks continued at least to 300 volts. These results were so much higher than common sense predicted that Milgram devised some alterations to the basic experiment to try to identify the factors which caused such high obedience.

First, many participants reported that they had continued to 450 volts because the experiment was being carried out at Yale, an important American university. Milgram then ran the same experiments in a rather dilapidated office building away from the university so that participants would not make any connection between the experiment and Yale University. The obedience level was still 49 per cent, a finding which suggests that although this reason was a factor in maintaining obedience, it had probably not been a major one.

A second factor was the nearness of the 'learner'. Would the same level of obedience be found if the 'learner' was in the same room as the 'teacher' and could be seen by him? What would happen if the 'teacher' was required to hold the 'learner's' arm down on the electrodes? One might expect that the obedience level in the first case would be considerably lower than in the basic experiment and almost non-existent in the second case. In fact the obedience level when the 'learner' was in the same room as the 'teacher' and could be seen by him was 40 per cent. When the 'teacher' had to hold the 'learner's' arm down on the electrodes, the obedience level was 30 per cent. In both cases there was therefore quite a large drop in the obedience level; nevertheless, it remained remarkably high considering the amount of information the 'teacher' was receiving about the effect of their reactions on the 'learner'. The nearness of the 'learner' was thus a factor, but not as important a factor as one might expect.

Milgram believed that the major factor was therefore the presence of the experimenter in his lab coat. In situations where he left the room and issued instructions by telephone, the obedience level dropped almost to zero: 'teachers' would pretend to press the shock buttons, or press the button for a lesser shock than they ought to have given. Somehow the presence of the experimenter with his 'prods' compelled the 'teachers' to carry on up to 450 volts.

According to Milgram, participants must have been obeying the experimenter's position rather than his personality, which had been suppressed by his use of a script. To the participants, the man in the lab coat appeared to know what was happening; many kept turning to the experimenter for advice or reassurance. One important factor emerged: the experimenter was scripted to reply 'yes' when asked if he would accept responsibility for what happened; once this had been established participants complained very little and carried on with the experiment. Thus the experimenter's absence gave the participants a greater feeling of personal responsibility for their own actions, and prompted them to obey their own consciences rather than his instructions. For Milgram, then, the experimenter's position as an expert was the major factor in inducing obedience. Participants knew little about what was happening, and therefore had to rely on the experimenter's word. When the experimenter accepted responsibility for what happened, this lifted the burden of uncertainty and fear that the 'teachers' felt. Milgram draws parallels between the behaviour of his subjects and that of the Nazi war criminals in the Second World War. Often their plea was 'I was only obeying orders' – in other words, 'I did it, but somebody else higher up accepted responsibility for it.'

Participants in Milgram's experiment often behaved as if they were locked into a role – that of somebody helping the experimenter with some scientific research. Some participants would use this role-playing as a defence mechanism, and would play the role of the perfect helper by reading the words with great care and clarity, and by pressing the shock buttons with great deliberation and precision.

The conformity and obedience experiments have been criticized because they are set up in laboratories, and are therefore not realistic. Critics point out that participants in conformity experiments are not allowed to discuss the problem with others, or to get more information. Crutchfield counters this by saying that in real life, too, discussion is limited, and that all the facts are not known; in some situations there are no facts or correct answers at all, only opinions. The fact that a group believes something may actually prevent its members from looking for further evidence about it.

A study by Hofling et al. (1966) shows that obedience to the dangerous requests of an authority figure are not confined to the laboratory. They tested nurses on normal duty at two American Hospitals. Each nurse received a phone call from a doctor that she had not met before but who was from the psychiatric department. The doctor explained to her that he would be up on the ward soon to see a patient. He asked the nurse to check the medical cabinet for a drug called Astroten. When she had done this the doctor asked her to administer 20 mg to the patient. The label on the container clearly stated that the maximum daily dose was 10 mg per day, but even so 21 out of 22 nurses went as far as pouring out the 20-mg dose before they were stopped by a confederate of the researchers. This was despite the fact that there was a hospital rule not to take instructions over the phone. The authority position of the doctor in the nurse–doctor relationship was enough to produce obedience rather than questioning.

Another objection to the conformity and obedience experiments is that they often involve deception on the part of the experimenter, particularly those of Asch and Milgram. Milgram points out that these studies could not be done without deception and argues that the results teach us things about human nature which outweigh the moral problem of deception.

This type of study always carries the risk that people will be mentally harmed by what they find out about themselves. Milgram recognizes this problem and is very careful to do a thorough *debriefing* of subjects after the experiment when they are allowed to meet the stooge learner to see that he is unharmed and it is pointed out that they have not behaved in an abnormal way. Participants are also guaranteed anonymity in any report of the experiment. In response to a questionnaire sent to them some time later, 84 per cent of the participants said that they were glad to have been in the experiment, 15 per cent were neutral and only just over 1 per cent said that they wished they had not been involved. Around three-quarters of them reported that they had learned something of importance about themselves and that further experiments of this nature should be carried out.

Conformity to Expectations

Milgram argues that much of our everyday behaviour is governed by roles. We expect students, teachers, publicans and hairdressers to act in different ways. The role makes certain behaviours permissible or expected in certain situations. My behaviour as a teacher is very different from the role I play as a bus passenger. If I stand up and give a talk in the classroom, that is perfectly OK because it is expected of me in that role; if I do the same thing on the top deck of the bus it is a different matter altogether.

A study performed by Philip Zimbardo of Stanford University in the USA shows, in a startling fashion, how people can become locked into roles from which they find it difficult to escape. Volunteers were asked to play the role of the prisoner or guard, and were assigned one of the roles randomly. They were then taken to a 'jail' and asked to play their role. The 'prisoners' were stripped and deloused and given prison clothing to wear. They were given numbers instead of being allowed to use their names. Guards were given uniforms, truncheons and sunglasses. Concealed cameras filmed what happened next. Although the simulation was supposed to run for 14 days, it had to be stopped after only six days, as both prisoners and guards were so locked into their roles that the guards made prisoners clean out toilet-bowls with their bare hands, or force-fed them, or put them in solitary confinement. The prisoners, far from fighting the guards, became apathetic and subservient and allowed the guards to do what they wished. The guards at their debriefing after the simulation were very surprised at how cruel they had been, but several mentioned that they had felt that they were locked into their role to such an extent that it overcame their normal moral aversion to behaving cruelly towards other people.

Much of our behaviour is affected by the expectations that we and others have of ourselves. Rosenthal warns against what he calls the *experimenter effect* which is the tendency for a researcher to confirm their own expectations in an experiment.

A good example of the experimenter effect is shown in a study by Rosenthal (1966). He asked students to train rats to run through a maze for a food reward and to record how well they did this. Some students were told that their rats were specially bred to learn quickly and others were told that their rats were genetically slow learners. Sure enough, the students with the 'bright' rats found that their rats did better than those with the 'dull' rats. This was despite the fact that the rats were in fact equal as far as maze learning ability was concerned and the only difference between the groups was the expectations of the students. The students with 'bright' rats had handled them more often and with more care than those with the 'dull' rats. When it was difficult to decide whether a rat had made a mistake, such as when it hesitated and turned first one way then the next at a junction, the 'bright' rats were more likely to be given the benefit of the doubt. The expectation that the rat will learn quickly becomes a *self-fulfilling prophecy*.

One of the 'classic' studies of the self-fulfilling prophecy was performed by Rosenthal and Jacobson (1968), and is very widely quoted. They gave schoolchildren a test which was supposed to pick out those children who were likely to increase their IQ over the following year. On the basis of these tests they identified a number of such children and informed their teachers. In fact the test was nothing more than a normal IQ test and the children had been picked out at random. When tested a year later, however, Rosenthal and Jacobson reported that the IQ of the chosen children had actually increased more than those of their contemporaries. It was argued that the teachers had behaved differently towards these children due to the expectation that they would improve. This self-fulfilling prophecy has obvious implications for teachers, especially those who work in areas where expectations are not very high. We must beware, however, of placing too much weight on the evidence of this study. Eysenck (1975) has pointed out that the result has not been replicated, and that in fact the conclusion of the study that expectation can improve IQ was only true for two age ranges studied.

Despite this problem with the Rosenthal and Jacobson study, the general concept of the self-fulfilling prophecy has been demonstrated many times. The roles that we voluntarily adopt in life carry with them expectations of how we should behave, and most of these are accepted at the outset. Some roles, however, are ascribed to us without any choice on our part. For example, we are all born male or female and usually this implies that we take on a particular *sex role* (see also p. 175). If a culture expects little girls to be like sugar and spice and little boys to be very different, then the self-fulfilling prophecy is likely to have effect.

False Confessions – A Special Case of Social Influence

In the early 1990s a number of infamous examples of miscarriages of justice were brought to light. Cases such as those of the Guildford Four and the Birmingham Six involved groups of people who were jailed for many years as a result of evidence which is now considered flawed. In a number of such cases part of the evidence was that one or more of the individuals had actually confessed to the crime under interrogation by the police.

Gudjonsson has made a study of cases where people confessed to crimes they did not commit. He has identified three types of false confession:

> voluntary confessions
> compliant confessions
> internalized confessions

It is not at all unusual for completely innocent people to go voluntarily into a police station and admit to a crime which they didn't commit. Some people do this over and over again and become well known to the police officers. This is so common that when publicizing a crime the police usually keep back a few crucial details so that if someone gives themselves up and confesses to the crime they can check the truth of their statement by reference to these hidden facts. Some people who make these voluntary confessions suffer from depression and have a general feeling of guilt which is then focused on the particular crime; others have a craving for the fame and publicity associated with such events; yet others suffer from disorders which make it difficult for them to distinguish between reality and fantasy.

In the cases of compliant and internalized confessions the individual admits to the crime during police interrogation and does this as a form of conforming to the demands of the interviewer. As in traditional conformity studies, these confessions may merely be made to deal with the immediate pressures of the situation (compliance) or they may be internalized as when the individual starts to believe what the interrogator is telling them ('We know you did it, you know you did it').

Most innocent people stick to their claims of innocence but report that being brought in for questioning is extremely stressful and that some types of interrogation can add to this. A few people under these conditions make confessions to escape the immediate stress. These people are often of low IQ and have a general tendency to comply with the wishes of others. When these characteristics are combined with extreme pressure and a personality that is extremely suggestible the individuals may come actually to believe that they committed the crime.

Gudjonsson gave evidence in the successful appeal of the Birmingham Six in 1991. HC, the eldest of the six, was the worse for drink when he was arrested and had been suffering from depression and a duodenal ulcer. Gudjonsson found that HC was an extroverted neurotic who had a great need for the social approval of others. HC reported that during interrogation there were up to six policemen shouting at him, that he was kept without food and that during the night he was not allowed to sleep. HC said that he felt totally disoriented and the pressure was so bad he would do anything to escape it – and that including signing a confession.

The police are also under some stress during interviews. In the cases we have referred to there was a great deal of media pressure to find the culprits for the bombings of innocent people in mainland Britain. Research has shown that police officers often go into interviews believing that they are talking to someone who is guilty and their resulting behaviour is designed to confirm this; undoubtedly this was true in these incidents. This in no way excuses the imprisonment of innocent people or the consequent escape of the guilty, but it does go some way to explaining why we need systems in place to protect against the false confession.

In the aftermath of these cases the rules for interrogation of suspects have been changed. Gudjonsson argued that training police officers to recognize individuals who are particularly vulnerable and adapting interview procedures will reduce false confessions but they will always occur. The law now requires additional evidence for a conviction.

Crowds and Crowding

Social Contagion
In his 1895 book, *The Crowd*, Gustave le Bon proposed that crowds were dangerous. He believed that individuals in a crowd lose their inhibitions and become impulsive, easily irritated, and irrational. The crowd itself seems to develop its own forms of irrational behaviour. Le Bon called this

development of a mob mentality *social contagion* because, as in a contagious disease, the individual 'catches' the mob behaviour.

However, crowds and bad behaviour are not inevitably linked. Benewick and Holton (1987) found no aggression or bad behaviour in a crowd of over 80,000 people gathered for the Pope's visit to Britain in 1982.

Deindividuation

Leon Festinger (1952) coined the term *deindividuation* to describe the effects of crowds on individuals' behaviour. In effect it means that individuals have their individuality removed from them. As a member of a crowd, the individual becomes anonymous (just one of the crowd). Consequently, fears about being judged as bad by others, fears about punishment, and feelings of guilt are all reduced. Zimbardo (1970) carried out an amended form of the Milgram electric shock study (see p. 118) to demonstrate this; two groups of women were tested to see what level of shock they would give. The two groups were prepared differently for the study, one group being put into the deindividuated condition and one into the 'individuated' condition, where they were treated as individuals.

Deindividuated condition	Individuated condition
• Wore bulky lab coats and . dark hoods.	• Wore normal clothing with large name tag.
• Spoken to as a group when given instructions.	• Given instructions individually.
• Not introduced to each other.	• Introduced to each other by name.

The deindividuated group gave, on average, twice the level of shock to the 'learner'. This study really shows the effects of anonymity rather than pure deindividuation, because the deindividuated women were not in a crowd or even a group when they pressed the shock buttons.

In addition, a later study by Johnson and Downing (1979) had the deindividuated group wearing nurses uniforms. Although still anonymous, they gave lower levels of shock than the individuated group.

Reduced lighting seems to increase deindividuation as shown in the following study by Gergen *et al.* (1978).

Both mixed groups of men and women students were told that they were to remain in a room together for an hour and that they would not meet each other again after the experiment was over. Group 1 was put into a normally lit room and Group 2 into a completely dark one. Both rooms were wired for sound, and all participants were interviewed afterwards. People in the lighted room stayed a reasonable distance from each other and chatted politely throughout the hour. In the darkened room, people explored their surroundings by touch and conversed with each other. The conversation faded over time, and over 90 per cent of the students reported that they had deliberately touched other people in the group, nearly 50 per cent said they had hugged somebody else, and 80 per cent reported becoming sexually aroused! Lack of light leads to anonymity which leads to deindividuation.

Bystander Intervention and Apathy

Another effect of crowds on peoples' behaviour is outlined in the work on bystander intervention and apathy on pp. 110–13.

Crowding

This is a form of stress resulting from unwanted excessive interactions caused by densely populated environments.

There is evidence from animal studies that living in crowded conditions can lead to an increase in aggression. A study by Calhoun (1952) demonstrates this. In a large, four-roomed enclosure, provided with adequate food and water, 48 rats were allowed to breed unchecked and their behaviour was observed as the population increased to 80. At this population density, aggression between animals increased significantly and there were frequent fights. Up to 75 per cent of the offspring died through neglect by the mother and some were eaten by other adult rats even though there was still enough food. A phenomenon which Calhoun called the *behavioural sink* occurred; rats would carry out certain normal forms of behaviour, but not as individuals. For example, there was a constant and adequate supply of food so that individual rats could feed whenever they felt hungry. With a high population density, individual rats stopped feeding by themselves and would eat only when there were several other rats present. Many of the rats developed physical illnesses and post-mortem examinations showed the effects of long periods of stress on for example, the rats' adrenal glands.

Can Calhoun's findings be applied to humans? The evidence suggests not. While high population densities in cities is often associated with crime, the causes of crime are at least equally likely to arise from poverty. Crime rates seem to be higher in areas where people are poor, whatever the level of crowding.

Crowding in a part of a city with a high density of people outside your home (called a *high outside density*) does not seem in itself to lead to raised levels of crime or aggression, but laboratory and field studies of crowding within a room (*high inside density*) show some effects. A field study by Loo (1979) showed that there was a positive correlation between the levels of verbal and physical aggression and the number of children in a room. Similarly, other researchers found that the degree of crowding in prisons was associated with higher levels of aggression. Freedman (1975) however, suggests that this is too simple a picture. In both field and laboratory studies, the exact mixture of participants can affect levels of aggression. For example, females are far more tolerant of crowding than are males.

Territorial Behaviour
It has been argued that, just as many species of animal have territories which they mark out and defend, so humans have territories too. Altman (1975) proposes that we each have three types of territory.

1 *Primary territories*, where the individual can enter, but very few others can (e.g. your own bedroom).
2 *Secondary territories* – areas which can be entered by many (but not all) people (e.g. a club or school).
3 *Public territories*, where anybody can enter, such as shopping malls or public parks.

We often mark out our territory, for example by using a bag or briefcase to separate our space in a library study area from other peoples' spaces. Felipe and Sommer (1966) carried out a study in a library, and found that when an experimenter sat at the same table as a female, territorial marking was much more likely when the experimenter sat in a chair next to the female rather than across the table or two chairs away. Females whose territory was invaded in this way showed other techniques too – some turned away from the experimenter, some folded their arms or hugged themselves to provide a barrier and some moved to another table. Only one out of 800 participants told the experimenter that he was crowding her.

E.T. Hall (1959) proposed that even within a primary territory, we have always around us four zones of 'personal space' – the distance at which we prefer different types of people to stay.

Zone 1, Intimate, 0–1½ feet. Into this zone we allow only intimate friends or close relatives.
Zone 2, Casual/personal, 1½–4 feet. Close friends or people at parties may enter this zone.
Zone 3, Social/consultative, 4–12 feet. In this zone, we allow working colleagues or people we have not met before.
Zone 4, Public, 12 feet and upwards. This represents the distance between say, a speaker and audience.

We would feel most uncomfortable if for example a colleague at work (who we would prefer to stay about 4 feet away) suddenly moved to only one foot away! These distances are of course very approximate and vary between cultures. Arabs, for example, stand much closer in conversation than do Swedes or Scots. A study by Jourard (1966) counted the number of times couples in cafes actually touched each other per hour. In London, for example, the number of touches per hour was zero. In San Juan, Puerto Rico, it was 180!

Note also that the role which a person plays can allow us to change our personal space distances. Because we view doctors, dentists and nurses in their roles rather than as individuals, we allow them into our intimate zone even though they may be relative strangers.

Privacy

Privacy does not necessarily mean always being alone. It is the amount of interaction which we prefer to have with others and it is the opposite of crowding. Privacy needs vary from individual to individual. Some people prefer constant interaction with others and feel lonely when this does not occur. Others feel the need to interact only relatively rarely and become stressed (crowded) when more than a few people are present. Our need for privacy can also vary over time. Altman (1975) who coined the term *privacy regulation* also said 'If I want to be alone, a colleague who comes into my office and talks for fifteen minutes is intruding and staying too long. If I want to interact with others, then the same fifteen minute conversation may be far too brief.' A study by Baum and Valins (1977) shows how individuals can regulate their privacy. Students who lived in rooms which were grouped around a central lounge area could reduce their privacy by sitting or studying in the lounge, have a medium level of privacy by sitting or studying in their room with the door open and have high privacy by staying in their room with the door shut.

Territorial markers and other techniques can be used to protect privacy: using books and bags as barriers, postural barriers such as folding our arms or turning away, avoiding eye contact with others, avoiding certain situations or places, or engaging in some task such as reading a book (or pretending to).

Defensible Space

Newman (1976) proposed that, while crime against persons and property are more common in areas suffering from poverty and unemployment, some techniques can be built into new housing developments which can help to make such crimes less likely to be committed. A development with 'defensible space' is less likely to suffer crime than a non-defensible space. Newman proposed that developers ensure that:

- The development should have no areas which do not clearly belong to somebody, or else these areas will tend to be neglected or vandalized.
- All areas should be easily kept under surveillance either directly by residents or by closed circuit TV (CCTV).

- There should not be any buildings or areas which look insecure, in order to deter opportunist thieves.
- Access into the development from outside must be secure and have surveillance, so that people will not feel that they are prone to attack as they enter or leave.

Summary

1 The mere presence of other people can have an energizing effect on behaviour. Allport called this *social facilitation*.

2 Latané and Darley showed that the likelihood that an individual will respond quickly to an emergency decreases when more people are present.

3 Conformity can be defined as 'yielding to group pressures'.

4 Sherif's experiment with autokinetic phenomenon showed how conformity can occur in a group, even when no members of the group have been told that they have to agree.

5 Asch's experiment showed that individuals will conform to the behaviour of a group of stooge subjects even when the group's response is obviously wrong. The minimum number of stooges required seems to be three; the presence of two real participants reduces conformity considerably.

6 Crutchfield's experiments modified Asch's so that more participants could be dealt with in a shorter time. They demonstrated a slightly lower degree of conformity, which increased with the difficulty of the task.

7 Milgram showed that conformity is affected by culture and that conformity decreases if the task is perceived as important.

8 Kelman proposed that there were two major types of conformity, *compliance* – paying lip-service – and *internalization* – believing. If an individual adopts a group's attitude after the experiment, it is internalization; if he returns to his former attitude, it is compliance.

9 Milgram tested obedience to authority: participants were given orders which they were told to follow. They showed obedience by giving electric shocks to another person. Milgram believed that the cause of the high obedience rate was mainly due to deference to the experimenter's role as an expert in that situation; when he accepted responsibility for whatever might happen, participants were more likely to continue.

10 Rosenthal showed that our expectations affect behaviour in such a way that the expectations are fulfilled. This is known as the *self-fulfilling prophecy*.

11 Social influence in the interview of subjects can lead to false confessions especially when highly stressful interrogation techniques are used with people of low intelligence and compliant personalities.

12 Le Bon argued that being in a crowd changed individuals' behaviour, usually for the worse. He called this *social contagion*. Festinger used the

term *deindividuation* to describe the increase in anonymity and consequent reduction in feelings of guilt caused by being in a crowd.

13 Crowding is the stress caused by unwanted excessive interactions with others. Calhoun found that crowding in rats could lead to severe behavioural disorders including cannibalism. The situation with human crowding is however, far more complex.

14 Altman believed that we all have primary, secondary and public territories. We can use markers like bags, books and coats to show the limits of our territories.

15 E.T. Hall proposed four zones of *personal space* – the distance which we prefer to be from other people.

16 Privacy is the amount of interaction which we wish to have with other people. Territorial markers and non-verbal signals allow us to regulate our levels of privacy.

17 *Defensible space* is a series of techniques which Newman proposed for new housing developments which aim to reduce actual crime and increase people's feelings of safety through better site design and surveillance.

Further Reading

Gudjonsson, G.H., *The Psychology of Interrogation, Confessions and Testimony* (1992, J. Wiley).

Chapter 7

Social Perception

Forming Impressions of Other People

We saw in chapter 2 how we don't necessarily perceive exactly what is 'out there', because we organize and translate the information from our senses, often using our previous experience. We saw, too, that similar previous experiences may be stored together as schema, and that these schema can affect our organization and translation of information. Just as these processes occurred with ambiguous information, so they occur with social information; that is, with information about other people. When we form impressions of other people, we do not automatically pay attention to all the information which we get from them – our schema lead us to assume certain things about them (based on similar people we have met in the past), and they alter what information we pay attention to. We may even not notice information which does not fit in with the particular schema we are using.

As an example, suppose you have been told that you are about to meet somebody for the first time, who is described to you as being an introvert. Your 'introvert' schema will probably have information such as 'prefers reading to meeting people, withdrawn, quiet, not a risk-taker' stored in it. When you actually meet the person, you already know (or rather, think you know), something about them. (Though how accurate an impression you gain depends on how accurately the word 'introvert' describes them, and also on how resistant your introvert schema is to change.) If you meet the person several times, you will probably develop a separate schema for that particular person, though if you gain any more information from them about what introverts are like, this information will probably be stored in the 'introvert' schema as well.

When we form impressions of other people, Asch suggested, there are some types of information which are more important than others in 'switching on' schema. Participants were given a list of seven words which they were told described a particular person. Half of the participants had 'cold' as one of their seven words, and the other half had 'warm'. All participants were then asked if the person described was generous and humorous. Of participants who had 'cold' in their list, only about 10 per cent described the person as generous or humorous. However, of participants who had 'warm' in their list, 90 per cent agreed with generous and 75 per cent with humorous. The words 'warm' and 'cold', therefore, were powerful in switching on different schema in the participants. When Asch used words like 'polite' and 'blunt' in place of 'warm' and 'cold' there was very little difference in their effects. Asch called such influential adjectives 'central traits'.

Kelley's study (see p. 25) was a follow-up to Asch's study, and showed the same effects.

Because each person has his or her own set of past experiences, they are likely to have different schema. For example, when parents are choosing a name for a new baby, there are often long discussions and even arguments about which name to choose. Although one parent may like the name 'Rosalind', perhaps because it was the name of a loved grandparent, the other may loathe it because of an unpleasant person they had met by that name. Each individual also has their own ideas on which characteristics seem to go together. In a study by Rosenberg and Sedlak, college students were asked to describe some of the people they knew. The most frequent words used were intelligent, friendly, self-centred, ambitious and lazy, but some of these words tended to be found together – for example 'friendly' and 'intelligent' were often found together, yet very few people described anybody as being 'friendly' and 'self-centred'. Schneider argued that we have a set of assumptions about which characteristics go together, but we rarely if every talk about it or even consciously think of it, though it affects the ways in which we judge other people. Schneider called these ideas our 'implicit personality theories'.

Since people tend not to be totally consistent in their behaviour, which bits of evidence about them do we use? Suppose somebody you have met only twice behaved in an extroverted way on your first meeting, but behaved introvertedly on your second meeting. What sort of person are they? Read the passage below, and answer the question at the end of it.

Jim left the house to get some stationery. He walked out into the sun-filled street with two of his friends, basking in the sun as he walked. Jim entered the stationery store, which was full of people. Jim talked with an acquaintance while he waited to catch the clerk's eye. On his way out, he stopped to chat with the school friend who was just coming into the store. Leaving the store, he walked toward the school. On his way, he met the girl to whom he had been introduced the night before. They talked for a short while, and then Jim left for school. After school, Jim left the classroom alone. Leaving the school, he started on his long walk home. The street was brilliantly filled with sunshine. Jim walked down the street on the shady side. Coming down the street towards him he saw the pretty girl whom he had met on the previous evening. Jim crossed the street and entered a candy store. The store was crowded with students, and he noticed a few familiar faces. Jim waited quietly until he caught the counterman's eye and then gave his order. Taking his drink, he sat down at a side table. When he had finished his drink, he went home.

[Luchins, 1957, pp 34–5.]

Question: What sort of a person is Jim? Is he an outgoing or a withdrawn sort of person?

This passage from a study by Luchins was designed to find out whether the primacy and recency effect was very strong – you demonstrated the primacy effect yourself if you described Jim as being 'outgoing'.

The first half of the passage described Jim as being a friendly, outgoing person, but after the sentence 'After school, Jim left the classroom alone', the passage describes him as an unfriendly or shy sort of person. Luchins gave the two halves (friendly/unfriendly) of the passage in different orders to different people. The impression that they got of Jim depended on which half of the passage came first (see table 7.1). Results like this show the importance of making a good impression early on.

Consider this example: two people are taking an examination and know equal amounts of information. Person A answers the questions he or she can do best first, whilst person B leaves his/her best questions until last. Who is likely to get the higher marks? Probably person A, because the examiner will have gained the impression that A knew his/her subjects, and is therefore liable to give the benefit of the doubt when marking the latter part of A's answer.

Table 8. Primacy/Recency Effect (as Shown by Luchins)

	Presentation of descriptions:			
	Outgoing description only	Outgoing, then withdrawn	Withdrawn, then outgoing	Withdrawn description only
% of people seeing Jim as outgoing	79	52	34	16
% seeing him as withdrawn	14	36	56	73

It may be that these effects are due to our schema. The first half of the above passage seems to switch on our 'friendly' schema, and assimilate 'Jim' into it. Once the 'friendly' schema is operating, it biases the way we look for other information about Jim – we may ignore or treat lightly the 'unfriendly' descriptions. Luchins found that participants who regarded Jim as friendly made excuses for his later 'unfriendly' behaviour, by saying he was probably tired after school. Just the sort of distortion, in fact, that Bartlett talked about (see p. 71). It seems that once we start to use a particular schema for a person, it is difficult, or takes a lot of opposing evidence, to make us switch to a different schema. Luchins found, however, that the primacy effect can be weakened if subjects are warned beforehand not to be too hasty in making their judgements.

Another way of reducing the primacy effect is to get the subject to do some other task between hearing the two parts of the story, or simply give he two halves on separate days. Under these conditions, though, there is sometimes a recency effect – the last half of the passage has more effect on our judgement than the first, probably because, like the recency effect in memory, it is the nearest in time to recall and is therefore remembered well.

The danger with the primacy effect in real life is that, if we meet somebody and don't like them, we may not want to meet them again and so gain information about them which may cause us to change our impression of them.

Schemas, Categorization and Stereotyping

Remember from the work of Bruner (chapter 5) that categorization is one of the ways in which we simplify the masses of information we receive, and which helps us to work out the 'recurrent themes' (the predictable occurrences) in our environment. We frequently categorize people for the same reasons. If you were told that Steve Heyes has red hair, you could find your 'red-haired people' schema or category, and from it extract other features likely to be found (in your experience) in red-haired people. You might, for example, find that red-haired people tend to be quick-tempered, and you may react to Steve as if he were a quick-tempered person (and you would be wrong, because he isn't). In this case, you would have stereotyped Steve – in other words, you would have stored him in your schema for 'red-haired people', a schema about an identifiable group. Like any schema, stereotypes tend to be resistant to change, because if you receive any information which does not fit into a schema, you distort it so that it does fit or simply forget it. So to you, Steve would probably continue to be a quick-tempered person.

The sort of stereotyping above is not particularly harmful, but other stereotypes are, because any individual you meet is unlikely to show completely the sorts of behaviour your stereotype of his or her group contains. Any stereotype is by definition an oversimplification of behaviour. Although stereotypes may be useful ways of categorizing people about whom we first know little, they are not a substitute for real knowledge of a person.

Simply being a member of a group (or simply regarding yourself as a member of a particular group) seems to be enough to make people stereotype any group other than their own. You are likely to know the people in your group (the 'in-group') quite well, but know less about people in other groups (the 'out-groups'), and you are likely to notice the similarities among members of your own group. This may be due to people's need to belong to a group, and to have a positive attitude towards it. You are more likely to treat people who are not in your group as an out-group – that is, to stereotype them, and as a result even to discriminate against them. An experiment by Tajfel shows this effect quite strongly, even though the group members did not even know or meet each other.

Participants in Tajfel's experiment (schoolchildren aged fourteen to fifteen years) were divided into two groups on some arbitrary basis (for example blue eyes versus brown eyes). Each child was told that he or she could give money to members of his/her own group, but they also had to give money to members of the other group. None of the children actually knew who was in which group, but they knew of course which group they themselves were in.

The children were given choices – for example, they could give 20 coins to a member of their own group and 15 coins to a member of the other group (in-group gets five more coins than out-group), or 15 coins to one of their own group and eight coins to a member of the out-group (in-group gets seven more coins than out-group). They tended to choose the second alternative, even though it meant that their group gained fewer coins than it could have, because the second alternative gives them a bigger advantage over the out-group than does the first. The same sorts of effects occur even when membership of a group is decided at random, by the toss of a coin.

This effect, of regarding oneself as a member of a group and of discriminating against out-group members is called social categorization. Social categorization results in the development of two important perceptual sets: firstly, people see their group members as being more similar than they really are, and secondly, they see the differences between the group and the out-group as being greater than they really are. This effect happens with particular strength in wartime – newspapers and films of the time of the Second World War frequently emphasized 'the British people' and contrasted them with out-group enemies, usually saying how much more courageous, inventive, and so on, the British were.

Categorization is the first step in stereotyping, and causes magnification of in-group similarities, and of differences between in-group and out-group. Stereotyping goes further, and encourages the development of strong positive or negative attitudes towards the out-group. Pennington believes that stereotypes have three main characteristics:

1 People are categorized on the basis of very visible characteristics, for example race, sex, nationality, bodily appearance, mode of dress, disability, and so on.

2 All members of a particular group are assumed to have the same characteristics.

3 Anybody who is seen to belong to a particular group will therefore automatically be assumed to have the same characteristics as the group.

The attitudes which people have towards stereotyped out-groups tend to be quite extreme, either favourable (positive) or unfavourable (negative). The strength of the attitude seems to depend on how simply the out-group has been defined – the more simply, the stronger the attitude.

Racial Stereotyping

One of the earliest studies of racial stereotyping was by Braly. He produced lists of adjectives, and asked which applied to Jews, Blacks, Germans and Americans. Common adjectives used for each ethnic group were:

Jews	Blacks	Germans	Americans
shrewd	lazy	scientific	shrewd
mercenary	musical	industrious	materialistic
	superstitious		

Later studies of ethnic stereotyping found that people were less willing to stereotype people, although stereotyping does still occur. The nature of the stereotyping has, however, changed (in the USA) since Braly's early work in the 1930s.

Table 7.2 shows how Americans' stereotypes of American Blacks and Jews changed over the years between 1933 and 1967. Notice how for example Jews were seen as less shrewd and mercenary in 1967 than they were in 1933 and how Blacks were seen as less lazy and superstitious but more musical.

Although stereotypes are grossly oversimplified descriptions, they may contain a grain of truth. In the USA, for example, the number of blacks in musical or athletic professions is much greater than the percentage of blacks in the total population – proportionately more blacks than whites are successful in music and sport.

The danger, however, in stereotyping is that we may distort what we see of people's behaviour so that it fits our stereotype. We may not do so consciously, for 'other people have stereotypes – we see things as they really are'.

Table 7.2

Ethnic group	Characteristics	Percentage who agreed with characteristics		
		1933	1951	1967
Americans	Industrious	48	30	23
	Intelligent	47	32	20
	Materialistic	33	37	67
	Ambitious	33	21	42
	Progressive	27	5	17
Jews	Shrewd	79	47	30
	Mercenary	49	28	15
	Industrious	48	29	37
	Grasping	34	17	17
	Intelligent	29	37	37
Blacks	Superstitious	84	41	13
	Lazy	75	31	26
	Happy-go-lucky	38	17	27
	Ignorant	38	24	11
	Musical	26	33	47

Sex-Role Stereotyping

An example of how subtle stereotyping can be was shown in a study by Goldberg in 1968. Female students were given articles on professional topics to read, and asked to say how well they were written, how persuasive they were, how technically correct and so on. Unknown to the students, the names of the authors had been slightly changed, so that some students received an article written by 'John T. McKay', and others received the same article, but written by 'Joan T. McKay'. Articles supposedly written by female authors received significantly lower ratings than exactly the same articles did when it was thought that the author was male. The students seemed to believe that women could not be as good at professional matters as men, but since this study in 1968, other researchers have found that the effect has become weaker, presumably because people are more aware of the dangers of sex-role stereotyping.

Children's books have frequently been criticized for supporting sex-role stereotypes, and a study in 1973 by Saario, Jacklin and Tittle in North America shows how widespread the unspoken assumptions about sex roles were in the elementary school books of the 1960s which they examined. They found:

Females appeared in books much less frequently than males.

Females tended to follow orders rather than to give them.

Females were more likely to be involved in fantasizing rather than problem-solving.

Females were more conformist than males.

Females were more verbal than males.

Females spent much more time indoors than males.

Positive events (e.g. success) were often attributed to the actions of males.

Positive events which happened after female actions were attributed to the situation or to the goodwill of others, rather than to the female's actions.

These differences in behaviour between the sexes increased with the age of child towards which the book was aimed.

Prejudice and Discrimination

Prejudice and discrimination are not the same thing. Prejudice is a positive or negative attitude towards a group or its individuals which causes us to think and feel in particular ways towards them. If, as a result of negative attitude towards a group, we behave unfairly or harshly towards them, we are said to discriminate against them. Prejudices lead to discrimination.

Allport argued that prejudice and discrimination are caused by four main factors:

1 historical and economic causes
2 cultural causes
3 situational (or interpersonal) causes
4 individual causes

HISTORICAL CAUSES

Much of the discrimination against blacks and Asians can be traced back to Britain's colonial days; blacks were imported into this country, and used in the colonies as slaves – and slaves by definition do not have equal rights or fair treatment. The British view of the inhabitants of its colonies was generally that they were inferior to 'true' Britons intellectually, socially and often in motivation. When workers were required, however, the colonies provided a readily available (and cheap) supply. Marxist sociologists see prejudice as a way in which the ruling classes maintain the attitude within society that a particular group or groups are in some way inferior, and therefore the ruling classes are justified in exploiting either the group or its resources.

CULTURAL CAUSES

Changes in the ways in which society operates may produce breeding grounds for racial prejudice. For example, increased urbanization (people being attracted to or forced to live in towns), mechanization and unemployment (and competition for jobs), the increased importance of training and qualifications, the increasing power of the media (so that people believe what they are told, rather than developing their own internal standards), changes in the structure of the family and in standards of morality, and the upward mobility (improvement in social position) of some groups are all thought by sociologists and anthropologists to have increased the level of prejudice.

Social processes, such as the law and education, may help to maintain prejudice by making formal and unequal treatment of particular groups. Because people and groups become crowded together, they are in competition for work and they are more easily affected by the media.

A beautiful demonstration of the effects of the educational system on prejudice was carried out at a primary school in America by Jane Elliott.

One day, blue-eyed Mrs Elliott announced to her class of nine-year-olds that brown-eyed people were more intelligent and better people than those with blue eyes. The blue-eyed children, although the majority, were simply told that they were inferior and that the brown-eyed children should therefore be the ruling class. Guidelines were laid down so the inferior group would 'keep their place' in the new social order. They were to sit at the back of the room, stay at the end of the line, use paper cups (instead of the drinking fountain) and so on. The 'superior' students received extra privileges, such as extra recess time for work well done.

Within minutes the blue-eyed children began to do more poorly on their lessons and became depressed, sullen and angry. They described themselves as 'sad', 'bad', 'stupid', 'dull', 'awful', 'hard', 'mean'. One boy said he felt like a 'vegetable'. Of the brown-eyed superiors, the teacher reported: 'What had been marvellously cooperative, thoughtful children became nasty, vicious, discriminating little third-graders ... it was ghastly.'

To show how arbitrary and irrational prejudice and its rationalizations really are, the teacher told the class on the next school day that she had erred, that it was really the blue-eyed children who were superior and the brown-eyed ones who were inferior. The brown-eyes now switched from their previously 'happy', 'good', 'sweet', 'nice', self-labels to derogatory ones similar to those used the day before by the blue-eyes. Their academic performance deteriorated, while that of the new ruling class improved. Old friendship patterns between children dissolved and were replaced with hostility.

The children reacted with relief and delight at the end, when the were 'debriefed' and learned that none of them was 'inferior' to others. Hopefully they had learned to empathize with those they might see being made targets of prejudice in the future. (Quoted in P. Zimbardo, *Psychology and Life*, 10th edn, 1979, p. 638.)

SITUATIONAL AND INTERPERSONAL CAUSES
Situational causes of prejudice include, importantly, conformity to group norms (see p. 113). Since people tend to conform with others so as not to appear different, to gain approval or to avoid punishment, we might expect that in a climate of prejudice, non-prejudiced people might conform with the prejudiced majority and behave in prejudiced ways. Before laws were changed in the southern states of the USA, restaurant owners often used the 'I'm not prejudiced, but my customers wouldn't like it' excuse as a reason for their refusal to admit blacks to their restaurants.

As situations change, so may prejudices. In the Second World War when the Soviet Union was an ally of Britain and the USA, people's opinions of the Russians were that they were not cruel, were hardworking, brave, un-conceited, progressive and intelligent. By 1948, with the advent of the 'cold war', opinions in the USA had changed; Russians were regarded by many more people as being cruel and conceited, and by fewer people as being hardworking, brave and intelligent. Now that the cold war is over opinions have changed again.

A study in South Africa by Pettigrew showed a relationship between prejudice and conformity. White students who were highly prejudiced against blacks also showed more conformity to social norms. In the USA southern states, the pattern was similar – highly prejudiced whites tended to be churchgoers, moving up the social ladder, and to have lower edu-cational attainment.

Milgram's study on the levels of conformity of French and Norwegians (see p. 117) suggest that there might be cultural differences in conformity (and possibly therefore in prejudice too).

INDIVIDUAL CAUSES
Two main theories have been put forward to explain why prejudice occurs in individuals. The first, the 'frustration-aggression hypothesis', was put forward originally by Dollard, and the idea is that, if a person is prevented from reaching a goal (that is, is frustrated by being prevented from getting something they want), or has something they want taken away from them (deprivation), they will experience an increase in aggression. If the original source of the frustration is not attackable, the aggression has to go

somewhere (that is, it has to be redirected), so it is likely to be redirected on to people or groups which are not able to fight back – in other words, when frustrated or deprived, people will find scapegoats. Feshbach and Singer, however, believed that the kind of frustration or threat was important. Something which threatened or frustrated the whole community, such as an attack by another country, or 'acts of God' like storms, tended to pull people together and to reduce prejudice. Personal threats or frustrations, however, such as losing one's job or being robbed, tended to increase prejudiced behaviour.

The second theory of individual prejudice takes the view that there are people who, because of some flaw in their personality, become prejudiced. Some of the earliest work in this area was carried out by Adorno and Frenkel-Brunswik. They tested over two thousand people in California – students at university, teachers, patients at the Langley-Porter Psychiatric Institute, nurses, union members, members of war veterans' clubs and inmates of San Quentin Prison. Test results from minority group members – blacks and Jews, for example, were excluded – Adorno and his co-workers wanted to find out what white, non-Jewish, native-born, middle-class Americans thought about Jews, how common anti-Semitism was, and if it was related to particular kinds of personality. (Adorno's and Frenkel-Brunswik's interest in anti-Semitism was not just an academic one – they were both Jewish, and had been students and teachers at the University of Vienna at the time of Hitler's rise to power.) Although their first researches were into anti-Semitism, they soon extended it into looking at what they called ethnocentrism – the tendency to dislike and reject all out-groups and aliens – a sort of general prejudice which would, of course, include anti-Semitism. (Summer, who introduced the term ethnocentrism in 1906, defined it as a tendency to accept rigidly the culturally alike, and to reject the culturally unalike.) After this, they investigated conservatism, the desire to keep things as they are, using a Political and Economic Conservatism Scale (PEC). Lastly, they developed 'The Implicit Antidemocratic Trends', or 'Potentiality for Fascism' or 'F' scale, which, although they did not call it so in their book, many psychologists have called the Authoritarianism scale. They gave to each subject questionnaires which consisted of statements (sample questions are shown in table 7.3) from the scales, and subjects had to show their agreement or disagreement with each statement using a Likert Scale (after Rensis Likert, who devised it):

+1 slight support, agreement −1 slight opposition, disagreement
+2 moderate support, agreement −2 moderate opposition, disagreement
+3 strong support, agreement −3 strong opposition, disagreement

Notice that there is no 'neutral' category – subjects had either to agree or disagree with a statement.

Table 7.3. Examples of Statements from Adorno's Research

Examples from the anti-Semitism scale:
'I can hardly imagine myself marrying a Jew.'
'No matter how Americanized a Jew may seem to be, there is always something different and strange, something basically Jewish underneath.'

Examples from the ethnocentricity scale:
'Blacks have their rights, but it is best to keep them in their own districts and schools and to prevent too much contact with them.'
'Certain religious sects who refuse to salute the flag should be forced to conform to such a patriotic act, or else be abolished.'

Examples from the PEC scale:
'A child should learn early in life the value of a dollar and the importance of ambition, efficiency and determination.'

'The best way to solve social problems is to stick to the middle of the road, to move slowly, and to avoid extremes.'

The 'F' Scale (the Authoritarianism Scale) tested nine different characteristics:

1 Conventionalism – How rigidly people stick to middle class, conventional values.
2 Authoritarian Submission – An uncritical acceptance and submission to their in-group's moral authorities.
3 Authoritarian Aggression – The tendency to look for and to punish or reject people who do not share traditional values.
4 Anti-Intraception – Opposition to the imaginative or tender-minded ('do-gooders').
5 Superstition and Stereotyping – Belief in such things as astrology – that our fate is controlled by some mystical process, and the tendency to think in rigid categories (seeing a problem as black or white, with no shades of grey).
6 Power and Toughness – Strong belief in the importance of dominance over submission, leaders over followers.
7 Destructiveness and Cynicism – Belief that people and events are generally bad – a hostility towards humans in general.
8 Projectivity – The projection of probably unconscious emotional impulses which are projected outwards. The belief that the world is a dangerous and unpredictable place, e.g. 'Wars and social troubles may someday be ended by an earthquake or flood that will destroy the whole world.'
9 Sex – A near-obsessive and puritanical attitude towards sexual behaviour.

So, is there an Authoritarian Personality, and if so, how does it relate to anti-Semitism, ethnocentricity and political and economic conservatism? When people's scores on each scale are compared (using the correlational statistical technique), it was found that ethnocentrism, anti-Semitism and authoritarianism were strongly interrelated – somebody who scored highly on ethnocentrism was also likely to score highly on anti-Semitism and authoritarianism. There was not such a strong relationship between political and economic conservatism and the others.

The second major part of the study was to interview some people in great depth ('clinical interviews') about things such as job aspirations and attitudes, religion, family background, relationships with parents, sexual behaviour patterns, educational interests, political attitudes and attitudes towards minority groups. Eighty people were chosen, 45 of whom had scored highly on the anti-Semitism scale and 35 who had scored low (we will call them 'highs' and 'lows' respectively). They were representative of the two thousand or more people originally tested and were roughly matched for age, sex, religion and political persuasion. They were not, however, matched for educational backgrounds. The interviews produced the clear differences (see table 7.4) between the 'highs' and 'lows' in personality and in previous (mainly childhood) experiences.

Table 7.4

High Ethnocentric Scorers	Low Ethnocentric Scorers
Personality differences	
Rejects socially unacceptable part of self.	Accepts socially unacceptable impulses as part of self.
Externalizes socially unacceptable impulses (fear, weakness, sex and aggressive feelings) through projection.[1]	Internalizes and ruminates about socially unacceptable impulses in self.
Holds conventional values and rules – conventional admiration of parents.	Holds more intrinsic and socially constructive values – realistic appraisal of parents.
Power-orientated in personal relationships.	Affectionate and love-orientated in personal relationships.
Rigid personality organization.	Flexible personality organization.
Differences in childhood situation	
Harsh, threatening parental discipline.	Reasonable parental discipline.
Parental love conditional upon display of approved behaviour.	Unconditional parental love.
Hierarchical family structure.	Egalitarian family structure.
Concerned about family status.	Unconcerned about family status.

[1] 'Projection' is a Freudian term – see p. 180. (From Adorno's *The Authoritarian Personality*.)

This was supported by a follow-up study by Frenkel-Brunswik, who studied prejudice in children and adolescents. Their main findings were that the most ethnocentric children and adolescents:

1 had undergone strict, rigid and punishment-centred discipline.
2 were liable to think of their parents as wholly good (at least in public – there were suggestions that in private, they thought the opposite). Unprejudiced children seemed more able to accept feeling love and hate for the same person.
3 tended to accept that parents' and teachers' main role was to discipline children and to make then behave properly.

There have been criticisms of Adorno's work which centre around two aspects of the studies. First, all the questionnaires except the Political and Economic conservatism scale were constructed so that if you agreed with a statement, you scored a 'point' on that scale. Questionnaire designers are aware of 'response sets' – Cronbach proposed in 1946 that some people may tend to agree with statements in questionnaires, whatever their content – maybe they just get into the habit of agreeing. If this happens, then such a person's scores on all the scales (except PEC) will be artificially high. A study by Bass showed how powerful this effect can be. He gave the Authoritarianism test twice to his subjects – once in the form used by Adorno, and once with each statement in reverse form (so instead of 'Science has its place, but there are many important things that can never possibly be understood by the human mind', Bass used 'All the mysteries surrounding our lives will sooner or later be cleared up through the progress of science'). If people's response sets had had no effect, they should have gained similar scores on the 'normal' and 'reversed' Authoritarianism tests, but in fact they scored much lower on the 'reversed' test. Response sets in their subjects are likely to have inflated the amount of authoritarianism shown by Adorno's subjects.

The second criticism is that the questionnaire results may be explained by the participants' educational level (the lower the level, the greater the ethnocentricity and authoritarianism) rather than by the idea of authoritarian personality type. A study by Hyman showed that there was a relationship between education and scores on the authoritarianism scale.

Although it suffered from the same response set problems as Adorno's study, a study by Rokeach provided an interesting development of Adorno's study. Rokeach believed that both politically left- and right-wing extremists were rigid in their thinking and would strongly reject views different from their own – in other words, they were dogmatic in their opinions. He devised a dogmatism questionnaire which he gave to English college students, and found that both extreme left-wingers (communists) and right-wing conservatives showed more dogmatism than the politically moderate students. Dogmatism (and maybe authoritarianism) may therefore be independent of political views – in other words, dogmatism (or authoritarianism) may determine the strength, rather than the direction (left- or right-wing) of political belief.

Adorno's idea, that prejudice is due to personality defects as well as to learning, is nicely demonstrated in a study by Hartley. If prejudice were solely due to learning or to conformity pressures, then prejudiced individuals should show prejudice towards groups they had learned or been pressured to dislike. But what would they do to groups they had never heard of, or which did not even exist? The 'prejudice = learning or conformity' theory would predict that no prejudice would be shown to unfamiliar groups. Adorno's theory, though, predicts that prejudice would be shown towards unfamiliar groups, because prejudice is a basic fault in the individual's personality, and prejudice will be shown to any out-groups. Hartley asked people questions about how close they would allow various out-group members to get (e.g. would they let them live next door, would they marry them, etc.). Some refused to give any answers to such questions about 'Danerians', 'Wallonians' and 'Pirenians', but many were prepared to give their opinions on these groups. Interestingly, the people who were most prejudiced against known out-groups (e.g. blacks or Jews) tended to express the most prejudiced opinions about 'Danerians', 'Wallonians' and 'Pirenians'. This clearly supports Adorno's theory – prejudiced individuals cannot have learned their prejudices about these groups because they don't exist.

Institutional Sexism and Racism – Two Case Studies

SEXISM

A report of the Equal Opportunities Commission shows how an institution may discriminate against women. The report showed that in a South Wales College of Further Education, the Principal and Head of Department of Business Studies had drawn up a list of criteria for use in deciding which staff should be promoted. In the Business Studies Department, there were fourteen men and nine women. All of the ten posts above the basic teaching grade were held by men. No women in the Business Studies Department had every been promoted. The reason were largely due to the ways in which the Principal (and sometimes the Head of Department) interpreted the criteria.

For example, the women had all had more teaching experience and industrial experience than the men. However, although both were on the list of criteria, the Principal decided that the women's industrial experience, though longer than the men's, was not as recent and so did not count as much as the men's. Similarly, their greater teaching experience was not given much weight as a criterion for promotion.

RACISM

Political and Economic Planning (PEP) carried out research financed by the Home Office and the Gulbenkian foundation. The research was into the current situation of racial minorities in Britain. One part of their research involved testing employers' attitudes towards employing racial minority members. A white actor, an Asian, a West Indian and a Greek, all fluent English speakers, were given carefully prepared similar (in terms of experience) but fictitious roles. In pairs, the testers would apply for non-skilled or skilled jobs. In the case of non-skilled jobs, the Asian and West Indian 'applicants' appeared to be discriminated against in 46 per cent of cases, and in applications for skilled jobs, they were discriminated against in 20 per cent of cases. The discrimination could not have been simply against foreigners, because the Greek was discriminated against only in 10 per cent of applications for non-skilled jobs, and in 9 per cent of skilled-job applications.

The Reduction of Prejudice – The Robbers' Cave Study

One of the most important studies in this area is Sherif's study of group formation, competition and cooperation on conflict and prejudice between American boys at summer camp.

In the study, trained observers first found out the patterns of friendship between the boys (who did not know they were in an experiment). The experimenters then formed two groups, so that two-thirds of best friends were in opposite groups. During the next week, the groups had little contact and separately took part in interesting and cooperative activities, e.g. cooking, transporting canoes. At the end of the week the boys were asked who their best friends were – and it was found that friendship choices had moved towards in-group members. This is how the rest of the experiment was conducted, and the results, in Sherif's own words:

> Next rivalry between the groups was stimulated by a series of competitive events. As predicted, this both increased in-group solidarity and produced unfavourable stereotypes of the out-group and its members. After losing a tug of war, the Eagles burned the Rattlers' flag. The Rattlers retaliated, and a series of bunkhouse raids ensued, accompanied by name calling, fist fights, and other expressions of hostility. During the conflict, a physically daring leader emerged to replace the less aggressive boy who had led the 'peacetime' Eagles. In this way relations with other groups will cause changes within a group.

An attempt was made to break down the hostility and induce the two groups to cooperate with each other. First, the rival groups were brought into close contact in pleasant activities – such as eating and shooting off firecrackers. The groups refused to intermingle, however, and the activities merely provided them with further opportunities for expressions of hostility, indicating that intergroup contact does not in itself decrease tension.

Situations were then contrived to bring about interactions of the groups to achieve superordinate goals – that is, important goals that required the combined efforts of both groups. The most striking episode in this period was one in which the tug-of-war rope, formerly the central object in a most antagonistic situation, served as a tool. On an overnight trip, a truck that was to bring their food stalled and the boys hit upon the idea of using the rope to pull the vehicle. After looping the rope through the bumper, the two groups pulled on different ends, and the next day, when the truck stalled again, members of the two groups intermingled on the two lines, obliterating group divisions.

Further evidence of the change in the boys' attitudes was obtained from friendship choices made at the end of the period of intense competition and again at the close of the experiment. Rattlers' choices of Eagles as friends went up from 6 to 36 per cent of their total friendship choice. Eagles' choices of Rattlers went up from 8 to 23 per cent. The boys were also asked to rate each other on six characteristics designed to reveal the presence of stereo-typed images. During the period of antagonism, Eagles received few favourable ratings from Rattlers, and Rattlers few from Eagles; but at the close of the experiment there was no significant difference in the ratings of in-group and out-group members. (Sherif and Sherif, 1936.)

What then can we conclude from Sherif's study? First, that simply bringing the two groups together was not enough to reduce the prejudices. Much more effective was bringing the groups together to achieve a series of goals which require the cooperation of both groups. Sherif stressed that the series of goals must be appealing to both groups, and that both groups should take an equally strong part in the activities – prejudice will not decrease if one group takes the role of leader, for example.

In addition to equal status, interaction between people and cooperative efforts, Cook proposed that two other conditions also bring about reduc-tions in prejudices:

1 Prejudice is reduced if the prejudiced person can meet individuals from the out-group who do not match the out-group's stereotype. For ex-ample, if a racially prejudiced person who believed that all blacks were unintelligent were to meet a black university professor, they would have difficulty in maintaining the prejudiced stereotype schema.
2 As an antidote to pressure to conform, support from the prejudiced person's friends or family for meetings with out-group members helps to reduce prejudice. This factor is supported by studies of racial prejudice in racially desegregated military units in Vietnam. In Vietnam, there was a reduction in racial prejudice, but when the soldiers returned home to people who were still racially prejudiced, they became more prejudiced again.

Summary

1 As in perception and memory, schema containing our previous experiences enable us to make predictions about the people we meet, and they also direct to some extent the sorts of information we look for in other people.

2 Asch's and Kelley's studies showed that some types of information (central traits) are more likely to switch on our social perception schema than are other types.

3 Schneider devised the phrase 'implicit personality theories' to refer to the assumptions, often unspoken, which we have about which personality characteristics go together.

4 Luchins demonstrated the effects of primacy and recency on impression formation. The primacy effect is important because it is from first impressions that our permanent attitudes towards other people may be formed.

5 Tajfel's study demonstrated social categorization – the discrimination of a group and its members towards people who are not in that group. The in-group sees itself as being more similar than it really is and sees the differences between it and the out-group as being greater than they really are.

6 Stereotypes involve people being categorized on the basis of visible characteristics and all members of a group are assumed to have the same characteristics.

7 Stereotyping can be dangerous because we may reject or distort information which does not fit our stereotype schema.

8 Goldberg studied how in the 1960s articles allegedly written by female authors were seen as being not as competent as the same articles written by male authors – thus demonstrating sex-role stereotyping. Saario, Jacklin and Tittle showed that children's books tended to stress this superior role of males.

9 Prejudices (positive or negative attitudes towards a group or individuals) can lead to discrimination (the unfair treatment of other groups or individuals). Allport suggests that there were historical, cultural, situational, inter-personal and individual causes of prejudice and discrimination.

10 Adorno *et al.* studied in great detail the extent to which prejudice was due to individuals' possession of an authoritarian personality.

11 Sherif and Sherif investigated the development, and more importantly, the reduction of prejudice among American boys at a summer camp. In order to reduce prejudice, opposing groups must be brought together to achieve, through cooperation, attractive goals, and the groups should also be of equal status. Cook suggested that experience of non-typical individuals would help to break down stereotypes, but that support from friends was also important in order to reduce the effects of conformity on prejudice.

Further Reading

Hinton, P.R., *The Psychology of Interpersonal Perception* (1993, Routledge).
Weber, A.L., *Social Psychology* (1992, HarperCollins).

Chapter 8

The Growth of Attachment

The close bond between the parents and offspring of many species has obvious survival value. There is a tendency for animals to be born in a vulnerable state the higher up the evolutionary scale you go. The offspring of insects and amphibians can usually fend for themselves the moment they are born, but human infants could not survive alone until much later. This prolonged period of childhood in the higher animals allows the offspring to learn from parents and others, so that each generation can build on the accomplishments of the past. In order to be successful, a strong attachment between parent and infant is necessary especially during early infancy. A group of scientists known as the *ethologists* have made a close study of this bonding process in animals. They have called the development of the bond *imprinting*.

Imprinting

The 'classic' demonstration of imprinting was performed by Konrad Lorenz, the Austrian ethologist. (*Ethology* is the study of animals' behaviour in their natural surroundings.) He was working with Greylag geese, and showed that imprinting behaviour consists of three main parts:

1 At a certain time after hatching the gosling will start to follow the first conspicuous object it sees. (This is called the 'following response'.)
2 After following this object for a period of time, often several hours, the gosling will develop an attachment to the object, and regard it as its guardian; in other words, it imprints on it.
3 Once an animal has imprinted, it develops a sexual preference, when it is mature, for the object on which it imprinted.

Lorenz believed that imprinting was a special form of learning because:

(a) It was very rapid – often occurring over a period as short as a few minutes.
(b) It was unreinforced – that is, no reinforcer was apparently necessary in order for the following response to occur.

(c) It occurred during a clearly defined time-period (the *critical period*). The critical period was of different length in different species.

(d) Once it had imprinted on an object, the animal would be unable to imprint on any other object – that is, imprinting was thought to be irreversible.

Lorenz's demonstration went as follows. He took a large clutch of goose eggs and kept them until they were about to hatch out. Half the eggs were then placed under a goose mother, while Lorenz kept the other half beside himself for several hours. When all the goslings had hatched and dried out, one group followed the goose, but Lorenz's goslings followed him. To check that this was not just chance, Lorenz put all the goslings together under an upturned box and allowed them to mix. When the box was removed the two groups separated to go to their respective guardians – half to the goose, half to Lorenz. The genetic instructions in the gosling's make-up must therefore prompt it to follow the first conspicuous object it sees. That object may be the mother goose; but Lorenz and other researchers induced goslings to imprint on many different objects, including boxes, balls and plastic watering-cans.

However, these genetic instructions are not active immediately after hatching; there seems to be a critical period during which imprinting can occur. Thus in 1958 E.H. Hess showed that although the imprinting response could occur as early as one hour after hatching, the strongest responses occurred between 12 and 17 hours after hatching, and that after 32 hours the response was unlikely to occur at all.

Goslings older than about 20 hours seemed to be very difficult to imprint. Lorenz and Hess believed that this is clear evidence for a critical period. The appearance of this 'imprintability' appears to be genetically determined. During the critical period, if there is a suitable environment stimulus, imprinting occurs. But they also believed that the disappearance of 'imprintability' is genetically determined, and occurs between 20 and 32 hours after hatching. Thus even if there is a correct stimulus, if it arrives after the genes have switched off the imprintability, imprinting cannot occur. From Hess's results, then, the phenomenon occurs between 9 and 12 hours, and disappears again at about 20 hours after hatching. The optimum time for imprinting appears to be 16 hours after hatching.

Not only does there seem to be a critical period for imprinting, but once it has occurred, Lorenz and Hess believed that it is not changeable. Once a gosling has imprinted on an object or model, it cannot be induced to imprint on anything else. The genes switch off the 'imprintability' by switching on avoidance responses in its place as soon as the gosling has imprinted on one model, it thereafter avoids other models.

However, other researchers do not accept that the critical period is in fact so predetermined. W. Sluckin (1961) and P.P.G. Bateson (1964) found that if ducklings are kept away from other ducklings, in social isolation, the imprinting period can be extended well beyond 20 hours. P. Guiton (1958) found that chicks kept in an unstimulated environment – particularly one lacking in visual stimulation – were able to imprint well after the end of the critical period. If the animal's experience can alter the length of the period of 'imprintability', the instruction for the disappearance of the phenomenon cannot be all genetic. Therefore Sluckin coined the term *sensitive period*, because although the appearance of imprintability may be genetically determined, the animal's experience can affect how long it lasts.

Figure 8.1 Simplified Graph Showing Times of Critical Period for Imprinting

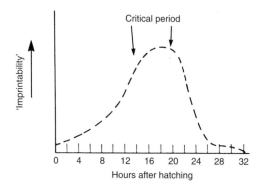

Lorenz believed that the model on which an animal imprints influences the animal's sexual preference when mature; for example, a gosling which imprinted on a farmyard hen would, when mature, regard itself as a hen, and try to mate with other hens.

Imprinting, though, has been found to be reversible. Guiton found that ducklings imprinted on chickens in farmyards tried to mate with other ducks when mature. He conducted a laboratory investigation in which ducklings were imprinted on a pair of yellow rubber gloves, and were much later gradually introduced to other ducks. They showed normal sexual preferences, which demonstrates that imprinting, once it has occurred, can be changed.

The earlier researchers believed that the beginning of the critical period was due to genetic factors – possibly to the maturation of the animal's ability to walk (so that it can make the following response), or perhaps to the maturation of its visual system. They believed also that the critical period was ended by genetic factors, which possibly caused the following response to be extinguished. The term *sensitive period* is now preferred because this refers to a period which may be started by genetic factors similar to those which were supposed to start the critical period, but its ending is not so predetermined and is governed by external factors. For imprinting the implication of a sensitive period is that the following response does not simply 'die away' as a result of genetic factors; instead it is 'cancelled out' by the development of the animal's ability to recognize objects as being unfamiliar. When it can recognize such objects, the animal avoids them. These contrasting views are shown in diagram form in figure 8.2.

Imprinting is only one example of a type of behaviour which is thought to have a sensitive period. Other forms of behaviour may also have sensitive periods; for example, language development and the formation of attachment bonds in humans and the determination of an animal's sexual preference when mature.

Conditioning Explanations of Attachment

At one time psychologists who attempted to use the ideas of conditioning to explain most of behaviour (the *behaviourists*) argued that the thing which caused the attachment between infant and parent was the fact that the parent fed the child and so became associated with food and pleasure; affectionate behaviour is reinforced by the food.

Figure 8.2. The Difference between Critical and Sensitive Periods

Harlow tested this idea by using two mother-surrogates or substitutes, one of which was made of wire and contained the food bottle while the other was covered with terry-towelling cloth – rather like the mother's fur – and did not provide food. Behaviourists would argue that the infant would spend most time with the wire-covered mother because 'she' supplied food. In fact the infants preferred the cloth-covered mother; it was also noticeable that monkeys reared with the cloth-mother showed much more exploratory behaviour than those reared with the wire-covered mother. These latter showed strange behaviour, they would only rarely embrace the wire mother, and most of the time stayed a short distance away, seeming very timid and clutching and rocking themselves for long periods of time. When both cloth- and wire-reared infants were, at maturity, placed with other monkeys it was found that they were largely inefficient mothers, they ignored or mistreated their own offspring.

Harlow believed that the preference for the cloth-covered mother showed an innate preference – possibly for the feel of monkey-fur rather than for the mother herself. In young monkeys such behaviour would have survival value: their mothers move around a lot, and this preference would keep them with their mothers, and therefore in safety.

Although conditioning may have some role to play in the growth of attachment to other people, Harlow's work shows that it cannot be regarded as the major factor.

A Critical Period for Attachment

In 1970 R.A. Hinde found that even brief separations of the infant from its true mother can produce long-lasting detrimental effects: the baby alternates between periods of great maternal contact and periods when it rejects the mother. Such effects were found by Hinde to continue for as long as two years after a brief separation. Thus if an infant monkey is deprived of its mother in infancy it cannot form an affection bond with her later. Harlow believed that there is a critical period for the development of this bond, and that this critical period is roughly from birth to eight months. Infants reared in isolation for more than eight months were unable to form strong bonds with a mother when they were introduced to her and showed no distress if she was parted from them.

Human infants take longer to develop than monkeys, but Harlow believed that the same principles still apply, except that the critical period for humans is up to about three years old. Maternal deprivation in infancy can therefore have severe effects on later development.

The Growth of Attachment in Humans

Babies show more interest in human beings than other objects from the moment that they are born. This may be due to the variety of movement, sound and touch that humans provide or it may simply be an innate preference. Fantz (1966) showed that babies as young as two weeks preferred to look at a picture of a human face with all the parts in the correct position rather than a jumbled face; this indicates that if recognition of the human face is not innate it is learnt very quickly.

Babies display their real social natures when they first start to smile which is usually noticeable during the fifth or sixth week. The smile is most often given to people rather than objects but Ahren (1954) showed that at about the age of five or six weeks a pair of eyes drawn on to the outline of a face was enough to initiate smiling. Later more details needed to be added, and by five months all the major features of the face, plus shading, to give a three-dimensional effect was required to elicit a smile. The most noticeable effect of the child's smiling is the way that it reinforces adults and maintains interaction.

Schaffer and Emerson (1964) studied 60 babies at monthly intervals during the first 18 months of life, and identified a regular pattern in the development of attachments. The children were all studied in their own homes to cut down any effect of unfamiliar surroundings. The level of attachment to their mother and other significant adults was measured in two ways. The first was a measure of the amount of distress shown by the child when separated from the mother, combined with the relief shown when she returns; this combined factor is known as *separation anxiety*. The second was a judgement of the extent to which the child showed *fear of strangers*.

They demonstrated the following pattern of development:

Birth to six months. This is the *indiscriminate attachment phase*. The child smiles at parents and strangers alike, and shows no particular preference about who picks him up.

Seven months to one year. This is the *specific attachment phase*. The child shows fear of strangers and great separation anxiety, usually in relation to the mother.

One year and older. The *multiple attachment phase*. The number of attachments to significant adults and children gradually increases. This phase usually starts about three months after the beginning of the specific attachment phase.

The ages are only a rough guide; in fact Schaffer and Emerson found children who started the second phase as early as six months and others as late as one year. The same pattern seems to occur in all cultures, and Kagan (1979) has shown it in cultural groups as diverse as Americans, Israelis and Kalahari Bushmen.

There is a tendency for us to use the word 'mother' whenever we are discussing the closest relationship that the young infant has with an adult, and in the majority of cases it is in fact the mother that holds this special relationship. Schaffer and Emerson showed, however, that it is not unusual for the infant to show its closest attachment to a different adult. Although the majority of the babies showed their major attachment to the mother, nearly one-third formed the primary attachment to the father, and one-sixth to another person such as brother, sister, grandmother, aunt or friend of the family. A couple of children showed no attachment at all. It is the quality of interaction between adult and child rather than the amount of time spent together which is the most important factor in determining attachment. The primary attachment figures were usually the people who fed and changed the child, but this was not always the case; and most important factor in the development of the relationship was the way in which the adult interacted with the child. The primary attachment figure was more likely to be sensitive to the child's behaviour and modify their own appropriately; in other words they are the ones who play and communicate with the infant. Schaffer used the term *reciprocity* to describe the way that a parent responds to the behaviour of their child and the child in turn modifies its behaviour in light of what the parent is doing.

Children of a very young age seem to be able to interact with adults; they are not the passive receivers of stimulation that we once thought they were. Meltzoff and Moore (1977) have demonstrated that babies of 12 days old and less were able to imitate their mother when she put her tongue out at them. In one film which they made, Meltzoff and Moore showed a 42-minute-old child who followed his mother's action of putting her tongue out with putting his own in and out, and when the mother then moved her mouth to an 'Ah' shape the baby frowned and changed to opening his mouth.

Stern (1974) showed that mothers and babies of three months old show many of the non-verbal signals that adults make to each other during conversation; they look at each other and move their heads in time with each other. He found that mothers and children maintain a lot of eye-contact and that it is the child which breaks off the interaction by looking away. Trevarthen describes the interaction of two-month-old babies and their mothers as conversations; the pair take it in turns to babble or make facial or body movements and do not interrupt each other. Schaffer argues that mother (or another primary attachment figure) and child develop a particular pattern of non-verbal communication, and that it is this that cements their relationship. The pattern that develops is unique to a particular adult/child pair. Once it has developed the child finds difficulty communicating with others, and it may be this that causes the so called 'fear of strangers' which occurs in the specific attachment period. This dialogue between the primary attachment figure and infant is known as *interlocution*.

Although strong fear of strangers is not shown until about seven or eight months, children show milder forms of the reaction much earlier. Sander (1969) showed that children as young as two weeks cried for longer than usual when their nurse was changed after ten days during which the nurse looked after the child for 24 hours a day.

Ainsworth observed the reactions of children in the specific attachment phase when they entered a new room with their mothers. The typical child when first entering the room stayed close to their mother, at first physically touching. Later the child moves away to explore, looking back from time to time. When a stranger entered the room the child tended to rush back to mother and would only play with the new person after some time-lapse. If the mother left the room at any time the child tended to cry and cease playing. Harlow found that young monkeys show very similar behaviour in strange environments. It is as though the primary attachment figure provides a base from which the infant can explore the world, returning from time to time for the assurance of the familiar, while he or she explores new places or meets new people.

Children vary greatly in the extent to which they show their attachments. Ainsworth, Bell and Stayton (1971) noted that the most common attachment relationship shown in situations like the strange room (above) was what they called *secure* attachment. These children tend to play positively with strangers, although they avoid getting too close early in the meeting. When their mothers return after an absence they go to her and then get on with playing. They contrast this with the *avoidant* child who tends to be unaffected by the position of the mother and ignores her when she returns after an absence, and the *resistant*, child who seems to be torn between seeking and resisting contact with the mother.

Observers tend to rate the mothers of secure children as more responsive to the child's behaviour. They tend, for example, to be consistent in the way that they respond to the child's crying, rather than varying their behaviour with their own mood. Ainsworth (1973) isolated four dimensions of maternal behaviour that are related to the type of attachment the child has. The four dimensions are:

Sensitive – Insensitive. Sensitive parents are more able to see things from the child's point of view.

Accepting – Rejecting. Accepting parents see the baby as making a positive change to their lives and don't show a great deal of resentment about the restrictions that babies impose.

Cooperating – Interfering. Cooperating parents tend to work with the child rather than imposing their own wishes.

Accessible – Ignoring. Accessible parents take more notice of the child.

Ainsworth showed that the mothers of secure children tended to be more sensitive, accepting, cooperating and accessible. The children with resistant and avoidant attachments both tended to have mothers who were rejecting, but this was combined with insensitive for the avoidant children, and with interfering and ignoring for the resistant children.

Ainsworth believes that the behaviour of the mother plays the most important part in determining the type of attachment that will be formed, but we must not forget the reciprocal nature of the relationship: both the mother and the child respond to each other. Some children are more easy to relate to right from the word go because they cry less, sleep longer, smile more, etc.

The attachments of early life are reflected in later behaviour. Waters, Wippman and Sroufe (1979) showed that children who had been classified as either secure or insecure in their attachments at the age of 15 months showed different social behaviour at three and a half years. The nursery school teachers rated the secure children as more popular, more likely to get involved in games, more self-directed and more eager to learn than children who had been categorized as insecure. Other studies have shown similar differences, but it is not possible to be certain that these behavioural differences are *caused* by the type of relationship that the child has with its parents. A child who is easy to get on with may start life with the sort of characteristics that encourage parents to be accepting, sensitive, etc., and these same characteristics may make him popular in later life.

Maternal Deprivation

In 1951 a paper for the World Health Organization by John Bowlby suggested that maternal deprivation could be a major cause of many social, emotional and intellectual disorders: 'mother-love in infancy and childhood is as important for mental health as are vitamins and proteins for physical health' (*Maternal Care and Mental Health*, 1951).

Bowlby's ideas were influenced by Freudian theory particularly the views:

(a) That the first five years of life are the most important in a person's development.

(b) That a child's relationship with its parents (particularly its mother) has a massive effect on its development.

(c) That psychological trauma ('trauma' means 'wound') in childhood has long-lasting effects.

(d) That loss of a parent, particularly loss of the mother or separation from her, is a major cause of psychological traumas.

Bowlby was also influenced by the ethologists' studies of imprinting, and the concept of Critical Periods (now called Sensitive Periods) in development.

This section will look at Bowlby's theory and the evidence for and against it.

In line with the results of Harlow's experiments (described on p. 159), Bowlby believed that if a child were not permitted to form an affection bond with its mother it would develop *affectionless psychopathy* – an inability to feel much emotion for anybody else and a lack of interest in anybody else's welfare. He also believed that children who had been deprived of a mother or mother-surrogate were far more likely to show delinquent behaviour later in life. Many people have assumed that, in order to prevent these tragic situations, full-time mothering is essential, but Bowlby never said this. He simply believed that there must be someone available with whom the child can form an affection bond; he did not say that this person had to be the mother.

Nevertheless, the findings of Bowlby and other researchers seemed at the time to point to the conclusion that lack of a mother or mother-substitute can lead to social, intellectual and general developmental impairment. We shall summarize some of the best-known findings.

Delinquency. In a study of 44 juvenile thieves, Bowlby found that 17 of them had suffered separation from their mothers for more than six months in their first five years of life. Only two people from his control group of disturbed adolescents who did not steal were found to have been maternally deprived.

Affectionless psychopathy. Two of Bowlby's maternally deprived delinquents showed this inability to form emotional relationships with other people.

Depression. In 1945 R.A. Spitz observed that maternally deprived children frequently showed apathy, slow development and general depression.

Dwarfism. In 1963 R.G. Patton showed that maternally deprived children often did not develop physically, and were undersized compared to normally reared children.

Slowed development of intelligence and language. In 1943 W. Goldfarb found that children raised in institutions were often retarded in their intellectual and linguistic development.

Enuresis. In 1970 J.I. Douglas studied children who were separated from their parents in the first four years of life due to hospitalization; they were liable to fairly persistent enuresis (bed-wetting) for several years.

All the above behaviour problems have thus at some time been lumped together under the heading 'caused by maternal deprivation'. But we shall now turn to an examination of each of these problems, to determine whether it is certain that maternal deprivation is the cause, and to investigate alternative explanations.

Delinquency

Bowlby's original study of 44 juvenile thieves has been much criticized. He tended to ignore the fact that more of his delinquents were not maternally deprived. Another problem related to his method of study: it was a retrospective study – that is, it took people who were already thieves and looked back on what had happened to them in the past. He therefore relied on the memories of the boys to discover what had happened to them in the first few years of life. In addition he was not able to see whether all people who suffered maternal deprivation later became delinquents. In 1961 L.J. Yarrow confirmed that there is quite a high positive correlation between broken homes and delinquency. However, the fact that two things correlate highly does not mean that one need cause the other – a third factor may cause both (see p. 306).

Broken homes often mean separation of a child from its mother; but not all broken homes lead to delinquency, which seems to depend more on the type of break-up. Death of a parent, which obviously disturbs home life, does not seem to lead to delinquency, while domestic upheaval as a result of a parental separation or divorce often does (Douglas, 1969). Thus it may be that divorce or separation causes delinquency; equally, however, divorce, or separation, and delinquency could all be caused by an unstable relationship between parents, or the child's delinquency might be a cause of the break-up of the home.

In 1965 M.M. Craig showed that families with a high level of internal conflict were those most likely to have delinquent children. Similarly, in 1971 M.L. Rutter found that delinquency and disturbance were found most commonly in children who had left unhappy homes.

Power and others (1974) studied children who had appeared in courts for juvenile crimes. Some children only appeared once but others ('recidivists') appeared in court several times. Power looked into the home situations of both 'once-only' offenders and recidivists. Why was it that some children committed crimes only once, while others kept on committing them? The answer seems to lie, as Craig and Rutter had suggested, in the amount of stress and conflict in the child's home – the higher the level of emotional stress, the more likely was the child to commit a crime. If the problems at home were solved, and the stress lowered, children would stop committing crimes (the 'once-only' delinquents). However if the levels of stress in the home stayed high, the child would continue to commit crimes (the recidivists).

In the studies that link maternal deprivation and delinquency, maternal deprivation is only one factor amongst others such as an unhappy home background and so it is not possible to say that maternal deprivation causes delinquency.

Affectionless Psychopathy

On the basis of the two maternally deprived delinquents who had severe problems in relating to other people, Bowlby asserted that affectionless psychopathy was caused by maternal deprivation. Simple separation does not seem to be a good enough explanation of this problem, however, since children separated from their mothers to go into a tuberculosis sanatorium did not show the disorder.

Maybe Harlow's study of infant monkeys could give us a clue here. The monkeys seemed to show affectionless characteristics after having been separated from their biological mothers. Rutter points out that Harlow's monkeys were not truly deprived of their mothers, because 'deprivation' implies having something and then losing it. Never having something is known as *privation*. Harlow's monkeys therefore suffered from privation, not deprivation. The monkeys had never been allowed to form an affection bond with their mothers and were later unable to do so with anybody. If, however, a child is allowed to form an affection bond with his mother, who then disappears, at least he has had some experience with bond formation. Privation does not permit any such experience.

Thus maternal deprivation cannot be identified as the cause of affectionless behaviour, while privation can be thus identified. But need it be maternal privation? Anna Freud and S. Dann (1951) investigated a group of six children left parentless by Nazi persecution and raised together, first in a series of concentration camps and finally in an English nursery. The children developed strong bonds with each other, because no parents or parent-substitutes were available. The children were all pre-school age at the start of their group life; as time went on, it became clear that, although some of the children showed various emotional problems, there was no sign in any of them of the affectionless character investigated by Bowlby.

At the age of 37, four of the six orphans were contacted again and their development investigated. Three of the four had been adopted between the ages of 5 and 8, and two of them were described as being happily married, effective and successful at work, and as having warm personalities. The third child was reported as still feeling insecure and was suffering bouts of depression. The fourth child, who was not adopted, was reported to be still upset and concerned about the damage and insecurities of his childhood. None of them, however, showed any sign of the affectionless character which Bowlby's theory predicts should have developed.

A pair of Czech twins were reared almost in isolation in cellars or even cupboards from 18 months of age until they were seven (apparently their mother had died and their father had married a woman who turned out to be a psychopath). When they were at last released from the cellar, they were taken into care and were studied by Koluchova (1972). On their release, they could hardly walk, showed almost no speech and were severely intellectually retarded. It was noted, however, that they were very attached to each other, and when they were adopted, both formed strong attachments to their foster mother. Koluchova tested them again when they were 14 years old, and it was found that their IQ scores were now average, and that they were happy, lively and popular at school. Although (not surprisingly) they were still afraid of going into cellars, they showed none of the affectionless psychopathy (nor any of the intellectual and language retardation) that Bowlby would have predicted.

If early experience does cause affectionless psychopathy it is as a result of never having the opportunity to develop an attachment to anybody. Schaffer showed that it is not unusual for children to make their closest attachments to their father rather than their mother. H.B. Biller (1971) even suggests that bond formation with the mother only may in itself be inadequate; he suggests that in order to be able to form stable relationships with both sexes in adulthood, the child needs the opportunity to form bonds with both parents. If a child develops a close relationship with its mother, or any other person, affectionless psychopathy is unlikely to result from later deprivation.

Depression

Spitz studied children who were long-stay hospital patients. He found that separation from both parents and from the home environment could cause general emotional upset. But these effects could be significantly lessened by counteracting the upsetting strangeness of the hospital atmosphere; this could be achieved either by providing interesting playthings (H. Jolly, 1969) – preventing boredom which could aggravate the problem – or by accustoming the child to the hospital before his actual admission, by allowing him to visit it with parents (J. and J. Robertson, 1955).

Death of a parent was found by Douglas to lead occasionally to long-term depression in the child, but this was only found in children who had been fostered after the parental death.

Maternal (or parental) deprivation can be related to long-term depression but cannot be regarded as the most important factor.

Dwarfism

Like the other problems we have examined, stunted growth is not caused simply by maternal deprivation. Two main factors seem to be at work here. First, the standard of care for the child, whether given by the mother or not, may be so low that the child is simply not given enough food to eat. Secondly even though enough food may be offered, the child may not eat it because it is emotionally upset. Again, this emotional upset may be caused by the lack of someone – not necessarily the mother – with whom to form an affection bond, or it may be caused by poor relationships between the child and parent or guardian – much scolding or spanking, for example.

Retardation of Language and Intellectual Development

Goldfarb asserted that the major cause of slow development was maternal deprivation. He compared the developmental rates of a group of 15 institutionalized children of the age-range 10–14 with a group – matched for heredity as far as possible – who were raised in foster homes, all children having been removed from their natural parents at a few months of age. The group kept in the institution were significantly regarded developmentally, compared with the other group. However, he had not considered other possible variables, in particular the amount of stimulation that the children received.

J.B. Garvin (1963) for example, found a gain in IQ of nine points in children going from unstimulating homes into institutions where they received more stimulation. H.M. Skeels (1966) found a similar effect occurring in children who were moved from a non-stimulating orphanage to an institution for the mentally subnormal where they received more stimulation. W. Dennis (1960) surveyed those institutions where children did not appear to gain much intellectually. He found that a 'poor' or non-stimulating institution was one where the children were rarely handled or talked with; where there were few toys or opportunities for play; and where there was a general lack of sensory, motor and linguistic experience for the children.

Perhaps in a way Bowlby was right: children whose mothers reject them are less likely to be receiving the right kinds and amounts of stimulation. But it is the lack of stimulation which seems to be the major cause of retardation, rather than the lack, or severance, of an emotional bond between mother and child.

Enuresis or Bed-wetting

Much of the evidence suggests that prolonged enuresis often occurs in children who have faced a great deal of stress during their first years, up to the age of six. In 1970 J.W.B. Douglas and R.K. Turner investigated the kinds of situation which may lead to stress in the child. Separation from the mother, father and home appears to be one factor; but there are many others. Like delinquency, enuresis was frequently found in children from homes where there was family discord, because discord produces stress. Stress is also obviously present in children who are in hospital for surgical operations, which often lead to discomfort. These children, too, show a high rate of enuresis. Burn and fracture cases, who usually suffer the most pain, also have the highest rate. Again, maternal deprivation may be one contributory factor, but it cannot be said to be a major one.

Conclusions

After reviewing the evidence, Rutter and Tizard suggest that Bowlby was wrong to take research carried out on poor-quality institutional care and to assume that its results applied just as strongly to day care or to any brief separation of the child from its mother. However, far more damning is that the evidence suggests that Bowlby's original theory (a mixture of psycho-analysis and ethological theories) was wrong. This section looks at the flaws in Bowlby's theory.

(1) Separation from the mother or mother surrogate does not seem to cause long-term damage to the child, as Bowlby predicted.

(2) The idea that the child's bond with its mother is always strongest (since babies have an innate tendency to imprint on their mothers) is not supported by the evidence. For example, in addition to Schaffer and Emerson's findings (see p. 155), Grossman and Grossman found that it is quite possible for a child to be securely attached to its father, but insecurely attached to its mother. Rutter found that children who had a good relationship with either parent were less severely affected by discord and conflict in the home. Similarly, Hetherington found that, if a child's parents divorced, children who stayed with the parent with whom they had a very good relationship were much less upset by the effects of the marriage break-up.

(3) Bowlby and Ainsworth believed that day care was harmful to the child, because it involved separation from the mother. (Institutional care was believed to be even more harmful, because it involved a longer separation.) However, Clarke-Stewart compared the results of 28 studies on the effects of day care and home care on the child's attachment to its mother. Only in one out of the 28 studies was it shown that day-care children were more likely to be anxious or insecurely attached to their mothers. Tizard believes that whilst some British research into day-care centres supports Ainsworth's views, this may be because in Britain, families with severe difficulties are given priority for day-care places which are in very short supply. Clarke-Stewart looked at research carried out in Scandinavia and in the USA, where day care is more easily

available. Day-care children, it was found, were more sociable and co-operated better with other children than did home-reared children.

(4) Bowlby and Ainsworth both stressed the tremendous importance of the mother's behaviour towards the child. However, research by Waters, for example, strongly suggests that the baby's behaviour affects the mother's, and that what is important is the two-way (or reciprocal) relationship between parent and child.

(5) According to Bowlby and Ainsworth, the first five years of the child's life were by far the most important; events which occurred during these years had a greater effect on the children than anything which happened in later years. Again, the research evidence does not support this point of view. Freud and Dann's study (p. 161) and the study by Koluchova (p. 162) show the limited effect of early experience. More evidence comes from a study by Tizard of children from residential nurseries who were adopted between the ages of two and seven years:

> Before this time the children were looked after by a large number of constantly changing nurses – on average 50 by the time they were four and a half – who were encouraged to relate to them in a detached, 'professional' manner. In other respects the care of the children was good. The staff–child ratio was high, the children were well supplied with books and toys, and their intellectual development was average. At 24 months, however, they tended to be excessively clinging to whoever was looking after them. By the age of four and a half 70% of the children still in institutions were said by the staff 'not to care deeply about anyone'.
>
> Nevertheless, after adoption most of the children quickly formed deep, reciprocated attachments to their new parents – evidence which seems to disconfirm Bowlby's belief that mothering is almost useless if delayed until after the age of two and a half. By the age of eight, their IQs and school work were well above average. On the other hand, about half of the children had difficulties at school and with their peers – that is, they were considered attention-seeking and restless by the teachers, and quarrelsome and unpopular with their peers. At age sixteen, their relations with their new parents in most cases continued to be good. But as a group they still had more problems with their peers than the control children, and they also tended to be more anxious. Whilst these differences could be due to some aspects of the children's current situation, on balance it seems more likely to be caused by the continuing effects of their unusual early social experiences. These effects, however, were much less drastic and of a different nature from those predicted by Bowlby – that is, those children who seemed to be affected had problems with their peers. They had experienced no difficulty in developing attachments to their parents.*

---

* Barbara Tizard, *The Care of Young Children – Implications of Recent Research* (1986, Thames Coram Research Foundation), p. 17.

(6) Rutter has proposed that, instead of early experiences being the only factor affecting an individual's development, events throughout life can cause behaviour problems – or reduce them. Early experiences, Rutter believes, may have a drastic effect, but only if the individual's behaviour or situation keeps him exposed to harmful effects. On the other hand, if the person's situation is changed, his behaviour may change and there may be no permanent damage.

A study by Dowding, Quinton and Rutter shows how this idea might work. Women who had spent most of their early life in care were studied as adults, and compared with a control group of women who had lived at home in early childhood. Thirty per cent of the 'in-care' women were described as having marked psychosocial problems, and 40 per cent were rated as being poor parents (because they tended to ignore their children's need for attention and they were not good at controlling their children, though they smacked them more frequently than home-reared women smacked theirs). So far, the results resemble Harlow's results from his 'Love in infant monkeys' study. However the results also showed that 20 per cent of the 'in-care' women did not show any psycho-social problems, and 31 per cent were rated as good mothers. Why were some women apparently affected by their institutional upbringing, and some not? Rutter and Quinton researched the lives of the women and found that what determined whether they developed behaviour problems and became poor mothers could not have been their early life in institutions, because they had all been institutionally reared. A whole range of factors was found stretching from childhood to early adulthood, which had affected the women's behaviour. For example, their experiences at school, how supportive their husbands were, and the levels of income and job security were all related to their behaviour problems. The women who did not show behaviour problems were the ones who had tended to have more pleasant school experiences, more supportive husbands, and were less likely to be under economic stress.

If Bowlby was right, children with happy and secure early experiences should be in effect inoculated against unpleasant events in later life – that is, they should be less harmed by them. Brown and Harris studied women from a range of backgrounds – some secure, some insecure – who had suffered the death of a parent during adolescence, or death of a husband in adulthood. According to Bowlby's theory, women from secure backgrounds should experience less psychological damage than women with insecure early experiences. Brown and Harris found that there was no difference in the frequency of depression between the two groups of women. Secure early experiences may not, therefore, inoculate us against psychological problem in later life.

Although Bowlby's theories are now largely regarded as being incorrect, he focused researchers' attention on the sorts of factors which may affect the child's development. Later researchers, instead of concentrating on the effects of maternal deprivation, now look at the effects which other people can have on the child, particularly on the child's relationship with its father, brother and sisters (siblings) and with other children of its own age (peers).

The Child's Relationship with Father, Siblings and Peers

Schaffer and Emerson (p. 155 above) showed that up to 30 per cent of children had formed their most important attachment to their fathers. Lamb found that the types of interaction between father and child tend to be different from those between mother and child; for example, mothers tend to hold the child more and to show more smiling and displays of affection than do fathers, who tend to become more involved in physically exciting play. Lamb found that these differences in parents' behaviour continue even when the father is the child's main caretaker. Maccoby suggests that fathers interact more with sons than with daughters, and may therefore be important in developing boys' gender roles. Lamb found that one of the major (though indirect) effects of the father is that the strength of his supports of the mother increases her sensitivity and responsiveness to the children.

It used to be thought that the main relationship between siblings was one of the emotional and physical rivalry. More recent research, however, suggests that siblings can be important attachment figures for the child, and may play a vital part in assisting the child's intellectual development.

In some cases, one-year-olds spend nearly as much time interacting with siblings as they do with their mothers. Dunn believes that older siblings are important to younger children because they provide a wider range of stimulation – for example they can act as teachers, playmates, protectors, comforters and as models for imitation as well as being aggressors and competitors for the parents' attention. Abramovich has shown that friendly behaviour between siblings is far more common than hostile or aggressive behaviour. Older siblings can also become attachment figures – Stewart found that in the strange situation test, over half of the 10–20-month-old children studied could be comforted by an older sibling when the mother left the room.

The importance of peers to a child's development obviously depends on the length of time the child plays with them, as well as on the intensity of the interaction. In the first year of life, although children will smile and touch other children of the same age, they do not usually form strong relationships with them. In their second year, however, children begin to be able to take turns with playthings (although there are sometimes squabbles over whose toy it is), and helping and comforting behaviour is shown between them. Ispa in the Soviet Union found that pairs of two-year-olds who had attended the same nursery group were able to comfort each other in the strange situation test, whereas solo children or children with another but unfamiliar peer, showed distress.

The Freud and Dann study (p. 161 above) showed how important a child's peers could become, and that attachment to its peers could almost act as a substitute for attachment to its parents. For children with parents, however, relationships with peers and siblings give a wider range of people to interact with and therefore give them wider opportunities for learning social behaviour and physical and intellectual skills.

From the evidence above, it seems that the child's relationships with a range of other people are what is important – the child does not necessarily have one all-important bond with the mother. These other relationships, as well as providing emotional comfort, can also be important in stimulating the child and in helping it to learn.

Summary

1 Attachment (the bond between parents and offspring) has survival value.
2 Harlow believed that there was a Critical Period for attachment in monkeys from birth to eight months of age (birth to 2 or 3 years in humans).
3 Schaffer and Emerson found three stages in the attachment of human babies to their parents: the indiscriminate phase, the specific phase and the multiple phase.
4 Schaffer and Emerson also found that many children can have fathers or other relatives as their primary attachment figure.
5 Meltzoff and Moore (1977) and Stern (1977) showed that babies can have non-verbal conversations with their mothers at a very early age.
6 Ainsworth discovered that some children form secure attachments with their mothers, some form insecure attachments and some children avoid or ignore their mothers.
7 Bowlby believed that maternal deprivation could have long-lasting and harmful effects on a child's development. In particular, he believed that maternal deprivation was a major cause of affectionless psychopathy, delinquency, dwarfism, enuresis, depression and intellectual and language retardation.
8 Much of the later research suggests that maternal deprivation is not a major cause of behaviour problems.
9 In recent years, researchers have stopped concentrating exclusively on the child's relationship with its mother, and have begun to look at the importance of the child's relationship with other members of its family and with other people.

Further Reading

Rutter, M.L., *Maternal Deprivation Reassessed* (1991, Penguin Books).
Tizard, B., *The Care of Young Children – Implications of Recent Research* (1986, Thomas Coram Research Foundation).

Chapter 9

Socialization

The human infant may be born into any of a vast number of different societies, all of which have different expectations of the way that he or she should behave. In most societies men and women are expected to behave differently; they have *sex roles* which, although they are rarely written down, have a great effect on behaviour. Sex roles differ from one society to the next (see p. 186), so we couldn't expect the young infant to be born with this knowledge.

Although there may be a lot of agreement that actions such as taking another person's life are wrong, the agreement is by no means universal and at times of war it seems to be possible to modify even this attitude. How is a new-born baby expected to pick up all the subtleties of morality? During the first few months of life it is quite acceptable to demand food and drink in the most outrageous manner whenever the child feels like it; this is not so acceptable later on, and an individual whose behaviour is governed only by his or her own immediate motivations is one who becomes a social outcast.

Socialization is the process by which we learn the patterns of behaviour which are expected of people in different positions in our society. It is how the values, attitudes, beliefs, and acquired behaviours of a society, institution or group are passed on to individuals.

There are a number of different theories of child socialization, many of which recognize the fact that the process goes on well beyond childhood, since adults have to be able to adapt to the expectations of new groups when they move to another area, another job, or do something else which involves taking up a new position in a group. In this chapter we look at two very different approaches to the problem of the mechanics of socialization: *Social Learning Theory and Freudian Theory*.

Social Learning Theory

The social learning approach to the explanation of socialization, as taken by writers such as Mischel, emphasizes the effects of the consequences of our actions on our later behaviour. In other words it applies the rules of reinforcement and conditioning that we discussed in chapter 3. Unlike

170

Skinner and the early behaviourists, who were only interested in the observable stimuli and responses, Mischel and other social learning theorists, such as Bandura, are quite happy to take into account the *expectations* of reward and punishment that the individual may have. The individual is not a passive recipient of all this reinforcement and punishment; Bandura emphasizes the extent to which individuals modify their environment and choose to do particular things so that they have a greater expectation of pleasant rather than unpleasant outcomes. In addition to reinforcement to guide behaviour, the social learning theorists also stress the role of observational learning or imitation. This form of learning can result in the production of complex patterns of behaviour without the need for an extended period of shaping.

One of the classic experiments demonstrating imitation was performed by A. Bandura. Nursery-school children were allowed to watch an adult performing aggressive acts towards a large rubber doll, such as hitting it with a hammer, kicking it, picking it up and throwing it. The children were then tested individually in a room containing the rubber doll and other toys; the experimenters noted the total amount of aggressive behaviour shown, and in particular the amount of aggressive behaviour which was copied from the adult model. The children who had been allowed to see the adult model performed a large number of aggressive acts towards the doll, about a third of these being direct copies of the adult's behaviour. The other children, who had not been allowed to see the adult model, demonstrated notably fewer aggressive responses, and of these actions, very few resembled those of the adult model. This suggests that the children who saw the model were copying him, because the behaviour of the control group did not resemble his. Imitation can therefore take place; but this is something most of us already know from our own experience.

Some Studies of Imitation

It is not enough simply to observe that imitation can take place, we must make some attempt to define under what circumstances it occurs.

Many conditioning theorists tried to explain imitation in terms of operant conditioning, and it is true that imitation will be increased if the child is reinforced each time an imitatory response is produced. The traditional forms of reinforcement are applied to the learner directly, but in many situations where imitation occurs it is the model that is reinforced for particular behaviours, and we tend to imitate behaviour which we have seen reinforced in somebody else. This has been termed *vicarious reinforcement*. It may be that seeing someone else reinforced leads the child to believe that they will be reinforced for the same actions.

Bandura, Ross and Ross performed the following test to see if vicarious reinforcement was responsible for imitation. First, the children were split into three groups; all the children saw a film in which a model behaved in a most bizarre and aggressive way, but the end of the film was different for each of the three groups.

Group A saw the model punished for his behaviour.

Group B saw the model rewarded.

Group C saw the model neither rewarded nor punished.

Conditioning theorists or behaviourists would expect that Group B, who saw the aggressive behaviour rewarded, would show the most aggressive behaviour when tested; that Group A who saw the model punished would show the least; and that the behaviour of Group C, whose model was neither rewarded nor punished, would be somewhere in between.

The actual results of the experiment *did not* uphold this prediction. Certainly the group of children who observed the punished model behaved less aggressively when they were tested, but there seemed to be no marked difference between the group whose model was rewarded and the group whose model was neither rewarded nor punished. From these results we can say that, although the sight of the model being punished seems to have prevented the children's imitation of his behaviour, the sight of the model being rewarded for his aggression (vicarious reinforcement), did not increase the likelihood that the children would imitate him.

Vicarous reinforcement, therefore, is not necessary for imitation to occur.

The children who saw the model punished did not imitate as much as the others, but does this mean that they hadn't *learnt* as much? Bandura, Ross and Ross tested the idea that the vicarious punishment had simply led the children to hide what they had learnt. The three groups of children tested earlier were thus put back into the test situation and were then given rewards each time they produced a piece of aggressive behaviour. All three groups showed approximately the same levels of aggression and, more importantly, roughly the same numbers of their aggressive acts were ones that the model had produced in the initial part of the experiment. In other words, all three groups must have learnt the model's behaviour equally, because they were all able to demonstrate the same number and type of aggressive acts in the second test. The group whose model was punished had presumably shown less aggressive behaviour than the other two groups in the first test because of the inhibitory effect of having seen the punishment of their model. They had nevertheless learnt as many aggressive acts as the other two groups, and were willing to demonstrate them when rewarded.

This study of the effects of vicarious punishment shows that we should make an important distinction between *learning* and *performance*: an individual may have learned something by observing a model, but may not necessarily show by their behaviour or performance that they have learned it (this distinction was also made in relation to latent learning on p. 50). A piece of behaviour that has been learned but inhibited in this way may never show itself. On the other hand, it may suddenly appear when the inhibition is removed. In chapter 11 we discuss the effects of the use of physical punishment to control children's behaviour; one effect of this is that the child may learn that violence is one method of getting your own way. The violent behaviour may be inhibited in the presence of adults, but show itself when the child is in the company or other, weaker, children.

Bandura has shown a range of factors which effect whether imitation is likely to occur. Imitation is most likely to occur when:

1 The model is similar to, but of slightly higher status than, the child.
2 The model is *not* punished.
3 The child is in an unfamiliar situation.
4 The child is rewarded for imitating.

We can increase the extent of a child's imitative behaviour simply by reinforcing it when it occurs, but this does not really help us to understand why we imitate in the first place. Reinforcement is not the cause, because even without it children still imitate. Why should this be? Babies show imitation very early in life. They appear to be able to copy an adult putting their tongue out before they are an hour old (see p. 156). It is quite likely that this predisposition to imitate is an innate characteristic of ourselves and other mammals. The ability to imitate would obviously have survival value simply because it enables one to learn adaptive behaviour more quickly and efficiently than is possible through trial-and-error learning or behaviour-shaping.

Sex Role

Mischel, and other social learning theorists, believe that children pick up the appropriate sex role by imitating the same sex parent and being re-inforced for behaving in a manner which the particular culture expects of a boy or girl. Bandura showed that imitation is most likely to occur if the model is perceived as similar to the imitator, making it most likely that little boys will imitate the behaviour of their older brothers or their father, rather than the behaviour of females.

Most children have a close adult of the same sex who they can imitate in order to pick up the appropriate sex role, but even in single-parent families social leaning theory can explain the development of sex role by the process of operant conditioning. By reinforcing masculine behaviour in a boy, both or either of his parents could ensure that he showed masculine behaviour, and that, similarly, feminine behaviour would be developed in a girl. It thus follows that the presence of either parent is sufficient to promote the development of appropriate sex-role behaviour in a child. So in the case of a woman living without a man and rearing her son, provided that she has an idea of normal male behaviour she should be able to reinforce any behaviour in her son which corresponds to this idea, and non-reinforce any feminine behaviour that the boy might show. According to the Law of Effect we should therefore expect the reinforced masculine responses to be performed more often than the non-reinforced feminine responses. Summarized in table form below are the principles by which behaviour – including sex-role behaviour – can be shaped. Remember that behaviour which is not reinforced tends to be extinguished.

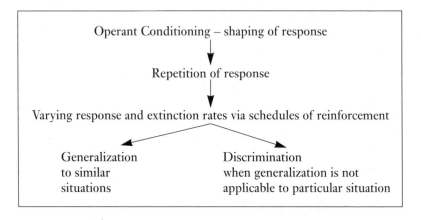

Note also the uses of positive and negative reinforcement here: desired behaviour is given positive reinforcement – such as a smile for saying please when asking for something – or negative reinforcement: for example, if a child has a temper tantrum he can be shut up in his room and only allowed out again when he calms down and apologizes.

Some people object to the social learning explanation of sex role on the basis that they don't believe that the sexes are treated differently. There is, however, a considerable amount of evidence that adults do behave differently to boys and girls.

Smith and Lloyd (1978) watched adults playing with children. The adults were all mothers of children less than a year old and were asked to play with a baby boy or girl for ten minutes. Smith and Lloyd noted that the first toy offered to the baby boys was usually a hammer-shaped rattle and the girls were offered a soft pink doll. When talking to the children the boys were more often encouraged to play vigorously but the girls were more often praised for their cleverness and attractiveness. If the babies became very active they were often imitated by the adults and encouraged if they were boys but the adults tried to calm down the same sort of behaviour in girls.

It is often argued that *if* adults do behave differently to boys and girls it is because the children themselves behave differently; this argument assumes that sex differences in behaviour are grounded in biological differences between the sexes. The interesting thing about Smith and Lloyd's work was that they had controlled for any possible sex difference in the behaviour of the babies by fooling the adults about the sex of the baby. They used male and female babies, but sometimes it was a boy who was dressed in pink and called Jane when it was handed to the adult, at other times it was a girl. The 'male' babies were dressed in blue and called John, but some of them were actually girls. The adults did not realize this deception was going on and their behaviour was shown to depend on the sex they *believed* the baby to be.

Lloyd points out that the play of two-year-olds reflects the stereotyped view of the behaviour of the sexes that is held in our society. She argues that this may result from the way that adults play with the children during the first year.

Parents have been shown to display disapproval when older children play in a sex-inappropriate fashion. Langois and Downs (1980) asked boys and girls between three and five years old to play with 'boys' toys' such as cars and cowboy sets in the way that boys do. None of the children had any difficulty doing this. Neither did any of the children asked to play with 'girls' toys' in the way that girls do. The children were quite aware of the differences between boy and girl behaviour. Langois and Downs were interested in the reactions of the children's parents when they came into the room after the children had been playing for some time. Most of the parents either joined in the play or were supportive in some other way, but some showed disapproval. It was interesting that nearly all the disapproval came from fathers whose sons were playing with girls' toys.

When it comes to aggressive behaviour, Rothbart and Maccoby showed that mothers were more likely to tolerate this from their sons than their daughters (see p. 212).

Effects of media on sex role

Parents, peers, brothers and sisters are undoubtedly major influences on the development of sex role, providing reinforcement of appropriate behaviours as well as being models for imitation. Other sources of role models include media such as books and television. Over the last 30 years there has been an attempt to reduce the amount of sex role stereotyping in which female characters take on passive roles and the males are always the ones taking decisive action. A comparison of children's books from the 1960s with those of today shows much more interchangeability of the roles of the male and female characters. Research into the effect of television on gender identity suggests that children do in fact pick up quite traditional ideas about sex role from their viewing. Primary school children asked about which jobs were usually carried out by men and which by women on television programmes tend to give answers conforming to traditional stereotypes: women nurses, male doctors etc. When asked about what they wanted to do when they grew up the children also picked traditionally sex-linked occupations. Other studies have been done which show that children who watch most television tend to show the most traditional sex roles as shown, for example, by observing the extent to which they chose toys related to their particular sex. These studies conform with the idea that television enhances traditional sex roles, but that they cannot be used as conclusive evidence of the role of the media; it is equally possible that the reason for the connection is that those who already have the most traditional sex roles choose to watch more television.

Aggressive Behaviour

Bandura's work illustrates how aggressive behaviour can be either increased or decreased by imitation learning in the laboratory, and the same factors can influence aggression in the real world.

Aggression is also affected by reinforcements and punishments: if a child has gained from aggressive behaviour in the past it is more likely that the child will become more aggressive generally and particularly in situations similar to those of his or her previous successes. Patterson, Littman and Bricker (1967) observed children over a period of ten weeks recording the outcomes of any aggressive interactions that they had. Their results showed clearly that children who had been successful in defending themselves by counter-aggression were less likely to remain passive in a new situation of attack than those who had been unsuccessful. Those who had been ignored by their victims when they attacked them were less likely to attack again than those who had been reinforced by the crying of their victim. (See also p. 211).

The View that Behaviour Depends upon the Situation

Mischel argues that the socialization process does not produce an individual with set characteristics which will be displayed in all situations. Rather, the resultant personality is largely controlled by the situation that the person is in; it is as though the person asks the following questions before deciding what to do:

Is this situation similar to one I have been in before?

What did I do last time?

What was the outcome?

Is the outcome likely to be the same this time?

Since people's experience will have been slightly different in different situations, their answers to these questions will vary and their resulting behaviour will be *situation specific*.

A classic study by Hartshorne and May (1928) demonstrates how behaviour such as honesty is situation specific, even though many people think of it as a personality trait that is a characteristic of an individual, irrespective of the particular situation.

About eleven thousand children participated in the Hartshorne and May study. The children were given the opportunity to cheat, lie, or in other ways be dishonest in many different situations. In one situation the children were given a multiple choice test and asked to circle the right answers; later they were given the correct answers and asked to mark their own work. A copy of their original answers had been taken without the child's knowledge and so it was possible to tell if he or she had cheated. Another exercise involved a set of puzzles, one of which included a coin; when the puzzles were returned the researchers checked whether the coin had been stolen. Many other situations were set up which varied in type and also in the likelihood of being caught and in the rewards for being dishonest. The results showed very little consistency of honesty for particular children across a range of situations: the children's honesty seemed to be governed by the situation rather than a consistent underlying characteristic of honesty or lack of it.

Mischel argues that the consistency that we notice in people's behaviour across many situations is largely in the eye of the beholder. He puts forward a number of reasons why this false perception is maintained:

1 In general the perception and memory systems try to see patterns in the world and ignore exceptions. (In chapter 2 we saw that the amount of information we can deal with at any one time is limited and how attention and other perceptual mechanisms dealt with this problem.)
2 We usually see people in the same sort of situation or role and then attribute the consistency of their behaviour to their personality rather than their role.
3 There is a tendency to believe that personality is consistent because other characteristics such as physical appearance have this quality.
4 Once we form an impression of somebody we are reluctant to alter it (see p. 133).

The work of social psychologists such as Latané and Milgram support this view of the importance of the situation and role in determining behaviour (see chapter 6).

Freud's Theories of Socialization

Freud was one of the earliest writers to emphasize the importance of the first five years in determining the personality for the whole of life. The first five years' experience were thought to have a dramatic effect on adult behaviour as divergent as nail biting, obsessive cleanliness and problems with relating to members of the opposite sex. The social learning theorists (see above), and others, would agree that early life is important in terms of the opportunity to learn from scratch, but they don't make the same emphasis because they believe that the effects of the early years may be changed by later experiences.

Freud's work spans the latter part of the last century and the first four decades of this century; it has had a great influence on our thoughts about behaviour, even though most psychologists do not accept his theories as a whole. The work of Bowlby, for example, was very much influenced by the fact that he followed the Freudian idea that the first few years were the most influential (see pp. 158–68).

Freud argued that development through the first few years followed a particular pattern for all children. As the pattern unfolds the child pays attention to and receives pleasure from different parts of its anatomy. The stages are as follows:

The Oral Phase. During the first year or so of life, children gain satisfaction from putting things into their mouth and sucking. The objects may range from the feeding nipple to anything which happens to be in reach. Smoking and nail-biting in adult life were seen by Freud as evidence of frustration or over-indulgence during this stage.

The Anal Phase. During the second and third years the child becomes capable of more control over its bowels and obtains great pleasure from the retention and expulsion of faeces. It is during this period that potty-training starts, and if parents approach this in too strict a manner or try to force the child too early into the socially acceptable methods of coping with defecation, Freud argued that this could result in the formation of the anal personality in adulthood. Individuals with 'anal personalities' are excessively concerned with order and cleanliness and cannot bear unpredictability or untidiness.

The Phallic Phase. Between roughly the ages of three and five the genitals become the area of the body from which the child derives pleasure. It is during this stage, according to Freud, that sex role and conscience develop as a result of the process of *identification* (see below).

These three stages are the most important in personality development and socialization. They are followed by a *latent phase*, which has no particularly important features for Freudian theory, and the adult *Genital Phase*, which starts at puberty.

Freud sees the adult personality consisting of three elements which interact with each other. The part which other people interact with directly is known as the *Ego*. Behind the Ego is a part of the personality that contains all our unconscious needs and wishes, the *Id*. The Id is the unsocialized part of our personality which wants to satisfy all our basic urges without waiting or being polite about things. If the Id were allowed out on its own it would be arrested in no time because as soon as it was hungry it would grab the first bit of food that it saw, whether it was from the fridge or in someone else's hand; if it fancied a member of the opposite sex...! (Of course, since the Id is simply one system within the personality and not something that could exist alone it could not in fact be 'let out'.) The other part of the personality is the *Superego* which is the socialized part of the personality which contains the conscience and an image of how the individual ought to behave. The Id and the Superego are often in conflict and the Ego is sometimes seen as a sort of referee. The behaviour and personality which is shown is a result of the interaction of these three systems.

It is important to note that Freud believed that the majority of factors which affect behaviour have an *unconscious* origin. The Id and the Superego are largely in the unconscious as are many of the memories of early life that have such a strong effect on our conscious personality. We are not aware, according to Freud, of most of the motives that drive us. Take an example of a woman who finds it difficult to get on with men; there are many possible reasons for this but one might be that as a young girl she was sexually assaulted, perhaps by a man whom she knew well. This memory would cause great anxiety to the young girl and so Freud would argue that it would be *repressed*, that is, the memory would be blocked in the unconscious and the older woman would not know of its existence. Although the memory itself is not available to conscious thought, it can still have an effect on behaviour, causing the adult woman's problems relating to men. The techniques of psychoanalysis including the analysis of dreams are designed to explore unconscious motivations and bring them to a conscious level in a therapeutic situation where the individual may be able to come to terms with them. Once the repressed memory of the sexual assault is brought to consciousness it can be seen for what it is and the woman will be more likely to cope with relationships with men.

Freud said that one principle governing the personality was that the Ego should be protected from anxiety and this is one reason that most of our motivations are unconscious. In the example above we talked about repression which is one technique by which the Ego can be protected from unpleasantness. Repression is just one example from a range of *defence mechanisms* which are techniques used to reduce Ego anxiety.

The Ego has an image of the sort of person that it thinks you are. If the image is unrealistically prim and proper it may be difficult to cope with the basic urges of the Id. The Ego will be protected in some way from recognizing this crude part of your personality but it may not be possible to bottle it up totally. In this type of situation the defence mechanism which helps avoid ego anxiety may be *projection*, that is, rather than accept your own basic aggression and sexuality, these characteristics are projected out onto the rest of society causing the individual concerned to notice these aspects of society much more than other people. Using this defence mechanism, the individual can pay attention to sexuality and aggression without disturbing the Ego because the Ego can interpret the world as being full of sex and violence and can criticize other people, rather than having to accept his or her own unconscious motives. The way in which projection makes the individual more likely to attend to some aspects of the world rather than others is similar to the concept of *Perceptual Set* which we discussed in chapter 2.

The defence mechanism of *identification* has some similarities to imitation and is an important factor in socialization.

Identification

Identification is much more than simple imitation, it involves the adoption of the model's whole range of attitudes, values and behaviour, rather than just specific actions. After identification, a child may act as they think the model would in a new situation.

Freud first used the concept of identification to explain the way in which children acquire their sex role – masculine behaviour in the case of boys, feminine behaviour in the case of girls. He put forward the idea that a boy's love for his mother increases greatly at around the age of four or five, to a point when he wishes to possess her sexually. The boy sees his father as a rival for his mother's love and develops a fear that his father will castrate him (*castration anxiety*). Freud called this unpleasant situation the *Oedipus Complex*; according to him, all boys – regardless of culture – go through this stage. Understandably, young boys would like to escape from the Oedipus Complex, and to do this they use the oldest trick in the book: 'If you can't beat them, join them.' Boys therefore identify with their fathers, becoming as like them as possible. Girls go through a similar process, known as the *Electra Complex*, which results in identification with the mother, though even Freudian psychologists admit that his theory of female identification is unsatisfactory and unclear.

Freud's description of the Electra Complex varied over the years of his writing and he admitted that he had problems with his theory of female socialization. At one point he suggested that his problem reflected the fact that women were actually less well socialized than men! The work of Sears *et al.* (p. 211) suggests that, if anything, the opposite is true. In one of its less confused versions the description of the Electra Complex goes like this:

At some time during the phallic stage the young girl realizes that she has not got a penis, and develops what Freud called *Penis Envy*. She realizes that her mother is also without a penis and believes that mum is responsible for her own loss. This produces a conflict between mother and daughter which is too much for the young child to cope with, and so she identifies with the mother in order to reduce this tension.

Whiting agrees that boys develop love for their mothers and girls for their fathers, but argues that identification occurs due to envy rather than anxiety. The child identifies with the same-sex parent in order to achieve the same status and control over the mother (in the case of boys) or the father (in the case of girls). This is known as the *status envy* theory of identification.

Bandura, Ross and Ross have managed to define more clearly what status envy means. It sees that the major factor behind it is that the person who is envied has control over resources; simply to be in possession of resources is usually not enough. Thus, in an experiment a child saw two adults involved in the following sequence of behaviour:

1 Adult A, who was in apparent control of a large number of expensive and elaborate toys, gave some of these to adult B.
2 Adults A and B then performed certain different striking patterns of behaviour which would be easy to recognize in the child if it imitated them.

Then the child's behaviour was observed.

If it is merely possession of the wanted objects which prompts imitative behaviour in the child then we might expect him to imitate the behaviour of both A and B. If, however, it is A's control of resources which is the major motivator, then only A's behaviour would be imitated. Observation of the child's behaviour showed that while he imitated some behaviour demonstrated by A and some demonstrated by B, recognizably more of A's behaviour, was imitated. This finding suggests that both control of resources and possession of resources act as motivators for imitative behaviour, but that control over resources is probably the more important of the two factors.

We could apply these principles to male sex-role identification:

1 A boy's father is seen by the child to control a valuable resource, namely his mother.
2 The boy envies his father's control of this much-desired resource.
3 The boy identifies with his father.

It is evident that a child is liable to find adults' presence, attention or praise reinforcing, and will imitate or perhaps identify with them if he can see that they control resources which he himself wants.

Many psychologists find Freud's theory of identification difficult to accept, for a variety of reasons. The theory would, for example, find it difficult to explain how the children of one-parent families can grow up to develop normal sex roles.

The following is a brief summary of some of the major criticisms of Freud's theories.

Source of evidence. Freud worked as a therapist and gained most of his insights into behaviour from his patients. These were a very limited and biased sample of the population in general. The sample has been described as consisting of middle-aged, middle-class, mid-European, neurotic women. He did study some males, such as the famous *little Hans* whose father wrote to Freud over many years recording the boy's behaviour in great detail. Given that so many of his patients were women, it is surprising that his theory of female socialization is so weak and this has led some people to suggest that his theories are based on his own childhood.

Since Freud was working as a therapist his main concern was the treatment of his patients, rather than the strict control of variables that is found in the laboratory. In this situation it is very easy to lead patients into saying things that fit in with the theory that you hold and when writing up the case afterwards memory is likely to be distorted in a way that fits the 'facts' to the theorist's existing ideas (see pp. 70–1).

Freud's theory is unscientific. Eysenck has argued that Freud's theory 'explains everything and predicts nothing'. It is a bit like the man who sits in the pub on Sunday lunch-time and can explain exactly why a particular horse won the race yesterday but is never any good at telling you which horse will win next week's race. To be scientific, a theory must make testable predictions in such a way that if the prediction proves false the theory would be discarded.

Some argue that it doesn't matter that the theory is unscientific, and point to other important theories such as the existence of God which have had a far greater effect on people's lives and the history of civilizations than most scientific theories. Following this line, the strength of Freudian theory lies partly in the fact that it helps people through the process of psychoanalysis.

Eysenck questions the effectiveness of the psychoanalytic method. He compared the recovery rates of two groups of patients, one who had psychotherapy and one who had no treatment, and claimed that after six months there was no difference between the recovery rates of the two.

Too many hypothetical notions. If there is no other way to decide between two theories the last resort is to accept the one that makes the least assumptions. Freud's theory is full of concepts such as the Id, Ego, Superego,

Oedipus Complex, and so on, which are not directly observable and are supported by questionable evidence.

The nature of conscience. Freud saw conscience as a quality of the individual that was fairly similar from one situation to the next. The work of the social learning theorists on the situation-specific nature of conscience directly contradicts this (see p. 177).

Aggression

Freud regarded aggression as a basic instinct that is present in the Id from birth. At first the aggression is relatively uncontrolled but with the development of the Ego and Superego it becomes channelled into socially acceptable behaviour. Unlike the social learning theorists, Freud saw aggression as inevitable and the only way to ensure that it is not destructive is to find an acceptable outlet such as sport or verbal conflict.

Sex Differences in Behaviour

At 6 years old Matthew said he didn't like girls (things were to change later). 'But you like Zoe,' said his mum. 'That's different,' replied Matthew, 'Zoe plays football'.

What makes a little boy think in this way? As a society we now put more stress on equality of the sexes and are more careful to avoid making assumptions about the way that people behave based solely upon whether they are male or female. Yet whether we are male or female is an important part of our individual identity and from an early age differences can be seen between the way that boys and girls interact.

Do behavioural and psychological differences between the sexes really exist? And if they do, where do they come from? Are they always there, fixed biologically at birth, or are they due to learning, that 'relatively permanent change in behaviour due to experience'? We have already looked at the way in which social learning and Freudian theorists consider sex-role development. In this section we will take a closer look at what differences have been shown between the sexes and consider the way that biological and cognitive factors influence them.

Some of the terms used by psychologists in studying this topic include the following:

Sex, the biological state of being male or female. Each cell of the body has a pair of chromosomes which determines your sex. If both chromosomes are the same (XX) you will be female, but if they are different (XY) you will be male. The female has a vagina and ovaries, whereas the male has a penis and testes. The balance of hormones in the body differs between the sexes with males having more testosterone and females having more oestrogen and progesterone.

Sex identity, the identification of an individual as male or female based upon the biological information. For most people this identification is not difficult since chromosomes, genitals and hormonal make-up all point to the individual belonging to one sex or the other.

Sex typing, picking up the behaviours that a particular culture expects from males or females.

Gender identity, an individual's inner sense of being male or female. This does not mean that the individual has to adopt all the behaviours normally associated with that sex, a female boxer may have no difficulty with her gender identity as a woman even though she participates in a sport that most people associate with men. Although gender and sex identity usually coincide, it is not always the case; people who undergo sex change operations usually report having felt trapped in the body of the opposite sex before having the treatment.

Sex or gender roles, the set of behaviours and attitudes which are more typical of one sex or the other. Sex-role behaviour is the exhibiting of behaviour that matches the culturally defined sex role such as choosing sex-appropriate toys, wearing appropriate clothes, etc.

Some Examples of Sex Differences
When considering reports of studies which show sex differences it is important to remember a number of points:

- The differences are averages and relate to comparisons of large groups; there is a great deal of overlap between the sexes.
- There is a tendency to report differences because they are newsworthy; similarities are often ignored.
- Out of the thousands of pieces of research into this area, sexual politics affects the choice of which ones are brought into any discussion
- Showing a sex difference does not tell you its cause; it may be due to biological or cultural differences or a combination of the two.

Some studies have looked at the social behaviour of adult men and women, often with predictable results. For example Buss and Schmitt (1993) report a field experiment on a college campus where an attractive man or woman approached strangers of the opposite sex and said 'I have been noticing you around campus. I find you very attractive.' They then asked one of three possible questions:

1 Would you go out with me tonight?
2 Would you come to my apartment tonight?
3 Would you go to bed with me tonight?

As expected there were sex differences in the responses of the person being asked (shown in table 9.1 below).

Table 9.1

Question	Proportion of men who said 'Yes'	Proportion of women who said 'Yes'
1 Would you go out with me tonight?	50%	50%
2 Would you come to my apartment tonight?	69%	6%
3 Would you go to bed with me tonight?	75%	0%

A more common type of study has looked at the behaviour of girls and boys during childhood. Maccoby and Jacklin (1974) noted that young males are more active and assertive than females. Boys from about 2 years old engage in more rough and tumble play than females, and at 5 they are more likely to respond aggressively to attack or give verbal insults. Malina (1987) reported that girls spend more time in small motor coordination (e.g. bead threading) and boys spend more time in large motor movement such as climbing. Boys, in general, show larger 'grip strength' from an earlier age than girls, whereas girls' general development seems to be slightly earlier than boys, so the baby's change from grasping things with the finger pressing against the palm to finally using the thumb in opposition to the finger probably occurs slightly earlier in girls.

Girls generally utter their first words earlier than boys, and this is reflected in a greater verbal ability throughout childhood.

Differences have been shown in perceptual abilities of children. Boys appear to have greater visual and spatial abilities than girls. Witkin (1962) studied the perceptual abilities of young children using the 'embedded figures test'. A child has to find a simple figure hidden in a more complex drawing. By becoming more able to ignore the background children generally become less field-dependent as they get older and are able to pick out the embedded figure more easily. Witkin found that, age for age, young girls were more 'field-dependent' than boys, and this difference has been shown in adults.

Many studies have shown differences in numerical ability between the sexes. Stumpf and Jackson (1994) studied the results of tests given to nearly 200,000 applicants to medical school in West Germany and showed that mean average scores for mathematical reasoning and scientific comprehension was greater for men than women but that women scored better on memorizing. Some people hope that sex differences will be reduced as cultures change; Stumpf and Jackson reviewed previous studies and reported that differences in mathematical reasoning showed no signs of decline over time although there was a slight reduction in the difference in memorizing. There is disagreement over whether sex differences are constant over time, with researchers such as Linn (1991) claiming a narrowing of the gap in mathematical reasoning. We will have to wait a while longer to get a more definite answer.

Even when there are no actual differences, our expectations of girls and boys may lead us to believe that they are not the same. Parsons *et al.* (1982) found that parents of children between 6 and 11 years thought that their daughters were less good at mathematics than their sons, despite the fact that their achievements did not differ. They believed that their daughters had to work harder to achieve the same results. Paulsen and Johnson (1983) showed that children of both sexes who had a positive attitude to mathematics did better on maths tests. So it seems that, to some extent at least, children's intellectual performance is shaped by parental and teacher attitudes and expectations as well as their own. These serve to exaggerate any small intellectual differences which may already exist.

Published results from the examination boards show that girls get better results at GCSE and A-levels and that the difference is increasing (in the 1970s boys did better in school exams). Unemployment rates in the UK and other countries are showing that young men are more likely to be unemployed. After a generation of looking at equal opportunities issues relating to sex as being a matter of removing barriers from girls and women, many now argue that we need to put more effort into doing something about the problem of underachieving boys.

Basic sex differences seem to occur all over the world. Maccoby and Jacklin studied the development of boys and girls in a number of different countries including Switzerland, India, Ethiopia and Mexico. They noticed that differences between the sexes in the extent of rough and tumble play and signs of dependency were very similar across all these cultures. Other *cross-cultural studies* have shown that sex differences are not totally universal – see Margaret Mead's study on p. 208.

Maccoby points out that differences between the sexes are not great and are much smaller than the similarities. The effect of parenting can magnify any cognitive differences that might already exist between the sexes, and (as we noted above) parents had preconceived ideas about the differences between boys and girls learning mathematics.

Biological Differences between Males and Females

At birth boys tend to be larger and heavier but are more vulnerable to disease than girls. There are differences in physical development, but these become magnified after puberty. Until then girls' development seems to be slightly faster and more regular and predictable than boys. Because these physical differences exist, it seems likely that some of the early behavioural differences between the sexes might be due to biological factors.

Each of the father's sperm contains either an X or a Y chromosome and the mother's eggs all contain X chromosomes, so the sex of the child depends on whether an X or a Y fertilizes an egg resulting in either XX (female) or XY (male). There are differences in the speed at which X and Y sperm swim, and in the conditions that they survive best and so the probability of a male or female child can be affected by the conditions inside the mother's vagina.

About two months after conception the presence of a Y chromosome causes the embryo to develop testes rather than ovaries. The testes or ovaries then produce sex hormones which control the development of the sex organs and which may also have an effect on later behaviour. In the absence of male sex hormones, the embryo will develop female genitals whether the chromosomes are XX or XY, but normally the presence of a Y chromosome means that there is a surge of male sex hormones (*androgens*) between 30 and 60 days after conception (a process known as *androgenization*).

On rare occasions there may be a hormonal problem in the development of the embryo, which means that an XX embryo gets too much androgen or an XY gets too little. In these cases the development of the sex organs is affected and the child may show poorly developed signs of both male and female sex organs; rather than being male or female they are hermaphrodite. Money (1980) studied the development of two genetically female (XX) hermaphrodite twins one of whom was brought up and treated as a son and the other as a daughter. Both seemed to adjust well to their allocated sex and were accepted by their peers showing the importance of social factors in the development of sex role. The daughter did however display what was called 'tomboyish' behaviour, supporting the idea that androgenization has an effect of increasing the rough and tumble behaviour usually associated with boys.

Another case study by Money and Ehrhardt (1972) involved two normally born identical male twins. One twin had a surgical accident at 7 months, and sex-reassignment was agreed on. From that time on, the twins were treated very differently, and by 4 years they also behaved very differently, according to their sex roles. Money and Ehrhardt report that the girl sat in front of the mirror, and the boy was very sloppy and wanted to be a fireman! Again gender identity seemed to be most affected by the way that other people treated the children but the effect of androgenization showed itself in the reports that the 'daughter' was unusually active for her age.

Most studies have shown that changes in allocation of sex before the age of 3 seem to be successful. At about 3 years children have achieved gender identity and it is more difficult to adapt. These studies suggest that, apart from levels of activity, the most part of sex role is affected by environmental factors rather than hormones but there are studies which appear to contradict this view. Imperato–McGinley et al. (1979) found a remote area in the Dominican Republic where many of the girl children changed to boys at puberty and took the male gender identity with no apparent difficulty including taking on female sexual partners. The children who 'changed sex' were all in fact biologically male, but they had a genetic defect which affected the balance of hormones before birth resulting in external features which made them appear female. At puberty the usual rush of male hormone resulted in the growth of the normal male appearance.

It could be argued that the ease with which the Imperato–McGinley children took on the male sex role was a result of being biologically male all along and that hormones rather than social factors eased the way that they were able to take on male gender identity. Although this condition is rare worldwide, it is not uncommon in this particular population due to inheritance of a 'faulty' gene from a common ancestor; in this situation the change of sex was not so unexpected, and it is questionable how consistently the children were treated as girls in their early years making this weaker evidence for the role of biological factors. In many cultures boy children are more highly prized than girls, probably due to economic factors, if the children had changed from boys to girls perhaps the transition would not have been so easy.

There is a suggestion that hormones may have a role in sex differences in cognitive abilities. Geschwind has linked spatial ability with the presence of large amounts of male hormone during pregnancy; Waber (1977) has noted that girls who reach puberty later are better at spatial tasks than those who mature earlier.

Hormones might be expected to play a part in sexual attraction but a number of studies have been performed which show no specific relationship between sexual orientation and adult hormonal balance (Meyer-Bahlburg 1984). There has been a suggestion that the brains of men and women are different and that androgenization results in the changing of a brain to give it male characteristics including a sexual preference for women. According to this theory male homosexuals may have received less testosterone (the main male sex hormone) during the critical period of development in the womb. The origin of this theory comes from work on rats where a specific part of the brain was damaged resulting in male animals which acted as females. It is going a bit far to assume that human sexual attraction is based upon brain structure simply by generalizing from such a study on rats, especially since what was being measured was particular behaviours rather than feeling or general orientation. It is easy to see why ethical considerations would prevent us from doing the same sort of study with humans.

Many newspapers reported the work of Hamer *et al.* (1993) who found a gene on the X chromosome which is more common in homosexual men; this was called by many of them the 'gay gene', and some readers gained the impression that this was a gene which *caused* homosexuality. Any relationship between a specific gene or androgenization and homosexuality is most unlikely to be a direct causal link, since studies show that nearly half the identical twins of homosexual men showed a heterosexual orientation despite the fact that they share the same genes and were in the same womb during androgenization.

In summary, hormonal factors do have a part to play in sex differences: there appears to be an effect on the greater activity levels shown in young boys; there may be effects on the difference in spatial and verbal abilities between the sexes and possibly on sexual orientation. It is likely that any effect of hormones is indirect, perhaps leading to a tendency toward so-called male or female behaviour. Remember that biological and social factors interact in their effect on human behaviour; parents reactions to a child will be affected by the way the child behaves, so if *he* is slightly more active or if *she* starts to talk earlier parents will interact with the two children differently exaggerating any minor differences that may have been there originally.

Cognitive theory of sex role development

In chapter 5 we looked at the theories of Jean Piaget who stressed that a child's understanding of the world progressed in stages, and that although experience was vital to development the effect of the experience was modified by the child's maturational readiness. Kohlberg based his theory of sex role development on the cognitive stages suggested by Piaget. He pointed out that children's understanding of their gender depends on their level of intellectual development; just as a child in the early pre-operational stage cannot conserve number or volume, so they have no idea of conservation of gender. The stages which Kohlberg suggested for gender development are:

Basic gender identity (approximately 2–5 years). At this stage children identify themselves as boys or girls but are not aware that this will always be so. Thompson (1975) showed that when children aged 2 are shown one same-sex picture and several opposite-sex pictures and asked 'which one is you?', they can pick out the same-sex picture correctly. By 3 years they can correctly answer 'which one is a boy?', etc. Katcher (1955) presented children with figures of clothed and unclothed men, women and children which were cut at the neck and waist so that each was in three sections. The children were asked to put the figures together and identify their gender. 3–4-year-olds did well with the clothed figures, but the unclothed figures confused them, and they seemed to think that girls could be boys if they wore boys' clothes and hairstyles.

Gender stability (approximately 5–6 years). At this stage children realize that they will stay the same sex when they grow up but still have some confusion if people wear opposite sex clothes. A man wearing a dress at a fancy dress party might be considered to have changed into a woman.

Gender consistency (approximately 6 years onwards). As the other constancies develop children see gender as a constant for any one individual which will not change over time or situation.

The cognitive development theory of Kohlberg stresses active involvement of the child in choosing role models of the same sex as their gender schema develops. Like other schema discussed in chapter 5 the schema for gender organizes the way that the child thinks, remembers and perceives matters to do with gender. A child who has basic gender identity as a boy will pick out males and choose to act like them.

Androgyny

Sandra Bem (1975) pointed out that we tend to view male and female as different and opposites, and that we have a tendency to bring up children conforming to one sex role or the other. She argues that masculinity and femininity are simply opposite ends of a spectrum and that people can display a combination of masculine and feminine characteristics; such people are said to be *androgynous*. Bem sees *androgyny* as the most psychologically healthy because it allows people to be flexible in their behaviour and not locked into a particular sex role.

Bem produced a questionnaire asking people to rate themselves on different aspects of their personality. Some of the adjectives used were traditionally feminine (e.g. affectionate, compassionate, warm, sensitive to the needs of others) and others masculine (e.g. competitive, forceful, acting as leader, analytical). She found that around a third of people showed signs of androgyny, rating themselves highly on some masculine and some feminine characteristics, and that these tended to be self-confident individuals.

Bem says that we have a gender schema and that this affects the way that we think and act. In chapter 4 we showed how people tend to put organization into the recall of randomly arranged words by grouping together those words that related to particular ideas or schemas. When asked to recall random lists of words Bem showed that people who were highly masculine or feminine (as rated by her questionnaire) tended to group together words with a masculine or feminine association (e.g. fighting, trouser, pilot or blushing, skirt, nurse). Androgynous people were less likely to group words in this way.

Spence and Helmreich (1978) used similar questionnaire showing that about 30 per cent of American college students were androgynous and that they were often the children of androgynous parents.

The idea that androgyny is the most psychologically healthy state has been questioned. Jones *et al.* (1978) found that high masculinity in both men and women was linked to better flexibility and overall adjustment. Others point out that androgynous individuals are likely to find difficulty if they live in a very traditional environment. Bem recognized this problem and argued that society as a whole should become less concerned with traditional sex roles.

Summary

1 The Social Learning theorists believe that the socialization process can be explained in terms of reinforcements and imitation learning.

2 Bandura found that children will learn to imitate actions from their observation of a model, and that although seeing the model punished affected the extent of their imitative behaviour, seeing the model rewarded did not. Rewarding the child for imitative behaviour showed that even when the child had seen the model being punished, it had still learnt the behaviour of the model; the punishment observed had simply inhibited the child's performance of it.

3 Mischel argued that behaviour depends more on the situation and the role that an individual adopts than upon stable personality characteristics.

4 Freud believed that children develop through a series of psychosexual stages, and that the first five years of life were most important for later adult personality.

5 Freud's idea that boys identify with their fathers in order to try to win their mothers' love is modified in Whiting's theory that boys envied their father's *status* and thus developed an appropriate sex role.

6 Bandura found that control of resources by a model made that model's behaviour more likely to be imitated than the behaviour of a model who did not control resources. This study can be used to back up the *status envy* view of identification.

7 Some of the major sex differences are:

• Young boys are more active than girls and engage in more 'rough and tumble' from around 2 years old.

- Girls spend more time practising small motor coordination. Boys spend more time displaying large motor actions.
- Girls are more advanced linguistically.
- Girls mature earlier.
- Boys have greater visual, spatial and numerical abilities.
- Girls do better on memory tests.
- Girls do better at GCSE and A-level.

8 When considering sex differences it is important to note that they are group averages and that there is a great overlap. Showing a sex difference does not tell us whether the difference is biological, cultural, or a combination of the two.

9 The presence of a Y chromosome usually results in a surge of male sex hormones between 30 and 60 days after conception. This process is known as androgenization and results in the development of male physical characteristics. Androgenization may also affect later 'rough and tumble' behaviour and the sex differences in cognitive ability.

10 Kohlberg suggested three stages of cognitive development with regard to gender role: basic gender identity, gender stability, and gender consistency.

11 Bem pointed out that masculinity and femininity are two ends of the same continuum. Many people have a mixture of both characteristics. Bem saw this androgyny as the most psychologically healthy state.

Further Reading

Hardy, M., Heyes, S., Crews, J., Rookes, P. and Wren, K., *Studying Child Psychology* (1990, Weidenfeld & Nicolson).

Mischel, W., *Introduction to Personality* (5th edn, 1993, Harcourt Brace Jovanovich).

Chapter 10

Theories of Personality

If asked to describe a friend – a woman, let's say – I might choose to say that she was five foot tall and overweight with long dark hair, but these are merely physical descriptions which might help pick her out in a crowded room and they don't really tell you anything about what sort of person she is or why I should choose to be friendly with her. The description of the sort of person she is, her psychological and behavioural characteristics, are the really interesting thing about her as a person. In some ways my friend is unique and like no one else that I know. This is often the case with very close friends, and perhaps I notice this because I know them so well. In other ways my friend is like a number of other people I know, being out-going and bubbly. When psychologists study personality they are looking at the psychological and behavioural characteristics that describe individuals and the way that they differ. Some psychologists are particularly interested in picking out common characteristics and use these to describe groups of people so that they can make predictions about how they might behave in particular circumstances. Others are more interested in the uniqueness of each individual and work with individuals to help them with personal difficulties.

Trait and Type Theories of Personality

Are you an extravert or an introvert? Are you an optimist or a pessimist? Are you a worrier or carefree? The idea behind trait and type theories is to find the basic characteristics of personality and then to describe individual's personality in respect to these. Thus one person might be an 'introverted pessimist worrier' while another could be an 'extravert carefree optimist'. These descriptions tell us something about the personality of the individual by placing them into groups. For example, all optimists look on the bright side of things. Listing an individual's personality traits may help us to predict their behaviour in some situations, but don't expect anything like certainty. The predictions we can make are only generalizations for that sort of person. For example, more extraverts smoke than introverts, but that doesn't mean that we can point to a smoker and be sure he is an extravert or indeed that we can find that someone is an extravert and predict that he will smoke. What we could reasonably predict is that if we used a questionnaire to identify extraverts and introverts we would find that more extraverts smoke that introverts.

If you are going to use this approach, the big question is how many characteristics are you going to use to describe people. This is where the disagreement starts. For some people the only way to describe the richness of personality is to break it into a large number of parts so that each individual may be measured against perhaps sixteen characteristics or *traits*. Each trait is a characteristic of personality which differs from person to person in a relatively permanent way. Others point out that some traits tend to go together: For example, two traits which could be used to describe people are *talkative/not talkative* and *open/secretive*, but talkative people tend to be quite open and those who are not so talkative are often more secretive. Rather than describe lots of traits it might be better to collect those traits that commonly go together and go for a small number of personality dimensions which we can then use to categorize individuals into a small number of *types* of people.

How many traits or types?
There are hundreds of words in the dictionary to describe people's personality, but using them all would make the description very complex and would have the additional problem that some overlap with others. In reality we don't have a common agreement about what exactly each one means. The technique used to arrive at an answer to how many traits or types are most useful is a complicated statistical technique known as *factor analysis*. The mathematics of this is not important to us but the technique involves getting lots of people to answer many yes/no questions about their personality. People who answer 'yes' to a question like 'do you like meeting new people?' also tend to do the same to 'do you like going to parties?', presumably because the question is dealing with a similar aspect of personality (a trait). Factor analysis picks out the questions which are related in this way and shows how many separate traits are being covered by the whole range of questions set. The two best known theorists who have used this approach are Cattell who has found sixteen personality factors (traits) and Eysenck who prefers to link together some traits resulting in three dimensions of personality.

Eysenck's Theory
The two main dimensions of personality which Eysenck describes are *extraversion/introversion* and *neuroticism*. The personality traits shown by the typical extravert and typical introvert are shown in table 10.1.

Table 10.1.

Typical extravert (major focus is toward the outside world)	Typical introvert (major focus is turned in toward self)
• Sociable	• Quiet
• Wants excitement	• Introspective
• Needs people to talk to	• Likes books
• Likes parties	• Reserved
• Gets bored easily	• Not easily bored
• Has lots of friends	• Has a few close friends
• Takes chances	• Doesn't like taking chances
• Acts spontaneously	• Tends to plan ahead
• Carefree easy going	• Keeps feelings under control
• Life and soul of party	• Reliable

The neuroticism dimension of personality refers to levels of emotionality. People at the stable end are calm, unflappable, well adjusted, reliable. At the neurotic end of the dimension are those who are temperamental, emotional, moody, worriers.

The third personality dimension is *psychoticism*, which relates to antisocial activity and levels of caring but most people have low scores on this. Using factor analysis, Eysenck showed that the three personality dimensions were independent by which he means that an individual's rating on one of the dimensions (say extraversion) has no effect on their rating on either of the other two dimensions (neuroticism or psychoticism). Most work has been done on the dimensions of extraversion/introversion and neuroticism.

Eysenck devised a personality inventory to measure personality. This consists of questions such as those in table 10.2 which are answered 'yes' or 'no'. Eysenck tested a lot of such questions on people who had been rated by those who knew them as definite extraverts or introverts. Each question was then examined to see whether introverts and extraverts generally answered it differently; if this was the case the question was retained in

Table 10.2.

Examples of the type of question asked in the EPI (adapted from Eysenck 1963)	Personality type tending to answer yes
Do you often look for excitement?	Extravert
Do you choose to have few but special friends?	Introvert
Are you often tormented by feelings of guilt?	Neurotic

the final questionnaire. In this way he built up the EPI (*Eysenck Personality Inventory*).

Many people are concerned that those taking questionnaire tests may lie and therefore give false results to the tests. Eysenck had a couple of responses to this:

- In one sense it doesn't matter. If, for example all extraverts answer 'Yes' to the question 'Do you like purple ice cream?' and all introverts reply 'No' then it doesn't matter whether anybody is telling the truth or not: it is still a good way of sorting out the extraverts from the rest.
- Some people do like to be seen in the best possible light and may lie to look better. To get round this Eysenck included a '*lie scale*' in the EPI and he disregarded the results from anyone who scores highly on this scale. The scale consists of a number of questions like 'Have you ever told a lie?' to which the vast majority of people answer 'Yes' if they are being truthful. Eysenck's lie scale would also exclude saints but very little questionnaire research has been done on this small group!

Few people are at the extremes of the introversion–extraversion or the neuroticism–stability dimensions; most will be toward the middle but with tendencies toward extraversion or one of the other extremes. As a result of taking the EPI an individual may be classed as one of four *types*: Stable Extravert, Stable Introvert, Neurotic Extravert or Neurotic Introvert (see figure 10.1).

Figure 10.1.

Eysenck thought that personality was largely inherited and that the personality types behave the way that they do due to differences in the nervous system. The difference between extraverts and introverts was thought to lie in the Reticular Activating System (RAS, see p. 306) which has an effect on the general level of activity (arousal) in the cortex (the top layer of the brain, see p. 308). In a paper called 'Eysenck's demon', Eysenck said that it was as though there was a demon sitting in the RAS with a lever at each hand; the left-hand lever increased general activity (arousal) in the cortex and the right-hand lever decreased it. Just as a car engine works best when it is warm and not so well when it is cold or overheated, so too the brain works best at an average level of arousal. The arousal of the cortex can come from two places:

1 From inside the nervous system itself.
2 Via the sense organs from the environment.

If there is too little arousal from the nervous system itself, the individual will feel bored and search for new stimulation from the world around. If there is too much, it will cause the individual to shy away from external excitement. Eysenck said that it was as though the 'demon' sitting in an extravert's brain was right-handed, causing the general level of brain arousal to be low and pushing the individual to search for new and exciting things in the world around. The introvert's demon would be left-handed, so that the general level of arousal would not need further increase from the outside world, allowing the introvert to be much more self-contained.

Eysenck demonstrated that introverts could be classically conditioned more easily than extraverts (see p. 35–40 for an explanation of classical conditioning). He used this finding to explain why criminals tend to score higher on the extraversion scale than the normal population. Eysenck and a number of the Social Learning Theorists (p. 170–3) saw conscience as a classically conditioned response (see figure 10.2). In an environment where exactly the same learning experience was available to everyone the introvert would develop the stronger conscience.

Figure 10.2.

The development of conscience through classical conditioning
(see chapter 3)

Bad Behaviour + **Puinishment** *leads to* **Feeling bad**
(conditional stimulus)   (unconditional stimulus)   (unconditional response)

After a number of pairings the 'bad behaviour on its own leads to 'feeling bad' (conscience).

Bad Behaviour *leads to* **Feeling bad** (Conscience)
(conditional stimulus)   (conditional response)

Costa and McCrae (1992) found a very close relationship between neuroticism and reported symptoms of physical illness. They studied a group of middle-aged men over a period of twelve years and recorded their reports of problems with aches and pains, eyesight, and a whole variety of other aspects of physical health. When they compared the rates of reported problems with personality they found that the greater the individual's neuroticism score, the greater the number of complaints, and they suggested that doctors might find an awareness of a patient's score on this personality dimension useful when making a medical assessment.

Eysenck's work has been influential in generating a lot of follow-up research. There is controversy about the number of dimensions or traits that is most useful in describing personality. Deary and Matthews (1993) reviewed the status of trait theories and pointed out that many theorists agree on the importance of extraversion/introversion and neuroticism dimensions, but that others such as openness, agreeableness and conscientiousness are also important.

Eysenck's views on criminality have been criticized as focusing too much on the individual and not enough on the society in which the criminals find themselves. Some studies have found prisoners to be more introverted; perhaps these introverts simply learnt well as part of a family and peer group that supports crime. Some have questioned the whole idea of a conditioned conscience being more easily gained by extraverts, especially since evidence for the conditionability of this group comes from the learning of very limited forms of response such as eye blinking.

Cattell's Theory

Where Eysenck preferred to describe personality in a way which divides people into a few basic personality types Cattell's descriptions analyse people on a larger number of traits. Cattell used factor analysis on three sorts of information which were:

1 A small group of students who were watched by trained observers over a period of six months. The observers rated each individual against a large set of personality characteristics which were taken from general and specialist dictionaries.
2 A large number of questionnaire items each having a choice of two or three answers.
3 A series of behavioural tests such as reaction time (this can be tested by asking people to press a button as soon as they see a light come on and measuring the time it takes them to do this).

From his research Cattell identified a number of personality factors, but he described sixteen of these in most detail and the questionnaire which he devised for research purposes is known as *Cattell's 16 PF*. These personality factors are like introversion/extraversion in the sense that people can be placed at one extreme or the other or some way between, but there are many more and each describes a smaller, more specific, piece of the personality. Some of Cattell's personality factors when combined together actually measure something quite close to Eysenck's introversion/extraversion; others combine to show something close to the neuroticism dimension. This adds some strength to both theories because both researchers worked independently.

Cattell's 16 Personality Factors (adapted and simplified from Cattell 1965)

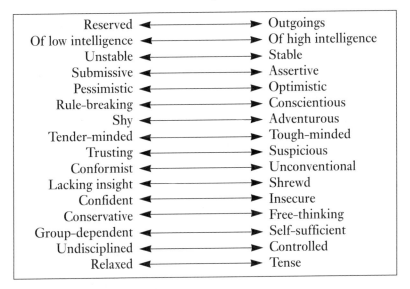

Reserved ◄──────►	Outgoings
Of low intelligence ◄──────►	Of high intelligence
Unstable ◄──────►	Stable
Submissive ◄──────►	Assertive
Pessimistic ◄──────►	Optimistic
Rule-breaking ◄──────►	Conscientious
Shy ◄──────►	Adventurous
Tender-minded ◄──────►	Tough-minded
Trusting ◄──────►	Suspicious
Conformist ◄──────►	Unconventional
Lacking insight ◄──────►	Shrewd
Confident ◄──────►	Insecure
Conservative ◄──────►	Free-thinking
Group-dependent ◄──────►	Self-sufficient
Undisciplined ◄──────►	Controlled
Relaxed ◄──────►	Tense

On taking the 16PF an individual is given a *personality profile*, i.e. a score against each of the traits showing where they lie on the scale between one end and the other, as shown in figure 10.3.

Figure 10.3. The relationship between Types and Traits

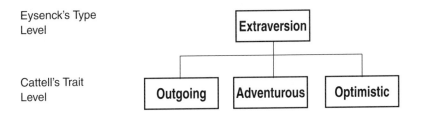

Eysenck's Type Level — **Extraversion**

Cattell's Trait Level — **Outgoing** | **Adventurous** | **Optimistic**

Mischel (1986) makes a general criticism of theories like those of Cattell and Eysenck. He said that they ignore the way that situation affects people. Some people may act in a very extraverted way when with friends on a social occasion but appear much more introverted when at work. He also quotes the work of Hartshorne and May (1928) who showed that honesty, which some might consider a personality trait, varies greatly from one situation to another (see p. 177).

Humanistic Theories of Personality

Nomothetic and Idiographic Approaches to Personality

The approaches of Eysenck and Cattell are deliberately scientific and result in general theories which give us insight into the way that particular types of people are likely to behave. When researching they purposely chose large groups of people to study so that they could get a general picture. This is known as the *nomothetic* approach.

Humanistic theorists disagree with the nomothetic approach because it disregards the uniqueness of each individual. They deliberately take a non-scientific approach and emphasize the way that each person sees and reacts to the world around them. This is known as the *idiographic* approach and is demonstrated by the theories of Rogers and Kelly.

Rogers' Theory

Rogers placed an emphasis on the way that the individual perceives the world and themselves. Each person's view of the world is unique to them, and one of the most important parts is the individual's view of themself which they gain from interaction with people around them. There are two important parts to the self:

1 *Self-concept.* This is the individual's beliefs about himself or herself; the answer to questions such as: 'Who am I?' and 'What am I?'.
2 *Ideal Self.* This is the desired self: 'Who I would like to be?'.

If the self-concept and ideal self are similar (Rogers calls this *congruence*), the individual is well adapted and will be able to achieve their full potential (Rogers calls this *self-actualization*).

Our interaction with those around us is governed by basic needs which we all share. These needs are:

• The need for *positive regard*. This is the need for love, affection and respect. Rogers saw this as something more than just a pleasant extra; it is a real need and people adapt their behaviour to get it. Most people have one or two individuals who can satisfy their need for positive regard in an unconditional way. For many this may be a parent who, though not always approving *what* the child does, always has a positive regard for that child. Rogers noted that many of his neurotic clients had parents who provided only conditional positive regard, i.e. their love was seen as dependent upon the child behaving in particular ways. He argued that this had caused his clients to adapt their behaviour to gain parental regard rather than to achieve personal growth.

• The need for self-actualization. Rogers saw this drive toward fulfilling our potential as something that we all have, and that for healthy personalities in an environment where positive regard is satisfied it is this which guides behaviour.

If there is incongruence between self-concept and ideal self, this causes anxiety, defensiveness and rigid thought patterns making it impossible to self-actualize. Rogers developed a therapeutic approach known as *client-centred therapy* to help. The therapist does not 'treat' the patient because Rogers believes that everyone can understand themselves and improve the balance between self and ideal as long as the circumstances are right. The therapist creates the right circumstances by showing unconditional positive regard for the client. In other words, the therapist shows love and approval no matter what the client says or does. This allows the client to bring hidden feelings to consciousness where they may be confronted. The regard has to be unconditional, because conditional regard will lead the client to do things which reduce the likelihood that the regard will be withdrawn rather than work toward reducing the difference between self and ideal self.

Rogers promotes a *non-directive approach* to ensure that it is the client that is working through their own problem rather than following the lead from the therapist. This means that the therapist doesn't tell the client what to do or even what the therapist thinks. To avoid leading the client therapists use techniques such as *paraphrasing*, which may be used at a point where the client has spoken for a while and wants some input from the therapist. It is important that the therapist does not put their own feelings into their response because this might influence and distort the client's problem-solving. Paraphrasing avoids this by simply summarizing what the client has said. This gives a chance for the client to pause as well as checking the understanding of what has been said and signalling that the therapist is listening and involved.

Example of Paraphrasing

Extract from client statement: I'm worried about my father. He has always been such a fit man and since he took early retirement he has been suffering from one thing after the other. Nothing very serious in itself but he never seems to be fully fit. He's not been well for a long time and now he seems to be getting depressed about his health.

Therapist's response: Your father's health and emotional state appears to be causing you a lot of concern.

Rogers has used the *Q Sort Technique* as a tool to investigate the self. People are given a lot of statements such as 'I am likeable', 'I am an obstinate person', and 'I am generous'. They are then told to sort the statements into order from those which are 'very like me' to those which are 'very unlike me'. This gives a picture of the individual's self-image. The ideal self can be measured in the same sort of way by asking the statements to be ordered against 'How I would like to be'. Comparison between the two sorts gives a picture of the congruence between the self-concept and the ideal self. Rogers and his students have used the Q sort technique to demonstrate that people coming for counselling do in fact have a greater incongruence between self and ideal self than do similar people who have not requested counselling. They showed that on completion of counselling congruence improves.

Note the difference between the 'scientific' work of Eysenck, who was trying to make generalizations about people, and that of Rogers who was talking about individuals working through their own difficulties. The role of the psychologist is also different. In Eysenck's approach the psychologist is the objective scientist categorizing and making predictions; in Rogers' approach the psychologist creates an atmosphere where each person can explore their own personality and grow as an individual. Rogers goes further than most psychologists in suggesting a philosophy of how the world should be. He argues that institutions, managers, teachers, friends, colleagues should all work to foster an environment of trust, security and positive regard, and that that will bring out the best in people.

Probably the majority of counsellors in this country take a person- (or client-) centred approach, and many take the Rogers philosophy that all are capable and motivated toward personal growth as an article of faith. Others are critical of the theory on the grounds that it is based upon concepts such as self-actualization which are ill-defined and woolly.

Kelly's Theory

When discussing Eysenck's and Cattell's theories we emphasized the scientific approach, i.e. making theories and predictions and testing them out. Kelly pointed out that scientists are simply doing in a formal manner what we all do throughout our lives. He emphasizes the way in which people act like scientists; they try to understand and predict the world around them. People make theories about what is going on at any one time and act in accordance with this theory. These theories are known as *personal constructs*, and when they prove correct they result in a well-adapted individual. It is the way in which each of us understands the world that is the basis for our personality, because it is that which determines how we will behave. For example, if I perceive the person coming toward me as angry and aggressive, I will behave differently toward them than if I think of them as warm and friendly.

Kelly said that everybody has their own way of interpreting the world. We classify objects, people, thoughts and feelings by using labels called *constructs*. These constructs always involve two opposites such as hot/cold, large/small, kind/unkind. Each individual has their own set of constructs which are used to understand the world and their own situation. An individual's set of personal constructs is used to make their theories about any situation that they are in, and this will determine how they behave. If the result of their behaviour confirms their theory, then this strengthens the personal construct system.

Similarity between two people's personal constructs helps them to get on but those with very different systems will not be able to communicate well. Constructs are not set in concrete and change over time, especially when the theories produced from the constructs are contradicted by experience. Many relationships break down when the constructs of each partner change. At the start of the relationship they may have shared many interests, but as they have different experiences in careers, family roles and pastimes their personal constructs may change so much as to make it difficult to relate. The one partner may construe success to be earning a big salary, driving an expensive car, and meeting other high-flyers, while the other may see it totally differently.

Kelly put forward the idea of *constructive alternativism*, arguing that the individual can deliberately change their constructs. For example, someone who is made redundant from a job that they have been doing for many years may construe this as awful. On the other hand, they may deliberately decide to see it as an opportunity. Using the 'awful' construct they are likely to act in the victim role, lose self-esteem, and look for evidence to back this up – quite often they will be able to find this and so the construct becomes stronger. The 'opportunity' construct may lead to a whole reorganization of life style and discovery of new pleasures – again it is quite possible that events will confirm this construct. This example shows how Kelly believes that individuals can shape their own destiny by changing their constructs.

Kelly's Repertory Grid

Like Eysenck and Cattell, Kelly has produced a device to measure personality but, following the more humanistic approach, this does not consist of a series of questions with limited choices of answer. For Kelly the basis for differences in personality is the personal construct system and his *repertory grid technique* is used to investigate this.

This is the sequence of activities to produce your own repertory grid:

- List things or people or activities that are most important to you. Kelly calls each of the items listed *elements*.
- Write each element on a card.
- Take three cards and choose some way in which two are the same and the third is different. (Here you are identifying a construct where two are at opposite ends of the construct, e.g. 'friendly', and 'not friendly'.)
- Take another group of three and do the same thing.
- Continue until you have produced all the constructs you can. Usually people produce around twenty or so.
- Now take each element and judge it against each construct so that it is placed at one end or the other of the construct, e.g. friendly or unfriendly. You now have a grid showing your personal constructs, the ones that mould your individual way of looking at the world.

Identifying your own personal constructs and seeing how they differ from others can be intriguing, but the technique can be used as a therapeutic technique by moving to the next stage.

- Take each of the constructs that you have identified and write them on a sheet of paper with the extremes at each end of a line. Now mark on the line where you see yourself and also where you would like to be (see the example below).

Ambitious _____ Not ambitious

             X   Y

   (Where I would   (Where I am)
     like to be)

- Now think about the changes that you want to make and think about the implications of doing it.

Note how, like Rogers, Kelly emphasizes action on behalf of the individual himself or herself rather than the psychologist being the activator. This stress on the changeability of personality is another characteristic of the humanistic approach. Trait theorists, particularly Eysenck, see personality as something more stable.

Summary

1 Eysenck's and Cattell's theories attempt to pick out the basic characteristics of personality which differ from person to person in a relatively permanent way. These characteristics are known as traits. Both Eysenck and Cattell have constructed questionnaires to measure personality.

2 Eysenck and Cattell both used factor analysis to pick out the traits which underpin personality.

3 Eysenck chose to concentrate at the level of description which groups together some of the more precise traits and produced a theory concentrating on four main personality types (stable extravert, stable introvert, neurotic extravert and neurotic introvert). He also proposed an additional personality dimension of psychoticism.

4 The fundamental reason for personality differences according to Eysenck was differences in the nervous systems. Extraverts require more excitement from the environment because their cortex is generally under-aroused. The cortex of the introvert is often at optimum arousal without the need for changing external stimuli.

5 Cattell's theory concentrated on 16 personality factors (traits).

6 Humanistic theories of personality such as those of Rogers and Kelly take an approach which stresses the importance of the individual. They are not concerned with classifying people. They stress the way that everybody sees the world in their own way. They generally display an optimistic view of human nature and the way in which people can change.

7 Rogers stressed the importance of the self-concept and the need for congruence with the ideal self. All share the need for positive regard and self-actualization.

8 Client-centred therapy allows individuals to move toward personal growth in a climate of unconditional positive regard. Individuals can bring themselves to personal growth in the right environment. The therapist is present to facilitate and not to lead or interpret.

9 Kelly stressed the role of personal constructs which underpin the way we understand the world. All individuals act like scientists trying to predict the world around them using their constructs and then testing their predictions against what actually happens.

10 The repertory grid technique was developed to explore people's constructs. This tool can be used to help personality change by comparing how an individual sees themselves against each construct compared with how they would like to be in relation to the construct.

Chapter 11

Child-Rearing Styles

There are many statements made about the treatment of children such as 'Children should be seen and not heard', They're only young once, so let them enjoy it', 'Spare the rod, spoil the child', 'Children must be protected', 'Children must be allowed independence'. Does it really matter how we rear children as long as their basic requirements of food, water and shelter are met? There are probably as many different ways of bringing up a child as there are children; psychologists, sociologists and anthropologists have tried to group these individual styles in categories, and have then studied the relationship between these categories and the development of certain aspects of personality.

It is a fact that the more advanced an animal is, the more helpless are its young, the more dependent and the more affected by experiences in early life. The newborn child is a defenceless object which attempts immediately to gratify any urge – such as the urge to urinate – as soon as it occurs. The child must learn to become more self-sufficient in order to survive, and to delay gratification of his urges in order to make his behaviour socially acceptable. The way in which parents help this process of growth inevitably affects a child's development, and as parents differ in the way they fulfil their roles, the later behaviour patterns of their children are also likely to differ.

Parents' treatment of children can vary in the following respects:

1 Their display of love and attention.
2 The type and consistency of their rewards and punishments.
3 The extent to which they give reasons for rules.
4 Their permissiveness.
5 Their control of children's aggression.
6 Their emphasis on behaviour appropriate to the sex roles.

This list is by no means exhaustive, but it includes some of the major categories that have been investigated.

One of the commonest methods of studying the effects of a particular child-rearing style on personality is simply to interview the individual or his parents to find out how they were brought up and to investigate some areas of their personality. If many people with a particular personality were discovered to have been brought up in a way noticeably different from the upbringing of people with a different personality, this would suggest that a certain child-rearing style might have caused the particular aspect of personality in question. However, this method often relies on an individual's memory of how they were brought up, and as we all know, such memories may be distorted. When an individual is asked to look back on their childhood in this way it is called a 'retrospective' study.

'Longitudinal' studies try to overcome the problem of distorted memory by selecting a group of children and following their progress over a number of years. The child-rearing style is thus characterized at the time it is happening, for example by interview or observation; the personality of the child can also be viewed as it is developing.

Both retrospective and longitudinal studies present a problem, which can be exemplified if we study the relationship between physical punishment and aggressive behaviour. It has been found that many aggressive adults have been brought up by parents who used physical punishment as a form of discipline, while the parents of many less aggressive adults used far less physical punishment. There are three possible reasons for this:

1 That physical punishment in childhood causes the development of aggressive tendencies.
2 That children who are naturally aggressive frustrate their parents so much that they resort to physical punishment.
3 That some other variable, such as the degree of affection that the parents show to each other, causes both the use of physical punishment and the development of aggressive personality.

Although we often assume that 1 is the explanation of the relationship, we cannot be sure that the real reason is not 2 or 3. This is once more the problem of causation: simply establishing a relationship between two variables does not tell us which of these was the cause or, indeed, if either one really did cause the other.

The only way to overcome this problem would be to set up an experiment in which we randomly allocated children to parents who would bring them up in strictly defined ways. If we still found that children brought up with the frequent use of physical punishment were the most aggressive this would be strong evidence that the punishment caused the aggression: the random allocation of children would have ensured that any naturally aggressive children would not all have been treated by physical punishment, while factors such as parental relations would have been controlled by having different types of parents using similar methods of upbringing. Unfortunately this sort of research is of course, impossible to do: who would volunteer to be a subject? However, some experiments can be done on a smaller scale by treating children in different ways for short periods of time and observing the effects (see the study by K. Lewin, R. Lippitt and R. White on p. 214). In such experiments we can be sure exactly how the child was treated, whereas an interview with parents may give us information simply about how they think the child ought to be treated: theirs will be socially acceptable answers rather than a reliable account.

In addition, many researchers have done cross-cultural studies which investigate the differences in child-rearing styles between different peoples of the world. We shall now examine in turn some aspects of personality or behaviour, and the studies of their links with methods of upbringing.

Sex Role

In our culture many people expect boys and girls to behave differently; they expect boys to be more aggressive, competitive and independent than girls. The characteristic behaviour expected of the different sexes, as we have already seen on p. 173, is known as sex role. Many people in our society now argue that we ought to break down the sex roles and allow males and females to behave in the same way; others argue that 'boys will be boys' and that they naturally behave differently from girls. The studies of Margaret Mead suggest that, far from being uniform, there are many variations of the sex roles in different cultures, and that the behaviour we can expect from boys and girls depends largely on the way they are treated as children.

Mead studied three groups of people in New Guinea – the Arapesh who live on hillsides; the Mundugumor who live by the riverside; and the Tchambuli who are lakeside dwellers. She found the following differences in the ways in which they were brought up to fulfil the sex roles:

THE ARAPESH
Both males and females of this tribe are brought up to act in what our society might call a feminine way, and in adulthood are gentle, loving and cooperative.

THE MUNDUGUMOR
Both men and women are self-assertive, arrogant and fierce. They continually quarrel, and Mundugumor mothers have little to do with their children apart from teaching them to taunt their parents.

THE TCHAMBULI
Girls are encouraged to take an interest in the economic activity of the tribe whereas boys are not. The result of this style of child-rearing is that men's and women's roles might be seen as the reverse of our traditional roles, the women taking care of trading and food-gathering and the men – who are

considered sentimental and emotional and not capable of taking serious decisions – spending much of the day in artistic pursuits or gossiping.

Conscience

Some people appear to be able to perform the most horrible atrocities without the slightest pang of guilt; others are worried by their consciences at the smallest dishonesty.

In 1938 D.W. Mackinnon studied the degree to which individuals felt guilt, and later related this to the forms of discipline used by their parents. His participants were set a series of problems to solve, working by them-selves in a room that contained answer-books, some of which they were allowed to use and others which they were not. Unknown to the subjects, Mackinnon was able to see by means of a two-way mirror that 43 of his 93 subjects cheated.

A few weeks later Mackinnon asked the participants if they had cheated; 50 per cent of those who had cheated admitted that they had. He found that very few of the cheaters reported feeling guilt or, among the ones who had not confessed, that they would have felt guilty if they had cheated. Most of those who were not cheats said that they would have felt guilty and that they often felt guilt about things they had done or failed to do. In a later enquiry he asked people about their childhood. He found two major types of punishment used by parents – physical punishment, which involved such things as spanking or withdrawing of physical objects such as pocket money; and psychological punishment, which involved, for example, telling the child that they had disappointed their parents, or simply becoming less affectionate, looking sad and being quieter than usual. Mackinnon found that most people use both kinds of punishment but employ one more frequently than the other. Most of the children who cheated had parents who favoured physical punishment, while the parents of those with stronger consciences used psychological punishment. His results are shown in the following table, which gives the percentage of cheats and non-cheats raised by parents who used physical and psychological punishment respectively.

The Types of Punishment Most Used by Parents

	Physical %	Psychological %
Cheats	78	22
Non-cheats	48	52

Do Mackinnon's results mean that the use of psychological punishment will result in a strong conscience? Let us look at some of the problems:

1 He was dealing with recall of childhood experiences; we cannot be sure these were accurate.
2 Even if their recall were accurate it may be that the parents who used psychological punishments were different in other ways from those who used physical punishment and that it was these other differences which caused the children to develop greater or lesser strengths of conscience.
3 We could reverse what seem the cause and the effect: a particular type of punishment might not have caused a certain type of conscience, but instead the children who did not quickly show strong consciences might have exasperated their parents so much that they resorted to physical violence.

It is difficult to overcome the last two problems but the first was solved in a study in 1957 by R. Sears, E. Maccoby and H. Levin, who asked mothers about their children's present behaviour rather than requesting adults to recall their childhood experiences. They questioned mothers about the behaviour of their children in situations when they were naughty. Did they lie or admit it, and did they feel guilty? From the mother's replies they graded each child for strength of conscience. They also asked the mothers about the way they punished their children for being naughty. This study also showed that children who received physical punishment usually had weaker consciences than those who were punished by psychological means.

If the use of different types of punishment determines the degree to which a child develops conscience, it is important to establish why it should have this effect. Winfred Hill suggests that the techniques of physical and psychological punishment require different responses from the child in order to end the punishment: the psychological type is normally ended when the child has performed some form of symbolic renunciation of his bad behaviour – apologized, promised not to do it again, or promised to make recompense; the physical type generally lasts for a shorter time and requires no such response. Psychological punishment therefore both stops the behaviour of which the parent disapproves and leads the child to perform a gesture of remorse to remove the punishment, while physical punishment simply stops the unacceptable behaviour and may even evoke feelings of resentment without requiring any gesture of remorse. Hill suggests that any form of punishment could lead to strong conscience as long as it induced a symbolic act of renunciation.

The results of studies such as those by Sears and Mackinnon show that children with highly developed consciences usually have parents who make firm moral demands on their children; explain and give reasons for those demands; use psychological rather than physical forms of punishment; and are consistent in their discipline. Children with weak consciences usually have parents who give little explanation for any rules or punishments; use physical or verbally aggressive forms of punishment; are inconsistent in their discipline so that they may punish behaviour simply because they are in a bad mood; and show little affection to each other and the child.

Aggression

Parents differ in their attitudes towards displays of aggression in their children. Studies like that of John and Elizabeth Newson, a longitudinal study of over seven hundred children in Nottingham, show that most parents object to displays of aggression towards themselves, although lower-class parents usually encourage children to 'fight back' and 'stand up for themselves'. As we might expect, studies have shown that the more permissive a parent's attitude towards aggression is, the more aggression is shown by the child.

Sears, Maccoby and Levin showed that another important factor in aggressive behaviour was the extent to which children were punished for it. They studied six-year-old children and found that those who were most punished for aggression were almost as aggressive as the children whose parents were highly permissive; these particular children were usually punished by physical rather than psychological means. Why should a child who is often physically punished be so aggressive? There are several possible interpretations of this finding. First, the parent may provide a model for aggressive behaviour (see pp. 171–3): the child sees that when their parents become frustrated they hit out, and he may then decide to imitate them. Such punishment might succeed in preventing aggression towards the parent, which would only result in further punishment, but it might also teach the child that they can get what they want if they are aggressive towards others, such as weaker children who cannot hurt them. On the other hand, the child of a parent who uses psychological methods, distracting their attention from the object of aggression or simply telling them not to hit other people, has to learn to cope with frustration by means other than aggression. Secondly, some children may be naturally aggressive and frustrate their parents to such an extent that they have to resort to physical punishment – the causation problem again. The results of a study in 1961 by Bandura, Ross and Ross refute this second explanation. They interviewed the parents of hyper-aggressive boys and argued from their findings that parental rejection and punishment occur before the child shows aggressive tendencies; this suggests that parental behaviour causes a child's aggression rather than the other way round.

When Sears examined the development of the children of the Sears, Maccoby and Levin study six years later, he found that although the children of permissive parents were still aggressive, those of the parents who had used physical punishment to combat aggression were much less aggressive than they had been at the age of six. It seems that by the time the child is twelve, continual physical punishment has been successful in inhibiting violent tendencies; however, the children who had thus been made more peaceable often showed great anxiety about aggression.

Boys usually show more aggression than girls; this may be caused by differences in the way they are treated by their parents. In 1966 Rothbart and Maccoby tape-recorded the spontaneous behaviour of parents towards their children rather than using the more usual interview technique. They found that mothers were usually more permissive towards aggressive acts committed by sons than towards those committed by daughters; fathers tended to be more permissive with daughters. Since it is often the case that the mother spends more time with the child than the father, at least in the early years, these findings may give one explanation of why boys are often more aggressive than girls.

Independence

The new-born baby is a highly dependent creature. By the time we reach adulthood, however, most of us have developed a fair degree of independence; we can make our own designs and look after ourselves. People do differ, however, in the degree of independence they attain; many adults seem able to live and take decisions without the help of other people, but some adults find it almost impossible to do so. The degree of independence a child is allowed will depend on two related variables – the child's ability to accept independence and the parent's attitude towards allowing it. These factors interrelate because a child's ability to accept responsibility for their own actions increases to a certain extent with the opportunities they are given for doing so. It is likely to increase further with age and cognitive development. Parents also differ – in the extent to which they allow their children to choose their clothes, go out alone and make decisions such as how to spend their pocket money. They may find it difficult to allow a child independence because they doubt that the child can cope, and fear that he may hurt himself. Most parents gradually begin to encourage independence in matters such as dressing, washing and playing alone without constant supervision. However, some find it difficult to allow their children complete independence even when they reach maturity, because this means such a dramatic change in their own life-style, after fifteen or sixteen years of being responsible for another individual. The change can be a sign of them growing old or, in the case of those mothers with few other interests, of losing their function in life.

We might expect that if a mother praised her child for independent behaviour and punished the child for dependent behaviour, she would produce an independent child capable of making decisions without relying on others, while the child of a mother who consistently rewarded dependent behaviour and rarely encouraged independence would be likely to remain 'tied to mother's apron strings'. In 1957 Sears, Maccoby and Levin found that rewarding a child for dependency does not necessarily cause dependency; it only has this effect when dependent behaviour is also punished. They found that mothers of the most dependent children sometimes lost their tempers over dependent behaviour and sometimes reacted favourably to it; or they might show irritation when the children turned to them but would eventually give them the attention they required. An example of a situation likely to increase dependency is one where a child cannot decide what to do and so asks the mother; she at first reacts angrily, but when she sees that this causes an upset she sits down with the child to play a game. Perhaps the contrast between the punishment and the reward makes the reward seem greater to the child. The mother who sometimes rewards dependent behaviour and sometimes punishes it may therefore simply be giving the child a variable-ratio reinforcement for dependent behaviour; as we have discussed on p. 45, this teaches a response which is far less likely to be extinguished.

Different types of parent can be graded on a scale according to how much they encourage independent decision-making in their children:

Autocratic or Authoritarian	Democratic	Permissive	Laissez-faire
The parent makes all the decisions; the child has no say.	The parent encourages the child to discuss what he wants to do.	The parent allows the child a great deal of freedom of action.	The parent leaves the child to go his own way.

In 1963 G. Elder questioned adolescents about the extent to which their parents explained and gave reasons for any rules that they imposed. He found that democratic and permissive parents were more likely to do this than autocratic parents. He then asked the children questions to test their confidence in their own beliefs and actions, and to gauge their independence in terms of their willingness to solve personal difficulties rather than turn to others. Most confidence and independence was shown by the children of the democratic and the permissive parents, who frequently explained the reasons for their rules, whereas the least confident and independent individuals tended to have autocratic parents who did not give reasons. It may be that autocratic treatment undermines a child's confidence in their own powers of decision-making while democratic and permissive attitudes allow a child to practise making his own decisions and to succeed in doing so.

In 1938 K. Lewin, R. Lippitt and R. White performed an experiment to investigate the effects of autocratic, democratic and *laissez-faire* adult behaviour on groups of ten-year-old schoolboys attending after-school clubs. Each club was led by an adult who acted in either an autocratic, democratic or *laissez-faire* manner. The autocratic leaders told the boys what sort of models they were going to make and with whom they would work, while the democratic leaders discussed the various possibilities for projects and team-work with the boys and allowed them to make their own decisions. The autocratic leaders sometimes praised or blamed boys for their work, but unlike the democrats they did not explain their comments; for example, an autocrat might say 'Good boy, Johnny', while a democrat might say in the same situation 'It's very good the way you have managed to make your plane more realistic by including windows'. The democratic leaders joined in with group activities; the autocrats remained aloof from their groups, friendly but impersonal. The *laissez-faire* leaders of course left the boys to their own devices, only offering help when asked to do so – which was infrequent – and offering no praise or blame.

The psychologists found that the boys' behaviour and their attitudes to work differed according to the degree of independence allowed by their particular leaders.

THE AUTOCRATIC APPROACH

The boys became aggressive towards each other, or simply apathetic. They were submissive in their approaches to the leader, which were often made simply to gain attention. If he left the room the boys stopped work and became disruptive. When frustrated by a problem the boys would blame each other rather than cooperate to solve it.

THE DEMOCRATIC APPROACH

Relationships between the boys were much better than in the autocratic situations: they showed less aggression and liked each other more. Approaches to the leader were usually task-related rather than attention-seeking. Although slightly less work was done than with the autocrat, the boys did not stop working when the leader left the room, thus showing that they were more independent of the leader than were the groups with the autocrat. When frustrated by a problem the boys would cooperate to solve it.

THE LAISSEZ-FAIRE APPROACH

These groups were chaotic. The boys' relationships were aggressive although not as much as in the autocratic groups. Very little work was done whether the leader was there or not. These groups did not even do enough work to encounter problems related to the task; they simply gave up when the work became in the least way demanding.

Later the children were grouped differently, and the leaders were asked to adopt one of the other kinds of approach. The behaviour of the children was thus proved to depend on the style of leadership and not on the particular personalities involved.

The study of Lewin, Lippitt and White had examined the effect on boys of the behaviour of adults other than their parents when these children had already experienced ten years of parental treatment. Thus it must be remembered that the fact that most of the boys preferred democratic leadership may have been because their parents were mostly democratic, while some less independent boys who showed preferences for the autocratic style might equally have been reflecting their parents' style. This study nevertheless suggests the possible effects on children of these three types of leadership when put into practice by parents.

Achievement Motivation

Some people have a great need to succeed in everything they do while others show little interest in achieving anything; thus people are said to differ in the extent to which they display *achievement motivation*. In 1938 D.C. McClelland showed how the 'thematic apperception test' or TAT could be used to measure achievement motivation. The TAT consists of a series of pictures. A subject is asked to take each picture in turn and to write a story about it. Because different people will write different stories, it is argued that the differences will be reflections of individual personalities. A typical picture used to test achievement motivation might be that of a boy holding a violin and staring vacantly into space. The tester would look for such things as whether a story deals with getting on in school or a career, and whether it involves success; the more it involves these, the greater achievement motivation the individual is thought to have. McClelland argues that if two people have similar abilities but one has greater achievement motivation, then that one is more likely to do well.

In 1953 Marian Winterbottom measured the achievement motivation of children by asking them to tell a story which would expand short sentences given to them, such as 'Two children were running a race when one fell over.' She interviewed the mothers of children with high and low achievement-motivation scores. Each mother was asked 'At what age did you expect your child to know her way around the city; try new things for herself; succeed in competition; and make her own friends?' She found that the mothers of high scorers had expected these things of their children at an earlier age than the mothers of low scorers. The mothers of children with high achievement motivation usually rewarded the child with physical affection; the mothers of low scorers placed more restriction on their children, giving many instructions about where they could go, what they could do and with whom they were allowed to play.

A study by B. Rosen and R. D'Andrade in 1959 also showed a relationship between the expectations of parents and achievement motivation of their sons. With his parents watching, a child was blindfolded and asked to build a tower of building blocks with one hand. His parents were asked how well they thought he would do; it was found that the parents of those with high achievement motivation had higher expectations. Parents also differed in their behaviour while the boys built the towers. The most notable behaviour of parents of children with high achievement motivation was that the mothers tended to encourage their children and to show great pleasure when they succeeded in placing a block. The most notable parental behaviour towards the children with low achievement motivation was that the fathers tended to tell their children what to do and showed disapproval when they failed.

The results of studies like these suggest that the child with high achievement motivation will have been encouraged to be independent and to seek reward, while the child with low achievement motivation will have been told what to do and will simply attempt to avoid punishment.

General Styles or Specific Practices?

In the preceding sections we have discussed general styles of child-rearing – authoritarian, permissive and so on – rather than specific practices such as toilet-training or breast-feeding. Freud suggested that the way a parent approaches the potty-training of the child may have a lasting effect on the child's personality. Although excessive emphasis on training, and punishment for failure to learn, may lead to signs of anxiety and even to delay in successful training, there is no strong evidence to suggest an effect later in life.

John and Elizabeth Newson argue that the reason for the difficulty in correlating specific practices with later personality is that these practices 'are a good deal less important in the long term than the spirit in which they are carried out'. The study of general styles and philosophies of child-rearing is thus likely to be more productive.

In presenting the results of studies on child-rearing, one is in danger of giving the impression that there is a formula by which to bring up children to be as moral, peaceable, independent and motivated as a parent desires. This formula obviously does not exist; these studies can only scratch the surface of the variables which affect behaviour. Most of the studies we have presented in this chapter supply correlational evidence and thus suffer from the causation problem, despite the convincing pronouncements of the psychologists involved.

We must also beware of accepting at face value the results of interviews with parents and children; there is always the possibility that some of them simply tell us what we want to hear rather than describing how they actually behave. Only when we find that the results of independent studies which involve interviews with children, such as Mackinnon's, give similar answers to studies involving interviews with parents, such as those of Sears, Maccoby and Levin, will this give us more confidence in the findings.

Despite such problems these studies do give us some useful insights into the social development of the child.

Summary

1 The relationship between child-rearing style and personality has been studied by retrospective, longitudinal and experimental methods.
2 Major problems include:
  (a) Memory problems.
  (b) The causation problem.
  (c) The problem that parents may be biased to give us 'socially acceptable' responses to our questions about the way they rear their children.
3 Mead showed that sex roles differ according to the ways boys and girls are treated in different cultures.
4 The studies of Mackinnon and of Sears, Maccoby and Levin suggest that strong conscience is a result of:
  (a) Firm moral demands on children.
  (b) Explanation of those demands.
  (c) The use of consistent psychological punishment.
  (d) An affectionate family relationship.
5 Sears, Maccoby and Levin showed that aggressive personality increases with parental permissiveness and the use of physical punishment.
6 Parents differ in the degree of independence they allow to their children. The most dependent children usually have parents who both punish and reward dependence.
7 Different types of parent can be graded on a scale according to how much they encourage independent decision-making in their child. The scale ranges from the autocratic parent, who makes all the decisions, to the democratic and the permissive parent, and finally to the *laissez-faire* parent who takes no responsibility for the child. Lewin, Lippitt and White showed that children were more likely to work on their own if in the charge of a democratic leader rather than an autocratic one; other differences in this situation included less aggression and greater willingness to cooperate.
8 Winterbottom demonstrated that the level of achievement motivation is highest in children whose parents expect earlier independence. Rosen and

D'Andrade found higher expectation and more encouragement in parents of those boys with high achievement motivation.

9 The studies of general styles of rearing – authoritarian, democratic and permissive – appear to be more productive than those on specific practices, such as toilet-training, in their contribution to our understanding of the development of adult personality.

Further Reading

Bee, H., *Growing Child (An Applied Approach)* (1998, Collins).

Chapter 12

Non-Verbal Communication (NVC)

Human *communication* occurs whenever a piece of information passes from one person to another, whether the message is intentional or not. It was noted in chapter 5 that Bruner argues that linguistic communication acts as an accelerator for intellectual development (see p. 99); without communication much human behaviour would be very different.

Verbal communication – speaking and writing – is a very efficient form of communication which allows the transmission of complex information from one person to another. While talking, however, people also communicate on a non-verbal level through posture, facial expression and gestures; communication without some of these ancillaries – as happens in a telephone conversation – may create many difficulties of interpretation and understanding. The basic difference between *verbal* and *non-verbal* communication is that the former makes use of language, using letters, words and sentences in both spoken and written form, whereas the latter does not. Apart from this difference, the two forms of communication differ in their capacity for ambiguity and in the extent to which they are voluntary. Usually individuals make their speech clear and unambiguous, although they sometimes use ambiguity for special effect, as in jokes, for example. With NVC, signals are less clear: a particular facial expression might signal either agony or ecstasy. We should assume from studying a photograph of adoring fans at a pop concert that they were in ecstasy because we should know about the situation they were in, but if we were told that they were at a funeral, the same facial expressions might successfully convey a totally different message. NVC must be interpreted in the context of the situation and the combination of all signals from the face and hands, body position and so on, to avoid this ambiguity. On the whole our verbal communication is voluntary; we say what we want to and refrain from saying things we want to hide. Perhaps because we attach so much importance to verbal communication we often give non-verbal signals without realizing it. The student who glances at his watch and yawns during a lesson would probably not say to his teacher that he wishes the lesson would end, but he might well convey the message all the same by unthinkingly using this set of non-verbal signals.

Animals have no known language and hence do not use verbal communication, but they are able to communicate in a non-verbal manner by employing smell, touch, sight and hearing; in humans a great amount of communication occurs on a verbal level but we have not lost our ability to use non-verbal communication, which performs a number of functions. Amongst these, it may replace speech; signal attitudes towards others; signal emotion; and aid verbal communication. Note that non-verbal signals may fulfil any of the above functions at a given time.

Michael Argyle (1967) sees social interaction in all its forms as a learnt skill. It requires the ability not only to send out messages to other people but also to discover from them how these messages are being received; in other words it requires *feedback*. Thus if A and B are in conversation and A is talking, he is at the same time on the lookout for feedback from B that indicates such things as agreement, understanding, interest and the wish to start talking himself. These signals may take a verbal form: B may say 'Yes, I agree' or 'Let me get a word in', but many of them will be non-verbal – head-nodding, looking at A, smiling and so on. To most of us, these non-verbal signals are so well learnt in childhood that we do not even notice that we are using them. They only become noticeable when something goes wrong; for example, if an individual is from a different culture which has different signals, or if someone has had a socially isolated childhood.

Figure 12.1. Interaction as a Social Skill

A may alter his behaviour as a result of feedback

B listens and gives feedback, either verbal or non-verbal

A

B

A talks

Methods of Study

The main method of studying NVC has been simple observation, watching people as they interact. When people know they are being watched they often become self-conscious and do not behave as they would normally. To overcome this difficulty many studies have used two-way mirrors so that the researcher can observe without being observed. Increasingly, researchers are using video to record the interactions of their participants. This has the great advantage that it can be viewed and re-viewed, slowed down and speeded up, to observe elements of behaviour that might be missed within the limitations of a single, normal-speed viewing.

Sometimes people are asked to behave in certain ways in order to study the effect on others; for example, increasing or decreasing the number of times a listener nods their head, to assess the effect on the length of time for which someone talks. Other studies have used a role-play procedure. A. Mehrabian (1968) instructed participants to talk to a hat-stand as if it were a particular type of person and found that when talking to 'people' supposed to be of higher status they raised their heads.

NVC as a Replacement for Speech

It is important here to distinguish between NVC and some forms of verbal communication that do not use the spoken word. Semaphore is not NVC: because it signals letters, words and sentences it is a form of verbal communication. Communication simply has to use language in some form to be verbal; a book or an essay therefore counts as verbal communication. NVC does not make use of the letters of the alphabet; it signals meaning without spelling words.

NVC can replace verbal communication when the latter is not possible, for example because of distance or noise. The single finger placed vertically over the lips does not require the verbal command 'Be quiet'. We all know how to signal 'Come over here' without using any words. In a car it is not possible to shout to other drivers that we are turning right or left and so we use hand signals or flashing lights.

The meaning of a signal may vary from culture to culture; for example to stick out the tongue, which in Britain is often regarded as an insult, in China is an expression of apology or surprise; in Tibet it is a sign of re-spect; and on the Marquesan Islands it means 'no'.

NVC to Signal Attitudes towards Others

An example of the way in which many signals combine to form a communi-cation is the signalling of friendship and intimacy. Argyle argues that the degree of intimacy is signalled by at least four factors – proximity; eye-contact; smiling; and personal topics of conversation. Young lovers in conversation will stand very close, perhaps even touching, look into each other's eyes a lot, smile, and talk about personal things. Two people who are relative strangers will stand further apart and make less eye contact; their topic of conversation is more likely to be the weather or some other impersonal subject. More intimacy is indicated by an increase in all four factors. However, sometimes external events may cause only one factor to change; for example, in a crowded London tube-train people's proximity increases and yet they are perfect strangers. They must therefore avoid signalling a degree of intimacy which is not there, and do so by decreasing the amount of eye contact that they have with other people. On a crowded tube the best way to do this is by looking up towards the ceiling – hence the location of advertisements on the tube.

If somebody gives inappropriate signals about intimacy this can be very embarrassing; people who have not learnt the 'rules' of NVC and stand too close or make too much eye-contact with others may find it difficult to make friends for this reason. Argyle argues that many people may be lonely or have social problems because for some reason they have inadequately learnt the language of NVC. These people may be helped by training.

Although in our culture proximity signals intimacy, it is common in parts of Africa and Asia for people in conversation to stand much closer together, even touching each other. When people from different cultures meet they have to cope with these differences.

The pupils of the eyes dilate when we feel happy or when we like something or someone. In 1963 E.H. Hess found that men preferred pictures of girls with dilated pupils to identical pictures in which their pupils were not dilated, even when the men could not say what the difference between the photographs was. This may be because we like people who signal they like us.

How much a listener looks at whoever is addressing them indicates the extent of their interest in what they are hearing; this can influence the amount of talking that the other person does. It is difficult to talk to someone who refuses to look at you. A student once reported that during his school life he had stopped talking to his teachers after class because they would talk to him endlessly. He found, however, that his friends did not have the same problem and he could not understand why. Apparently the reason was that this student continued to look at his teachers while in conversation, which was interpreted as the normal signal to continue. It is actually quite difficult to stop talking while somebody does this. Once his problem was discovered this particular student became adept at stopping conversation by lowering his gaze and looking away.

The type of interest – for example, whether we like or dislike the person – is signalled by facial expression, which can also indicate our emotional state, as described below.

NVC to Signal Emotion

I. Eibl-Eibesfeldt argues that many of the facial expressions characteristic of states of emotion such as anger, sadness and happiness are innate and do not need to be learnt, because children who are both blind and deaf show basically the same facial patterns of laughing, smiling, crying and sulking as do normal children. The top half of the face around the eyes and eyebrows seems particularly important in signalling emotions: the eyebrows are raised in surprise; the brow is furrowed when we are worried.

Facial expression alone is often not enough to give a precise understanding of which emotion is being felt; we need to know more about the context in which the expression is being given. It is for this reason that participants in experiments often make as many as 40 per cent errors when asked to judge the emotions expressed by faces in photographs. However, H. Schlosberg (1952) showed that people were unlikely to mistake contempt for fear, disgust for surprise, or happiness for anger; they were much more likely to mistake disgust for contempt, happiness for surprise, and fear for anger.

S. Kasl and G. Mahl (1965) have examined the non-verbal aspects of speech itself – not what is being said but the messages that can be understood from how it is being said. As well as signalling such things as class, sex, age, and place of origin, we can also express emotions such as anxiety by the way in which we speak. Errors in speech can also be significant: Kasl and Mahl distinguished between 'ah' errors, when the speaker inserts an 'er', 'ah', or 'um' into the sentence, and 'non-ah' errors which involve repetition, stuttering and slips of the tongue. 'Ah' errors occur more when a speaker is talking on a subject that they find difficult; it is as though they give time to think. 'Non-ah' errors increase with anxiety and can therefore communicate it. We have a fair degree of voluntary control over the muscles of the face and can use it to disguise our feelings, but we seem to be far less successful in concealing our emotions by control of our voice and hands.

NVC as an Aid to Verbal Communication

It was noted earlier in this chapter that when talking on the telephone we emit certain sounds to show that we are still listening, but in face-to-face conversation we are also able to do this by using such signals as head-nods and eye-gaze. In 1967 A. Kendon filmed people in conversation and established different patterns of eye contact in speakers and listeners. The listener spends more time looking at their partner than does the speaker, who starts by looking away from the listener, glancing up from time to time and looking back at the listener at the end of the utterance. Head-nodding and smiling on the part of the listener act as reinforcers because, as we have seen, they increase the length of a speaker's utterances. When the speaker glances up at their partner they not only receive messages to stop or go on but also information which tells him how to continue; a facial expression of doubt, disbelief or boredom is likely to prompt a different response from that prompted by agreement or interest. When speaking on a difficult subject a person looks up less, probably because they need to attend more to the subject than to its effect on the listener. During these conversations Kendon observed that listeners often mirror the gestures and facial expressions of speakers.

The end of an utterance is often signalled by a change in the positions of the speaker and listener. The power of this gesture as a form of communication can be illustrated by the case of Clever Hans, an 'intelligent' circus horse who appeared to be able to solve arithmetical problems. If Hans was asked to give the answer to the problem 'two plus two' he would strike the ground four times with his hoof. Hans could solve an amazing range of such problems and many believed that he could really think mathematically, but in 1911 A. Pfungst showed that if the questioner hid from Hans's view the horse would go on striking the ground even after he had reached the correct answer. The horse had learnt to stop 'counting' when his questioner made the slight change in posture that we all make when we have received the desired answer and believe that a communication has ended.

In 1967 P. Ekman and W. Friesen argued that cultures and classes differ in the signals they use to accompany conversations; other people may appear rude or difficult to talk to simply for this reason. In emphasizing points in their verbal conversations, the Italians use arm gestures far more than do the British. Because Arabs stand much closer – often touching – during conversation, they can make use of changes in position and pressure of touch more effectively than can the British or Germans who stand further apart. Although we do not have a precise translation for NVC, many teachers of language see the need to teach both verbal and non-verbal aspects of communication to their students. Gestures such as head-nodding or head-shaking often accompany the words 'yes' or 'no', but even this is not universal. Visitors to Greece may very well have problems, since when Greeks says 'no' they raise their head in a way that the British could mistake for a 'yes' signal, especially since the Greek word for no, 'ochi', sounds like 'OK'.

Summary

1 For successful social interaction individuals need feedback about the effects they are having on others. This feedback may take the form of verbal or non-verbal communication.

2 Although some facial expressions of emotion may be innate, much of NVC is learnt. Differences in NVC shown by people of different cultures or

those who have not learnt adequate non-verbal skills may cause difficulties and embarrassment in interaction.

3 NVC may replace speech, signal interpersonal attitudes, express emotion or simply aid verbal communication – functions which are not mutually exclusive.

4 NVC may be correctly understood only in the total context of the situation. Signals such as those for intimacy can be understood only by attention to a combination of characteristics of behaviour.

5 We signal, receive and understand many forms of NVC without being consciously aware of it.

Chapter 13

Emotion, Arousal and Stress

Psychologists have a great deal of difficulty in defining emotions because they are such subjective feelings and have instead preferred to try to establish the types of events which occur in emotional situations.

Arnold (1960) suggests that the sequence goes as follows:

Perception. We perceive something and assess whether it is harmful or helpful.

Experience. We experience a feeling of emotion.

Physiology. Bodily changes occur; for example, increased heart rate, faster breathing (the fight or flight response).

Behaviour. Our facial expression and body posture may change and we may move away or towards different things.

Measuring Emotion

Each of these events can to some extent be measured. In order to study the 'perception' element above, individuals could be asked to view a series of pictures or videos and to report (called a 'self-report') to the experimenter either orally or in writing, the extent to which they see the various stimuli as being pleasant or unpleasant. Self-reports can also be used to investigate the type and strength of emotions felt by people in a particular situation. Physiological changes, particularly arousal, can be measured by several techniques – the Galvanic Skin Response (GSR) (see p. 303) pulse and respiration rates, blood pressure and voice stress analysis, where tightening of the vocal cords as a result of arousal can be measured by computer analysis of voice recordings. All of these physiological measurement techniques can be taken together with a 'polygraph', which is used as a 'lie detector' in the USA, for example. The behavioural part of emotion can be measured by taking still or video pictures of facial expressions, body postures or physical activity in emotional situations.

All of these measures have problems associated with them which affect their accuracy. Self-reports have an obvious flaw. We cannot be sure that the person given the report is telling the truth about what they really think or are experiencing, either because they do not want to reveal it or are unable to find the correct words to do so.

Physiological measurements of arousal can be made inaccurate if the individual has recently been exercising, or if the room is too hot, or if they are engaged in a task which interests them (all of these lead to increases in arousal, independent of any emotions being felt). In addition, measurement of arousal by different physiological techniques do not often agree highly with each other. For example, a person's arousal might appear to be high when measured by the GSR, but only medium when measured by the increase in heart rate. It is also worth noting that those physiological measurements really only tell us about levels of arousal. It is extremely difficult, if not impossible, to tell by physiological measurements alone exactly which type of emotion a person is feeling.

Facial expressions are largely controllable. Because a person's face seems to be signalling fear, we cannot be certain that they are actually feeling it. In Japan, for example, expressions of anger, sadness or grief in public are thought to be bad manners; people are taught to smile or laugh to hide their anger or sadness when in public. Michael Argyle (1967) found that emotional expression through the face and through general behaviour was encouraged for women more than for men and encouraged in Mediterranean communities more than in Northern European countries. So the type and degree of emotion displayed by a person may be greatly influenced by their country of upbringing or their gender.

Despite the lack of a generally accepted definition of what emotion is, most psychologists agree that the psychological feeling of emotion results from the brain combining two sorts of information.

The Work of Schachter and Singer

There are many types of emotion: happiness, sadness, joy, love, hate, anger, fear, anxiety, etc., and each of these can be experienced in a range of different intensities from mild to extreme. They can be categorized as positive (for example, happiness, joy, love), or negative (for example, hate, anger, fear). Most people actively seek positive emotional feelings and attempt to avoid the negative ones.

There are a number of studies which suggest that there are two separate components to each emotion that we feel.

The psychological feeling of emotion results from the brain combining two sorts of information:

1 Information from the senses about what is going on around you. This combined with memories about what happened in similar situations in

the past helps to decide which *type* of emotion will be felt. This is often known as the *cognitive processing*.

2 Information from the body concerning its general level of arousal (is the heart beating quickly, is the liver releasing sugar into the blood, are the blood vessels to the voluntary muscles dilated?). This information is used to determine the *level* of the emotion. If the body is highly aroused we will feel *very* emotional, if it is at a moderate level of arousal we will feel only *slight* emotion. General arousal is controlled by the level of activity of the autonomic nervous system (see p. 302), and can vary from very low, when the body is relaxed and dozy, through to the high arousal of extreme emotion when the sympathetic section of the autonomic nervous system puts the body into the fight-or-flight response (see p. 302).

Although our actual experience of emotion doesn't feel like two separate processes, Hohmann's (1966) study of Vietnam War casualties backs up the idea that the unified feeling that we get usually results from a combination of two types of nervous activity.

Figure 13.1. How We Feel Emotions (Schachter and Singer's Model)

Hohmann interviewed casualties who had spinal injuries which severely limited the amount of information that their brains received about the general state of arousal of the body. He found that although these patients could still feel angry or sad or happy, they did not feel their emotions to the same extent as before their injury. The patients reported that their emotions lacked the intensity that they had previously had. Before the injury the brain had apparently combined a decision about what emotion to feel with information from the body about general arousal, to give the resulting emotional state. After the injury the brain still knew what emotion to feel, but not how much of it.

A study by Schachter and Singer in 1962 backs up the idea that the decision about the *type* of emotion felt depends upon cognitive processes (see point 1 above). They injected people with adrenalin which activates the autonomic nervous system and produced the same physiological changes that normally accompany emotion. They found that the increased heart-rate, flushed face and trembling hands caused by the adrenalin were interpreted in different ways depending upon the information available. Some participants were told that they had been injected with a vitamin compound. Each was then put into a room with another person who was actually a confederate of the experimenter and was scripted to act in either a happy or an angry fashion. He was known as the 'stooge'. Schachter and Singer found that participants accompanied by a happy stooge interpreted their bodily changes as an emotion of happiness, whereas those accompanied by an angry stooge felt angry. Another group was informed of the physiological side-effects of the drug; these participants were not affected by the behaviour of the stooges.

A control group was injected with a *placebo* (simple saline solution which has no effect on arousal). This group showed slight emotional change, but not as great as the incorrectly informed adrenalin subjects.

The results from Schachter and Singer's experiment can be interpreted as follows:

Those injected with adrenalin but not informed of its effects. These people experienced general bodily arousal for no obvious reason. They therefore needed to search for more information, since nothing else was available they looked to other people in the same situation and conformed with them. This conformity in situations that are unclear is a well-known phenomenon (see p. 115).

Those injected with adrenalin and informed of effects. These people experienced general bodily arousal but were able to put this down to the effect of the drug and so no further search for information was needed.

Those injected with saline solution. These people experienced no general arousal and showed only slight emotion. This shows that although the influence of the stooge subject alone was enough to alter emotions, physiological arousal is necessary for a strong effect.

Schachter and Singer were among the first people to put forward the theory that cognitive factors are important in determining the type of emotion, and that general bodily arousal determines the strength of the emotion. This view is now widely accepted, but it must be noted that their original experiment has been criticized on a number of grounds:

1 Other researchers have had difficulty replicating Schachter and Singer's results.
2 In each condition there were a number of people whose results were different to that expected by the theory.
3 Schachter and Singer did not check the moods of their participants *before* the experiment.
4 Schachter and Singer used two measures of emotion. The first was a self-report in which the participants answered a questionnaire which asked them to rate their emotions on a four-point scale. The second was an activity-rating which was produced by observers who awarded points for each piece of emotionally-related behaviour. In the anger condition both measures of emotion showed that the uninformed group were most emotional, but in the 'happy' condition only the activity ratings showed the expected differences. In this condition there was no significant difference between the self-ratings of the uninformed and placebo groups.

The final criticism above reflects a general problem with research in the field of emotion. The psychological experience of emotion as measured by questionnaire does not necessarily correlate with other measures of emotion. Some studies have measured emotion by taking physiological measures of things such as pulse-rate and levels of adrenalin, but Schachter's study shows that this may not always tell us anything about the type of emotion being felt. Observer ratings of people's emotions are hampered by the fact that some people hide their emotions more than others, and in many situations people prefer to *look* calm even though they don't feel it.

What Causes Arousal and Why Are Some People More Emotional Than Others?

Mandler has pointed out that emotions occur when something unexpected happens, or when we are blocked in achieving a particular goal; he calls this *interruption theory*. Interruptions of this nature cause arousal, which results in an emotional experience. Some people's autonomic nervous systems are more responsive to interruption. The ease with which these people can be aroused means that they can show extreme changes of emotion; one moment they are happy and excited, the next they are depressed or angry, as the situation changes and thereby causes a new interpretation of the type of emotion linked with the underlying arousal. Mandler points out that athletes often show extreme emotional reactions to news given to them immediately after a race. The emotion can be positive or negative depending on the nature of the news, but it is extreme because general arousal is high as a result of running the race.

Arousal is affected by the general level of stimulation around us; we become bored and dozy when 'nothing is going on', and studies which pay people well for doing absolutely nothing in conditions where there is very little to watch or listen to, show that most people cannot stand this for more than a short period. Mandler argues that we are motivated to achieve what he calls *autonomic jags* – that is, increases in general arousal – and that this is one factor which causes us to change from one activity to another. Most of us can receive our autonomic jags from everyday social interactions, but some people have very unresponsive autonomic nervous systems which can only be 'jagged' when they put themselves into positions of extreme danger. These people appear to be very calm and in control of their emotions; nothing seems to upset them, but they may perform acts of great cruelty simply to receive the same level of autonomic jag that is available to the rest of us much more easily. These people, sometimes known as *psychopaths* or *sociopaths*, appear to experience no guilt for their actions, which can be explained by the fact that in order to feel this emotion with any intensity, a state of general arousal is required.

Historical Theories of Emotion

Throughout this century psychologists interested in emotions have argued about the role of the autonomic nervous system (ANS), and it is only in the last twenty-five years or so that there has been a general level of agreement. The idea that the ANS is in some way responsible for the feeling of emotion was first put forward by W. James and C. Lange at the turn of the century, but they overstated the case by arguing that interpretation of bodily arousal was the *only* factor determining emotion.

Sherrington (1906) produced experimental findings that contradicted the James-Lange theory. He showed that dogs could display emotions such as fear, anger and joy, even when he had operated on them to cut the nerves which pass information to the brain from the viscera (gut, liver, etc.) and most of the skeletal muscles. These dogs showed the same facial expressions as normal dogs in conditions that usually evoke anger. The fact that the dogs performed all the behaviours normally associated with emotions (such as attack when angered) led Sherrington to conclude that the dogs actually felt the emotion in the same way as normal dogs, and that they were not simply giving the facial expression without experiencing the emotion. Sherrington did not, however, cut all the nerves from the body and this may explain why his dogs still showed full-scale emotion. On p. 228 we discussed the effects of damage to the nerves passing information from the body to the brain in human subjects. Unlike Sherrington's dogs, Hohmann's patients with high spinal injuries did not display emotions to the same extent as people without such damage.

If the James-Lange theory were correct, each separate emotion would have to result from a different combination of bodily changes. Physiological investigations at the time were unable to differentiate between the states of the body in different emotions. Even now there are very few studies which show differences in the physiology of the different types of emotion. One study that does, however, is that of Ax (1953).

Figure 13.2. The James–Lange Theory of Emotion

Ax found some physiological differences between the emotions of fear and anger. He induced fear or anger in his participants and measured the changes that occurred. One problem in this sort of research is finding a way to get your participants into the right emotional state. Ax did this by acting in two different ways while he attached his participants to the measuring apparatus. In the fear condition he 'accidentally' gave his participant a small electric shock, became alarmed and hinted that the apparatus might be dangerous. In the anger condition he was rude to the participant and continually grumbled and handled him roughly.

Ax found that the pattern of physiological changes which occurred during the emotion of fear was similar to that produced by injections of noradrenalin, but the changes associated with anxiety were like those resulting from an injection of adrenalin *and* noradrenalin (both adrenalin and noradrenalin are transmitter substances which affect the firing of nerves – see p. 297).

W. Cannon, the man who coined the term 'fight-or-flight response', put forward an alternative theory which states that autonomic activity has no role to play in the feeling of emotion. He argued that the body changes that occur during strong emotion are vital to ensure that the individual can cope with the situation, but that the feeling of emotion is simply a result of the brain's interpretation of what is going on in the environment.

If Cannon was right, however, then spine-damaged patients would feel emotion in the same way as the rest of us, rather than losing the intensity of the experience as Hohmann showed.

Today's theories recognize the role of the ANS, both in the determination of the feeling of emotion and in the extent to which it is responsible for ensuring the body's capacity to react to threatening situations. In a way, present ideas are a modification of the James–Lange theory, in that they recognize the role of arousal in the degree to which emotion is felt, but combine this with an interpretation of both internal and external factors made by the brain to determine the type of emotion felt.

Figure 13.3. Cannon's Theory of Emotion

Emotion-producing stimulus

Interpretation of the stimulus by the brain causes feeling of emotion

Stimulation of the autonomic nervous system causes bodily changes

The Effects of General Arousal

As Cannon said, the state of the body during the fight-or-flight syndrome (increased heart-rate, sugar being released from the liver, more blood available to the limb muscles, etc.) helps us to cope with physical danger. It may be that the evolution of the autonomic nervous system has lagged behind social evolution, in that it is hard to see how some of these bodily reactions to stress help us to cope with such 'dangers' as job interviews or exams. The increase in blood-flow to the brain is likely to be useful in these instances, as indeed may be a general arousal of the cortex. The general arousal of the cortex is analogous to the effect of heat on a car engine: when it is very cold or boiling over, an engine does not work very well, but at intermediate temperatures it is fine. The cortex is most efficient at an intermediate level of arousal; at low levels of arousal the individual is sleepy, and high levels indicate over-excitement or high tension. This arousal can be affected by environmental stimulation and by what Mandler called 'interruptions', which were discussed earlier.

People who suffer from 'exam nerves' often find that they are so aroused in an examination that they cannot think of anything relevant to the questions; yet later on, when the exam is over and they have calmed down, it all comes flooding back. Those who don't suffer so badly find that, although they have difficulty at first, they are able to jot down well-learned pieces of information first and this makes them calm down, allowing the remembrance of more difficult information. Although high levels of arousal can lead to poor performance in exams, a medium level of anxiety probably results in a better level of performance than none at all.

A similar relationship between arousal and performance can also be seen with physical skills such as driving a car. Accidents are more likely when a driver is drowsy or in a state of heightened emotion rather than at a medium level of arousal.

The rule governing the relationship between arousal and performance on a task is known as the Yerkes–Dodson Law, which states that medium levels of arousal produce the best performance and that, for a complicated task, performance levels drop quickly if arousal either increases or decreases; simple tasks are only disturbed by extremely low or high levels of arousal (see figure 13.4).

Figure 13.4. The Yerkes–Dodson Law

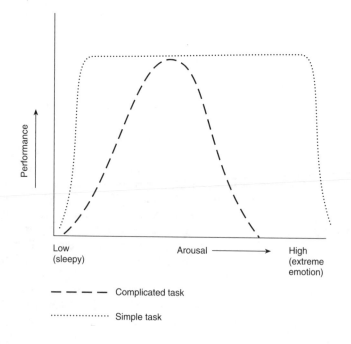

Of course, whether a task is simple or complicated depends very much on the individual concerned; a learner might find driving complicated, whereas this task is simple for an experienced driver. The same is true in exams: the person who learnt the material well in advance and has become familiar with it may be performing a 'simple' task as far as the Yerkes–Dodson Law is concerned, and will be relatively less affected by exam nerves. Someone with the same level of exam nerves who only learnt the material recently is likely to give a poorer performance.

The precise level of arousal that produces the best performance depends on the type of task as well as on its complexity. Optimum levels of arousal for physical tasks may be higher than those for mental tasks.

Stress

While everybody has felt stress at some time and researchers recognize its potential for harmful effects on people's physiological and psychological health, there is as yet no generally accepted definition of it. Instead, researchers have tried to identify and explain the main processes involved when we say we feel stressed.

Early explanations were based on engineering principles – a piece of metal would eventually break if enough external force were applied to it. This approach assumed that, in humans, stress is caused by the actions of external stimuli, or stressors. A development of this idea by Selye introduced the idea that external stressors affected the body's physiology. But, as in the section earlier on theories of emotion, most psychologists now think of stress as being the result not just of external stimuli or physiology but of an interaction between both of them with cognitive factors.

Cox (1975) proposed the transactional model of stress, in which he pointed out the relationships between external stimuli, our perception of them (and of our own ability to cope with them) and physiological changes. Cox believed that stress occurs when a person perceives that the demands of a situation (the extent of which it is likely to cause us harm) are greater than the person's perception of their ability to cope with the situation.

The physiological changes which occur in response to stress were termed the 'fight–or–flight syndrome' by Cannon. Selye (1979) called it the *alarm reaction*. Selye was interested in what happens if the stress continues for longer than the initial alarm reaction. Experimenting with laboratory rats, Selye found that there were three stages of physiological reaction, together called the *general adaptation syndrome*:

1 *Alarm reaction*. This comprises two events. First there is a shock phase where blood pressure, body temperature and muscle tension all decrease for a few seconds. Next comes the countershock phase, the fight-or-flight response, when the body's resistance to stress is at its highest. However, the body cannot resist stress indefinitely, which leads to the second stage.

Table 13.1. Possible Sequence of Events in the Perception of Stress

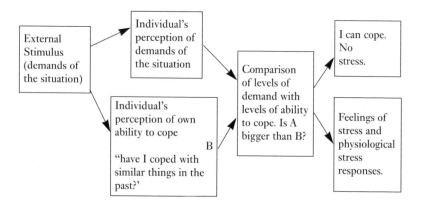

2 *Resistance*. If the stressor continues for a few days, the physiological changes which occurred during the alarm reaction seem to disappear. If however the stressor continues for longer than a few days (and especially if a new stressor is introduced), the animal enters the last stage.

3 *Exhaustion*. The animal can no longer resist and there is a breakdown of physiological functions. During this stage the adrenal glands become damaged, the immune system's efficiency is reduced, and stomach ulcers develop. Physiological breakdown can be so severe as to lead to the animal's death.

Brady (1958) showed that stress could lead to the development of stomach ulcers in monkeys, which are physiologically more similar to humans than are rats. Pairs of monkeys were tested together, one monkey acting as the 'executive' and the other as the control. The executive monkey's task was to press a lever at least once every 20 seconds. If it failed to do so, both it and the control monkey received electric shocks. Brady believed that the extra responsibilities of the executive monkeys would cause them to suffer more stress than the controls. This belief was confirmed – he found that the majority of the executive monkeys developed stomach ulcers, whereas the control monkeys did not. It later became apparent that Brady had selected the most active monkeys to be executives, so it could be that it was the higher levels of activity rather than the additional stress, which led to ulcer formation.

Friedman and Rosenman (1974) became interested in the possibility that some people are more prone to suffer illness through stress than others, and that certain patterns of typical behaviour could act as indicators to future illness. They investigated the typical behaviour patterns of people suffering from coronary heart disease and found consistent types of behaviours kept appearing. These are called *Type A* behaviour patterns.

Typical Type A Behaviours
Some typical Type A behaviours are:

- Thinking of or doing two things at once.
- Hurrying the speech of others.
- Becoming unduly irritated when forced to wait in line or when driving behind a car you think is moving too slowly.
- Frequent knee jiggling or rapid tapping of your fingers.
- Explosive speech patterns or frequent use of obscenities.
- Becoming impatient while watching others do things you think you can do better or faster.

People who did not behave like this were said to be showing Type B behaviour. According to an 8½ year study of 3,000 men by Rosenman (1975) Type A men were 2½ times more likely to have a heart attack than were Type B men.

It may be that people can be taught to overcome their Type A behaviour (and hence lessen their chances of having a heart attack) to some extent. Gill (1985) taught an experimental group of middle aged American military officers to reduce their Type A behaviours (for example, by practising relaxation when standing in queues). After 4½ years, the heart attack rate amongst the experimental group was only half that of the control group who also showed Type A behaviour but who had had no training. This study also showed that the Type A behaviours most strongly associated with heart problems were those involving aggression or hostility (for example, 'explosive speech patterns …', 'becoming impatient whilst watching others …', 'becoming unduly irritated when forced to wait in line …').

There is some evidence that stress can affect humans' immune systems. Jemmott (1985) found that, in students taking examinations, the levels of a particular antibody which defended against respiratory infections was lowered. However, successful coping with stress may actually strengthen parts of the immune system. Jemmott and Locke (1985) found that people suffering long-term stress but coping well with it, showed much higher levels of natural killer cells (which help to prevent tumours from growing) than did people suffering from similar levels of stress but who showed high levels of anxiety and depression.

Psychological Reactions to Stress

The main reactions are anxiety/fear, anger/aggression and depression. (Psychologists find it difficult to define how fear and anxiety differ, so the two terms are used interchangeably. The same is true for anger and aggression. We shall use 'anxiety' and 'aggression' as shorthand.)

Anxiety is a normal helpful reaction to situations which we interpret as threatening; sometimes, however, anxiety can reach such high levels that it prevents us from coping with situations. If we accept Cox's transactional model, different people will interpret the same stimulus in different ways.

This agrees with Freud's personality theory (see pp. 178–83). Freud believed that unconscious conflicts between the Id and the Superego (where the Superego is attempting to prevent unpleasant or unacceptable urges from the Id becoming conscious) lead to anxiety. So a person who has strong Id–Superego conflict will be more likely to interpret a situation as threatening than someone with a weaker conflict.

In chapter 3 we discussed the development and treatment of the irrational fears known as phobias. One of the earliest behaviourists, John Watson, felt that most of our emotions were developed by Classical Conditioning based on a few reflex emotions to painful or pleasant experiences (see pp. 35–41 for a discussion of Classical Conditioning). To demonstrate this idea, Watson and Rayner (1920) conditioned an emotional response in a young child who is often known as 'little Albert'.

They first tested Albert's emotional reactions at the age of nine months. They found that Albert showed no fear to a range of stimuli which included a white rat; he did, however, start crying and showing other fear reactions when Watson made a sudden loud noise by banging a steel bar with a hammer.

When Albert was eleven months old Watson and Rayner paired the white rat with the loud noise of the hammer on the steel bar. After a number of pairings, which were spread out over a period of fifty days, Albert showed a fear response to the white rat on its own.

They demonstrated generalization of the fear response to other (similar) stimuli such as a rabbit, a dog and cotton wool. None of these stimuli had evoked fear before the study. These fear responses were still shown a month later, though they were not as strong. Most people nowadays would have qualms about this sort of research, because it might have long-term effects on the child. Watson and Rayner did not see Albert again after this final test and so they were not able to extinguish the response.

In chapter 3 we talked about phobias as an example of classically conditioned responses. There is also an operantly conditioned component to the behaviour of a phobic patient, which is part of the reason why phobias can stay for years without getting any better. This combination of the two forms of conditioning can most clearly be seen in the laboratory study of *avoidance learning*.

Most dogs will learn very quickly to avoid an electric shock if a light is turned on just before the shock is given, and if there is an escape route, such as being able to jump over a small barrier. This form of learning is called avoidance learning and is very resistant to extinction. The bell and the shock become associated, leading to a classically conditioned fear or anxiety response to the light.

$$\text{CS} \quad + \quad \text{UCS} \longrightarrow \text{UCR}$$
$$\text{(Light)} \quad\quad\quad \text{(Shock)} \quad\quad\quad \text{(Anxiety)}$$

When the animal then jumps the barrier, the anxiety is reduced and so the jumping response is negatively reinforced and is more likely to occur again. The jumping response is therefore operantly conditioned.

$$\text{Light} \longrightarrow \text{Anxiety} \longrightarrow \text{Jump} \longrightarrow \text{Reduced Anxiety}$$

The reason why this response is very resistant to extinction is that the animals do not stay around long enough when the light is turned on to learn that the shock is no longer associated with it. This, of course, is very like the condition of a person with a phobia and is the reason why phobias can last so long. Although the original phobia may have been caused by classical conditioning, the later avoidance responses are operantly conditioned, and since they reduce anxiety they are unlikely to extinguish. This combination of operant and classical conditioning is very powerful.

The only way to extinguish the avoidance response in the light and shock experiment is to prevent the animal escaping, so that it learns that the shock is no longer associated with the light; once the anxiety response is extinguished there is no motivation for the jumping response so this ceases too. This is very similar to the technique of flooding as a treatment for phobias (see p. 39).

Frustration

The frustration-aggression hypothesis of Dollard (see p. 140) suggests that when somebody or something blocks our path to a goal which we are trying to reach, aggression is often the response to this frustration. This aggression can sometimes be redirected towards other people or objects if the original frustrator cannot be directly attacked. For example, suppose a parent smacks a child. The child cannot hit the parent and get away with it, and so redirects his or her aggression on to toys. Frustration does not seem automatically to lead to aggression though. It may be that one person learns in childhood that aggression is successful or that aggression brings attention from parents. Other children's early experiences (having aggression punished or ignored, for example) may make them less likely to show aggression as a result of stress and instead retreat into apathy or depression.

Learned Helplessness

Animals in avoidance learning experiments usually show signs of emotional arousal. If the arousal is not too great it helps the animal learn to avoid the shock. Seligman and Maier (1967), however, showed that under some conditions animals do not show this arousal and fail to learn.

On the first day of the experiment, dogs were given electric shocks at random intervals. The dogs could not avoid or escape the shocks which lasted for five seconds at a time. On the second day the shocks were preceded by a signal and the dogs could avoid the shocks by jumping over a small barrier. Most dogs in this experiment never learnt to avoid the shock. It was as though they had given up, many simply lay down and passively received the shocks. Seligman called this phenomenon *learned helplessness*, the dogs seemed to have learnt that nothing they did would have any effect.

The same sort of thing can be demonstrated with human subjects and Seligman argues that depressive illnesses may result from a past history of being in situations where the individual had no control over his environment and experienced prolonged failure. The important thing is whether the individual perceived the situation as one in which they had control, those suffering from depressive illness are most likely to have thought that others controlled their fate, rather than seeing any failures as due to themselves.

Zimbardo (1979) puts forward the case that it is possible to 'immunize' against the onset of learned helplessness. He points out that if the dogs in the Seligman study had been in a lot of situations where their behaviour affected what happened to them, then they did not suffer from learned helplessness and were able to avoid the electric shock in the second part of the study. Zimbardo draws the conclusion that parents and teachers need to give children responsibility and provide them with activities and experiences which allow successful control over their environment, so that they are less likely to fall into the learned helplessness condition later in life.

Once learned helplessness has occurred, it is not easy to treat. Seligman managed eventually to get *some* of his dogs to learn by dragging them away from the shock, so that they could see that it was only given in one part of the apparatus. Some dogs were dragged like this up to two hundred times before they were able to break out of the helplessness and learn to avoid the shock themselves.

Human depression has many different forms, and although some people display symptoms similar to those of the animals suffering from learned helplessness, it would be overstating the case to use this as an explanation for all depressions.

Life Changes and Hassles

Holmes and Rahé (1967) believe that the amount of readjustment which we have to make in order to deal with changes in our lives may predict our levels of stress and hence our likelihood of suffering illness. Using 'marriage' as a typical life event which requires us to readjust our lives, Holmes and Rahé gave it an arbitrary value of 50. Eight hundred volunteers (males and females of different ages) were then asked to compare other life events (both pleasant and unpleasant) with marriage. For example, does being sacked from your job rate higher or lower than marriage in the amount of readjustment which you have to make and in the length of time over which readjustment is necessary? The mean average values for a whole range of life events is shown in table 13.2. Holmes and Rahé call this the Social Readjustment Rating Scale.

The scale appears to have some use as a predictor of illness. Over 50 per cent of people who experienced more than 200 points worth of life event changes became ill during the following year. 79 per cent of people scoring over 300 became ill in the following year. Small but significant correlations have been found between high scores and the occurrence of fatal and non-fatal heart attacks, tuberculosis and leukaemia. But (see p. 366) correlation does not imply causation. It could be that the onset of a serious illness predisposes people to be sacked from work or undergo a marriage break-up, rather than that these life changes cause illness, or a third factor could be causing both illness and life changes.

Stress does not always come in large, life-changing events. Daily life is full of smaller stresses, such as losing one's keys, missing a bus, or having to fill in bureaucratic forms. De Longis (1982) found that measuring an individual's total of daily hassles over a period of time proved a better prediction of later illness than did life change events. He also found that pleasant events which he called 'uplifts' (the opposite of hassles) could reduce the likelihood of future illness.

Table 13.2. The Social Readjustment Rating Scale (after Holmes and Rahé, 1967)

Life event	Life-change value	Life event	Life-change value
Death of spouse	100	Trouble with in-laws	29
Divorce	73	Outstanding personal	
Marital Separation	65	achievement	28
Jail term	63	Wife begins or stops work	26
Death of close family member	63	Begin or end school	26
Personal injury or illness	53	Change in living conditions	25
Marriage	50	Revision of personal habits	24
Fired from job	47	Trouble with boss	23
Marital reconciliation	45	Change in residence	20
Retirement	45	Change in school	20
Change in health of		Change in recreation	19
family member	44	Change in church activities	19
Pregnancy	40	Change in social activities	18
Sex difficulties	39	Change in sleeping habits	16
Gain of new family member	39	Change in eating habits	15
Business readjustment	39	Vacation	13
Change in financial state	38	Christmas	12
Death of close friend	37	Minor legal violations	11
Change to different line			
of work	36		
Foreclosure of mortgage	30		
Change in responsibilities			
at work	29		
Son or daughter leaving home	29		

Coping with stress

According to Lazarus (1984) strategies for coping with stress fall into two categories:

Emotion-focused coping occurs when an individual is enabled to reduce their feelings of anxiety

Problem-focused coping occurs when the individual is able to reinterpret the situation as being less threatening, or is able to change or avoid the situation.

Problem-focused coping

Kobasa (1986) developed a system of training which uses a two-stage-training model. In stage 1, the individual is trained to realize that they are feeling stress by becoming aware of their heart rate and muscle tension changes. This enables them to recognize the situation or type of situation as one which causes them stress. In stage 2 they are taught to reconstruct in their mind stressful situations which they have experienced. They are taught to concentrate on the reality of the situation (how could it have been better? how worse?) rather than the emotions felt at the time. Starting with simple situations and progressing to more complex ones, they are taught coping strategies, the idea being that successful coping with simpler problems leads the individual to develop confidence that they can control a situation or cope with it. In effect, it increases the likelihood of an 'I can cope' outcome in Cox's model on p. 235 by increasing the 'have I coped with similar things before?' self-perception.

Emotion-focused coping
The application of classical conditioning for the treatment of phobias outlined on pp. 37–40 is one useful way of dealing with cases of extreme anxiety. operant conditioning too can be used, as Biofeedback, to reduce arousal (see p. 52).

Antidepressant and tranquillizer drugs can also be used short term (days) to medium term (months) to reduce a person's levels of depression or anxiety. In practice, emotion-focused coping strategies are often used to reduce the individual's level of anxiety enough, so that problem-focused coping strategies can then be used.

Environmental Effects

Temperature
A study by Harries and Stadler (1988) showed a link between high temperatures and increases in people's arousal – and hence their aggression. At a mean average temperature of 50–59°F, there was a mean average of 14 daily assaults in Dallas, Texas; at a temperature of 70–79°F, there were 16 assaults; and when the temperature averaged 90–99°F, there were 18 assaults on average per day.

Noise
Noise is simply unwanted sound. Like temperature, noise can increase arousal and stress. Apart from the obvious physical damage which loud noise can cause to the body's hearing apparatus in the middle ear, lower volumes of noise can cause some psychological reactions to stress, notably loss of attention and ability to process information.

A study by Moser (1988) in Paris shows some of the effects. In situations with high levels of traffic congestion and noise from road construction activities, pedestrians were asked to do one of three things. Some pedestrians were asked to complete a questionnaire; some were observed to see if they picked up and returned a set of keys which an experiment had dropped in front of them; other pedestrians were asked for directions to a metro station. Only 41 per cent of those observed reported the dropped keys, and 35 per cent completed the questionnaire. 100 per cent of those asked for directions complied with the request. This suggests that the noise and congestion had not made people less helpful but had reduced people's ability to process information; they were less likely to notice the keys and less likely to cope with the demands of answering the questionnaire.

A Milgram-type experiment (see p. 118) by Geen (1969) showed that people in the teacher situation gave higher levels of shock to 'victims' in noisy conditions compared with quiet ones.

It is not just the volume of noise which causes stress, however. People living near busy motorways soon adapt to the constant noise and cease to be affected by it. However, a noise which varies in intensity (the noise made by jet aircraft on a take-off route over your house) is more difficult to adapt to; studies in the USA have found that children subjected to such noise still showed difficulty in concentrating even after they had moved away from the airport one year previously.

Pollution

Oborne (1983) found that people's results on tests of cognitive abilities showed deterioration if the tests were conducted in a room filled with cigarette smoke. Some people may be so stressed by cigarette smoke that they are discouraged from taking part in some social activities. Bullinger (1989) studied people from two towns in Germany. Both towns had only moderate sulphur dioxide pollution, but one city's level was slightly higher than the other. People from the second city showed more stress and emotional response and performed worse on cognitive tasks than people from the first city.

Since all the people tested had been resident in their respective city for more than two years, it seems that there is no adaptation to stress caused by such chemical pollutants as sulphur dioxide.

Architecture

The term *sick building syndrome* became commonplace in the 1980s. It referred to the detrimental effects on workers of buildings with inadequate natural lighting, ineffective ventilation, and too much or too little heating, as well as to the physical symptoms encountered by some people which were triggered by materials used in the building's construction. One of the major factors in worker dissatisfaction was open plan architecture, where private offices disappeared and low partitions were all that separated workers.

Block and Stokes (1989) carried out a study to test whether people worked better and were more satisfied in open plan, compared with private offices. Open plan offices, where many people are working closely together should increase arousal. According to the Yerkes–Dodson Law (p. 234) performance on complex tasks should be hindered by an increase in arousal, whilst performance on simple tasks should not be affected. Therefore, performance on complex tasks should be worse in open plan offices than it would be in private offices. The simple task was clipping tax forms together using paper clips, whilst the complex task was actually filling in tax forms.

As expected, Block and Stokes found that performance on complex tasks was indeed better in private offices than in open plan ones, and people doing complex tasks were much less satisfied with the work environment when they were tested in the open plan office. So office architecture does not automatically lead to stress – we must take into account the complexity of the work being done, too.

Summary

1 There are no agreed definitions of what individual emotions are. Instead, psychologists have examined the cognitive processes involved from stimulus to feelings of emotion.

2 All stages, (perception, physiology, behaviour) can to some extent be measured, but all measurement techniques have flaws, and different techniques do not always agree on the amount (and particularly the type) of emotion being experienced.

3 Mandler argues that we are motivated to seek 'automatic jags', temporary increases in ANS activity as a result of environmental stimulation. Those with a very responsive ANS appear very emotional because this governs the physiological responses that determine the degree of emotion felt.

4 Historically, there have been conflicting theories about the role of an ANS in emotion. James and Lange argued that the physiological changes brought about by ANS activity are responsible for the feeling of emotion. Cannon argued that the physiological changes that occur as a result of ANS activity have a role to play in determining the degree to which an emotion is felt.

5 The Yerkes–Dodson Law describes the relationship between arousal and performance on simple and complex tasks. Complex tasks are more affected by changes in arousal levels.

6 Classical Conditioning may explain the way that normal emotions develop, as well as the development of phobias.

7 Some forms of depression may result from experiences of lack of control over the environment. The result of lack of control may be learned helplessness, a condition which impairs future learning.

8 Stress results from our perception that our ability to deal with a particular situation is not great enough.

9 Physiological changes in stress (the General Adaptation Syndrome) can lead to long-term health problems. Some people (showing Type A behaviours) may be more prone to coronary heart disease.

10 Psychological effects of stress are anxiety, aggression and depression.

11 According to Holmes and Rahé, the amount of readjustment which we have to make in our lives can indicate how likely we are to suffer physiological damage through stress.

12 Emotion-focused coping involves reducing the individual's feelings of anxiety, while problem-focused coping involves getting the individual to change their perception of the situation in order to see it as less threatening.

Chapter 14

The Nature/Nurture Debate on Intelligence

The Nature/Nurture Problem

At conception every animal is provided with a mix of genetic material from its parents which governs much of its later development, such as whether the new being will develop into a frog or a toad, a male or a female; many other major or minor physical characteristics are also genetically determined. For some animals these hereditary factors determine most of the behaviour performed during a lifetime.

For example, a digger wasp lives for only a few weeks, during which it has to hunt, dig a nest hole, mate, lay eggs and provide next year's generation with a store of food. The wasp then dies; there is no adult to teach complicated behaviour patterns to the young, nor time for them to learn by trial and error. Life is very different for the human infant, but to what extent are we controlled by inherited factors?

The nature/nurture debate is about the relative importance of inherited and environmental influences on human and animal characteristics.

The debate is not just of academic interest, since presumably if it was decided that human intelligence was limited by inherited factors this might affect educational policy in a different way than if environmental experience was considered to be most important. Extreme right-wing political parties have selected some of the studies that we will quote later, to argue that some races are genetically inferior to others. If the selection of evidence is biased in a different way, studies show that the way we treat people is the most important determinant of behaviour. It is not surprising that, superficially, studies appear to give contradictory results, since the question 'is nature more important than nurture?' is rather like asking whether the length of a rectangle is more important than the width in determining its area. If either the width or the length is taken away you have no rectangle; keep the length constant, then variation in the width will change the area just as the length will determine the area if the width is constant. Human behaviour and characteristics are an interaction of nature and nurture.

Even in cases where we know the hereditary factors associated with a particular human quality, as with Phenylketonuria (PKU), it is not possible to separate nature and nurture

PKU is a genetic disorder which occurs when an individual receives a particular pair of genes at conception. Genes are small elements of the genetic code that are carried in their thousands on each of the string-like chromosomes contained within the nucleus of every cell in the body. Most people have a pair of genes that successfully control the breakdown of phenylalaline, a protein contained in many everyday foods, but the PKU sufferer has a pair of genes which cause phenylalaline to be broken down into a substance which is poisonous to the developing nervous system, resulting in mental retardation. Surely this is an example of genetic factors controlling intelligence since we can trace the problem back to the pair of 'defective' genes? The controlling factors, however, are not so clear, for if the disorder is detected by a routine blood test soon after birth, and the child is raised on a diet free of phenylalaline, the child develops normally and may have an IQ anywhere in the normal range. The PKU example shows how the effect of genetics depends upon the environment; it is not possible to say that genetic factors *caused* the low intelligence of a particular person with PKU since we know a different environment, in this case a simple change of diet, would lead to a different IQ. It would be equally foolish to claim that environment had *caused* the retardation. The intelligence of the PKU patient and the rest of us is a result of an *interaction* between genetic and environmental factors.

The nature/nurture problem has been discussed for centuries. Once the question of whether genetics *or* environment cause particular qualities or behaviour has been disposed of, there are a number of more sensible questions that can be asked: do babies perceive the world in the same way as you and I, or was William James right in saying that the newborn baby's world is 'one blooming, buzzing confusion'; are there any particular experiences that infants need in order to ensure a properly functioning adult perceptual system, or do they have a fairly inflexible system which is relatively unaffected by environmental factors? In the area of intelligence, to what extent are the *differences* between people in a particular population due to genetics?

The major contributions that psychologists have made have been in the field of practical studies performed to test the hypotheses that result from taking particular positions in the debate. At its simplest, the argument is between the *empiricists* who stress the role of learning and environmental influence on human characteristics and the *nativists* who stress genetic (hereditary) influences.

In this chapter and the next we shall look at some aspects of the nature/nurture debate as they apply to the areas of intelligence and perception.

What is Intelligence?

It seems reasonable first to ask the question, *what is intelligence?* The simple answer is that we do not know.

Consider two different people – a university professor and a lorry driver. Can both of them show 'intelligent' behaviour? We would assume that they can: the university professor may talk 'intelligently' and the lorry drive may be an 'intelligent' driver. Have they then the same amount of 'intelligence'? People might feel inclined to say that the professor is more intelligent than the lorry driver. What, then, is there in the professor's behaviour which might lead us to believe that he is more intelligent?

This is where the problems of definition begin. Most people have an idea of what they mean by intelligence – 'cleverness', 'understanding', 'the ability to think', 'the ability to cope', 'inborn brilliance', and so on. But such definitions do not really enable us to judge whether certain behaviour is either intelligent or unintelligent. The difficulties arise because we are wrongly assuming that intelligence is a thing: accepted descriptions of people – 'He went to university because he's intelligent' or 'She's intelligent: she's got a high IQ' – assume that we each possess a quantity of something called 'intelligence'. But psychologists study behaviour, and most of them therefore really use the term 'intelligence' in the sense of intelligent behaviour. It is impossible to have an amount of intelligence. In grammatical terms, perhaps we should think only of 'intelligent' as the adjective, describing behaviour, rather than of the noun 'intelligence', which would denote an object.

All the psychologists' attempts to define what is meant by intelligent behaviour have had their critics. C. Spearman believed that intelligence was a 'general capacity for thinking and reasoning'. L.L. Thurstone, on the other hand, saw intelligence s a series of separate abilities. He believed that abilities such as numerical ability, memory and word fluency together made up intelligent behaviour. Some psychologists have gone further than Thurstone. J.P. Guildford, for example, claimed that intelligence is made up of 120 different factors. The argument about the number of abilities involved in intelligence still continues.

Alice Heim, a psychologist working at Cambridge University who developed several intelligence tests, devised the following definition of intelligence: 'Intelligent activity consists in grasping the essentials in a situation and responding appropriately to them.' This definition – or perhaps more accurately, description – of intelligence, although necessarily vague-sounding, does not make intelligence into a thing; it can include most if not all acts of intelligent behaviour; and it is still compatible with common conceptions. Thus Heim's description of intelligent behaviour seems the best way of characterizing intelligence available in our present stage of knowledge. You will note too that it has fairly close parallels with the ideas of Piaget and Bruner on cognitive development – the idea of the individual making efforts to deal effectively with his or her environment.

Most researchers have wanted to quantify intelligence in some way and have used so-called intelligence tests to do this. These tests involve a series of numerical, verbal, spatial and reasoning problems, the successful solution of which can be termed intelligent behaviour. The score on this test is considered as a measure of intelligence. In practice, when studies are performed the operational definition of intelligence is 'that which is measured by intelligence tests'; although this is a circular definition, it gets over the problem of the disagreement on a general definition by saying exactly what measure is being used in the study and limiting the research conclusions to this definition of intelligence, rather than attempting the impossible and studying all the different 'intelligences' at the same time.

Intelligence tests allow us to calculate an individual's *Intelligence Quotient* (IQ), a numerical value which allows us to make comparisons between people. For youngsters, IQ can be calculated by comparing an individual's real (chronological) and mental ages. Mental ages are worked out by giving the IQ test to children of different ages and working out the average score for each age group; somebody scoring the same as the average eight-year-old is said to have a mental age of eight, irrespective of real age. Obviously a six-year-old with a mental age of eight would be considered bright but the same would not be said of a ten-year-old with the same score. To work out IQ the following formula is used:

$$IQ = \frac{\text{Mental age}}{\text{Chronological age}} \times 100$$

A child with a chronological age of eight and a mental age of eight will thus have an IQ of 100 (average IQ), but a ten-year-old who gets the same number of correct answers and therefore has the same mental age as the previous child has an IQ score of only 80.

IQ tests were first widely used by A. Binet in the early 1900s as an instrument for the Education Department of Paris. Their major purpose was to single out those children who were unlikely to benefit from the school system of the day. In effect, the Binet test was a test for mental retardation: children who failed to gain high enough scores were not allowed to go to school. More modern versions, in particular the Terman-Merrill version, are still being used today for selection and counselling purposes.

The Nature/Nurture Debate on Intelligence

D.O. Hebb in 1949 argued that much of the misunderstanding about intelligence arose because two separate facts were not recognized:

1 Humans have brains and brain cells for whose structure and function there must be some genetic blueprint. Presumably also encoded in the genetic blueprint is the ability of these cells to join together to form cell assemblies which allow us to store memories and solve problems. In effect, we have an innate ability to form cell assemblies.

2 Although we may have the potential for forming such brain connections, we may not necessarily actually do so to the fullest extent: the environment may help or hinder their formation.

In other words, not only must we have brains and potential neural connections within the brain, but we must also actually make these connections. Therefore, according to Hebb, we ought to recognize two distinct types of intelligence.

Intelligence A

This means potential intelligence – the genetically-determined structure of the brain and the potential ability of the brain neurons to connect. This potential intelligence is laid down in an individual's genetic blueprint. The fertilized egg has the genetic blueprint or potential for the development of the ten thousand million brain neurons and their ability to connect. What happens to the organism after conception can either help this potential to be realized, or hinder it; it cannot alter the potential itself.

Intelligence B

This describes the extent to which this genetic potential has been realized as a result of the interaction of an individual's genetic makeup with the effects of environment.

To indicate how complex the interaction between heredity and environment is, consider what happens to the newly fertilized egg. In minute one it is immediately affected by the environment – the conditions of implantation in the womb, and food and oxygen supply, for example. It is now no longer a simple reproduction of genetic information: some of the genetic blueprint has been reproduced, but some has either not been reproduced at all or had been reproduced imperfectly. The organism at minute two no longer shows only genetic potential: it is the result of the effects of the environment at that time on the structures which are currently developing. It is a different organism from minute one. But at minute two this new organism is still being affected by its environment, to produce yet a different basis at minute three, on which the environment will have further effects. At minute four it will be different again, and so on.

Intelligence B is thus, according to Hebb, the way in which the brain functions after the environment has helped or hindered its development from the genetic blueprints of its cells: it is the average level of performance or comprehension on the part of the developing individual that we infer from his or her behaviour

We cannot directly study intelligence A: how can you study a potential until it has been realized? We could perhaps devise systems for measuring the neural 'connectability' of an individual's brain, but because we could not do this until neurons had formed, the environment would already have had an effect. Nor is intelligence B measurable. Hebb regards intelligence B as the normal functioning of the brain; thus although it is theoretically possible to monitor separately the activity of each brain neuron, the complete process for an entire brain would take roughly fourteen million years. Even then we should not know what connection each of the neurons had with intelligent behaviour.

Intelligence tests, Hebb said, measure only a sample of intelligence B, so that it is impossible for them to give us reliable information about the nature of intelligence A.

Intelligence C

Philip Vernon, a British psychologist, has proposed a third type, intelligence C. This, he says, is an unknown amount of intelligence B which can be measured with IQ tests. IQ tests cannot measure the whole of an individual's intelligence B, as we have seen, because intelligence B is the way the individual responds to the environment as a whole. Vernon therefore argues that because intelligence C is an unknown proportion of intelligence B, and B is an unknown proportion of A, it is most unwise to use IQ – intelligence C – scores to find out about intelligence A; we do not know anything about the relationship between intelligence C and A (see figure 14.1).

Family Studies

Towards the end of the 19th century, Francis Galton performed a series of family studies. He found that intelligent (high-IQ) parents tended to have offspring with high IQs and that tracing a family over a series of generations showed a remarkable consistency in the type of people in each generation. At first sight many people might take this as evidence of the importance of heredity in characteristics such as intelligence. A longer consideration makes us question this. Intelligent parents may pass on 'intelligent' genes

Figure 14.1. The Hebb–Vernon Model of Intelligence

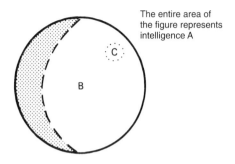

The entire area of
the figure represents
intelligence A

to their children, but their environment may also differ from the kind provided by less intelligent parents: a child may see more books, have a different kind of conversation with parents, and so on. However, precisely because of this, we cannot use family studies alone for valid evidence in the nature/nurture debate: the child's IQ may be a result of either nature, or nurture, or both.

Twin Studies

Ideally, a study which attempted to separate the effects of genetics and environment would compare people with the same genetic makeup but different environmental experiences, or it would do the opposite, comparing individuals who have different genetic makeup but the same environmental experiences. The use of twins allows both these kinds of studies since there are two types of twin. Monozygotic (MZ) twins develop from the same fertilized egg which splits to produce two individuals with the same genetic makeup; these are identical twins. Dizygotic (DZ) twins develop from two separately fertilized eggs and are not genetically identical; they are only as genetically similar as any set of brothers and/or sisters, but since they are the same age their environments are likely to be more similar than is usual for separate individuals.

As we argued earlier, an individual's IQ results from an interaction of environmental and inherited factors and it is not logically possible to say which is most important. The twin studies do not attempt to tackle this logical impossibility – they are designed to produce a heritability estimate, an estimate of the extent to which inherited factors are responsible for differences between the IQs of people in a particular population. If the heritability estimate for IQ in this country was 90 per cent it would mean that 90 per cent of the differences between people's IQ scores was due to inherited differences passed on through the genes, and only 10 per cent of the variation was due to environmental factors.

COMPARISON OF MZ TWINS REARED TOGETHER WITH MZ TWINS SEPARATED IN EARLY CHILDHOOD

MZ twins brought up together have very similar IQs. This is not surprising since they share the same genes and environment. To get an idea about what effect the environment can have on IQ differences we could look at MZ twins who were separated at birth and brought up in very different environments; if these twins also have very similar IQs then it could be concluded that environment has very little effect on IQ differences. In other words, the heritability estimate would be high, If the twins brought up separately had very different IQs this could only be due to environmental differences, and so the heritability estimate would be low.

In theory this sort of study sounds ideal, but in practice not many MZ twins are separated at birth, and many of those who were have been reared by relatives in the same town – hardly a totally different environment.

COMPARISON OF DZ AND MZ TWINS

Another sort of twin study tries to counter these problems by comparing the similarity of IQ of MZ twins brought up together with that of DZs brought up together. The theory behind this is that if DZs brought up together are as similar in their IQs as are MZs then the important factor must be the similarity of environments, since DZ twins do not have identical genes. If, however, DZ twins reared together are not as similar as MZ twins reared together this would suggest a high heritability factor, since it must be genetic rather than environmental similarity that causes the MZ twins to have nearly the same IQs.

Unfortunately, this type of study also has problems: can we be sure that DZ twins are treated as equally as MZ twins who look the same and may often be mistaken for each other? Many people argue that boys and girls are treated differently by adults; yet both members of an MZ pair will be the same sex, but half of all DZ pairs consist of one boy and one girl. To improve the likelihood of DZs having an environment as similar as MZs, studies should not include mixed-sex pairs – though many have failed to exclude them.

The correlation coefficients shown in the results of C. Burt in 1953, H.H. Newman, F.N. Freeman and K.J. Holzinger in 1928 and Bouchard and McGue (in a summary of studies published in 1981) indicate the degree of similarity found between their subjects: the nearer to one the correlation coefficient is, the more similar are the individuals in terms of IQ. Thus the correlation of 0.9 between the IQ of monozygotic twins shows that if one twin has a high IQ then the other is very likely also to have a high IQ. You will notice that the IQs of dizygotic twins and siblings (or brothers and sisters) have lower correlations: the lower the correlation, the less similar are the IQs of the individuals in each pair.

Study of	Burt	Correlation Coefficient Newman, Freeman & Holzinger	Bouchard & McGue
Monozygotic twins reared together	0.92	0.91	0.86
Monozygotic twins reared apart	0.84	0.67	0.72
Dizygotic twins reared together	0.53	0.64	0.60
Siblings reared together	0.49	No figures available	0.47

In the early days of twin studies many mistakes may have been made in identifying twins as MZs or DZs. Twins are often thought to be identical because they look the same. A large number of physiological tests are required to be sure that twins are MZ; looking the same is not enough because even unrelated people can look identical if they happen to have a relatively small proportion of similar genes, those affecting external physical characteristics of the face and head.

Although MZ twins are regarded as genetically identical it is now known that there are very small genetic differences between them.

All these problems reduce the value of what originally looked like a very valuable method for investigation of the nature/nurture debate.

Some of the most influential studies in this field were those performed by Sir Cyril Burt, who concluded that 80 per cent of the differences between the IQs of people in Britain were due to inherited factors and only 20 per cent were due to environmental differences. Many psychologists used Burt's data in producing their own heritability estimates and there was some degree of agreement that an average eight out of every ten IQ points of difference between people in white Western European and American populations were due to genetic variation. It is now generally accepted that Burt falsified at least some of his results and so any heritability estimate produced from them must be re-evaluated. The Newman, Freeman and Holzinger studies produced heritability estimates of about 50 per cent, and other researchers have produced even lower figures.

Even if the twin studies were perfect it would not be surprising if different studies came up with different results, since the heritability estimate is an average for a *particular* population. For a group of people who stress conformity and treat their children as similarly as possible, any differences in IQ are more likely to be due to genetic differences, but if their culture promotes independence and the treatment of children as individuals then there is much more room for environmentally induced differences; the heritability estimate that you find will depend on which group you study.

Adoption and Fostering Studies

Imagine this situation: a man and woman who both have low IQs, have a child. This child is adopted at birth (or fostered from birth) by a high IQ couple. When the child is older, its IQ is measured and is compared with its real (biological) parents' IQs, and also with its adoptive parents' IQs. If heredity is the most important factor in IQ, the child's IQ should be similar to its biological parents' IQ. However, if the child is found to be more similar to its adoptive parents in IQ, then this suggests that environment is more important in determining IQ.

Early studies which followed the above procedure found an average correlation of 0.44 between the child and its biological mother (the figure for children who are brought up by their biological mother is approximately 0.50). This figure of 0.44, however, masks some evidence: although the correlation looks as if the children's IQs are similar to their biological mothers, if you look at the actual IQs involved, the children made big gains in IQ after being fostered or adopted. For example, Scarr and Weinberg (1976) studied disadvantaged black children who were adopted or fostered by white families. The black parents were usually poorly educated and below average in IQ. By 4–7 years old, the children's IQs were 110–112 – much higher than their biological parents, and much more in line with their adoptive or foster parents.

Similarly, Schiff studied children who were moved (before the age of six months) from low-status families to families of a higher social status. Schiff compared the adopted children's IQs with brothers and sisters who had stayed with the biological parents. The average IQ of the adopted children was 111, whilst the average IQ of the children who had stayed with their natural parents was only 95.

Fostering and adoption studies seem to suggest that environment can have a large effect on the development of children's IQs, but a recent review of this area by Locurto (1988) finds that such improvements are not obviously caused by the child moving to a more stimulating environment. Locurto believes that what is also important is that the adoptive parents are more sensitive to the child's particular needs – it is not *more* general stimulation which the child needs, but the right specific stimulation, and sensitive adoptive parents can find and provide this stimulation.

Race and IQ

From the early days of IQ testing there has been an interest in the comparative scores for different races. R. Lynn has recently shown that Japanese schoolchildren score about four and a half points more on IQ tests than do Americans.

In a controversial paper in the *Harvard Education Review* in 1969, Arthur Jensen looked at reasons why American blacks score, on average, 15 points less than whites on IQ tests. Before discussing these reasons it is worth emphasizing that we are only talking about averages and that there is a great deal of overlap between the scores of the different races, many blacks having a greater IQ than many whites. Remember also that the discussion is about IQ, a very limited definition of intelligence.

Jensen argued that the 15 points difference between whites and blacks was too great to be explained by environmental factors; he backed this up by quoting heritability estimates of 80 per cent for intelligence. He felt that specialized education programmes for children of different ability groupings should be devised, to allow the full development of each child. This idea was seized upon by many white Americans in the southern states as an argument to continue segregated schooling of black and white children, which was a hot political issue at the time; it was conveniently forgotten that Jensen was talking about average scores and that many black children have greater measured IQs than many whites.

Jensen's position has been heavily criticized. Leo Kamin has demonstrated problems with a lot of the studies used to produce the heritability estimates, including the fact that some of the work originated with Burt and therefore cannot be relied upon.

Hebb put forward an analogy to show the difficulty in using heritability estimates to look at the differences between populations:

Suppose we kept all baby boys in barrels from birth and fed them through the bung-holes until they were mature. If we then tested their IQs and compared them with the IQs of the girls who were reared normally, we should probably find that the girls' IQs were much higher than those of the boys. Because all the boys had been brought up in identical environments, any differences in their IQs should be caused by genetic factors. Could we then say that the boys were less intelligent than the girls, and therefore that, because the differences among the boys' IQs were largely created by genetic factors, the differences between boys and girls were also caused by genetics? Of course not. Firstly we would be comparing IQs, not intelligence as a whole. Also we could not compare the role of heredity in determining the boys' and girls' IQs unless both groups had been reared in identical environments.

If we apply this analogy to the race and IQ debate, we cannot compare the effects of genetics in the determination of blacks' and whites' IQs unless we are sure that they have been brought up in identical environments. Jensen claimed that because he compared middle-class blacks with middle-class whites, and working-class blacks with working-class whites, he had held the environmental variable constant. We do not yet know enough about the effects of the environment to be certain which factors are important in IQ, but there is considerable doubt that using social class as a yardstick is a sufficiently sophisticated way of ensuring that the environment is constant.

I.I. Gottesman has shown that large differences in IQ can result from environmental differences: in one study of identical twins the average IQ difference was fourteen points. J.R. Flynn compared IQ scores of different generations and showed that today's white American children score 15 points more than did their equivalent in 1928, something that is most likely due to changes in education.

Kamin and many others have pointed out that IQ tests are *culture-bound*, i.e. they favour people from particular backgrounds, using language and setting problems that reflect white middle-class educational and other experiences. The discrepancy between different races in IQ score may simply reflect this, and so there have been attempts to produce *culture-free* tests though none has been unanimously accepted.

A. and E. Hendrickson have shown a close relationship between IQ and brain-wave patterns shown on an electroencephalograph (see p. 301) in response to a series of tones. C. Brand has shown a similar relationship with inspection time; people with higher IQs take less time to make simple decisions such as which is the longer of two lines presented to them. Brand argues that these techniques may be used as fairer measures of intelligence.

The arguments about heredity, race and intelligence rage on because there are no definite answers and may never be; it is important, however, to be aware of the shortcomings and counter-claims in this area, if only to be able to rebut the claims of those with extreme views who carefully choose the evidence which supports their case.

Environment and Intelligence

What aspects of the environment have an effect on intelligence? We have already said that schooling can change measured intelligence, and studies of Learning Sets (p. 58) suggest that the more experience of different types of problem, the more likely we are to be able to 'grasp the essentials in a situation and respond appropriately to them'. Remember that environment includes the food we eat and the air we breathe, and the chemical nature of these can have an effect (as it certainly does with PKU patients – see p. 248). The environment has an effect before birth; smoking and drinking during pregnancy are known to have some effects on the unborn child, as are particular maternal illnesses such as German measles. Environmental effects which cause strong emotions in the mother or child can have lasting effects which seem out of proportion to the original event. A programme to devise the best environment for development of intelligence would have to take all these factors into account, and it might be that what is best for one aspect of intelligence is detrimental to another. The optimum environment for one individual with a particular genetic makeup may not be best for us all.

We now turn to examples of procedures in this field of study. One obvious need for a developing human being is food, and in particular protein, which is necessary to build brain cells. If an adult is starving to death the last area of the body to lose weight is the brain; any other organ will be sacrificed first. But in babies this is not the case: if during the period of brain development the baby is deprived of protein, the brain suffers along with the rest of the body. Although the genetic potential for development might exist, the material with which the body's structures can be built is absent, so that it does not develop properly. J. Cravioto, in studies of Mexican children deprived of protein and stimulation, has found that such children show impairment not only of intellectual functions but also of physical development. Moreover, even such simple forms of behaviour as cordination between hand and eye – in catching a ball, for example – are affected adversely. Studies are continuing now to attempt to distinguish more clearly between the effects of protein deficiency and stimulation deficiency. Early results suggest that both factors can have separate detrimental effects on the development of intelligence.

At the University of California M.R. Rosenzweig and D. Krech have devised experiments to investigate the effects of the lack of environmental stimulation on normally-fed rats. Rats reared with several other litter-mates in a stimulating environment – with treadwheels, ladders, swings, roundabouts, and daily changes in these toys – showed marked differences in both brain structure and behaviour compared with litter-mates who were reared in an unstimulating environment with one rat to each sound-proofed cage and no toys. The differences were that 'enriched' rats showed a significantly larger brain size with more transmitter molecules – in other words, larger and more active brains – than the 'deprived' group, and that 'enriched' rats were significantly better at solving discrimination-learning tasks than were 'deprived' rats. A stimulating environment, then, seems to help the intellectual development of rats. Hebb's daughter reared rats as household pets, and these animals performed significantly better on maze-learning tasks than litter-mates housed in normal rat cages who were not treated as pets.

Steven Rose goes one stage further. Not only can deprivation of protein and stimulation in infancy affect a person's intellectual development, but it may also affect the intellectual development of her children and perhaps even of her grandchildren. Malnutrition in a female rat in infancy, for example, may affect her physical and behavioural development: her womb may not develop properly, and she may not develop normal patterns of rat behaviour. Even if she is well fed in later life, the conditions in her womb and her maternal behaviour may be sub-standard, so that the offspring which she rears will themselves be in a deprived environment. This *transgenerational transmission* – so called because it can affect the animal's development before birth – looks like a genetic effect but is in fact an environmental effect. Rose believes that this same process may occur in humans and can be a contributor to the apparently genetic factor in the development of intelligence.

Conversely, however, it is very difficult to pinpoint specific environmental factors which will improve intelligence, because any one environmental alteration may help the development of some intellectual abilities but hinder the development of others; also the timing of the stimulation is crucial (see sensitive periods, pp. 152–3). Any 'good' environment, therefore, may only be good if it occurs at a particular time in development. It seems that the only basic rule which can be applied is therefore something like, 'As varied and stimulating an environment as possible, as early as possible.'

Summary

1 Intelligence is not a 'thing': it may be a whole number of different abilities, but should best be regarded as a descriptive term, used of behaviour which is appropriate to the environment.
2 Psychologists use the Intelligence Quotient (IQ) as the operational definition of intelligence; this indicates how well an individual compares with others in tests involving logical thinking.
3 It is not possible to find out whether genetics or environment is the major influence on an individual's IQ, but we can try to find out how much they cause differences in IQ.
4 Twin studies are the major research tool for this, but there are severe practical difficulties in carrying them out which make their results rather unreliable.

5 Probably no universal perfect environment exists to help the development of intelligence, because it is not a single ability. Varied stimulation, as
early as possible, seems the best recommendation at present.

Further Reading

Rose, S., Lewontin, R.C. and Kamin, L.R., *Not in Our Genes* (1984,
    Penguin).

Chapter 15

The Nature/Nurture Debate on Perception

Introduction

We experience the world through our sense organs which send information to the brain in the form of nerve impulses. For most of us this experience is something that we take for granted; the brain produces a model of the world without our thinking about it – it just happens! This disguises the fact that the brain does a very complicated job of organizing and interpreting information from the sense organs, a process known as *perception* (see chapter 2).

In the process of perception the brain has to make decisions about shape, size, distance, colour, brightness and many other factors. In this chapter, we are looking at how it is that we come to have perceptual abilities. Before we do, though, try this:

Look at figure 15.1(a). What is it? It can be perceived in a number of ways but many would say that it is simply a jumble of black blobs. In fact

Figure 15.1.(a)

it is a picture of a long-haired man with a beard, but simply being given this information is unlikely to change your perception. Now turn the page to figure 15.1(b), which is a 'cleaned up' version of the picture; it is not exactly the same but when you look back at the original, you will be able to 'see' the long-haired man. (If this doesn't happen immediately, compare the two figures for a little longer.) The message from your eye hasn't changed but now the brain is interpreting it in a different way. It may be that what you first saw in the picture was something like William James's 'blooming, buzzing confusion'. But now, experience has enabled you to perceive it differently. Some people argue that babies perceive the world in the sort of way that you first perceived figure 15.1(a) and that it is only through experience that the brain learns to interpret what it sees.

The Nature/Nurture Debate on Perception

Like the debate on intelligence, this discussion is about the relative import-ance of inherited and environmental influences. (Before reading this section you should consult the general introduction to the nature/nurture problem on pp. 247–8.)

The empiricist side of the debate stresses the role of experience in the development of perception; in its extreme form it maintains that only the simplest form of perception, *figure/ground* (the ability to perceive that there is 'something there' standing out from the background), is innate, and that all the rest of our perceptual abilities are learnt or are determined by the environment.

The nativist side of the debate stresses that, under normal circumstances, perceptual processes develop in an orderly manner controlled by the genetic 'blueprint'. If the baby's perception at birth is not the same as that of an adult it is largely because the perceptual system is immature and needs time to develop.

Until the 1960s many psychologists held the empiricist view that infants had very little perceptual ability. The idea was that although the eyes worked, the brain was not able to make much sense of the information it received until it had had the chance to learn from experience. As our methods of studying infants have improved we have found that their capacities are far greater than was previously thought.

Babies use gestures rather than words to communicate, so we can find out what they perceive by studying what they do.

Infants often fall down steps and it had been thought that one of the reasons for this was that they could not perceive depth. The work of E.J. Gibson and R.D. Walk in 1960 demonstrated that they can, in fact, tell that one surface is lower or further away than another. They constructed an

Figure 15.1.(b)

apparatus known as the 'visual cliff' (see figure 15.2). Towards one end of the apparatus, immediately under the glass 'floor', was stuck some black-and-white check material; towards the other, the material was placed about four feet below the glass. The effect was therefore of a visual cliff on the right hand side of the apparatus in the figure.

Figure 15.2. The 'Visual Cliff' (Gibson and Walk's Experiment)

Shallow side   Baby   Deep side

Gibson and Walk studied babies aged between six and fourteen months. They were placed on the central plank and their mothers then called them from the 'deep' or the 'shallow' side. The infants would crawl to their mothers over the 'shallow' side, but would not move over the 'deep' side. Occasionally babies would fall on to the glass over the 'deep' side; they were alright until they looked down, when they showed obvious signs of fear. It seems, then, that if infants of this age fall down steps and off chairs it is not because they do not see the depth but because they have yet to develop adequate control of their movements. This study cannot be performed until the child is old enough to crawl and so it does not tell us whether the child has developed this particular ability or whether depth perception is possible from birth. Other animals, such as cats, sheep and chickens can be tested a few hours after birth and all show an avoidance of the deep side.

Campos (1978) placed babies on to the visual cliff apparatus and found that infants as young as two months old showed a change of heart-rate when placed on the deep side but not when placed on the shallow side. Infants of this age could obviously perceive the depth but they showed no fear, suggesting that this fear has to be learnt by experiences of falling.

When you move your head or your eyes, objects which are close to you move quickly across your field of vision but objects that are at a distance move more slowly. This can be seen most clearly when moving in a car. A hedge at the side of the road seems to fly past but a tree two-hundred yards beyond the hedge seems to drift slowly across the visual field. The brain can use this information, amongst others, to help perceive distance; if an object swings wildly across the visual field when the eyes are moved the brain assumes that it is close, if it moves more slowly it must be further away. This clue to distance is known as *motion parallax*, and Gibson and Walk suggest that this is the main way in which depth is detected by young infants.

The *visual preference method* has been used by a number of researchers to discover the quality of infant perception. Using this method babies are shown two pictures at the same time. If these two pictures are exactly the same, babies should, on average, spend the same amount of time looking at each of them; if, on the other hand, they are very different it is likely that the baby will prefer one to the other and will spend more time looking at that picture. If infant perception is poorer than ours we might find that objects which look different to us appear the same to a baby.

R. L. Fantz (1961) was one of the first people to use this method. He showed that babies between one and fifteen weeks old were able to distinguish many patterns; for example, he found that a bull's-eye pattern was preferred to stripes, checks and geometrical shapes, and that a drawing of a human face was preferred to all these patterns. Fantz suggested that babies may be innately programmed to prefer human faces to other objects, although others have argued that they simply prefer complicated patterns to simple ones and that in this study the faces were the most complicated pictures.

Fantz presented diagrammatic versions of faces like those in figure 15.3. On average the 1–15-week-olds preferred to look at the 'normal' rather than the scrambled face. This does not definitely mean that there is an innate preference to the human face; the preference may simply develop quickly due to exposure to faces.

Figure 15.3. Face Shapes of the Type used in Fantz's Experiment

(a) Organized face

(b) Scrambled face

(c) Shaded face shape

More recent research has shown us that newborn babies do seem to take particular notice of human faces and can distinguish between them. Bushnell, Sai and Mullin (1989) have shown that two-day-olds show a preference for their mother's face compared to that of a stranger.

The visual preference method has shown us that before the age of six months infants cannot see fine detail. This ability to see fine detail is known as *acuity*. If you have had difficulty telling the difference between C and G in the small letters of an optician's chart you have experienced the limits of your own visual acuity. Young babies show no preference between a grey card and a card with thin black and white lines on it. The pictures that a baby experiences would seem very fuzzy to us because their acuity is between ten and thirty times poorer than ours.

Size constancy is a perceptual process which allows us to judge correctly the size of objects no matter how close or how far away they are. An elephant on the other side of a field looks big, and a ladybird on your hand looks small, yet the images of them both on the retina of the eye may actually be the same size. With increasing distance an object's image size decreases, but size constancy enables us to overcome this false information from the retina, and to realize that the elephant is not really as small as the ladybird but is just much further away. Without size constancy, objects would appear to grow or shrink as they moved towards or away from us. Some investigations by T.G. Bower in 1967 showed very young babies do in fact have the size constancy mechanism.

In figure 15.4 the two-month-old baby is placed on the table in a comfortable cot from which he can see an object. He comes to learn that if he turns his head to one side he is rewarded by an adult playing peek-a-boo and tickling him. This is an example of operant conditioning (see p. 47). Once the baby has been conditioned in this way he will give many head-turns when the original object is placed in front of him, but if the object is changed for something completely different he will give far fewer head-turns. The number of head-turns given to an object will tell us how similar the baby considers the new object to the original one.

Figure 15.4. General Layout of Bower's Experiment

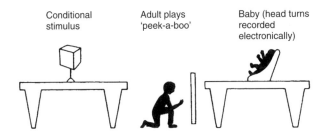

| Conditional stimulus | Adult plays 'peek-a-boo' | Baby (head turns recorded electronically) |

Bower conditioned babies to turn their heads when a 30 cm cube was placed one metre in front of them. He wanted to know whether the infant would recognize this cube when it was shown further away or whether they could confuse it with a 90 cm cube placed three metres in front. The reason for using a 90 cm cube at three metres is that it produces an image on the retina of the eye which is exactly the same size as the image produced by the smaller cube at one metre.

If babies cannot use the size constancy mechanism, the 30 cm cube at three metres would seem like a new object and therefore stimulate few head-turns. To a baby without size constancy the 90 cm cube at three metres would look very like the original cube and would be greeted by many head-turns.

Bower showed that his babies (aged two months) did in fact use the size constancy mechanism. They were able to recognize the 30 cm cube even though it had been moved further away. They were not confused by the 90 cm cube and gave far fewer head-turns to this stimulus when it was placed at three metres. They gave a few more to the 90 cm cube at one metre, presumably because they recognized that although it was a new cube it had some similarities to the original and was placed in the same position. By far the most head-turns were given to the 30 cm cube whether it was at one or three metres.

Figure 15.5. Cubes Used in Bower's Experiment

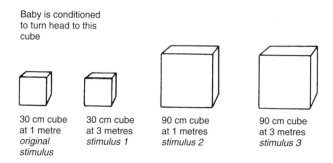

Baby is conditioned
to turn head to this
cube

30 cm cube	30 cm cube	90 cm cube	90 cm cube
at 1 metre	at 3 metres	at 1 metres	at 3 metres
original	*stimulus 1*	*stimulus 2*	*stimulus 3*
stimulus			

Although Bower showed that two–month-old infants have the size con-stancy mechanism, there has been much disagreement about whether the mechanism is present at birth (the nativist view) or has to develop with experience (the empiricist view).

Slater, Mattock and Brown (1990) have provided evidence for the nativist view by showing that newborn infants are able to recognize objects at different distances. They used a method known as an *habituation procedure* which relies on the fact that if an infant is shown an object for a long period of time it loses interest in it and will prefer to look at a new object. On many occasions they showed cube A to babies at a number of different distances from the child. When cube A was later shown together with a different size cube (B), the babies preferred to look at the new cube even though A and B were placed at different distances so that they both produced the same size image on the retina. If the newborns were not able to use the size constancy mechanism there would be no reason to prefer one cube to the other.

Studies of babies have shown that they have a much more well developed perceptual system than many of the early empiricists believed. William James's description of the perceptual world of an infant as a blooming buzzing confusion seems to be a great exaggeration but nevertheless we should not assume that the infant's perceptual experience of the world is the same as ours. We have the advantage of being able to use our previous experiences to relate what is in front of us now with what we have seen before. Our previous experiences help us to pick out the most relevant parts of a visual image and pay attention to them while ignoring irrele-vancies. The view of an infant may therefore be far more confusing. Gordon (1989) suggested that an infant's normal perception may be very like our own during the first few seconds of waking up in a strange room: 'we see everything but nothing makes sense'.

Deprivation Studies

It would be wrong to assume that because the infant has a fairly sophisticated perceptual system, experience does not have a great influence. There is a sensitive period during the first two or three years during which children must have a variety of active visual experiences if they are not to suffer lasting perceptual damage. Most of the studies which show the effect of visual deprivation were done with animal subjects because it is not ethically acceptable to deliberately deprive children in order to see the effect. There is a widely held view, with which we have sympathy, that it is not right to subject animals to the sort of deprivation that occurs in some of these studies no matter what the value of the findings.

In 1947 A.N. Riesen kept a group of chimpanzees in darkness from birth until they had matured, and compared them with normally reared chimpanzees. The group deprived of light showed markedly inferior perceptual abilities. L. Weiscrantz found that this was due to the fact that the retinas of the chimps reared in darkness had not developed properly and contained fewer retinal cells. Riesen's experiment shows that light is necessary to maintain the visual system or to help it mature.

Riesen then tested chimps which had been raised wearing translucent goggles, which allowed only diffused light to enter the eye. The experience of wearing translucent goggles is like looking through thick bathroom windows: light comes through but there are no clear images. Under these conditions the retina was not damaged but the chimps still had very poor perceptual abilities compared with normally reared animals. At the time of the study it was felt that this result could be used as evidence that perceptual abilities develop as a result of experience rather than being present at birth.

D.H. Hubel and T.N. Wiesel (1962) found that kittens reared in translucent goggles did not develop normal connections between the retina of the eye and cells in the visual cortex of the brain. In normally reared animals, particular cells in the visual cortex are stimulated when a line of light pointing in a particular direction is shone into a particular part of the retina. This area of the retina is known as the *receptive field* of the cortical cell. Some cortical cells have receptive fields which stimulate them when a vertical line is shone on to the retina; others are only stimulated by horizontal or diagonal lines. Receptive fields are very important in the perception of shape because differently shaped objects will stimulate different combinations of cells in the cortex.

In 1966 C. Blakemore and G.F. Cooper brought up cats in a 'vertical world', a drum which had only vertical lines drawn on it. The cats were therefore presented with images, but these were very specific, being vertical only. When the cats had matured their perceptual abilities were tested, and it was found that they were unable to perceive horizontal lines. Their receptive fields had developed, but only those which registered vertical lines would operate: horizontal lines had no effect on them. Suggestions were made that this result showed that line recognition has to be learnt. But it is more likely that receptive fields capable of registering lines at all angles are present at birth but that unused fields deteriorate, or are 'taken over' by fields registering vertical lines.

Thus it seems the type of environment is important in the development of perception: this in turn suggests that learning plays at least some part in perception, and that it is not all innate. However, visual experience alone is not enough. R. Held and A. Hein (1963), for example, showed that for perceptual development to take place fully the tested subject must be allowed to use its eyes and also to manipulate, or at least move around in its environment. In figure 15.6 both kittens, A and B, are given exactly the same amount and type of visual experience. Kitten A's movements are transmitted via a system of pulleys of kitten B's basket so that any movements made by kitten A are transmitted automatically to kitten B. Both kittens have exactly the same amount of movement in their environment,

Figure 15.6. The Apparatus used by Held and Hein

the only difference being that kitten A's movements are active (it moves itself) and kitten B's are passive (it does not control its movement).

The passive kitten showed much less perceptual development than the active kitten, which suggests that activity in, or interaction with, the environment is necessary for full perceptual development.

Although it is not possible to conduct experiments which deliberately cause deprivation to humans, there are examples of people who have suffered deprivation through illness or accident and the effect of this on later perception can be seen. One of the best known studies of this type is that described by R.L. Gregory in 1963. In this case a 54-year-old man who had been blind since birth was given his sight as a result of the development of a new surgical technique to remove cataracts from the eye. At first the patient could only experience the figure/ground phenomenon: he was aware of objects standing out against a background but was unable to recognize them by sight alone. When allowed to handle objects he found it much easier to see them. This ability to use information from one sense to assist a different sense is known as *cross-modal transfer*. After a fairly short period of time the patient was generally able to overcome the initial problems and to perceive fairly normally.

Annis and Frost (1973) studied Cree Indians in Canada. Some Cree Indians are still reared in traditional tents made of wooden poles covered in animal skins. Viewed from inside the tent, the poles are at a variety of angles, not just horizontal and vertical. Cree Indians reared in towns have much more experience of vertical and horizontal lines. If groups of 'tent' and 'town' Cree are tested on their ability to decide whether pairs of lines were parallel, we might expect the 'town' Cree, because of their early experience, to be better at deciding when the lines were vertical or horizontal than when they were at different angles. Similarly, 'tent' Cree, reared in a visual environment with lines at all angles, may be expected to be equally good at judging whether sets of lines are parallel, whatever angle they were presented at. This is exactly what Annis and Frost found, supporting the idea that early experience can affect our perception.

Children who are born with bad squints are deprived of the normal input to the brain from both eyes working together, and as a result can lose their ability to focus using both eyes and may have impaired depth perception. Studies show that damage is much more likely if the squint is not treated early. In the past it was thought best to delay treatment until the child was older and more ready to withstand the rigours of surgery, but now the operation is performed much earlier.

Distortion or Readjustment Studies

The aim of this type of study is to show that adult perceptual systems are not inflexible and can adjust to a new visual environment. If this can be shown in adults then it is likely that newborn babies also possess such a flexible perceptual system which is shaped by learning rather than one which is inflexible and innately determined.

Lower animals – lizards, frogs and chickens for example – do not appear able to adjust to a distorted visual world. Chickens wearing goggles that distort their vision by 10 degrees to the right never adapt enough to compensate for the distortion and miss the grain at which they are pecking by 10 degrees each time (E.H. Hess, 1956).

However, studies of adult humans wearing distorting goggles have shown that humans have a much greater ability to adapt to a changed visual world. Ivo Kohler wore goggles in which the left half of each lens was red and the right half green. At first his visual world appeared red when he looked to the left and green when he looked to the right. After only a few hours this apparent division was no longer experienced: he had evidently adjusted to compensate for the change. However, when he removed the goggles, Kohler found that his visual world seemed to be coloured in the opposite direction to that experienced when first wearing goggles, but only for a short time, after which it returned to normal. Once more he had been able to adjust. Kohler also experimented on himself and others using goggles which inverted or displaced objects in their visual world. At first he experienced great disorientation and nausea, but after several days he was able to adjust and live reasonably normally.

G.M. Stratton performed similar experiments on himself using inverted goggles. After a few days' adaptation he was able to move around normally and his visual world appeared to be the right way up except when he really concentrated. On removal of the goggles there was again a reversed after-effect, which lasted only a short time.

Such evidence from readjustment studies shows that human perceptual systems retain a flexibility and an ability to alter in the light of experience even in adulthood. The perceptual system is certainly not inflexible, as some of the early nativists believed.

Cross-Cultural Studies

Cross-cultural studies demonstrate the effect of different life experiences on some aspects of perception. Many studies show that people from different cultures are affected differently by illusions such as the *Muller-Lyer illusion*. To most of us the horizontal line at the bottom of figure 15.7 looks longer than the one above it, even though in fact the horizontal lines are the same length. Segall, Campbell and Herskovits (1963) found that members of African tribes living in jungle conditions were much less susceptible to this illusion and tended to see the lines as the same length.

There have been numerous explanations put forward for the differences in the susceptibility to illusions, but it is probably due to the extent to

Figure 15.7. The Muller-Lyer Illusion

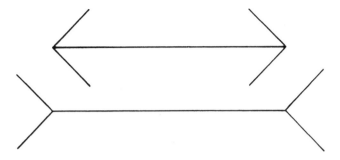

which people are accustomed to interpreting two-dimensional drawings and pictures (a skill which we take for granted in our world which is so full of photographs).

Some studies have shown that size constancy (see p. 13) is not used for far objects by people whose normal experience does not include distant views. Turnbull (1961) reported an experience with a pygmy from the rain forest of the African Congo. He took the pygmy to an open plain and pointed out a buffalo in the distance; the pygmy refused to believe that this was a large animal, arguing that it looked like an insect. Only when Turnbull drove the pygmy over to the animal did he believe that it actually was large. The pygmy's perceptual system had not applied size constancy to the small image on the retina of his eye to take account of the fact that the animal was far away. This is probably because the pygmy had no experience of seeing great distances and so his perceptual system had not learned to recognize the clues to distance contained in the view; with no recognition of distance the size constancy mechanism will not be used.

Conclusions
The research on the nature/nurture debate on perception has shown us that animals which are low on the evolutionary scale have very inflexible perceptual systems which are preset from birth. For example, certain species of frogs have genetically determined perceptual systems which, without any need for learning, make them very sensitive to small dark images which move quickly. When the frog detects such a stimulus it automatically extends its tongue and is therefore very efficient at catching flies. If such a frog were surrounded by dead flies it would starve to death because its innate, inflexible perceptual system is not sensitive to still flies, only to moving ones.

As we move up the animal kingdom, perceptual systems become more flexible and able to learn from experience. The human newborn has a perceptual system which, although it cannot detect fine detail, has a fair level of competence in skills such as shape, size and depth perception. These develop as the nervous system matures and becomes capable of more detailed processing. We now believe that infants are able to recognize the face of their mother at a very early age, although, it is likely that this is as a result of much less detailed analysis of facial features than that performed by an adult.

The development of the perceptual system requires a variety of stimulation and active participation of the individual with their environment, and it looks as though there is a period during the first two or three years when the developing perceptual system is most sensitive to those experiences.

The studies that we have discussed show that it is not sensible to take an extreme nativist or empiricist position on the nature/nurture debate. Perception develops as an interaction between innate and environmental factors.

Summary

1 Perception is the process by which the brain organizes and interprets information from the sense organs. In this chapter we have concentrated on visual perception which involves the interpretation of information from the eyes to determine qualities such as shape, size, colour and distance.

2 Nativists stress the importance of genetic factors in the development of perception and tend to regard the perceptual system as fairly fixed and unalterable. Empiricists stress that it is much more flexible and is altered as a result of experience. The debate between people holding these two viewpoints is known as the nature/nurture debate.

3 Studies of babies' perceptual abilities demonstrate that although the 'picture in their head' is fuzzy they are able to make judgements on shape, size and distance amongst other things.

4 Deprivation studies, in which an individual is reared without being allowed to practice normal perception, suggest that the environment does play an important part in the development of perception. Deprivation may lead to a degeneration of existing perceptual systems, especially if it occurs early in life. To develop normally an individual must have an active involvement with a variety of visual stimuli.

5 Distortion studies, which show that an adult can readjust and learn to perceive the world accurately again after his vision has been distorted, demonstrate the flexibility of the perceptual system.

6 Cross-cultural studies reveal that individuals from different cultures have differences in their perceptual abilities.

7 The range of studies considered suggests that innate and environmental factors interact to produce a well-functioning mature perceptual system.

Further Reading

Bee, H., *Growing Child (An Applied Approach)* (1998, Collins).

Chapter 16

Language, Problem-solving and Creativity

Explanations of Language Development

This is another example of a 'nature-nurture' debate. B.F. Skinner, the developer of operant conditioning (see p. 41), was an *empiricist* (one who studies the role of learning and experience in language development). Noam Chomsky put forward the most influential nativist theory, that language development occurred because of innate factors.

Skinner's Approach

Skinner believed that children developed language through Operant Conditioning (see p. 41). In particular Skinner believed that there were three types of early language responses which children could make.

1 *Mand (from 'demand')*. A mand is when a child wants something (for example, milk) and makes a sound (e.g. 'muk') which is reinforced by being given some milk or by the parents becoming excited by their child's use of a new word! In future, this sound can be shaped (see p. 47) into the correct word.

2 *Tact*. A tact is a name for an object or action. Children hear language all around them, and adults often link words and objects (e.g. 'here's the cat!') Children can learn to associate words with objects and are reinforced by praise or attention from adults.

3 *Echoic response*. An echoic response is when a child imitates or practises a word which it hears and is reinforced by adults.

Most psychologists agree with the idea that children can learn words through some form of operant conditioning. However, several experiments show that operant conditioning does not appear to work for the development of grammar (the child's understanding of the rules of language.) For example, Jean Berko gave children aged less than four years figures such as:

Figure 16.1 Jean Berko's Wug

This is a wug.

Now there is another one
There are two of them.
There are two ＿＿ .

All children said 'wugs' (even though they had never come across a wug before), showing that they grasped the rule about adding an 's' to make a plural. Similarly, Berko showed a picture of a man swinging an unidentified object over his head. She told the children that the man was 'glinging', and asked them what he did yesterday. The children said 'glinged', showing they had learnt the rule of adding 'ed' to a word to indicate the past tense. (Adults, who have learnt more rules, give answers such as 'glang', 'glung' and even 'glought' in addition to 'glinged'.)

Tizard studied children whose parents were encouraged to correct faulty grammar and reinforce correct usage. According to Skinner, such children should show improved grammatical skills; in fact Tizard noted no improvement in the children's grammar. Slobin found that parents generally did not operantly condition a child's grammar. Instead they reinforced true or correct statements, even if they were not grammatically correct.

Chomsky's Approach

Chomsky believed that Skinner was wrong; operant conditioning can teach words, but not grammar. He coined the statement 'Colourless green ideas sleep furiously'. This is grammatically correct but, said Chomsky, could not have been uttered if language development occurred only through operant conditioning. It is extremely unlikely that anybody would ever have been conditioned to link 'colourless' and 'green', 'sleep' and 'furiously'. There must be some underlying process in humans, which allows us to learn not just words but the rules of grammar. Chomsky believed that all humans have an innate *Language Acquisition Device* (LAD) – some form of innate ability to extract the rules of grammar from the language we hear around us. The LAD gives us the competence to use grammatical rules correctly even with words which are new to us; it also allows us to utter sentences which are unique. ('Colourless green ideas sleep furiously') but which are still grammatical. Operant conditioning gives language performance only (a parrot can perform language in that it can imitate human language, but it does not have the competence to generate sentences of its own).

The LAD, according to Chomsky, allows us to translate the meaning of something (the *deep structure*) into a number of different ways of expressing it in language which Chomsky called the *surface structure*. For example, there is a wonderful Monty Python sketch in which John Cleese finds lots of different ways to explain to a shopkeeper that a parrot which he has just bought is dead, ending in '... this is an ex-parrot!'. Similarly, the LAD allows us to interpret surface structures which can have more than one deep structure. For example:

'Visiting relatives can be boring'. (Surface Structure)

Deep Structure 1   Deep Structure 2

'Going to visit these people can be boring.'   'Relatives who visit me can be boring'.

The LAD is responsible for our understanding of syntax, the rules of word order. For example, the sentences with 'the boy chased the girl' and 'the girl chased the boy' both contain exactly the same words, but their similar surface structures have different deep structure meanings.

If language competence in the form of the LAD is innate, as Chomsky believed, all humans should possess it, and should develop it in similar stages, though not necessarily at the same time. Lenneberg found that language development in normal and Down's syndrome children occurred in the same stages, but Down's syndrome children moved through the stages more slowly. They also developed motor skills such as walking and the ability to manipulate objects more slowly than other children, though in the same sequence. This supports the idea that language, like motor development, is due to the maturation of some physiological structures, and is therefore probably innate.

Lenneberg believed that there is a critical period (see p. 151) for language development, from birth until about the ages of 10 or 11 years. If language has not developed during this time, it cannot develop after it. During the critical period however, the child needs only to be able to hear language and does not have to be taught it. However, studies by Bishop (1988) on people who lost their capacity for language (aphasia) through brain injury showed that, whilst children under the age of 11 could redevelop language, so also could people in early adulthood. For this reason (see also Sluckins work, on p. 152) the term *Sensitive Period* is now used, rather than *Critical Period*.

A study by Bard and Sachs (1977) provides some evidence in support of a sensitive rather than a critical period. They studied a boy named Jim, who had normal hearing but who had parents who were deaf and used only sign language to communicate with each other and with Jim. Jim had access to TV and radio, which allowed him to hear language spoken. Jim had learnt enough sign language by 3¾ years old to communicate with his parents, but did not use spoken language at all. So mere exposure to language is apparently not enough to enable the LAD to extract the rules of language. However, at 3¾ years of age, Jim was sent to a speech therapist and by the age of 4, he was able to speak normally. Moving from zero speech to normal speech in only 3 months suggests that there is some maturational process at work - Jim was clearly ready to speak, but had not been exposed to language in the proper way. What seems to be necessary is interaction with other people rather than just hearing language spoken, as Lenneberg believed. While there seems to be some role for maturation in the development of language, innate factors by themselves do not lead to language development. Some learning must take place and the Jim study showed that interaction with other humans seems to be necessary.

Bruner (1975) showed that mothers use language with a child in context; that is, they use language to refer to things that the child is doing or to objects which it is manipulating ('Here's your teddy'). The child is therefore able to link its own understanding of what it is doing to the language which its mother is using. Harris *et al.* (1986) found that mothers of 16-month-old children spent 78 per cent of their total talking time speaking about what the child was doing or what it was looking at. Mothers of children whose language development was regarded as poor by the age of 2, however, spoke about such things only 49 per cent of the time. Unsurprisingly, from the evidence so far, it seems that language abilities are neither wholly innate nor wholly learnt; both are necessary for normal development.

Sequences of Language Development

The classic study of stages in language development was carried out by Roger Brown (1973). He studied three infants, Adam, Eve and Sarah, in their normal (home) environments over a period of three years. Brown's study clarified the stages through which children pass and examined the role of adults (particularly the mother) in language development.

According to Bee (1980), the general sequence of language development occurs as outlined below. However, it should be noted that the ages given are a general guide only – while all children go through the same sequence, they do not do so necessarily at the same age. Before the first word is uttered at about 10 months of age, the child is said to be pre-linguistic.

Birth to 1 month of age. The baby's vocal sounds are limited to crying, and parents can often interpret different forms of their child's cries as hunger, pain or fear, for example.

1 month to 6 months, cooing. In addition to crying, the baby introduces sounds which seem to indicate pleasure or contentment. These sounds are usually long vowel sounds ('aaa', or 'uuu') and are called cooing. Trevarthen (1974) showed (by simultaneously filming the faces of mothers and babies in interaction) that babies as young as 8 weeks old could imitate their mothers' facial expressions and mouth movements and were able to take turns with their mothers in doing so. This suggests that, whilst the baby is not yet apparently learning to speak, it is already learning how to take turns in conversations!

6 months to 10–12 months, babbling stage. In addition to crying and cooing, the child begins to use some consonant sounds, particularly 'd', 'g' and 'k'. These consonants become linked with vowel sounds, so that sounds like 'da' are produced. These sounds become repeated towards the latter part of this phase (and the child gains pleasure from doing it) so that it produces strings of sounds like 'dadadada'. Linguists call this repetition of a sound *echolalia*. The sounds produced by the child are not linked to the child's native language. For example, Japanese babies in the babbling phase use the '1' sound, which adult Japanese do not; English babies make vowel sounds which are common in German but not in English.

10 months to 14 months, first word stage. A child's first word may not resemble the adult version very closely at all. What makes a group of sounds into a word is the child's consistent use of it to refer to a specific thing. Thus a child may use the sound 'ag' to refer to food. Although 'ag' in no way resembles the sound 'food', linguists would still call it a word. After the first word, a period of approximately 3 months passes before the child's vocabulary reaches 4 words. After this, progress is rapid, so that at the age of about 18 months, children's' vocabularies usually total 40 or 50 words and at 24 months 300 words.

Although many of these words are names for objects or people, children can use them to substitute for whole sentences. For example, a child who says 'milk' usually makes facial expressions and gestures too so that the single word is clearly interpreted by the parents as 'Give me some milk'. Speech which uses single words to stand for whole sentences is called *holophrastic* speech – 'milk' in the example above is a holophrase.

Even in the one-word stage, children have some understanding of sentences. In a study by Sachs and Truswell (1978), children showed by their behaviour that they could follow simple instructions such as 'kiss dog', 'bang car' and even 'tickle book'.

18 months to 30 months, two word stage, telegraphic speech and early sentences.
During the early part of this stage, the child develops the ability not only
to use pairs of words, but to do so grammatically as sentences. For example,
'see truck', 'all gone milk', 'Daddy go'. Such sentences are called telegraphic speech because they include only the key words, just as if they were
a telegram. You wouldn't send a telegram saying 'Please send some money
to me at the Excelsior Hotel where I'm staying'. You would include only the
key words (usually nouns or verbs or adjectives) 'send money Exelsior
Hotel'. Although telegraphic speech is still simple, just like holophrastic
speech, a two-word sentence can mean different things in different contexts.
For example, in different circumstances 'Daddy go' may stand for 'Daddy
is going', 'Daddy, please go' or 'Is Daddy going?'. Bee (1980) terms this
stage *Stage 1 Grammar*. Towards the end of this stage, the child becomes
able to produce longer sentences. In figure 16.2 the graph is adapted from

Figure 16.2. Roger Brown's Analysis of Language Development in
Young Children

Roger Brown's study of three children, Adam, Eve and Sarah. The mean average number of words which each child could speak in a sentence is shown (as *Mean Length of Utterance* (MLU)) on the vertical scale.

Note from this graph that the pattern of development for each child is similar (the lines all climb at similar rates), but that the age at which each child develops differs. In this case, Eve has developed a mean length of utterance of 4 words by age 25 months, approximately, whilst Adam and Sarah do not develop an MLU of 4 words until 41 months of age.

However, until the next stage, the child cannot use plurals, or past tenses.

Stage 2 Grammar, 30 months+. These forms of grammar develop during this stage and continue developing for the next two or three years. During this stage, the child learns the grammatical rules for things such as prepositions ('but', 'and'), plurals, irregular verb endings such as went (rather than 'wented') or saw (rather than 'seed'). Later in this stage, possessives (such as 'its', 'hers', 'theirs') develop. The study by Berko on p. 277 shows clearly that children develop grammatical rules because they can apply them to situations or objects which they have never seen before. Once a rule is learned, it is often applied to every possible similar situation, or overgeneralized. This overgeneralization occurs during this stage and gives rise to some of the language errors which parents find so enchanting ('I goed to school'). Later in this stage, too, the grammatical rules for questions (which, why, when, where?) develop as does the ability to deal with the passive tense. For example, the child can understand that in the sentence 'the dog was hit by the boy' it is the boy who is doing the hitting. Full understanding and use of passive sentences does not occur, however, until after the age of 6 years. By the age of 5 or 6, though, the child has developed most of the grammatical rules which it will need while vocabulary continues to grow throughout life.

Is Language Restricted to Humans?

The nativists believe that language is a species-specific ability, unique to humans. They think that it is not just quantitatively different from animal languages (that is, there is more of it), but that it is also qualitatively different – it is based on different principles and operates in a different way. The major method of testing this hypothesis has been to try to teach human language to non-human species. If they have the LAD, or language competence, they should be able to learn it. If they can learn it, this shows that they have a (presumably innate) competence, even though they may not use it in the wild.

We must first have some yardstick against which to measure the animals' language learning abilities: at which point can we agree that they have learnt a human language? The ability to speak it turns out to be not very useful. Dumb humans cannot speak the language, yet are assumed to have it. Similarly, parrots and mynah birds can speak but do not apparently understand language, largely because they cannot use it flexibly.

C.F. Hockett (1958) produced a list of criteria for human language, which he termed 'design features'. He believed that human language, and human language users, show all these features. It is these which have become widely accepted as the criteria by which non-human attempts at language development should be measured.

CRITERIA FOR HUMAN LANGUAGE
Note that features 1 to 4 are concerned with the ways in which speech carries information (there are ways of using language other than speaking).

1 *Vocal/auditory:* it is carried by sound, which is made vocally by one individual and received auditorily (through hearing) by another.
2 *Broadcast transmission/directional reception:* the sounds made are broadcast, and individuals receiving them should be able to tell from which direction the sound is coming.
3 *Rapid fading:* a vocal utterance fades rapidly (unlike written language, which can be read and re-read).
4 *Total feedback:* when you speak, you can hear what you are saying. (You could not see what you were saying if you were using semaphore, but you could hear what you were saying when using speech.)
5 *Interchangeability:* a speaker can send and receive information.
6 *Specialization:* the speech function is for communication only. It should not be a by-product of some other form of behaviour.
7 *Semanticity:* language has meanings.
8 *Arbitrariness:* language does not need to look like or sound like the things it symbolizes.
9 *Traditional transmission*: language can be transmitted from one generation to the next.
10 *Learnability:* language can be learnt. (Humans can learn languages other than their native one.)
11 *Discreteness:* information is not coded by the length of the utterance, but by the position of the phonemes.
12 *Duality of patterning:* language has a double pattern:
    (a) Phonemes are organized into words.
    (b) Words are organized into sentences.
13 *Displacement:* language enables the user to refer to objects or situations which are displaced in time or space.
14 *Openness/productivity:* language is capable of generating an infinite number of new meanings (novel utterances).
15 *Prevarication:* language enables the individual to lie, or to talk about things which are impossible.

16 *Reflexiveness:* using language, an individual can talk about language.

Whether or not non-human primates possess language abilities can now be tested against these criteria.

TEACHING HUMAN LANGUAGE TO NON-HUMAN PRIMATES

The earliest systematic attempt to teach human language to a non-human species was undertaken by Hayes and Hayes (1951). Using Operant Conditioning with their baby chimpanzee, Vicki, they managed to get her to speak four words ('mama', 'papa', 'cup' and 'up') by the age of three years. Kellogg and Kellogg (1933) reared a chimpanzee called Gua with their own child. Gua was able to understand seventy words or commands, but was unable to speak.

Allen and Beatrice Gardner (1969) thought that the failure of these early attempts meant either that chimpanzees could not develop language, or that they had language competence but were physiologically incapable of speaking. The various gestures which Vicki used in trying to speak gave them the idea of using a human sign language with a chimpanzee. The Gardners' chimpanzee, a female named Washoe, was born wild, and her language training began when she was about nine months old. The language used with Washoe was '*Ameslan*', short for *American sign language*, developed from Red Indian sign languages. Ameslan was the Gardners' sole means of communication with Washoe, and they were quickly impressed with her ability to imitate signs. If her signs were not accurate enough, the Gardners used behaviour-shaping techniques and their own development of these, *moulding*, which involved their actually manipulating Washoe's hands, in order to make the correct signs. Three years after training began, Washoe knew 85 signs, which increased to 160 by the time she left the Gardners two years later. Only ten months after the start of training, when she was approximately twenty months old, Washoe made her first combinations of signs ('Gimme sweet', and 'Come-open'). She showed an early ability to name objects (something which was previously thought to be unique to humans), and the Gardners used a *double-blind* technique to avoid bias in their results, as follows. They presented a series of photographic slides of objects, in random order, to Washoe, who had to make the appropriate Ameslan sign for each of them. Washoe's signs were observed and noted by an experimenter who was unable to see the slides himself. Consequently, if Washoe's sign was clear enough for him to understand and interpret, and it was also correct, Washoe must have learned to name an object correctly. This technique controlled for the possibility that Washoe might simply be making sloppy or ambiguous signs which the Gardners wishfully interpreted as being correct.

After she left the Gardners Washoe went to Oklahoma, where she now lives with other Ameslan-using chimps under the care of Roger Fouts. He has compared the chimpanzees' performance with Hockett's design features, and believes that the chimps have demonstrated enough language ability to seriously damage the assertion that language is unique to humans. Of the other chimps in the colony, Ally is particularly interesting, since he is a very clear 'signer', learns very quickly, and can apparently translate spoken words into Ameslan signs.

Below is a summary of some of Fouts' findings and research techniques. Note that some of the design features are inapplicable to Ameslan-using chimpanzees: design features numbers (7), (8), (10) and (11) listed on p. 283 are properties of their language, not of the speaker, and numbers (1), (2) and (3) are inapplicable because Ameslan is not a spoken language. This means that the main design features for comparing animals and humans are interchangeability, displacement, openness/productivity, traditional transmission, prevarication and reflexiveness.

Interchangeability   In the Oklahoma chimp colony the chimps use Ameslan among themselves even when no human is visible, both for sending and receiving messages.

Displacement   Fouts has designed an investigation to see whether his chimps can show displacement. One chimp is taken out of sight of the others, who are caged. This chimp is shown two hidden 'presents'. One is food, and the other, something which chimps dislike (a stuffed snake, for example). The chimp is then put back into the cage with the others and left with them for a while. After this the other chimps are released and the original chimp kept in the cage. If the original chimp has managed to convey where the hidden 'presents' are, Fouts believes that this is evidence for displacement. (If only the whereabouts of the stuffed snake is conveyed, this might be evidence of prevarication!)

While with the Gardners, Washoe would sign 'time eat', which may suggest that she has some concept of time (the formation of which requires some displacement abilities). However, to date, displacement has not been conclusively demonstrated.

Openness/productivity   Washoe invented her own sign for 'bib', since the Gardners did not know the proper sign – and Washoe's invented sign turned out to be close to the correct Ameslan. Lucy, one of Fouts' chimps, coined her own name for radishes – 'hurt-cry fruit' – and she also calls watermelons 'candy-drink' or 'fruit drink', even though she knows the correct Ameslan sign for watermelon.

Koko, a female gorilla taught by Francine Patterson, has devised her own form of swearing. Washoe shows displeasure with somebody by signing 'dirty' before their name. Koko goes one better: her favourite phrase is 'You big dirty toilet'.

Traditional transmission Washoe gave birth to two babies, but both died in infancy. At her new home in Fouts's chimp colony she adopted an infant. Fouts claimed that there was clear transmission of signing from Washoe to the adopted infant, since that infant was able to produce signs that were not learnt from a human.

Prevarication Koko seems to have demonstrated this in her answer to the request 'Tell me something you think is funny'. She signed 'Nose there', pointing to a bird puppet's tongue; 'That red', and pointed to a green plastic frog. Francine Patterson also reports that when she puts a stethoscope to her ears, Koko smirks and puts fingers over her eyes.

Reflexiveness Michael, a male gorilla who lived with Koko, was trying to ask Francine Patterson to let him enter Koko's caravan. Patterson insisted that he make the correct signs, but he could not. Koko, watching through a window, demonstrated the correct signs which Michael copied, and he was then admitted. When she saw him enter, Koko signed 'Good sign Michael'.

Other researchers have used different techniques. Duane Rumbaugh at the Yerkes Primate Research Centre in Atlanta, Georgia, has investigated chimpanzees' abilities to deal with syntax. Lana, the chimp he used, lived with a computer, which would give her what she wanted only if she pressed the correct sign-buttons in the correct order. Thus, for example, she had to say 'Please machine give piece of apple' (full stop), but 'Please machine make music play' (full stop) or 'Please machine make window open' (full stop). Lana performs very accurately on these tests and can apparently tell the difference in meaning between 'Lana groom Tim' (one of her trainers), and 'Tim groom Lana' – a difference in meaning which is entirely due to syntax.

David Premack has devised a plastic sign language for use by his chimpanzee, Sarah. Using plastic symbols, she has been able to demonstrate her understanding of interrogatives, negatives, conditionals (if-then phrases) and full sentences, as well as object naming.

Such studies have not been without their critics. Despite the Gardners' use of double-blind techniques with Washoe, the decision as to whether or not a particular piece of behaviour satisfies one of Hockett's criteria is often a subjective one, and experimenters and critics differ on these judgements, and even on which criteria to use for judgement. Criticism of the experiments themselves has often been concerned with the degree to which the experimenters might have led the animal into signing what was required; for example, when Washoe signed 'Baby in my drink', H. Terrace, who himself attempted to teach Ameslan to a chimpanzee, claimed that he saw the Gardners 'cueing' Washoe. Other researchers, on looking at the film, disagree with him.

The feelings among the researchers themselves seem to be that interchangeability, productivity, reflexiveness and prevarication seem to have been demonstrated by the various primates, but that there does not seem to be enough evidence yet that displacement and traditional transmission have definitely been shown. Researchers still disagree about the extent to which primates can acquire human language. (See **Stop Press** on p. 366.)

Problem-solving and Creativity

Problems come in many shapes and sizes; from 'fun' problems such as crosswords and chess problems in newspapers through mathematical problems at school to serious problems such as 'How can we prevent global warming?'. Problem-solving involves: trying to reach a goal (a solution to the problem), a sequence of steps towards that goal (not just a single one like catching a falling cup for example) and requires thought (sorting knives, forks and spoons into a cutlery drawer is a fairly automatic activity and so would not be classed as problem-solving).

Algorithmic problem-solving

The earliest computers designed to play chess tended to be slow and not very successful against humans. They had been programmed with all the rules of chess including which moves were possible by each chess piece. In addition, they had been programmed to calculate all the millions of possible results of each move by themselves and by their human opponents. This is called *algorithmic* problem-solving. Try the problem in figure 16.3.

Figure 16.3. The Problem of the Bird and the Train

Train A
45 mph

Bird
20 mph

Train B
55 mph

← 100 miles →

A bird flies from train A towards train B at a constant speed of 20 miles per hour. When it reaches train B, it immediately turns and faces back towards train A (you can assume that the turning does not take any extra time) and this process is repeated until the trains meet. The question is: by the time the trains meet, how far will the bird have flown in total? The algorithmic way of solving this problem is to calculate how far train B would have moved by the time the bird reaches it, then calculate the distance travelled by train A whilst the bird was flying towards train B, plus the distance train A travelled whilst the bird was flying back towards it, and so on. A computer, suitably programmed, could do the calculation in a fraction of a second, because this type of repeated algorithmic calculation is exactly what computers are good at. However, there is a short-cut to the solution of this problem which humans can use but computers (unless specifically programmed to do so) cannot. The short-cut is this: how long does it take for the trains to meet? Once you know this, look at the bird's speed of flight!

Heuristic problem-solving

The short-cut described above is an example of *heuristic* problem-solving. Heuristic problem-solving involves using short-cuts or rules of thumb to look only at selected parts of the problem which are more likely to be the important ones. Modern chess computers are now programmed to use heuristic models; they are now much faster and can beat human chess grand masters. Newell and Simon (1972) described problem-solving as being a sequence of stages involving *operators* – actions or thoughts to solve problems.

1 *The problem* (Newell and Simon call this the *initial stage*).
2 Carry out *operators* which move you towards the solution. Try them all out – algorithmic or use rules of thumb to select the most promising until:
3 *Solution* (Newell and Simon call this the *goal state*).

The gap between the initial state and the goal state has been called the *problem space* by Newell and Simon.

In practice, humans use far more heuristic techniques than they do algorithmic and there are two major types of heuristic problem-solving techniques: *means-ends analysis* and the *analogy approach*.

Means-ends analysis

Using Newell and Simon's terms, this means crossing the problem space from the initial state to the goal state by choosing only operations which move you closer to the goal state perhaps by enabling you to reach a sub-goal. Imagine this scenario:

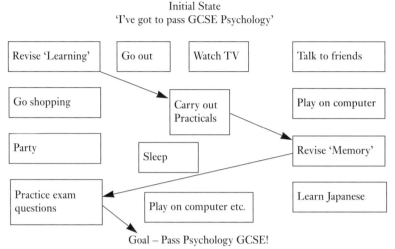

Initial State
'I've got to pass GCSE Psychology'

| Revise 'Learning' | Go out | Watch TV | | Talk to friends |

| Go shopping | | Carry out Practicals | | Play on computer |

| Party | | Sleep | | Revise 'Memory' |

| Practice exam questions | | Play on computer etc. | | Learn Japanese |

Goal – Pass Psychology GCSE!

Each time you have to make a choice, you do so on the basis of 'does doing this move me towards the goal or not?' If it does, do it! In the diagram above, 'revise learning' leads you to a sub-goal (you now know about the psychology of learning which is a sub-goal, a part of the whole psychology syllabus).

A means-ends analysis is one therefore where you choose the operators (the *means* by which you may solve the problems) which take you farthest towards your goals (the *ends*).

THE ANALOGY APPROACH

This heuristic technique can act as a very powerful short cut to a solution. The technique is to use an operator which has been useful in the past for solving a different problem, by asking yourself the questions – 'Have I ever come across this type of problem before?' and 'Which techniques worked then?' – or 'Have I ever experienced anything which could help to solve this problem?' The analogy approach has led to the development of two of the most influential scientific theories of all time. Albert Einstein developed the Theory of Relativity which changed physics. He reported that the lay idea (that the speed of light is constant) came to him as a sort of daydream. He was imagining what it would be like to ride on a beam of light, and while doing this he realized that if he did so, the light would appear to be stationary to him. The analogy ('What would it be like if I could ride a beam of light?') provided an extremely powerful short-cut to his understanding of the problem of relativity. Similarly August Kekule discovered the general principles of how atoms join together to form molecules. He was staring into the fire, and saw a pattern which looked like a snake eating its own tail. Wondering whether atoms could form such rings led Kekule to discover the structure of the benzene ring, which revolutionized chemistry. The analogy approach seems to depend on experience – and expertise – the more of each you have, the more able you are to use the analogy method.

Factors Affecting Problem-solving

Mental set

Previous experience of solving similar types of problems can be useful as we have seen. However, it is possible for previous experience to make it more difficult to solve a problem if the previous experience produces a 'mental set'. This occurs when a person becomes so used to utilising a particular type of operator that they tend to use it if even when there is a different or even simpler approach. A study by Luchins (1942) shows this. The problem is to get a fixed amount of water into a container (the goal amount). Containers of different sizes and unlimited water are provided. As an example:

Goal amount	Container A	Container B	Container C
18 litres	100 litres	40 litres	2 litres

Participants were given several similar problems. The solution is to fill container B twice from container A. This removes 80 litres, leaving 20 litres in container A. Filling container C from container A leaves 18 litres in container A. Most participants quickly learned to solve this type of problem. (There is a close analogy here with Harlow's theory of learning sets on pp. 57–8.) However, participants were then given a further problem, such as:

Goal amount	Container A	Container B	Container C
14 litres	23 litres	62 litres	9 litres

They still try (because of their mental or learning set) to use three containers. In fact, the solution is simply to fill container C from container A. In this case the mental set has hindered, rather than helped problem-solving.

Functional Fixedness

This is our tendency to assume that particular objects have a specific use and that they cannot be used for something else. Functional fixedness is like a mental set for the uses of objects. In a study by Duncker (1945) participants were placed individually in a bare room except for a table, a candle, a box of matches and a box of tin tacks. The problem they had to solve was to fix the candle to the wall. Because of functional fixedness (that boxes' only function is to contain things) many participants failed to solve the problem because they attempted to fix the candle to the wall by using melted wax or tin tacks. The solution is to empty the box, use one or two tin tacks to fix the box to the wall, then fix the candle to the box. As we shall see later (p. 292), one of the tests for creativity is to see how far people can overcome functional fixedness in thinking up alternative uses for everyday objects.

The Gestalt psychologists believed that humans have innate ways of processing information which cause us to see things in particular ways and therefore try to solve problems in ways which may not always be successful if we apply them rigidly. The Gestaltists called this rigidity of perception and thinking *einstellung* (einstellung can be translated as 'attitude' or 'view'). To see it in operation for yourself, solve this problem. Join all the dots with four straight lines, without going over a line twice or taking your pencil off the paper. (The solution is on p. 293.)

Even though you were not told that you had to keep your lines inside the nine dots, there is a tendency to assume that you must. This is the Gestalt principle of closure (see p. 292).

Convergent and Divergent Thinking

J.P. Guilford (1956) distinguished between two types of thinking.

Convergent thinking where the aim is to narrow down (converge) a number of possible answers to questions or solutions to problems to one 'correct' one. For example, many IQ test questions require convergent thinking ('what comes next in the series A,E,I,M,... ?).

Divergent thinking is the opposite: starting from one piece of information the aim is to produce many alternatives. For example, a popular question in tests of creativity is 'How many uses can you think of for a brick?'.

MacKinnon (1962) investigated the relationship between IQ (convergent thinking) and creativity (divergent thinking). He found that up to about IQ120, people with higher IQs tended also to be more creative, than people with lower IQs, '... but above a certain required minimum level of intelligence which varies from field to field, and in some instances may be surprisingly low, being more intelligent does not guarantee a corresponding increase in creativeness.' In other words, IQ and creativity tend to increase together up to about IQ120. An IQ of more than 120 is no guarantee of a higher level of creativity.

A study of famously creative US scientists in 1953 by Ann Roe showed that IQ tests, along with personality inventories, provided poor measurements of creativity. 'Indeed' she remarked, 'there are a number of subjects for whom none of the test material would give the slightest clue that the subject was a scientist of renown.' Famously creative people such as Darwin (low numeracy) and Einstein (not very good at maths) show that the lack of factors which contribute to high IQ does not seem to reduce creativity.

Creativity Tests

The classic creativity test is the 'uses of objects' tests. People are asked to write down as many possible uses as they can for a particular object (bricks are very popular). The test is usually scored on how many different uses a person can think of. Convergent thinkers tend to come up with a limited number of fairly conventional uses, such as 'building a wall', 'laying a path', whereas divergent thinkers produce much longer lists often (though not necessarily always) with more original uses (for example, 'use it as a desk ornament to keep paper clips in, 'propped up on a peg with cheese underneath as a mousetrap', and even 'psychology teachers can put it on a table and ask their students how many uses they can think of for it!')

The uses of objects test, however, measures originality and divergent thinking ability, but does it measure creativity? There may be some truth in this assertion. Roe found that scientists for example, tend to be convergent thinkers, but the more creative scientists (as measured for example by number of papers published, honorary degrees and prizes awarded for their work) tended to show more divergent thinking than their less creative counterparts. MacKinnon found that creative people in all fields (not just science) showed more divergent thinking than people without such records of creativity.

Summary

1 Skinner's theory of language development argued that children learned words through behaviour-shaping, with reinforcement from adults in the form of praise or attention.

2 Other research showed that children seem to learn grammatical rules which they can apply in new situations, rather than simply learning chains of words. Attempting to correct children's grammatical mistakes does not seem to improve their grammar significantly.

3 Chomsky's theory of language development proposed that all humans have an innate language acquisition device which allows children to extract the rules of grammar from the speech they hear around them.

4 Lennenberg believed there was a critical (or sensitive) period for language development from birth to 10 or 11 years of age.

5 Some maturation seems to be involved in language development, but there evidence that the verbal interaction of adults with children (rather than simply talking at them) is also essential for normal language development.

6 Language development seems to occur in stages: prelinguistic, first-word (holophrastic) stage; two-word (telegraphic speech) stage; grammar stage.

7 The two main types of problem-solving are algorithmic (working out all possible alternative steps towards the problems solution) and heuristic (looking at only those parts of the problem which are most likely to produce results).

8 Means-end-analysis and the analogy approach are the two commonest forms of heuristic problem-solving.

9 Mental set (the tendency to use techniques used before even when they are less effective), functional fixedness (the tendency to assume that objects can only be used for the purpose for which they were designed), and einstellung (innate perceptual rules which steer us towards certain occasionally inappropriate ways of solving problems) can all hinder our problem-solving abilities.

10 Convergent thinking (moving from many possibilities to one solution) and divergent thinking (moving from one possibility to many alternatives) were thought by J.P. Guilford to be two of the factors involved in IQ test success. MacKinnon found that above IQ120, IQ scores did not indicate people's levels of creativity.

11 Creativity tests often involve 'uses of objects' tests, but may be measuring originality, not whether the ideas generated are useful or genuinely creative.

Solution to the nine-dot problem:

Chapter 17

The Biological Bases of Behaviour

The behaviour of any object, whether it is a computer, a radio or a human being, must to a great extent depend on its structure. The room in which you are sitting at the moment is full of radio waves, and yet you cannot sense them because your structure is different from that of a radio set. Your picture of the world is different from that of a colour-blind person: he finds it difficult to distinguish between red and green because his eye does not contain some chemical contained by yours. Damage to the brain can cause a grown man to act like a babbling infant or to lose the ability to remember things for more than a few moments. Some drugs act on the brain to give the individual a feeling of elation or depression, anxiety or rage.

Which parts of the brain are responsible for the control of eating, sleeping and mating? Where are memories stored? How do we form our visual, touch, smell and sound model of the world? These are some of the questions that psychologists are trying to answer in an area of study known as 'physiological psychology' in which the main emphasis is on discovering the structure and functions of the brain and nervous system and of the endocrine system.

The Nerve Cell or Neuron

The basic 'building block' of the brain and nervous system is the *nerve cell* or *neuron*. It is through neurons that information can pass from a sense organ to the brain and from the brain to the muscles. It is estimated that the brain itself consists of about twelve billion neurons whose activities make possible the remarkable range of behaviour and experience that we all share.

Neurons vary in structure but there are three major types – *sensory*, *motor* and *connector neurons*. Sensory neurons carry information to the brain from the sense organs; motor neurons carry information from the brain to the muscles; connector neurons, which are found in the brain and spinal cord, link these two types. The three types consist of a cell body with

Figure 17.1. Uses of Sensory, Motor and Connector Neurons

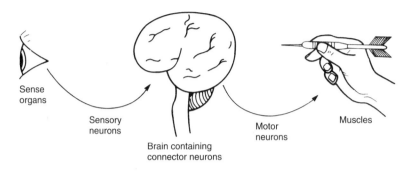

many branching filaments called *dendrites*; one of these is often very long and is termed the *axon* and it is along this that the nerve impulse travels away from the cell body towards the next neuron in the chain, or to a muscle (see figures 17.2 and 17.3). An impulse can be produced by the excitation of a sense organ or the reception of an impulse from another neuron. When an impulse passes along an axon – always in the same direction – the neuron is said to *fire*. The *myelin sheath* around the axon has an insulating effect; it also causes the speed of conduction of the impulse to be greater than that for neurons without myelin. The speed at which an impulse passes along a neuron may be as fast as 120 metres per second for large-diameter, myelinated axons, or as slow as one metre per second for small-diameter, non-myelinated axons.

Figure 17.2. A Sensory Neuron

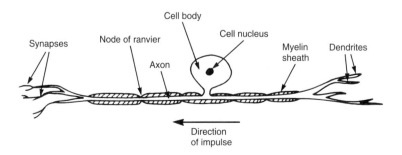

The stimulus to the neuron must be large enough to produce an impulse, i.e. must be above the *threshold of response*; once this threshold is passed the impulse travels without any weakening to the end of the axon. The strength of the impulse in an axon never varies, for it is either present or not; this is known as the *all-or-none rule*. A strong stimulus produces a more rapid burst of impulses than a weaker one; it cannot produce a stronger impulse in an individual neuron, but may stimulate more neurons. After each firing

Figure 17.3. A Motor Neuron

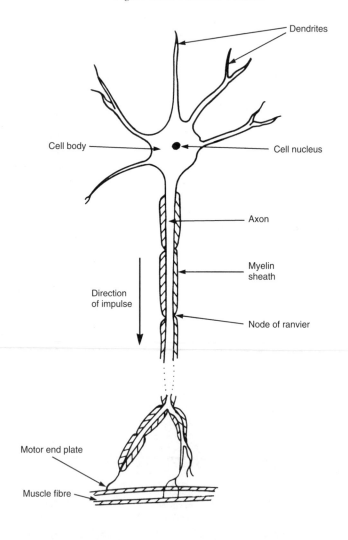

there is a very short period of time, one or two milliseconds, during which no further impulse can pass no matter how strong the stimulus; this is known as the *absolute refractory period*. It is followed by a short period when the neuron can only be caused to fire by strong stimuli, i.e. the threshold of response is higher than usual; this is known as the *relative refractory period*. Because a strong stimulus can create an impulse as soon as the absolute refractory period is over, it may prompt a firing rate of up to a thousand impulses per second, whereas the delay caused by the relative refractory period means that the firing rate for a weak stimulus can be as low as 25 impulses per second.

All messages in the nervous system are carried in the form of nerve impulses, but their interpretation depends upon which part of the brain receives the message: in one part an impulse might be interpreted as a spot of light, in another as a sound. Imagine the effect of plugging the nerves from the ear into the visual areas of the brain!

The Motor End Plate

The axons of the motor neurons which terminate on muscles end in a series of branches. These are tipped by *motor end plates*, each of which is attached to a single muscle fibre. An impulse at the motor end plate causes the muscle to contract, which may thus result in an arm being raised, a movement of the tongue, or any one of thousands of other responses, depending on which muscle is stimulated. Physical activities produced by the stimulation of muscles by nerves are called *motor responses*.

The Synapses

Neurons are not in direct contact with each other; there is a small gap between each cell and its neighbour known as a *synapse* across which the nerve impulse has to pass. When an impulse reaches a *synaptic knob* (see figure 17.4) it causes the release of chemicals known as *transmitter substances* which pass across the gap, the *synaptic cleft*, and stimulate the next cell. If enough transmitter substance is received the next cell fires. Conduction across a synapse can occur only in one direction.

Many synapses separate each neuron from other neurons; it may be necessary for transmitter substance to be received from several of these synapses at the same time, or from one synapse fired a few times in rapid succession, in order to reach the thresholds of response. The process whereby the firing of a few neurons adds up to the production of a stimulus strong enough to fire another neuron is called *summation*.

The synapses so far described are known as *excitatory synapses* because they 'excite' the next neuron, causing it to fire, but some synapses prevent the firing of the next cell; these are called *inhibitory synapses*. Whether or not a cell will fire depends on the relative activity of the excitatory and

Figure 17.4. A Synapse

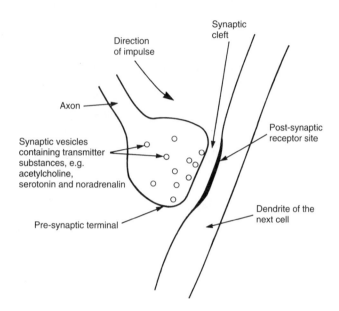

inhibitory synapses of its dendrites: if the excitatory activity is greater than the inhibitory then it will fire.

After a transmitter substance has reached the next neuron it is destroyed and so does not continue to stimulate the cell. Many of the so-called 'nerve gases' produced for warfare work by preventing the destruction of the transmitter molecules; death results from the continual excitation of many neurons which causes prolonged contraction of all the muscles of the body. The hallucinatory drug LSD is very similar to *serotonin* which is a transmitter substance in some brain synapses; the presence of LSD can thus cause neurons to fire even though no impulses have been passed from the sense organs, which is why LSD takers 'see' things which are not really there.

Inhibitory synapses use different transmitter substances from those used by excitatory synapses and they play an important role in the nervous system. Inhibition controls the spread of excitation through the highly interconnected nervous system and keeps activity channelled in appropriate networks or 'circuits'. Epileptic fits may be due to the excitation of many different brain circuits at the same time. The possible connections with other cells are astronomical in number; the connector neurons in the spine, for example, may each be stimulated by up to two thousand synapses.

Figure 17.5. Many Synapses Terminating on one Neuron

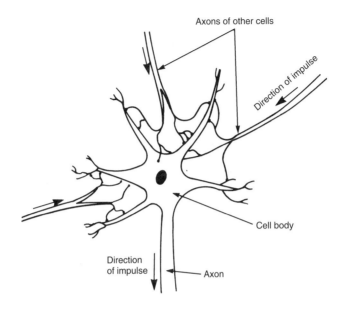

It is changes in the connections between cells in the nervous system that allow both learning and memory.

Methods of Studying the Brain

A simple study of the anatomy of the brain does not tell us very much about the functions of its different parts. However, it might lead us to make educated guesses; for example, if it can be seen that a particular nerve is connected to the retina of the eye and leads towards particular areas of the brain we might guess that that nerve is passing visual information. A lot of information has come from Sir Gordon Holmes's studies of accidental injuries to the brain such as those suffered by soldiers during the First World War. Holmes found that patients with shrapnel lodged in the rear of the brain could not see objects that were placed in some positions in front of the eye. An object moved in front of the eye might be visible, then disappear, only to reappear after passing the blind area. This suggested that the rear of the brain dealt with vision. It is difficult to draw conclusions from studies of accidental injury, however, because we do not know exactly where the damage is until the patient dies; nor can we set up an accident and ensure that it will damage only one part of the brain in order to determine exactly what caused the change in behaviour that occurs.

Figure 17.6. Methods of Studying the Brain

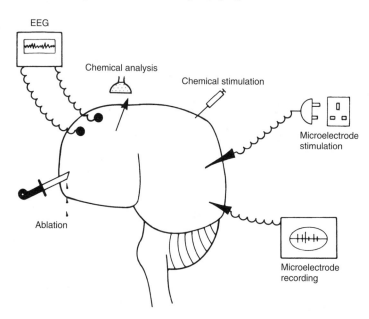

Surgical removal of parts of the brain, either by a cut of the knife or by burning out certain neurons with electrodes, has supplied a great deal of information about the functions of many parts of the brain. This technique is known as *ablation*: the idea behind it is that if, for example, removal of a particular area of the brain leads to overeating on the part of the subject, then that area must have been responsible for controlling eating activity. The results of ablation and other studies have to be considered carefully and in the light of information from several sources, because the fact that a certain operation causes a particular change in behaviour does not definitely prove that the affected part of the brain was the control centre for that behaviour; the area may simply be one part of a larger system, or the behaviour change may have been brought about by general shock to the nervous system.

Other studies involve the insertion of *microelectrodes* – very fine needles which conduct electricity – into single neurons in the brain. These electrodes may be used either to record the activity of a cell while the animal being studied performs some activity, or to stimulate the cell with a small electric current to gauge the effect of this on behaviour. Chemical studies fall into two similar principal categories – those that analyse the chemicals present in the brain and those in which injected chemicals, often similar to trans-mitter substances, affect the brain.

For more general studies the *electroencephalogram* or EEG is used to measure the electrical activity of large areas of the brain rather than indi-vidual neurons. Characteristic patterns of brain activity are found during different kinds of behaviour, for example when the subject is active, relaxed or dreaming.

To summarize then: the major physiological methods of approach to the study of the brain are anatomy, accident, ablation, electrical and chemical analysis, electrical and chemical stimulation, and recording of the activity of larger parts of the brain.

The Nervous System

The cell bodies of most neurons are contained within the brain or spinal cord. The elongated axons of many neurons pass information either in from the sense organs or out to the muscles. Some of these axons are over one metre in length; they are grouped in bundles known as *nerves*, which are usually large enough to see with the naked eye in a dissected animal. Those leaving the brain or spinal cord through holes in the skull are known as *cranial nerves*; others situated between the vertebrae of the spine are called *spinal nerves*. Most contain both motor and sensory neurons.

The brain and spinal cord contain the majority of cell bodies and are therefore termed collectively the *central nervous system* or CNS; the nerve fibres outside the brain and spine are known as the *peripheral nervous system*.

The Peripheral Nervous System

The peripheral nervous system consists of two main sections, which have different structures and functions – the *somatic nervous system* and the *autonomic nervous system* or ANS.

THE SOMATIC SYSTEM

The somatic system comprises the nerves that carry impulses from the sense organs – the eyes, ears, nose, tongue and skin – and that affect those muscles which are under voluntary control. Any part of the body that you can move of your own volition, such as your fingers or face, is therefore controlled by the somatic section of your nervous system. The cell bodies of these neurons are mostly contained in the central nervous system; only those axons with a myelin sheath are present in the periphery.

THE AUTONOMIC NERVOUS SYSTEM, OR ANS

The autonomic nervous system controls the internal organs and glands of the body – those activities which require no conscious effort, for example heartbeat, blood pressure and pupil size. You cannot decide to alter the size of your eyes' pupils because they are not under voluntary control (although you could of course do so indirectly by looking towards a bright light). 'Autonomic' axons do not have thick myelin sheaths and the cell bodies are outside the central nervous system.

There are two sections of the ANS, the *sympathetic* and the *para-sympathetic divisions* both of which connect with most of the glands and organs of the body, usually with opposing results, for example impulses in the sympathetic system cause an increase in heart-rate but impulses in the parasympathetic system cause a decrease in heart-rate.

During strong emotion the ANS is very active and its action produces what Walter Cannon described as the *fight-or-flight syndrome*. When you are in a threatening or stressful situation the sympathetic section of the ANS becomes active, increasing blood flow to the brain and muscles so that these organs can function more effectively; at the same time, the bronchioles of the lungs are dilated so that more oxygen can be taken into the bloodstream. In such situations the action of the sympathetic nervous system also inhibits bodily processes which are not needed to prepare for action, such as digestion. Thus when the sympathetic nervous system is active the body is excellently tuned either to stay and fight or to flee, hence Cannon's term. The effects of the sympathetic system can be quite long-lasting because it also causes the adrenal glands to secrete *adrenalin* into the bloodstream. Adrenalin is very similar to the transmitter substances in the sympathetic synapses; it induces increased firing in the sympathetic nervous system. For this reason you may feel your heart beating heavily for several moments after a dangerous situation, such as a near-accident in a car, has passed.

The parasympathetic division of the ANS controls the conservation and restoration of the body's energy resources; because its effect is normally opposite to that of the sympathetic system most of the organs and glands are controlled by a balance of the two systems.

Consider someone wandering around an isolated, dimly-lit country house. Suddenly there is a sound of creaking floorboards and the candles blow out. At this moment his autonomic nervous system is highly active, especially the sympathetic section: his heart beats faster; his blood pressure rises; his mouth feels dry; the pupils of his eyes dilate; the blood vessels serving the voluntary muscles of his trunk and limbs are enlarged; the blood vessels to his stomach and intestines become smaller; and contractions of the stomach and intestines cease or may even be reversed. In addition the *galvanic skin response* – the electrical resistance of the skin – will decrease due to the greater production of sweat. (This galvanic skin response or GSR may be measured by a simple battery-operated device known as a GSR meter.) He experiences a strong emotion of fear. Imagine, on the other hand, that a friend has died. Again your autonomic nervous system is active, but this time it will be predominantly the parasympathetic division; you experience the emotion of sadness. With other emotions such as anger and joy both sections of the autonomic nervous system may be highly active (see chapter 13).

Some of the Functions of the ANS Showing the Opposing Action of the Sympathetic and Parasympathetic Sections

Organ or Gland	Effect of Sympathetic Action	Effect of Parasympathetic Action
Heart	Heartbeat increased	Heartbeat decreased
Liver	Sugar released into blood	Sugar stored
Intestines	Peristalsis (muscular action causing food to move along intestine) slowed	Peristalsis accelerated
Salivary gland	Secretion suppressed	Secretion stimulated
Pupil of eye	Dilated	Contracted

The Central Nervous System (CNS)

The CNS consists of the brain and spinal cord; it is believed to contain not only some twelve thousand million neurons but ten times as many *glial cells*, which fill the spaces between neurons and probably supply them with nutrients and their myelin sheaths. R. Thompson maintains that the number of possible interconnections between the cells of a single human brain is greater than the number of atomic particles that constitute the entire universe.

At birth the brain contains the adult number of neurons but weighs only half that of an adult brain. By the age of two and a half the brain reaches 75 per cent of its adult weight; it is during these early years that the brain is most vulnerable to the effect of malnutrition, according to J. Dobbing and G. Sands. The average weight of the adult brain is, 1,250 grams for females and 1,375 grams for males; it increases in weight after birth because of the multiplication of glial cells, the process of myelination of axons and an increase in the number of interconnections and the size of neurons. Brain size itself does not reflect intelligence and neither, it seems, does the ratio of brain weight to body weight; what seems to be important is the number of *cortical neurons* and the connections between them. (Cortical neurons are the nerve cells in the *cortex*, the area forming the surface of the top part of the brain, which is responsible for processes such as thinking and memory.)

If the central nervous system simply provided direct connections between sense organs and muscles, the number of responses to any situation would be extremely limited; the same response would always be elicited by the same stimulus. However, the connection is not direct; there are both excitatory and inhibitory synapses in the system, which act like switches, so that a particular stimulus may trigger one pathway in a particular situation, but if that pathway is being inhibited for some reason, it may trigger a different pathway.

This characteristic of indirectly linking sensation and response means that most animals – and humans – have a huge behavioural repertoire and can produce different responses to the same stimulus. For example, the smell of baking bread may make you feel very hungry one day, but the next day – perhaps because you have overeaten, or have had a severe fright – it may make you feel sick.

Figure 17.7. The Relationships and Functions of the Parts of the Nervous System

Central Nervous System (CNS)
Consists of the brain and spinal cord and serves to interpret signals from the periphery, store information and control motor responses

Peripheral Nervous System
Somatic Section
Serves the sense organs and skeletal muscles, i.e. the voluntary muscles such as those of the legs and arms.
Most cell bodies of this system are contained in the CNS and the axons have myelin sheaths

Peripheral Nervous System
Autonomic Section (ANS)
Serves internal glands and organs, i.e. those parts of the body over which there is little voluntary control

| **Sympathetic Section** | **Parasymphathetic Section** |
| Serves to prepare the organism for activity | Serves to conserve or restore bodily energy resources |

Most cell bodies of the ANS are outside the CNS. The axons do not have the thick myelin sheaths.

Figure 17.8 shows the parts of the central nervous system, each of which has a slightly different function. It appears that the lower sections deal with simple autonomic behaviour such as reflexes, control of breathing and digestion, and the passage of information to higher centres of the brain. The higher centres of the brain control complex voluntary behaviour and it is here that processes such as thinking and remembering occur.

Figure 17.8. The Brain

THE SPINAL CORD

The *spinal cord* is about the thickness of a little finger and passes from the brain stem down the whole length of the back encased in the vertebrae of the backbone. This cord connects the central and peripheral nervous systems, providing a pathway between the brain and the body. Some of the very simplest reactions to stimuli, the *reflexes* – the reactions you give when you quickly pull your hand away from a hot object or when your knee jerks in response to the doctor's hammer – are controlled by the spinal cord. Reflexes are extremely primitive items of behaviour because they are involuntary and always take the same form given the same stimulus; yet because they are so fast they can prevent the sort of damage we might do ourselves if, for example, we did not let go of a hot object until nerve impulses had been transmitted to the brain, processed and then passed down again.

In the knee-jerk reflex a sensory neuron fires when the correct part of the knee is tapped; this message passes into the spine where the synapse of the sensory neuron transmits the impulse to a motor neuron. The firing of this causes the knee muscle to contract and the leg to jerk forward. Most reflexes involve a connector neuron between the sensory and motor neuron; this simple system of connection is known as a *reflex arc*. The two or three neurons of the reflex arc do, however, have synapses with others which pass up and down the spine and it is through these pathways that we actually become aware of the reflex.

Figure 17.9. A Simple Reflex Arc

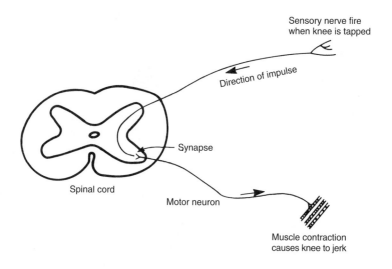

THE BRAIN STEM

The lower part of the brain – the *brain stem* – which is linked to the spinal cord, contains structures with a variety of functions. However, one of its main purposes is to control those kinds of internal behaviour over which we have little or no voluntary control, such as breathing, heartbeat and digestion. One structure of the brain stem the *reticular formation*, which is sometimes known as the *reticular activating system* or RAS, has connections with the whole of the cortex and receives stimulation from the sense organs. It is thought to be important in the maintenance of wakefulness and attention in the cortex; many sleeping pills therefore work by restraining its activity.

THE CEREBELLUM

The *cerebellum* is involved in the maintenance of balance and the performance of skilled actions like walking or riding a bicycle, and similarly aids the coordination of flight in birds and of swimming in fish. The cerebellum thus allows us to perform complicated actions 'without thinking'; if it were damaged such activities would require great concentration and might even become impossible. People with damage to the cerebellum display a noticeable loss of muscle control.

THE HYPOTHALAMUS

This structure, no bigger than the top part of a little finger, has an essential role to play in the motivation of behaviour. The *hypothalamus* is extremely well supplied with blood and contains neurons which are sensitive to changes in blood temperature and content. A fall in the amount of sugar in the blood causes part of the hypothalamus to become active in passing impulses to the cortex which may prompt the person or animal to search for something to eat; at the same time impulses are transmitted to other parts of the nervous system and to the pituitary gland, causing physiological changes such as the release of sugar from the liver into the blood (see p. 303). The process of maintaining a fairly constant level of blood temperature, sugar and salt concentration, hormones and so on is known as *homeostasis*; without it we would not be able to survive. Electrical stimulation and ablation studies have shown that the hypothalamus plays an important part in controlling the activity of the autonomic nervous system and emotion.

THE THALAMUS

The *thalamus* is a relay station for nerve pathways leading to and from the cortex. The impulses passed to the cortex concern sensory information such as vision and hearing; those passing down are directly towards the cerebellum and concern complex limb movements. Another part of the thalamus influences sleep and wakefulness.

THE LIMBIC SYSTEM

This lies just below the cerebral hemispheres (see the following section) and consists of a collection of individual structures involved in motivation, emotion and memory. Ablation of various parts of this system in monkeys can result in either an increase or a decrease in aggressive behaviour, while damage to other parts in humans has been shown to limit severely the length of time for which a patient is able to remember new material. Nerve pathways link the limbic system with both the thalamus and the hypothalamus.

THE CEREBRUM AND THE CORTEX

On examination of the surface of the brain, the most striking feature is the extremely wrinkled surface of the *cerebrum*, which is split by a large crevice from front to rear suggesting the appearance of a walnut. The two *cerebral hemispheres*, one on each side of the crevice, are joined by a mass of nervous tissue called the *corpus callosum*. Although the cerebral hemispheres are the largest structures of the brain the most important part, the cortex, consists only of the top few layers of cells; it is here that control of intelligent behaviour largely originates. The major concerns of the cortex are perception, learning and memory, and control of motor functions. In humans the cortex also controls the production and understanding of language.

The wrinkled surface of the cerebrum appears to be divided into four lobes as shown in figure 17.10, and some forms of behaviour can be localized to particular areas on those lobes. The *visual cortex* is found in the *occipital lobe*, and cells in this area receive input from the light-sensitive cells of the eyes' retinas. The *auditory cortex* in the *temporal lobe* receives information from the ear. There is a strip of cortex at the front of the *parietal lobe*; this receives input from all over the body, and when a part of the body is touched it is stimulated and produces some sort of sensation. The sense of bodily feeling with which this area is involved is known as *somesthesis*. This strip of cortex is organized so that the strip on the left hemisphere receives information about the right side of the body while that in the right receives information from the left side of the body. Information from the feet is received by cells at the top of the strip, whereas information from the face is dealt with lower down. The amount of cortex dealing with particular parts of the body depends not on the size but on the sensitivity of an area. Patients with damage to this strip of the cortex report that they

Figure 17.10. Lobes of the Cerebrum

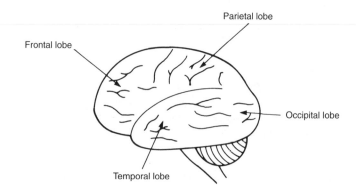

feel as though they have lost part of their bodies. In mice, the cells connected to the whiskers occupy most of this strip. The motor control strip lies just in front of the body-feeling area and behind the *frontal lobe*. Cells in this strip directly regulate particular muscle movements and their organization is also inversely related to the physical areas they control. They are distributed in proportion to the number of muscles in the various parts of the

Figure 17.11.(a) The Area of Cortex Dealing with Muscle Control and Bodily Feeling

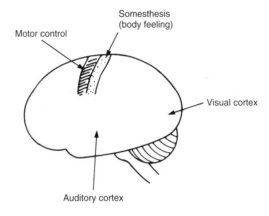

Figure 17.11.(b) The Area of Cortex Dealing with Bodily Feeling

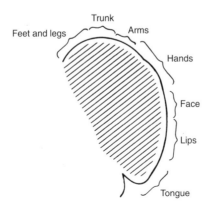

body. Damage to the motor area of the cortex results in paralysis of the area of the body controlled by the damaged part.

A large proportion of the human cortex does not have a sensory or motor function; this is called the *association cortex* where the processes of learning, remembering and thinking occur. There is a greater proportion of association cortex in humans than in any other animal and this may well account for our greater intelligence.

In a series of classic experiments by Karl Lashley during the 1920s, the effects of damage to the cortex of rats on learning and memory were studied. Although very specific areas of the cortex can be shown to deal with motor control and reception of information from sense organs, Lashley discovered that none could be located which specifically dealt with learning. In one experiment he trained rats to find their way round a difficult maze and then damaged fifteen per cent of the cortex in each animal. When tested again on the maze these rats were no longer successful, but he observed that they could re-learn the maze with ease. This showed that although one area of the cortex was used for learning the maze in the first instance, a different area could do the same job. Lashley coined the *Law of Mass Action* which states that for the learning of difficult problems the effect of cortical damage depends upon the amount, and not the position, of the damage; the more cortex affected, the more difficulty the rat has in learning the maze.

Language, the ability to communicate with words, is a peculiarly human ability and possibly originates from certain specialized areas of the cortex on the left hemisphere. A sharp blow on the left of the head might result in an inability to understand or produce the spoken word, whereas a blow on the right would not.

In 1865 Paul Broca found that patients with damage to the part of the brain now known as *Broca's Area* (see figure 17.12) lost their ability to speak properly, although they could still move tongue, jaws and vocal cords. The speech of such patients is very slow and crude: instead of producing full sentences they tend to miss out small words and the endings of nouns and verbs. When asked what he did the previous night, a patient might reply 'Go ... cinema.' It appears that Broca's Area is necessary to prepare words for speaking, but not for understanding them; such patients have no difficulty in comprehending. Behind Broca's Area, however, is a part of the cortex known as *Wernicke's Area*, damage to which does prevent a person from understanding language; nevertheless he may still be able to hear and enjoy music. While damage to Wernicke's Area does not prevent talking, the patient may forget some words and substitute others: he may ask for a pen by saying 'Please pass the thing you write with.' Damage to Wernicke's Area causes problems in the understanding of both written and spoken language; damage to another area, the *angular gyrus*, causes the loss of reading ability whilst having no effect on comprehension of the spoken word.

Patients with damage to the angular gyrus are able to see the written word but it has no meaning for them; it has been suggested that this part of the cortex must therefore convert the visual patterns of the written word into auditory patterns which are then passed along to Wernicke's Area for comprehension.

Figure 17.12. Language Areas of the Brain

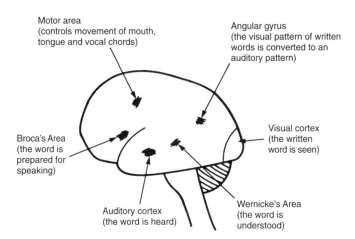

Psychologists sometimes study the performance of a person in the production or comprehension of language in order to help them locate specific areas of damage to the brain which might have resulted from an accident or tumour. It must be remembered, however, that an inability to use language may result from such things as the lack of an opportunity to learn, as well as from specific brain damage.

To summarize: if you were to read this sentence aloud, the presence of these marks on the paper which we call words would produce activity in your visual cortex; this would be passed on to the angular gyrus and then to Wernicke's Area which would enable you to understand the words; the activity would then spread to Broca's Area, and finally to the motor area which would cause your speech muscles to produce the sounds that you would then utter.

The Endocrine System

We have discussed one communication system within the body, the nervous system, but there is another, complementary system – the *endocrine system*.

This releases chemicals known as *hormones* from the endocrine glands into the bloodstream. Because every cell in the body is either directly or indirectly in contact with the blood system, hormones can reach every cell, whereas nerves only pass messages to the muscles and from the sense organs. As the messages of the endocrine system pass in the bloodstream this system is obviously slower than the nervous system, which can pass messages in a matter of milliseconds; but it is more suited to transmitting steady, relatively unchanging messages over a long period of time. Behaviour such as catching a cup before it falls to the floor and smashes must be controlled by the nervous system because of the need for speed. On the other hand, behaviour demonstrating an increased inclination for courtship during certain months of the year in birds and other animals has a hormonal basis.

The endocrine system consists of the glands shown in figure 17.13. The pituitary is known as the master gland because it releases hormones which in turn stimulate the other glands to produce their own hormones.

The pituitary gland is connected by many nerve pathways to the hypothalamus; the nervous and endocrine systems closely interact to control the functioning of the body. This interaction takes place, for example, when someone has not had anything to drink for a while. The fall in liquid content of the body is registered by the hypothalamus; it sends nerve impulses to the cortex, which interprets the message as a feeling of thirst and may prompt the person to look for something to drink. At the same time the

Figure 17.13. The Endocrine System

hypothalamus passes impulses to the pituitary gland; this releases an anti-diuretic hormone which controls the extent to which water is reabsorbed into the blood from the kidneys after blood filtration; this in turn causes less water to be excreted into the bladder. The combined actions of the cortex and the pituitary gland therefore produce a reaction to water deficiency on both a behavioural and a physiological level.

The endocrine and nervous systems also interact in stressful situations. As seen, the sympathetic section of the ANS is highly active when we are under pressure, producing the fight-or-flight syndrome and mobilizing all the body's emergency energy resources. The adrenal glands are caused to secrete adrenalin and *noradrenalin* into the bloodstream; because they are the transmitter substances for the sympathetic nervous system they have the same effect on the organs of the body, maintaining the fight-or-flight syndrome.

The adrenal glands have two parts – the *adrenal medulla*, which secretes adrenalin and noradrenalin, and the *adrenal cortex*, which secretes a range of other hormones. One of these is *hydrocortisone*, which functions to adjust the level of sugar stored in the liver after the amount has fallen because of stress.

Female cats that have not been neutered 'come on heat' about three times a year, during which time they attract and accept willing males; yet at other times a male that comes too close encounters only hostility. The chain of reaction during the 'heat' periods starts with the production of *follicle-stimulating hormone* in the pituitary gland, which stimulates the growth

Table 17.1. Some Pituitary Hormones and their Effects

Hormone	Stimulates	Effects
Growth hormone	Body tissues	Increases growth
Gonadotrophic hormone	Testes or ovaries	Stimulates production of sex hormones and sexual characteristics
Vasopressin	Blood vessels	Causes the blood vessels to contract
Thyrotrophic hormone	Thyroid gland	Stimulates production of thyroxin which increases metabolic rate
Corticotrophic hormone	Adrenal gland	Stimulates production of adrenalin affecting emotional behaviour
Antidiuretic hormone	Kidneys	Reduces excretion of water

of eggs and the production of *oestrogen* by the ovaries. The presence of oestrogen in the bloodstream causes changes in the reproductive system, such as thickening of the uterus walls; it also stimulates the hypothalamus which, in connection with other parts of the nervous system, prompts the female to lift her rump, move her tail to one side and make treading movements with her rear legs when a male appears. The stimulus to the nervous system during copulation reaches the hypothalamus and is passed on to the cat's pituitary gland; this then releases *luteinizing hormone* which effects the release from the ovaries of eggs to be fertilized by the male's sperm.

Thus sexual activity in animals is also governed by the action of the endocrine and nervous system in conjunction, to cause both physiological and behavioural changes.

Summary

1 The nervous system consists of millions of neurons connected by excitatory and inhibitory synapses.

2 Each neuron has a threshold of response, and once stimulation exceeds this it fires. The firing obeys the all-or-none rule.

3 The firing of a neuron is followed by the absolute and then the relative refractory periods.

4 Physiological psychologists have used various methods of studying the brain – anatomy, accident, ablation, microelectrode recording and stimulation, and chemical analysis and stimulation.

5 The central nervous system (CNS) consists of the brain and spinal cord. The peripheral nervous system consists of the somatic nervous system which passes messages in from the sense organs and out to the voluntary muscles, and the autonomic nervous system (ANS) which deals with emotions and involuntary functions. The autonomic nervous system has two sections, the sympathetic and parasympathetic.

6 Activity of the sympathetic nervous system puts the body into the fight-or-flight syndrome.

7 The parts of the central nervous system perform different functions: the spinal cord is responsible for reflexes and the transmission of messages from brain to body; the brain stem, including the reticular formation, affects wakefulness and attention; the cerebellum enables balance and the co-ordination of skilled actions; the hypothalamus governs motivation and emotion; the thalamus acts as a relay station between the sense organs, the cortex and cerebellum; the limbic system influences motivation, memory and emotion; and the surface of the cerebrum, the cortex, controls intelligent behaviour.

8 Functions such as visual and auditory awareness, bodily feeling, motor control and language control, are related to specific regions of the cortex.

9 Lashley showed that no specific region of the association cortex is involved in learning and memory of specific behaviour.

10 The endocrine system affects the state of the body by the release of hormones. Its effects are slower but more long-lasting than those of the nervous system.

11 Both nervous and endocrine systems are important in the control of, among other things, thirst, emotion and sexual activity.

Chapter 18

Studying Animal Behaviour; Ethology

Why Study Animals?

All psychology is concerned with animal behaviour since humans are animals, but some psychologists spend a great deal of time studying non-human animals. In this section we shall use the word 'animal' to describe any non-human living organisms other than plants. Part of the definition of science is 'the pursuit of knowledge for its own sake', and for some people this is sufficient reason for this type of research; but, apart from pure academic interest, these studies may help to control animals for commercial and domestic purposes and give some clues about the behaviour of humankind. Animals have provided food, comfort, and protection for humans for thousands of years. Studies of selective breeding have increased the efficiency of farm animals for food production, and behavioural studies have helped choose and train dogs for guard duty and sheep gathering, as well as for entertainment in circus acts and advertisements. The most controversial reason for studying animals is that it may lead to an understanding of human behaviour; this immediately raises the question, Why not study humans directly? The short answer to this is that it is not always possible to study humans directly, because there are greater moral and ethical restrictions on the type of research that can be performed using humans as subjects. Also animals are less complex and therefore easier to understand (it is a basic principle of science to start with the simple and progress to the complex). In particular, animal studies have the following advantages. First, it is possible to administer greater rewards and punishments with animals and to use experimental techniques such as rearing in isolation which are not possible with humans. However, it is worth noting that a growing number of people argue that animals suffer too much in the cause of the search for knowledge, and there is a recognition that much research in the past has involved cruelty which can no longer be tolerated. Secondly, with animals it is possible to study instinctive behaviour, little or none of which remains in humans. Similarly, it is possible to study the evolution of behaviour, since animals can be crossbred in tightly controlled environments and usually have shorter gestation and maturation periods than humans, allowing research into many generations in a short time.

Still, we cannot be sure that research into the causes of animal behaviour is applicable to humans. If we study part of the brain of an animal, we cannot be sure that it has the same function as in humans, although experimenters try to take into account differences between animals and people by using an animal whose brain is similar in structure to human's. Then again, even if the structures are similar, their functions may be different. In addition, although there may be similarities between a species and humans, there may be differences we have not yet found. Some of these problems can be reduced by careful choice of experimental animals; for example, the frog's eye works in a similar way to the human eye, so it is used in visual experiments. It is known, however, that a frog's brain attends to different classes of stimulus than a human's, and so although some of the findings of visual experiments on frogs may be generalized to humans, those in the field of perception may not.

Some people argue that, even if the structures of an animal and humans are identical, it is still not valid to generalize the results to humans because of the unique possession of consciousness and power of thought. However, psychologists generally agree that all mental processes are ultimately dependent on physical structures and chemical changes within those structures (see chapter 17). Animals have nerves and brains; the messages passing along those nerves do so in the same way as in humans; and the similarities in the structure and function of nerves and brains are more noticeable than the differences. It is possible to argue that human uniqueness is not a qualitative difference from animals, but a quantitative one. In other words (and with the possible exception of speech), the elements of behaviour displayed by humans are also displayed by animals, although in a simpler form. Hebb argues that animal findings are not, by themselves, directly applicable to humans, but they may be used as hints – to give clues and to generate hypotheses which can then be tested directly on humans.

When studying humans, we can ask for verbal reports of their experiences in experiments. Since animals do not talk, we have to get an animal to report its experiences by its behaviour. Thus, in order to find out whether a rat can discriminate between two colours, we would condition it to press one lever when a red light comes on and a different one when a blue light comes on. If the rat can do this, it must be able to distinguish between the two lights. Bower used similar procedures with human babies to test their perceptual capacities.

One of the biggest 'sins' that an animal researcher can commit is that of *anthropomorphism*, the tendency to see human-like qualities or motives in non-human organisms or objects. It can be seen in statements such as 'the rat is pleased' and 'the cat thinks she will get a reward'. We may be right when we think the animal is happy, but we can never know this with certainty. The case of 'Clever Hans' is a classic example of the mistaken application of anthropomorphism. Hans was a circus horse which could apparently compute arithmetic equations. If asked to solve the problem 'two plus two', the animal would answer by striking the ground four times with its hoof. The number of problems that Hans could answer suggested that the horse was doing more than recalling the responses to a few stand-ard questions, and many scientists took the view that it actually worked out the calculations just as humans do. It was only after exhaustive research by Pfungst (1911) that it was discovered that Hans was simply responding to clues given by the questioner. Pfungst showed that if the questioner hid from Hans's view the horse would go on striking the ground even after it had reached the correct answer. The horse had learnt to stop 'counting' when its questioner made the slight change in posture that we all make when we have received the desired answer and believe that a communi-cation has ended.

The common brown rat showed apparently 'intelligent' behaviour when it avoids a favourite path when a farmer puts poison on it. If, however, a harmless paper parcel is placed on the path rather than poison, the rat will still avoid the path: rats simply avoid new objects.

Although animal behaviour has interested people for a long time, it is only in recent years that systematic studies have been carried out on it. A two-pronged investigation has taken place, using rather different research techniques. These two sets of techniques, ethology and experimental psychology, will be discussed next.

Ethology

In the 1930s and 1940s Konrad Lorenz and Niko Tinbergen founded the group of researchers who now call themselves *ethologists*. The group was made up of Europeans, mainly zoologists, who had in common a wish to study a wide range of animals, preferably in their natural habitat.

In the 1950s and 1960s, a spirited debate took place between the ethologists and the (largely behaviourist) experimental psychologists on the relative merits of their approaches to the study of animal behaviour. The ethologists were often concerned with investigations into the function of the animals' behaviour – how and why certain kinds of behaviour furthered the survival of the individual or species. To this end, they examined a wide range of animal behaviour during such times as the establishment of territories, courtship and parenthood.

The Ethogram

It is very difficult to observe and manipulate variables in the natural habitat of an animal, so ethologists have developed a research tool, the *ethogram*, which is a detailed catalogue of the behaviour of an animal. This catalogue of behaviour is made up of two kinds of description:

- *Description by motor patterns*, literally the description of the physical movements made by the animal. This had the advantage that it is relatively objective, since it avoids the possibility of anthropomorphism and is accurate. It has the disadvantage that it does not relate the animals's movements to its environment, and that it can also be cumbersome to use often all individual limb movements have to be described.
- *Description by consequence*. In this method the consequences of the animal's behaviour are described in relation to its environment. As an example, consider the description 'the rat approached the lever'. Were this activity being described by motor pattern alone, it would have been concerned with the limb movements, and how the animal moved. Description by consequence is more concerned with why the animal moved – what the consequences were of the movement. Description of behaviour by consequence is a more economical form of description; it relates the animal to its surroundings, but it has the disadvantage that it is not appropriate to the study of detailed differences in behaviour, or of motor patterns, between different animals. In order to obtain a full description of animal behaviour, ethologists usually use both forms of description.

The example below is taken from Niko Tinbergen's (1952) work on territorial and courtship behaviour in the stickleback. The description by motor pattern is enclosed in square brackets; the description by consequence is enclosed in round ones.

> The threat display of male sticklebacks is of two types. (When two males meet at the border of their territories, they begin a series of attacks and retreats. Each takes the offensive on his own territory, and the duel seesaws back and forth across the border. Neither fish touches the other, the two dart back and forth) as though attached by an invisible thread.

> When the fight grows in vigour, however, the seesaw manoeuvre may suddenly change into something quite different. [Each fish adopts an almost vertical head-down posture, turns its side to its opponent, raises its ventral spines and makes jerky movements with the whole body.]

Experimental Psychology

The experimental psychologists, unlike the ethologists, studied a limited range of animals, usually using the experimental method, in laboratory settings. They were more concerned with animal learning; so much so that one unkind wit compared behaviourists with magicians: one pulls rabbits out of hats, while the other pulls habits out of rats! Probably as a result of their choices of methods of study, the ethologists and experimental psychologists quickly came into conflict. They were really interested in two different areas of the development of behaviour:

Phylogenesis. The ethologists were interested in the functions of animal behaviour and how such behaviour had evolved in a particular species, a process known as *phylogenesis*.

Ontogenesis. In the early days, the ethologists were not much concerned with the investigation of how behaviour develops within the individual; such development being known as *ontogenesis*. On the other hand, ontogenesis was a primary concern of the experimental psychologists.

In the end the main arena for debate took place over ontogenesis, with the experimental psychologists stressing the role of learning and of the environment, and the ethologists, having seen so much stereotyped behaviour among individual species, reintroducing the term 'instinct' as a means of explanation for these stereotyped acts of behaviour.

The Instinct Debate

In order to survive, an animal must be able to cope successfully with its environment in order to find food and a mate, and to rear its young. Such adaptive behaviour was often thought by the ethologists to be instinctive; that is, it was thought the behaviour was due to the genetically determined structure of the animal, usually of its nervous system. The experimental psychologists criticized the use of 'instinctive' as an explanatory term, preferring instead to stress the importance of the animal's learning and experience. Out of the instinct debate came the attitude which now prevails in studies of animal behaviour: the attitude that behaviour develops, with both hereditary and environmental factors being necessary. The task of research should then be to investigate how these two factors together contribute to development. It is worthwhile examining in more detail how this change of attitude came about.

The rise of 'human instincts' seems to have begun with Darwin. His theory of evolution postulates that there has been a continuity of development of man from the animals. However, Darwin was faced with the prevalence of the view that humans were qualitatively different from animals, particularly in the existence of human reasoning ability. To try to merge these opposing views he argued that humans had instincts like animals and that animals had primitive reasoning ability like humans. William James, who was influenced by the evolutionary movement, insisted that humans have more instincts than any other animal. McDougall in his famous book *Social Psychology* listed many human instincts (for example, flight, repression, repulsion, parental feeling, reproduction, self-abasement and others). Even Thorndike, originator of the Law of Effect, thought that human behaviour was an expression of instinctive drives or needs. There was, however, little agreement about the number of instincts.

The constant use of 'instinct' as an explanatory term, when it really is only a descriptive term, led to a revolt against its use. In the 1920s and 1930s, Z.Y. Kuo fought against the use of the concept, but still admitted the existence of unlearned *units of reaction* (reflexes). By doing this, he admitted the learning-versus-instinct split, and had to try to find learning explanations for everything except a few reflexes. The real question, as will become apparent, is not 'Innate or learnt?' but 'How does behaviour develop?'

Criteria for Instinctive Behaviour

Lorenz and Tinbergen were ethologists who argued that much behaviour is hereditarily determined. In order to provide some means of investigating such behaviour they produced a list of criteria, by which behaviour can be determined as innate or instinctive.

- The behaviour must be stereotyped and constant in form.
- It must be characteristic of the species (that is, *species-specific*).
- It must appear in animals which have been reared in isolation from others.
- It must appear fully developed in animals which have been prevented from practising it.

That some animal behaviour conforms to these criteria is clear, but a lot more which is claimed to conform is found not to do so, when studied more closely. First, an example of behaviour which does fulfil the criteria – swimming in the frog tadpole. Carmichael (1927) kept the eggs in an anaesthetic solution which prevented any movement by the developing larvae. When the tadpoles had long passed the stage at which they would normally have begun to swim, they were placed in fresh water. When the effects of the anaesthetic had worn off, they were able to swim as well as any non-anaesthetized tadpoles in about half an hour and apparently without practice. To control for the possibility that the anaesthetized tadpoles might have had some practice while the anaesthetic was wearing off, Carmichael anaesthetized the group that could already swim, and then removed the anaesthetic. It took this group approximately half an hour to begin swimming again, suggesting that the originally anaesthetized group were not practising.

The second example of 'innate' behaviour, however, is by no means as clear-cut as that example. It was a study by Reiss (1951) of maternal behaviour in the rat. Rats were reared in isolation from other rats, and Reiss found that they developed the normal 'maternal instinctive' behaviour – nest building, and retrieval and licking of the young. This, at first glance, seems to be another example of behaviour satisfying the criteria for innateness. But because a rat has been kept isolated from other rats does not mean that it has been kept in isolation from its species' normal environment. Is it a reasonable assumption that the only way in which behaviour can occur without being innate is by learning from others? Experimental work on maternal behaviour in the rat suggests not.

Reiss (1951) reared rats which were prevented from carrying anything in their paws (faeces fell through the floor-grid and food was powdered, not in pellet form). When such rats had litters they did not build nests, nor did they retrieve their young. If female rats are prevented from licking their own genital organs (which they apparently do to obtain salt), they do not lick or retrieve their young, and in fact eat a high percentage of them (Birch, 1948). Environment may thus drastically affect behaviour.

Tinbergen argued that the pecking response of the laughing gull was innate, and also demonstrated how specific the appropriate sign stimulus had to be. The chick would peck only at the red spot on the parent's beak, who would then regurgitate food for it: it would not peck at the red spot if it was moved from the beak to the forehead. However, Hailman (1967) showed that this specificity only occurred when the chicks were a few days old. Newly hatched chicks would peck at the forehead. He showed that, although the laughing gull chicks had an innate tendency to peck at the red spot on the parent's beak, this was at first a very crude piece of behaviour, which improved with experience and food reinforcement.

Hailman suggested that the development of the pecking response and other 'instincts' involves a component of learning. It is necessary only that the learning process be very much alike for all members of a species for a stereotyped, species-specific behaviour to occur. Given that the structure of an animal (hereditarily determined) is relatively standard between individuals of a species, and given also that the type of environment which the individuals share is also relatively similar, it is perhaps no surprise that stereotyped behaviour patterns emerge.

It should be seen from this that several environmental factors play a part in the development of 'instincts'; but once the ontogenesis of the behaviour is studied more closely, it no longer appears to be quite so innate. In addition, some doubt is cast on Lorenz and Tinbergen's criteria. It is as well to remember that if behaviour is to be classed as innate, it must occur even though the animal is held in entire isolation from the normal environment of the species.

What then is 'genetically determined'? Is the behaviour pattern present in the fertilized egg? Or do the genes set out certain possible patterns of development, during which the organism affects, and is affected by, its environment? Lehrman said: 'The interaction out of which the organism develops is not one, as is so often said, between heredity and environment. It is between organism and environment. And the organism is different at each stage of its development.'

In view of the disagreements about whether or not 'instinct' is a valid term with which to explain behaviour, the term *species-specific* is now preferred, since it does not pre-judge the issue of whether the behaviour is innate or not. The sections which follow, on *fixed action patterns* and *behaviour sequences*, deal with forms of behaviour which earlier would have been called instinctive but which are now know as species-specific behaviours.

Fixed Action Patterns (FAPs)

Fixed Action Patterns (FAPs) is the term coined by Lorenz to describe those forms of behaviour, often taking the form of courtship or aggressive displays, which are extremely stereotyped. This means that different individuals of the same species will perform the same actions in the same way in the same circumstances.

FAPs are more complex than reflexes, as the three following examples illustrate.

1 The first instance is that of egg retrieval by the greylag goose. If one of its eggs is moved out of the nest, the female stretches her neck out so that her beak goes beyond the egg. She then uses the underside of her beak to roll the egg back to the nest. All greylag females perform these same movements in the same situations. So stereotyped is this behaviour that, if the egg is removed by the observer, the female continues to make the retrieval movements.

2 The second example is from one of the classical ethological investigations by Tinbergen (1937) mentioned earlier. Ethologists are interested in determining what stimuli trigger (or, as they put it, *release*) certain forms of behaviour, and Tinbergen's studies provided some of the earliest clarification of the nature of these *sign stimuli*, as they are called. He found that the male sticklebacks he was studying, even those reared in isolation, would attack other males in spring. They would also attack their own image in a mirror, showing that the sign stimulus for attack did not involve smell. He built a series of models, ranging from those roughly shaped like a male stickleback to some which were almost circular in shape. Some of these models were painted to imitate the red underbelly of the male stickleback. Tinbergen found that the major sign stimulus was not the shape of the model, but the red underbelly: models with the

red underbelly were attacked much more frequently than those without. There was also a second sign stimulus: the models were more likely to be attacked if they were near the centre of the male stickleback's territory.

3 Thirdly, as we have seen, the red spot near the tip of the beak of the adult laughing gull releases pecking behaviour from the chick, which then eats the food regurgitated by the adult. Tinbergen showed that the chicks would also peck at a pencil with a red dot on it; but when the pencil had three red bands on it, it released even more pecking than did the natural stimulus. Such extra-powerful releasers are known as *super-releasers*.

Egg retrieval by the greylag female, the attacking of a male intruder by the male stickleback, and pecking at the red spot on an adult's bill by the laughing gull chick, are thus all examples of Fixed Action Patterns. All FAPs are released by sign stimuli – in these cases, respectively, the sight of the egg outside the nest, the intruding male's red underbelly and the red spot.

Behaviour Sequences

Although FAPs are fairly simple pieces of behaviour, they can be chained together to form more complex sequences, such as the courtship behaviour of the three-spined stickleback studied by Tinbergen. The function of the sign stimulus or releaser, he believed, was to release the appropriate innately determined behaviour via the *innate releasing mechanism* (IRM) (see figure 18.2). This, however, would only happen if the animal was in a state of 'readiness'. In the case of the male stickleback this was thought to be some kind of hormonal change, associated with the onset of spring. Figure 18.1 shows the sequence of fixed action patterns which are chained together to form

Figure 18.1. Courtship Dance of the Three-spined Stickleback

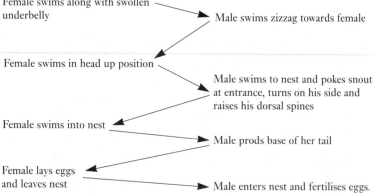

Female swims along with swollen underbelly

Male swims zizzag towards female

Female swims in head up position

Male swims to nest and pokes snout at entrance, turns on his side and raises his dorsal spines

Female swims into nest

Male prods base of her tail

Female lays eggs and leaves nest

Male enters nest and fertilises eggs.

the courtship dance of the three spined stickleback. Each action of the female fish acts as the sign stimulus for the next action of the male and vice versa.

The Hydraulic Model of Motivation

The ethologists produced a *hydraulic model of motivation* in order to explain the variations in behaviour which they had observed in animals. They particularly wanted to explain:

Variation in the strength of responses. Sometimes the FAP was performed very vigorously, at others it seemed almost half-hearted.

Variation in strength of sign stimulus needed to trigger the response. They noticed that at some times a particular form of behaviour was easily released and was performed intensely (at some times, a sign stimulus was not even necessary, the behaviour appearing apparently spontaneously and being know as *vacuum activity*). At other times, however, even the appearance of the appropriate sign stimulus would not release the behaviour, or would do so only in a weakened form.

Displacement activity. This was often observed in conflict situations. It takes the form of a type of behaviour which seems to be irrelevant to the activity in progress. For example, two gulls engaged in threat displays may suddenly break off and begin to preen their feathers.

The hydraulic model of motivation (sometimes called the *psycho-hydraulic model*) was an attempt to explain these variations in response strengths, vacuum and displacement activities. It is important at this point to note that, although the model is a hydraulic one, this does not imply that animals have taps and valves inside their heads; the idea is that animals behave in the way that they would *if* they were built in this way.

Each different FAP or behaviour sequence was assumed to have its own *Innate Releasing Mechanism* represented by the valve in figure 18.2. The Innate Releasing Mechanism (IRM) was opened by the appropriate sign stimulus (represented by the weight), to release the fluid (*action-specific energy* or ASE), which then 'powered' the behaviour. The container permitted the build-up of ASE, or 'readiness'. This model supplied explanations for the questions that had been raised from observation of behaviour.

1 Response strength depended on the level of fluid in the container (the more fluid, the more strongly the behaviour was performed); and on the strength of the sign stimulus, or the amount of weight pulling the valve open. The stronger the stimulus, the more the valve would open, thus the stronger the behaviour.

Figure 18.2. The Hydraulic Model of Motivation

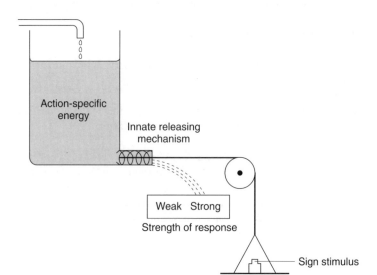

2 If the amount of fluid in the container was large enough, the pressure of the fluid alone might be enough to force open the valve, so vacuum activity, activity without a sign stimulus to release it, would occur. As the behaviour occurred, it used up ASE, so that there was less pressure against the valve and a stronger sign stimulus was required to release the same behaviour again, until the ASE had had time to build up. If all the ASE had been used up, no sign stimulus, however strong, would release the behaviour; this explains the variations in thresholds.

3 Displacement activity was thought to occur when two mutually incompatible hydraulic systems were released simultaneously, as they would be in a conflict situation where tendencies both to fight and to flee were present. Since the two systems were incompatible, they inhibited each other, and the ASE in each overflowed (or *sparked over*) into another hydraulic system or form of behaviour (preening, for example) which then occurred, more or less as a vacuum activity, with no relevance to the current situation.

CRITICISMS OF THE ETHOLOGISTS' HYDRAULIC MODEL
OF MOTIVATION
Despite its explanatory powers there have been substantial criticisms of the ethologists' hydraulic model, the most fundamental ones being aimed at

the model's emphasis on the ASE which is only available for one type of behaviour and on the predictions which the model makes about displacement activity.

If ASE is used up only by performance of the particular behaviour, how could the hydraulic model explain the results of the following 'classic' experiment by Adolph (1939)? Water was placed directly into the stomach of a thirsty dog via a tube, so that the dog did not need to perform any drinking activity. It was left for 10–15 minutes, and it was then offered water to drink in the normal way. (The 10–15 minute waiting period was necessary for the water to be digested.) The hydraulic model would predict the dog would still be thirsty, since it had not performed any drinking behaviour and so had not used any 'drinking ASE'. In fact, the dog in Adolph's experiment did not drink, so a prediction based on the hydraulic model was incorrect.

According to the hydraulic model, displacement activity is performed without relevance to the situation at hand, so the strength or absence of a sign stimulus for the displacement behaviour should not affect how much it is performed. This prediction is not borne out in practice; for example, Manning reports work by Van Iersel and Bol, in which nesting terns who were in a conflict situation (between staying on the nest and fleeing) performed displacement preening more when their feathers were wet than when they were dry.

THE DISINHIBITION HYPOTHESIS

A more recent attempt to explain displacement activity has been the *disinhibition hypothesis* (Van Iersel and Bol). It explains why behaviour which occurs as displacement activity is affected by the stimuli which affect that behaviour under normal circumstances. They put forward the idea that at any given time the animal has a hierarchy of possible responses available, and that the response at the top of the hierarchy will be performed and will inhibit those below them in the hierarchy. If, as can happen in a conflict situation, the top two responses are incompatible, they will mutually inhibit each other, and also remove their inhibitions on the next-highest response. For example, Van Iersel and Bol's terns could have had 'remaining on the nest' and 'escape' responses at the top of their hierarchy. Since these two responses inhibit each other, they would also release each others' inhibition of the next-highest response, preening. The stimuli for preening would probably have been present all the time, and wetting the feathers would increase the stength of the stimuli. If, however, the next-highest response had been feeding, instead of preening, feeding would have taken place as a displacement activity, but still in response to external or internal stimuli, not as a piece of behaviour irrelevant to the situation.

Social Behaviour

At some time in their life cycle most animals interact with others of their species, even if only for the purpose of mating. Species vary in the extent to which they mix in groups, from the highly social animals such as humans, and the social insects (bees, ants and so on), which spend most of their time in the presence of others and have evolved complex methods of communication which allow individuals to perform different roles within their society, to animals such as the digger wasp, whose only contact with others occurs in order to mate. Between these extremes are a wide variety of levels of social behaviour.

Some writers have suggested that animals form groups purely for the sake of the pleasure of being with other individuals, but there are in fact sound biological reasons for grouping. Social groups make it easier to find a mate, and larger groups have a greater range of genetic make-up, making genetic adaptations to environmental conditions more likely. There is more safety from predators because there are more 'lookouts', and some hunters seem to be confused by large groups. Vegetarian animals spend most of their time eating, and groups may be more efficient in finding food. For example, sparrows tend to land where they can see other birds feeding, so that large flocks form around good food sources. Barnard (1979) showed that individual scanning for predators decreased as the size of the sparrow flock increased, thus giving each bird more time for feeding; the random scanning of each bird in a large flock ensures that there are always a few lookouts to warn of approaching danger. Carnivorous animals such as the lion are far more successful when hunting in groups than they would be individually, since a group may approach the prey from different directions; and smaller animals increase their physical advantage over their victims by sheer numbers.

V.C. Wynne-Edwards argued that the major reason for the development of social grouping in animals is the control of population level, for grouping ensures that this level is in equilibrium with the available food supply. Many forms of social behaviour have evolved to meet this end. The study of voles by Krebs and Boonstra (1979) is an example of how population control can be achieved by animals. They found that when the numbers of a particular type of vole, *Microtus pennsylvanicus*, caused a high population density, only the larger animals were successful in their mating attempts. The larger animals were more successful because of their greater aggressiveness, which forced smaller animals to migrate. The remaining voles did not, however, reproduce fast enough to maintain the population numbers, and as the number of animals decreased, so the smaller ones were again allowed to mate. In this way the vole population fluctuated but never became too overcrowded for the available food.

Chapman (1928) demonstrated the way in which flour beetles are able to keep their population in a very precise ratio to the food available. He put an equal number of beetles into closed containers with different amounts of food. The food in each container was continually renewed so that it was never exhausted. Chapman found that after six months each environment contained a different number of beetles but that the ratio of beetles to food was constant: there were 44 beetles for every gram of flour in the container. Those in the container with a lot of food bred rapidly, but those with limited resources kept their populations low by laying fewer eggs and by cannibalising the eggs and larvae. This experiment has been repeated with other animals such as mice, rats and guppies, with similar results.

Wynne-Edwards suggests that many forms of social behaviour have evolved to allow population control. He suggests, for example, that starlings flock at night in order to monitor their numbers and compare this figure with the available food supply: if the numbers in the flock are too high, some members leave and migrate to other areas. The synchronised 'morning chorus' of birds may fulfil a similar purpose. Phenomena such as *dominance hierarchies* (see p. 335) ensure that at least some members of a group will survive at a time of food shortage. Rather than all members receiving a small, insufficient amount of food, those high in the hierarchy eat reasonably well at the expense of lower individuals. Since animals with dominance hierarchies know their position, they do not waste energy fighting over scarce resources, which could result in survivors too weak to benefit from their winnings, and which could thus cause the whole group, and perhaps the whole species, to become extinct.

Many writers (most recently the group known as *sociobiologists*) attempt to explain social behaviour with reference to its hereditary basis. They argue that some forms of social behaviour make it more likely that an animal will successfully reproduce and pass on its genes. This is easy to see if the behaviour is something like cooperating with others in the hunt for food, but it is more difficult to credit in the case of *altruistic behaviour*, which is discussed on page 337.

The sociobiologists point to human evolutionary connections with apes and monkeys and the similarities in responses that result from this. They also argue that behaviour today is influenced by the fact that we have evolved through a million years and were formerly engaged in hunting and gathering, and that although this was largely abandoned ten thousand years ago, it still affects social behaviour today. This evolutionary history has its effects in two ways: first, genetically, because those genes that favour hunting and gathering are likely to have been maintained in the population; and secondly, culturally, in the form of the socialization of successive generations (see chapter 9 for a full discussion of the socialization process).

The sociobiologists argue amongst themselves about the degree to which cultural rather than genetic evolution determines human behaviour today. Those who stress the biological origins of human behaviour have been heavily criticized on political grounds. It is argued that their approach is an attempt to justify inequalities by saying that they are a result of 'human nature' which has evolved over centuries, and by saying that deviations from this nature are abnormal. Edward Wilson, whose book *Sociobiology* sparked off much of this heated debate, replies that his critics are falling into the naturalistic fallacy of ethics which uncritically concludes that what is, should be. He points out that it may be human nature to rear as many children as possible, or to indulge in warfare under certain conditions, but that in our present environment these behaviours are likely to lead to ultimate destruction; he argues that evolutionary explanations should be an addition to, rather than a replacement for, other viewpoints on human and animal behaviour.

Whatever the reason for the formation of groups and societies, it is obvious that forms of behaviour must develop to regulate activity in these collections. The next few sections consider some of these forms of social behaviour, looking at courtship and parental and aggressive behaviour.

Courtship Behaviour

Especially in those species of animals which do not form permanent male–female relationships, the particular displays or FAPs which act as a prelude to mating are vital for the reproduction of the species. In such solitary species the male and female may meet only to mate, and at all other times act aggressively towards one another. In some species hormonal factors, perhaps influenced by temperature or day length, provide a means of general synchronization of the onset of the reproductive period. However, a more precise synchronization is usually required if the pair is to mate successfully, and this process of synchronization must also inhibit both sexes' aggressive behaviours. Courtship displays therefore seem to have evolved to both synchronize reproductive behaviour and inhibit aggression, the enabling mating to occur.

Observational studies had suggested that courtship displays take place when an animal is in a state of *approach-avoidance conflict*. For example, the male chaffinch, several weeks after he and the female have formed a pair-bond, loses his dominant status over her and becomes her subordinate. When he approaches her, two sets of drives appear to be present: one drive is to mount her, and to copulate, while the other is to flee from her. These drives are obviously in conflict. Hence when he approaches her, he does so hesitantly, with small steps and in a zigzag route, instead of directly.

Similarly, as we have seen, Tinbergen's work on mating in the stickleback showed that the zigzag display dance of the male had attack components in it (when it swam towards the female; occasionally it might even nip her) and also escape components (when it swam away from her).

Since conflicts between attack and escape tendencies are often present in courtship, it might be expected that displacement activities would occur too, for their occurrence also depends on this same situation. In fact, displacement activities of a sort do occur. For example, the male mallard reaches back with its bill, behind its slightly raised wing. Instead of performing normal preening, it wipes the tip of its bill across the stems of the feathers, producing a loud rattling noise. It can also dip its bill briefly in the water and raise its head suddenly, producing a spray of water. But these displacement activities are not normal ones – the 'preening' display is not normal preening in its displacement form, but a highly stereotyped and simplified version of it. Neither is the 'drinking' display real drinking – the male does not actually take in any water. These displacement activities have become ritualized by natural selection: they have become common to a particular species and are stereotyped; that is, always performed in the same way. In addition, they have become emancipated from the original stimuli which in the past elicited them. They are now elicited by the escape and avoidance stimuli emitted by the female, instead of by wet feathers or thirst. The displays are performed with what is known as *typical intensity*; that is, no matter how strong or weak the stimuli from the female, the male will perform the courtship display with full intensity. A weak stimulus will release a short-lived display, and a strong stimulus a longer display, but whether long or short, the display will be performed just as intensely.

Most ritualized courtship displays have the effect of making the animal (usually the male) more conspicuous, for the obvious reason that the male is then much more likely to be recognized by the female.

Maternal Behaviour

In some species, the male may share or take major responsibility for the young, but in mammals the female is more likely to care for them. The young of relatively advanced species are born at an immature stage in development, cannot fend for themselves, and consequently depend for survival on parents. Parental behaviour is of evolutionary significance because animals which look after their young ensure their survival and that of the species; animals who do not, or who display inadequate maternal behaviour, are not likely to have young which survive. When the young of inadequate parents do survive to maturity they are frequently incapable of attracting a mate, mating or rearing young of their own. Parents provide defence, protection from exposure, food and water, and sometimes some form of behaviour shaping.

Several researchers have noted quite clear phases in the feeding and nursing behaviour of mammals towards their young. The length of each phase varies from species to species. Rosenblatt and Lehrman (1963), for example, describe three phases.

1 The first is a phase where the mother takes an active part in presenting the nipple to her young.
2 Secondly, the infant is the more active in initiating feeding, actively seeking the female's attention; the female readily assists feeding by remaining fairly still in the nursing position and making the nipples available.
3 In the third phase, the female becomes increasingly reluctant to assist the young with feeding and eventually takes active steps to prevent it (weaning).

Harlow (1963), in studies of maternal behaviour in rhesus monkeys, found three stages analogous to those above. The earliest stage is that of attachment, where the infant clings to its mother's underside, spending much time at the breast even though it is not necessarily actually feeding. The mother increasingly grooms the infant. (Grooming is at first performed only by the mother, but later other animals do it. As well as preventing parasites and cleaning, grooming has social significance since it helps to maintain pair bonds and patterns of friendship.) The second phase involves the young becoming more active, spending less time clinging to her, and being groomed by her less. The mother at first restricts the infant's activities, preventing it from straying too far, but later allows more independence. At this stage the young approach the mother more than she does them, often leaving her to explore new situations but always returning to her. The final stage is that of separation, where the mother punishes and rejects the young more often. Most male young, for example, are separated by the end of the second year. Male adult rhesus monkeys may approach and touch the young while in their mother's arms, and may carry the young during long treks. They are highly sensitive to the distress calls of the young and would, for example, attack a human observer who came between the young and the rest of the group.

Hinde (1966) showed that disturbance of these processes, by forced separation of mother and infant, could have drastic effects on the infant's development. Harlow (see p. 154) had shown that separation of an infant from its mother only twelve hours after birth had a profoundly damaging effect on the infant's social and sexual responses, even when mature. Hinde suggested that separation may occur much later, and be much briefer, yet still have damaging consequences. Six-month-old rhesus monkeys can fend for themselves. If the mother is removed from the group, even though a young monkey may be 'fostered' by other adults, it still shows signs of gross distress (much distress calling, reduced exploration, and occasional bouts of sitting hunch-backed in corners). When the mother returns, there is a very swift reunion, and the baby monkey spends more time than usual clinging to its mother. This pattern may last for several weeks, following a separation of only a few hours. Hinde believes that such effects are still observable years later, for 'separated' young appear to show more fear in new situations than normally reared young.

In sub-primate species, much research has been concerned with the development of maternal behaviour, mainly in rats and mice. Although this research is probably not directly applicable to humans, it does give a useful impression of how physiological and behavioural factors interact. Female mice, when pregnant, build nests. Weisner and Sheard (1933) showed that injections of *prolactin* (a hormone produced by the pituitary gland during late pregnancy which stimulates milk production) stimulated maternal behaviour such as nest building and the retrieval of young, even in virgin females, and to a lesser extent in males.

However, it would be wrong to think that all maternal behaviour is totally controlled by hormones. Rosenblatt and Lehrman (1963) found that the young, once born, acted as stimuli to release maternal behaviour in rats. Normally, female rats continue nest building for two weeks after the birth of the young; if the young are removed from the mother at birth, however, nest building declines immediately. It seems that hormonal changes are necessary to initiate nest building, but that once it has occurred the presence of the young is necessary to maintain it. The gradual decline of maternal care seems to be associated with two factors: first, the increasing size of the young; and secondly, perhaps the reduction in prolactin production. However, Noirot (1964) has shown, with mice, that the same gradual diminution of care occurs even if given by virgins who do not produce prolactin. The young themselves may therefore be more important as stimuli in the cessation of maternal behaviour. Hinde suggests, for example, that young rhesus monkeys gradually become rejected because, as they get older and larger, their nipple-biting and hair-holding become painful to the mother.

Previous experience of motherhood, or certain forms of environmental stimulation, may have an effect on maternal behaviour; with the possibility that this is more so in the higher mammals than the lower. Rats and rabbits show very little change in maternal behaviour between the first and subsequent litters, when 'maternal behaviour' is defined as interest shown in the young, the level of aggression response and the length of time devoted to nest building. The rate of survival of the first litter does not differ significantly from that of later litters, although Calhoun (1962) has demonstrated that, in rat colonies, environmental variables such as overcrowding can lead to breakdowns in maternal behaviour and infant mortality rates close to 100%. Primates also rear young adequately on the first litter, but do show greater improvements in infant care with subsequent litters. Mitchell *et al.* (1966) showed that first-born infants play less with their parents and show less emotion, but appear to be more disturbed by strange environments than later infants. Maternal behaviour, then, has obvious survival value for the individual and the species. However, in species whose young are mobile shortly after birth there is the danger that the young will wander off, or fail to form attachments with their parents. The section, on *imprinting*, in chapter 8 looks at the means by which the young may be kept close to their parents.

Agonistic (Aggressive) Behaviour

The responses that animals make when involved in social conflict are known as *agonistic behaviour*. These responses include attack, threat, fight, flight and submission. Lorenz points out that it is useful to distinguish between aggression that takes place between members of the same species and that between animals of different species. Different rules apply to the two situations, and the motivation for aggression is usually different. In the former case agonistic behaviour is often motivated by rivalry, and rarely results in fatal injury, whereas aggression shown between species often involves hunting, which may well result in the death of the prey.

Agonistic behaviour is often prompted by competition for such things as food, water, sex and status; it is also a common reaction to frustration and pain, but is most regularly seen in the establishment and protection of territories. The males of the majority of birds and mammals establish an area at the beginning of the breeding season which they defend against males of the same species. A piece of land may contain the overlapping territories of many different species, for it is rare that animals will need to defend them against other types of animal unless they share the same food requirements. The possession of a territory is an advantage, because the possessor will not then have far to search for food and will not encounter competition for scarce resources. Not all animals use their territories for feeding. For example, the herring gull has a territory of only a couple of square yards, which it uses only as a nesting site. Territories are usually breeding areas, and since there is usually not enough space to go round, some animals miss out and may not breed. In times of food shortage animals which feed within territories need larger areas for food gathering; consequently fewer but larger territories are developed, so fewer birds can breed.

Observers have noted for many years that an animal in its own territory seems to have an advantage in a conflict with an intruder which outweighs any physical differences between the two. Yasukawa (1979) demonstrated this phenomenon experimentally with dark-eyed junco birds which were matched for sex, size, colour and age. He put groups of birds into different aviaries for a week, during which time each group established a dominance hierarchy. Dominance hierarchies (mentioned earlier) are found in many species which live as a group within territories; those animals at the bottom of a hierarchy are subservient, and allow higher-ranking animals their pick of desirable commodities, such as food and sex. After a week, some of the birds were moved to other cages. When a group of birds was introduced to an aviary containing residents that had lived there for a week and formed a dominance hierarchy, they took their position at the bottom of the hierarchy with relatively little fighting. When birds from two different groups were introduced to a neutral cage, however, there was much more fighting, and the resulting dominance hierarchy was a mix of the hierarchies of the original groups. Individuals maintained their position relative to members of their original group. If the original ranks had been A, B, C and 1, 2, 3, the resultant dominance hierarchy might be A, 1, B, 2, 3, C. Yasukawa argued that introduction to a neutral cage had resulted in more physical fighting because there was no obvious advantage for any of the birds on account of their having been matched for physical characteristics and having no home territory advantage. When one of the groups was on home ground this had been enough to determine the outcome without escalation of the conflict.

Two competing drives are usually present when performing agonistic behaviour. The first is the *attack* (or *fight*) *drive* fuelled by the need to defeat an opponent; the second is the *submission* (or *flight*) *drive* which is a result of the fear of personal injury. The response elicited in a particular confrontation depends on the strength of these two drives. An animal is most likely to fight when it is inside its own territory, the drive being strongest at the centre and decreasing towards the boundary. As the tendency to fight decreases, the flight motive increases; on the edge of a territory the two drives may be equal, resulting in the production of displacement activity. Some fish and birds display *pendulum fighting*, which is when an animal on its own territory swims or flies at an intruder which flees, followed by its attacker, across the border into its own territory. At this point the relative strengths of the fight and flight drives in each combatant reverse, so that the original attacker is chased back into its own area, and the sequence may start again. Animals rarely kill other members of their own species because they use elaborate rituals rather than actual fighting to determine which animal should win the dispute. Factors such as relative size, territory and the possible rewards or losses determined by the outcome affect the extent to which each individual is willing to escalate the conflict. Within established groups the dominance hierarchies limit the extent of intra-group aggression because low-ranking individuals quickly submit to those higher in the scale.

A dispute usually starts by one or both animals demonstrating a *threat display*. These differ between species. For example, dogs bare their teeth, snarl, raise the ears and stiffen the tail, standing with a characteristic posture that is recognizable even to humans. Threat postures are most often seen in territorial animals at the border between adjacent territories; since neither animal is likely to advance into the other's territory, the result may be nothing more than a demonstration of displacement activity.

If there are no obvious deciding factors such as territory to determine which animal should win, the episode may escalate into actual physical contact, although rules still apply. Bernstein and Gordon describe the behaviour of 36 rhesus monkeys which first met as adults introduced into a single enclosure. The fighting appeared to be bloody and unrestrained, but an inspection of the wounds showed that they were limited to areas of the body such as the shoulders, face and tail rather than those parts where injury might be fatal, such as the throat and abdomen. Monkeys withdrew from fighting by adopting an *appeasement display*, which involves crouching and turning away from the attacker. This type of display is common to most animals and inhibits further attack; it is usually obviously different from any threat posture, and often involves the exposure of vulnerable parts of the body. Natural selection favours animal species which can terminate their aggression in this way rather than those which continue until the death.

Some appeasement displays seem to work by eliciting behaviour from the attacker that is incompatible with aggression: baboons adopt the female sexual presentation posture and may be briefly mounted by the dominant animal, but they are usually allowed to slink away. Bernstein noticed that submissive monkeys allowed small bites by an aggressor, but would immediately resume fighting if these bites involved the use of the potentially lethal canine teeth. It is therefore advantageous to a winning animal to discontinue its attack on sight of an appeasement display: he can then enjoy the rewards of his victory, which may be territory, food, a mate or long-lasting establishment in a dominant position.

The introduction of new animals to an existing group, or the first formation of a group, are the surest ways of producing violent fighting. Once the group is established and the newcomer has been ejected or assimilated, most disputes are quickly resolved by reference to the existing dominance hierarchy. Throwing a piece of food between two monkeys may result in agonistic behaviour, but usually this is one-sided, with the dominant animal chasing off its subordinate. Bernstein argues that in the case of monkeys, fighting occurs more often between animals of roughly equal status than between those with a great difference in rank. This means that adult male monkeys rarely attack juveniles because they are not perceived as a threat, whereas another adult male may be chased away if it approaches too close when a dominant male is eating. Shortage of food may increase aggression briefly; but, as we mentioned earlier, the dominance hierarchy ensures that high-ranking animals survive to maintain the species without suffering the weaknesses produced by starvation, or the sorts of injury that might result from unrestrained fighting, while the lower-ranking animals seem to starve and even die so that the group can survive.

This seemingly altruistic behaviour on the part of some members of the group has presented problems from evolutionary theorists, because an animal that dies in this way cannot pass on its genes to the next generation, whereas a selfish animal might live to produce offspring, so that surely any genes that favour altruism would disappear after a few generations. John Maynard Smith points out that members of groups are usually related, sharing common genes, and that any behaviour which allows a group to survive ensures the maintenance of those genes; so in this way natural selection favours altruism toward relatives. He argues that it is the survival of genes rather than individuals that is evolutionarily important. The evolutionary advantage of some forms of altruism can be seen most easily in the case of parents risking their lives for their offspring. A bird which flies noisily away from its nest to draw an intruder away from its young is more likely to be caught than one which slips away quietly, but its young are more likely to survive. The genes associated with this form of protection of the young may be present in the offspring and therefore be passed down to more and more individuals of succeeding generations. This is known as *kin selection*.

Bernstein's work shows how dominance hierarchies are built in groups when individuals are introduced as adults, but most individuals are born into existing groups. Manning argued that the emergence of dominance within a group is largely dependent upon maturation. The animal which matures earliest will for a time be bigger and stronger than the others and will therefore be able to dominate them; this dominance is maintained even when all the others have matured. Brown noted that lion trainers put themselves at the head of the dominance hierarchy by intimidating a harnessed young lion until it indicates submission by appeasement gestures; then the lion will still respect the trainer's rank when it is adult. Bernstein describes the assimilation of young monkeys into a dominance hierarchy as a socialization process, which differs from species to species. For most monkeys, rank position is maintained by alliances with other individuals, so that an old animal may maintain a high position because its offspring and peers support it. Since a young monkey is seldom attacked because it is not perceived as a threat, its socialization will consist of learning its mother's position in the hierarchy, which monkeys support her, and which responses it can get away with without provoking older animals.

Most species show a sex difference in the type and frequency of aggressive responses, though males are usually more aggressive. This fact has been linked with the male sex hormone, testosterone. Castrated rats usually show a decrease in aggression towards other rats, although they still attack mice, which reinforces the argument that there is a difference between inter- and intraspecies aggression. Bernstein pointed out that adult male monkeys are more often involved in the less restrained fighting that occurs when two groups meet, but that at other times they show very little aggression, though females and juveniles may involve themselves in threats and chases. He argued that natural selection probably favours this difference, for if the lethal fighting abilities of females and juveniles were used within a society this would make group survival less likely.

Agonistic behaviour is influenced by an animals's habitat. Southwick showed that aggression was more frequent in captive groups of rhesus monkeys than in those living around rural villages, and that it occurred least in forest-dwelling groups. He noted that food shortages did not lead to increased aggression; the changes seemed to be caused by crowding, though social changes such as the introduction of a stranger into a group had the greatest effect. Calhoun (1962) studied the effect of crowding on the behaviour of rats. He placed 32 rats into a room 10 ft × 14 ft room in which they were given adequate food and opportunity for play. The animals reproduced, but the amount of space was not increased. Once the number increased to about 80 rats the social patterns changed, there was an increase in aggression and homosexual behaviour, and the young were neglected and sometimes eaten by the males.

COMPARISONS BETWEEN ANIMALS AND HUMANS IN AGGRESSIVE BEHAVIOUR

Some writers see man as an innately aggressive animal who has lost the ability to control his agonistic behaviour in the way that is common amongst lower species. Ethologists have tried to explain why humans appear to be an exception to the rule as far as killing members of their own species is concerned. Tinbergen and others pointed out that human behaviour is heavily influenced by cultural factors which affect the expression of any genetic relationship with the lower animals. For example, cultural heritage may have upset the balance between fight and flight drives, because combatants are taught that it is 'cowardly' to run away and in many armies the punishments for desertion are greater than those for staying in battle. Also, modern warfare often involves killing at a distance: the bomb-aimer cannot see the victims and any appeasement displays they might produce. Lorenz (1966), using his hydraulic model to explain the motivational basis of aggression, argued that people have an inborn tendency towards aggressive behaviour, which inevitably finds an expression, no matter what the physical environment. As the action-specific energy builds up, the strength of stimulus needed to release it in the form of aggressive responses becomes less and less, and unless it is diverted into some socially acceptable behaviour such as sport or political argument, aggression will spontaneously erupt as a form of vacuum activity.

Lorenz backed up his assertion that aggression is inevitable by referring to examples such as the cichlid fish. This fish can only mate successfully when other males are present, because in the absence of another fish to attack, the male will fight with its female partner. When another male is present as the target of aggression, little agonistic behaviour is found between the courting pair, and they successfully mate. Lorenz argued that the cichlid fish attacks its partner in the absence of another fish because the action-specific energy has to find an outlet. However, Hinde argued that other explanations are possible which do not stress the inevitability of aggression: he pointed out that all courtship behaviour involves a conflict between the agonistic and sexual drives elicited by the mate. When another cichlid fish is present, the agonistic arousal can be redirected away from the mate, but this is not possible when they are alone. Hinde pointed out that cichlid fish are exceptionally aggressive compared with most other animals, whose sexual arousal during courtship usually outweighs any aggression. Heiligenberg found that even in cichlid fish the aggressive drive decreases after a few days when presented with no arousing stimuli; this is the exact opposite of Lorenz's expectations.

Wilson (1976) argued that human and animal aggression is more affected by factors such as crowding, food shortage, and frustration that any innate inevitability. He pointed out that it is common to find closely related species of birds or mammals who differ greatly in their levels of aggression, and so it is unwise to assume that it is a deeply rooted instinct in animals as diverse as cichlid fish and man. Humans have a capacity for aggression which may have had an evolutionary advantage, but that behaviour is finely adjusted to circumstances, and capable of remaining dormant for long periods in the correct environment. Human cultural heritage and experiences of socialization are the most important factors in determining aggressive behaviour (see chapters 9 and 13).

Many of the animal aggression studies have suggested human parallels which have been further studied. For example, Calhoun's work on the effect of crowding on rats prompted Ehrlich and Freedman (1971) to study the effect of room size on human groups playing games which could be performed in either a cooperative or a competitive manner; they found that in small rooms males were more likely to be competitive, dislike each other and give more severe sentences in a mock trial. In a large room, male behaviour was less competitive, the participants like each other more and gave less severe sentences.

Hinde criticised the way in which Lorenz and others drew parallels between the behaviour of man and other animals. He pointed out that the ethologists are careful to describe animal behaviour fully, determining the functions and causes of responses by close observation and experimentation. By comparison, their analysis of human behaviour is very crude, grouping together such diverse activities as playing games and contributing to political argument under the general heading of aggression. The use of the ethologist's techniques in the study of actual humans is likely to be more useful than these crude comparisons between human and animal behaviour.

Summary

1 Animal behaviour is studied for many reasons including: for its own sake, for commercial reasons and to help with the understanding of human behaviour. Great care needs to be taken in generalizing from animal to human behaviour but our knowledge of animals may be used to generate hypotheses which might then be tested on people.

2 Ethologists studied the behaviour of animals in more natural situations than did most experimental psychologists. They developed the ethogram to describe animal behaviour.

3 Ethologists reintroduced the concept of instinct. To be considered an instinct behaviour must be more than a simple reflex, it must be inherited and must be:

- stereotyped and constant in form.
- characeristic of the species (that is, *species-specific*).
- appear in animals which have been reared in isolation from others.
- appear fully developed in animals which have been prevented from practising it.

4 The term *species-specific behaviour* is preferred to 'instinct' because it allows for at least the possibility of learned components to behaviour. Most animals in a species share common environments and it is both hereditary and environmental similarites which produce the behaviour typical of the species.

5 Lorenz put forward the ethologists hydraulic model of motivation to explain species-specific behaviour. The model is successful in explaining a number of characteristics of behaviour but has been criticized for the way it assumes that energy is reserved for particular actions and cannot be used for others. The disinhibition hypothesis provides a better explanation of displacement activity.

6 Courtship and maternal behaviours are highly characteristic of the particular species and have often been regarded as instinctive. Most studies have demonstrated environmental influences and these behaviours are better termed species specific.

7 Lorenz distinguished between inter- (between) and intra- (within) species aggression. Concepts of dominance hierarchy, appeasement displays and territoriality are important controls on aggression within species and make it unlikely that animals are gravely hurt.

8 Humans are most unusual in the extent of harm that they do to each other. This may be due to the development of weapons which make appeasement displays less visible or may be due to the effect of culture.

9 The ethologists have been criticized for the way that they overemphasise the similarity between humans and other animals and the extent to which they overemphasize the hereditary component of behaviour. The ethological approach to studying behaviour in detail in its natural environment can be applied very usefully to the study of human development.

Chapter 19

Psychology Practicals

Psychology is a practical subject. You will have noticed in previous chapters that we do not simply sit in our armchairs and *think* about how people behave; we go out and test our theories either in the laboratory or in the real world.

Psychology practicals can take many forms. In some cases we simply *observe* behaviour in its normal setting. For example you might want to know whether there is any difference between boys and girls in the types of games they play. This could be done simply by watching a variety of different playgrounds and recording which games were being played by each sex. It would probably be better if the children didn't know that you were watch-ing and recording because if they knew this they might 'behave properly' or 'show off' and not behave normally. The way in which people change their behaviour when they know that they are being observed is known as the *Hawthorne Effect*, and many observational studies are done without the subject's knowledge in order to avoid this.

Another way in which we could study sex differences and games would be to *interview* boys and girls and ask them questions about how often they played certain games. We could even write these questions down in the form of a *questionnaire* and let children fill it in themselves. One major problem with these techniques is that we can't be sure that children (or adults) will tell us the truth; they may forget or they might not want to admit that they play some sorts of games. The interview/questionnaire techniques can often, however, be very useful, especially since they tell us about how people feel about things as well as what they actually do.

Lots of people talk about *experiments* and *practicals* as if they were the same things. But it is important to realize that the term 'experiment' has a specific technical meaning and that many practicals such as Observational Studies or Interviews are not experiments.

Before embarking on any piece of research you should search through the published literature to see what has already been written about your area of work. Be systematic in your search of the library, archives or Internet, so that you build up your skills of finding relevant material. Design your study in the light of what you find in the search perhaps by replicating a study, modifying it or designing something new resulting from the ideas that the reading stimulates.

The Experimental Method

In observational studies all you do is *look* at what is going on. The experimental method, however, involves changing things to see what happens. You start off with an idea about what might happen if the participants did one thing rather than another. This is known as an *hypothesis*. For example, you might put forward the hypothesis that children would drink more orange juice if they were in a hot room than if they were in a cold room. To test this hypothesis experimentally you would simply put some children into a hot room and other (similar) children into the same room when it was cold. Both groups would be supplied with as much orange juice as they desired and you would measure how much was drunk.

The thing that you change in an experiment (the temperature of the room in this one) is known as the *independent variable* and we note the effect of this change by measuring the *dependent variable* (how much orange juice was drunk). Of course, there are lots of other things that might affect the amount of juice that was drunk and we would have to make sure that these did not upset the experiment. It would be silly to allow one group to have crisps if the other group only had the orange juice, or to have some children who had just been playing football and another who had been sitting down in a classroom. These other variables are known as *extraneous variables* and we try to *control* them so that they have the same effect in both conditions.

The great advantage of the experiment is that it is the only method that directly studies cause and effect.

Formula for an experiment

EXTRANEOUS   +   INDEPENDENT ——▶ DEPENDENT
   variables   variables   variables

All experiments can be fitted into this 'formula'. In an experiment to test the hypothesis that there is a difference in the speed that people react to visual and auditory stimuli the independent variable would be whether the stimulus was a sound or a light, the dependent variable would be the time taken to respond to these stimuli. In an experiment to test the effect of a drug on memory the amount of drug received by the child would be the independent variable and the dependent variable would be some measure of memory.

Examples of Extraneous Variables and their Control

In the auditory and visual reaction-time experiment above, you would probably decide to use the same people in both conditions: if you used different
people in each condition any difference in the results might simply be due
to ability differences between these two groups of people rather than
anything to do with the difficulties of the two types of task. Using the same
people to react to both visual and auditory stimuli, however, introduces
another set of extraneous variables; these are called *order effects*. If all
people responded to the auditory stimulus first, then it could be argued
that any difference in the results of the two conditions were due to practice
(if visual reaction time was best) or fatigue (if auditory reaction time was
best). This would be a confounding nuisance when it came to interpreting
the results of the experiment; uncontrolled extraneous variables are called
confounding variables. Order effects can usually be controlled by *counterbalancing*, which involves half the people doing condition A first and the
other half doing condition B first. You will notice that this does not get rid
of order effects, it simply makes sure that they have the same effect on each
condition.

There are some extraneous variables that can be simply *eliminated*. These
are such things as noise or distractions. We can't get rid of other variables
such as sex or time of day, but we can make sure that these don't effect the
difference in the results of the two conditions by making sure that they are
the same for both. If all the participants in one condition are boys then all
those in the other condition should also be boys (unless of course you are
studying the difference between boys and girls). This method of control is
known as *matching* or *constancy*.

When we put some people into one condition and the rest into the other
it is important that the two groups are as similar as possible. The most
usual way to do this is by *random allocation* which can be done by putting
the people's names into a hat and picking them out at random to see who
goes into each condition. In this way there should be no bias built in to the
groups; other techniques such as asking all the children who sit in the front
of the class to be in condition A and the rest in condition B have the
disadvantage that the sort of people who choose to sit at the front may
be different from those who sit at the back. If the experimenter makes a
personal choice, all sorts of things might affect the choice and so it is best
to rely on random allocation.

In all experiments people should, as far as possible, be treated the same
way in each condition and care should be taken to avoid such things as
competition between people or letting them know how you expect the
experiment to turn out, unless of course this is what you are investigating.

It is impossible to control all extraneous variables but we must design
our experiments to avoid any constant difference between the conditions

other than the independent variable. Some variables change in a random manner; these are chance factors and cannot be controlled because we can't predict them. Chance variables make life interesting and are the basis of gambling but they are a pain in the neck for experimenters. It is these uncontrollable factors that produce the need for *statistical tests* which are used to make an estimate of how likely it was that any difference between the results of the experimental conditions was due to chance.

A survey of the statistical tests that are available to researchers is beyond the scope of this book. Any reader who would like to know more about statistical tests should read *Starting Statistics* (see the end of the chapter for a full reference).

EXTRANEOUS   +   INDEPENDENT ⟶ DEPENDENT
  VARIABLES   VARIABLES   VARIABLES

                         Condition A   Result A*

                         Condition B   Result B*

* The difference here is due to the difference in the variables on the left. If *extraneous* variables were controlled to prevent *confounding* variables, then the difference in the result of the two conditions is due to the *independent variable* or to *chance*.

Experimental Design

Sometimes we use the same people in both conditions of an experiment; at other times this is not possible. Experimental design refers to the way that we use people either in one or both of the experimental conditions.

(a) *Repeated measures design.* In this design, each person performs in both the control and the experimental condition (i.e. in both condition A and condition B).

(b) *Independent subjects design.* In this design, some people perform in condition A and others in condition B. (Note that psychologists sometimes use the term *subject* to refer to a person who is taking part in an experiment.)

(c) *Matched pairs design.* From the results of a pre-test, the participants are sorted into matched pairs (pairs of equal abilities on the task to be measured). One from each pair performs in condition A and one in condition B.

*Table 19.1. An example of Allocation of Children to Conditions in
Repeated Measures and Independent Subjects Designs*

(a) Repeated Measures		(b) Independent Subjects	
Condition A	Condition B	Condition A	Condition B
Tim	Tim	Tim	Ben
Matthew	Matthew	Matthew	Sally
Carol	Carol	Carol	Isabelle
Tom	Tom	Tom	George
Laura	Laura	Laura	Jenny

Advantages and Disadvantages of the Designs

(1) As you can see, you need twice as many people for an independent subjects design.
(2) Since the same people are tested in conditions A and B in the repeated measures design, this method automatically ensures that there are no personality or ability differences between the two groups.
(3) In some experiments, performance in one condition changes the subject in such a way that they could not reasonably be included in the other. This is often the case in learning experiments. For example, it would not be possible to use repeated measures design to investigate difference methods of learning to drive a car.
(4) Matched pairs design controls for personality and ability differences between conditions by the method of constancy (see page 344), and can be used in situations where repeated measures design is not possible.
(5) The choice of characteristics to match in matched pairs design is a subjective decision and pre-testing can take a long time. Independent subjects design is more commonly used in situations where repeated measures is not appropriate.

Populations and Samples

Before you perform an experiment you should decide which *population* you want your results to apply to; you might want them to apply to all humans (good luck!), or just to males or females, to students or to children under the age of seven, etc. It is usually impossible to study the whole of a population, so you must choose a smaller group from within the population. This is known as a *sample*. If you decide that you wanted to study students at a college it might be tempting to simply ask the people that you know to take part in the experiment. This might not be a good idea because they are a special group within the population of college students and might be different from students in general. You must choose a *representative sample*, i.e. a sample which has the same characteristics as the population. Remember that if you take an unrepresentative sample of the population you might not be able to generalize your results.

There are two main types of methods by which you can achieve a representative sample. These are *random* and *quota sampling*.

Random sampling. For this method a sample is drawn in such a way that every member of the population has an equal chance of being selected, for instance the use of a pin stuck at random into a list of names or drawing names out of a hat. This should produce a representative sample.

Quota sampling. For this method the population is analysed by picking out those characteristics which are considered important as far as the research is concerned. Individuals are then systematically chosen so that the sample has these same characteristics. The system will produce a representative sample as long as the right characteristics were chosen in the first place.

In practice you may be limited when choosing your participants from people who are available in a college library or refectory. Try to avoid personal bias in choosing who you will ask to become involved in your experiment. Decide before you go into the library or refectory that you will ask (say) every tenth person that you pass as you walk up the aisle. In this way you should at least get a representative sample of people in those rooms. We don't recommend the system used by one or two of our students which is to choose only the most attractive members of the opposite sex they can find; that is useful for many things, but doesn't help obtain a representative sample for an experiment!

Experiments – a General Planning Sequence

1 Decide what you want your experiment to find out. This means producing a hypothesis which can be tested to see if it is likely to be true; for example 'A group of participants asked to recognize words from a list previously learned will remember more than participants asked to recall the words.' When you have done the experiment you can either accept this hypothesis (if they did recognize more words than were recalled) or reject it (if they didn't).
2 Decide which population you want your results to apply to and how you will obtain a representative sample.
3 Design the experiment. This involves making decisions about whether the participants will perform in both conditions (repeated measures design) or whether half of them will be in one condition and the other half in the other condition (independent subjects). Also think about

possible extraneous variables and design the experiment to control them using methods such as elimination, matching, counterbalancing and randomization.

4 Write down your instructions so that you give the instruction in the same way to each participant. Make sure you know exactly how you are to record the responses. If there is more than one experimenter check that you all agree about everything you are going to do.

5 Always perform a pilot study. This means doing the practical with a small group of people before going ahead with the full-scale study. The pilot study often shows up weaknesses in things like instructions to subjects or difficulties in measurements; these should be sorted out before continuing with the real thing.

6 Collect your participants together. Act in as professional a way as possible – if you take the experiment seriously they will.

7 Perform the experiment.

8 Debrief your participants. Thank them for their involvement in the study and give them a brief explanation of what you were doing. If you are going to get some more participants later it might be wise to ask this group not to discuss the experiment with anybody else. Assure your participants that they will not be named in any report that is written.

Some experiments involve deception and can embarrass participants; Milgram's study of obedience is an example (see pp. 118–21). Under these conditions the debriefing sessions are most important to reassure the subjects that they are not abnormal and that their embarrassment will not be made public. An even better way of reducing people's embarrassment is, of course, not to practise deceit on them. Such experiments are thought to be ethically wrong by the majority of modern psychologists.

9 Organize your results into a form which makes them clear (see pp. 358–66) and decide what they mean. Do they support the original hypothesis or not? Remember that it is possible that the difference in the results of the two conditions is due to chance; this is especially likely if the difference is small. If other people in your group have done the same experiment and got the same answer it makes it less likely that it was a chance result, but the best way of finding out is by performing one of the statistical tests to be found in *Starting Statistics*. (Heyes, Hardy *et al.*, 1993.)

10 You must now decide how your findings relate to other comparable psychological studies. If you are performing a replication of a previous study, the comparison of findings is relatively straight-forward, even most non-replication studies are highly likely to have similarities with other studies.

If your results are substantially different from other studies you will need to offer explanations for this difference. Consider the following possibilities:

(a) Was your participant sample biased/unrepresentative/too small?
(b) Were your instructions standardized? Were they the same or similar to those used by previous researchers?
(c) Did you use different measurements of the dependent variable?
(d) Did you use the same type of experimental design?
(e) Be honest! Were there flaws in the design or the way the study was carried out?

If none of the above checklist gives you an idea for the discrepancy between your results and other published work *always consider the possibility that you may be right and they might be wrong!*

11 Write up your report.

Cross-sectional, Longitudinal and Cross-cultural Studies

If you wanted to study a question like: 'does watching TV alter children's behaviour?', how could you do it? Firstly, you'd need to find some way of measuring the amounts and types of TV which children watched, and secondly, you'd have to find some way of measuring children's behaviour. But which children would you study, and over how long a period would you study them?

You might decide to study a group of 5-year-olds, a group of 6-year-olds, 7-year-olds and so on, for as many ages as you wished. If you obtained a *representative sample* of each age-group, the results of your study of each age could be applied to all children of that age; that is, you would be able to say how TV affects the behaviour of all children aged 5, 6, or 7. This is known as the *cross-sectional method*. It is a fairly quick method to use (you could carry out your study in a few days only) – but it does have one main disadvantage. Suppose you found that 7-year-olds' behaviour was much more affected by TV than 5-year-olds. Does this mean that TV really does have more effect on 7-year-olds. Possibly, but it could mean that there was something in the 7-year-olds' upbringing which makes them respond more to TV, and that 'something' was missing from the 5-year-olds' upbringing. Using cross-sectional studies, you cannot be sure that your various age-groups have had the same upbringing; what may be true for the 7-year-olds now, may not be true of today's 5-year-olds when they become 7.

Longitudinal studies are a way of overcoming this problem. Instead of studying groups of children of each age-group, you could test a group of

5-year-olds, and then retest them when they were 6, again at 7, and so on. (A Granada TV series called '7 up' used this method. A group of 7-year-olds were studied, and they were studied again at ages 14, 21, 28, 35, and most recently 42.) This method has the advantage that you can see how children are affected by TV over a period of time, so you can see how changes both in a child's age and in its environment affect its behaviour.

There is a big drawback to longitudinal studies, however – if you were studying children from 5 until they were 20 years old, your study would take 15 years to complete, and you may well lose touch with some of your subjects over that length of time. What started out as a representative sample of subjects aged 5 may be very far from representative when they reach the age of 20.

Whether you use the cross-sectional or the longitudinal method of study, you would probably be studying British children, so your results could only be applied to British children, not to children from different cultures or countries. The cross-cultural method of study allows you to see if children from different countries or cultures behave differently from British children. So, in your TV study, you could find out whether children in Britain are affected as much by TV as children in the USA, or Greece, or wherever, by testing samples of children in each country. Cross-cultural methods tend to be expensive (you have to travel a lot), and they suffer from one other disadvantage: suppose you had studied a group of British children and were comparing them with a group of children from country X. If you found that children from country X became more aggressive after watching TV than the British children did, can you be sure that children from country X respond differently to TV than do British children? Unfortunately not – it may be that country X's TV allows more aggression than does British TV; or it may be that parents in country X are more prepared than British parents to allow their children to be aggressive. Cross-cultural studies are also really just cross-sectional studies of different countries, so they suffer from the deficiencies of cross-sectional studies, too.

Observational Methods

There are many situations where behaviour is so complex that it cannot be isolated clearly enough to be manipulated experimentally. In addition, when researchers are starting to look at a type of behaviour not previously studied, observational studies must first be made before any hypothesis about the causes of such behaviour can be tested.

A major problem with observational studies is the lack of time which an observer has in making a record of his/her observations. If the observer also has to record the type of behaviour seen, so much time has to be spent in writing that observations may be missed altogether. To overcome this problem, *behavioural categories* can be developed. Before the study begins the observer decides what types of behaviour are to be recorded, and then draws up a table of categories which can simply be ticked when the particular behaviour occurs. Operational definitions of behaviour must be devised so that the observer has clear criteria for what constitutes a particular category of behaviour.

For example, if you were conducting an observational study of the behaviour of males and females on zebra crossings, you would need an operational definition of what constitutes 'correct' use of the crossing. If, for example, an individual walks across the road one metre to the side of the crossing, have they used the crossing correctly? You would need to define exactly what constitutes 'correct' and 'incorrect' methods of crossing, and agree this in advance, so that all observers record the behaviour in the same way.

Figure 19.1.

Correct use (pedestrian
on the crossing for 75%
or more of the journey
across the road)

Incorrect use (crossing
used for less than 75%
of the journey across
the road)

Once the definitions are agreed, observers simply use ticks on a tally record to show how many male and females used the crossing correctly and how many used it incorrectly. For example:

Male correct	ɪɪɪɪ ɪɪɪɪ	(9)
Male incorrect	ɪɪɪɪ ɪɪɪɪ ɪɪɪɪ ɪɪɪɪ ɪɪɪ	(23)
Female correct	ɪɪɪɪ ɪɪɪɪ ɪɪɪɪ ɪɪɪɪ ɪɪɪɪ ɪɪɪɪ ɪ	(31)
Female correct	ɪɪɪɪ ɪɪ	(7)

When devising categories, make sure that they are meaningful and not so large that they ignore important differences in behaviour, or so small and numerous that they are impossible to use.

Observational Studies – A General Planning Sequence

1 Having decided the behaviour(s) to be observed, draw up a checklist for observers in order to make the recording of the behaviour easier and more reliable. The most common type of checklist is one which uses behaviour categories (see above).

2 Make sure that all your observers are using the checklist in the same way. Get them all to watch the same event and record it on their checklists. If they do not all agree, discuss any differences and get them to agree what should have been recorded. Then watch and record another event, repeat this until all your observers agree. When they all agree, you have established *inter-observer reliability*.

Estimate the minimum observation time needed for accurate recordings of the behaviour. This will vary according to the complexity and frequency of the behaviour, but, as a general guide you should spend a minimum of two hours on your observations.

4 *Time Sampling.* You may not have time to observe behaviour for 24 hours each day – or the behaviour you wish to observe may only occur at a particular time each day. Consequently, you can often only make observations of samples of behaviour. Two main methods are used to obtain representative samples of behaviour:

(a) The length of time over which the behaviour occurs is divided into 'time units', usually of a few minutes each. You then decided what proportion of the total time units you wish to observe, and select the required number at random. For example, if the total time of 240 minutes were made up of 40 time units of six minutes each and you decide that you wanted to sample 30 per cent of the total time, you would need to choose 30 per cent of 40 = 12 time units at random, to observe.

(b) As an alternative, you could record observations at (say) every three, or five or ten minutes throughout an hour, and choose a different hour each day.

5 As with experimental designs, it is often very useful to conduct a small-scale pilot study first, in order to sort out any 'bugs' in your techniques.

Probably the major advantage of observation studies over experimental methods is that you can observe people performing naturally in their normal environments – this is particularly important for example in studies of children's behaviour (especially if the children are with parents or other children) and for studies of animal behaviour. Do remember, however, that experiments can be carried out in the 'normal environment' rather than in the laboratory, though it is more difficult to control extraneous variables.

Asking Questions

If you want to ask people questions about their thoughts, feelings or behaviour, rather than observe or experiment, the same guidelines apply regarding the sample of people you choose and your professional approach.

Make sure any questions are clearly phrased and unambiguous, and encourage the interviewees to answer truthfully. Closed-ended questions which simply require a choice of predetermined answers such as Yes or No are easy to record and quantify, but may not give as much information as more open-ended questions which allow the subject to expand on his answers. The interpretation of answers to open-ended questions may be difficult and can be affected by your own biases. If you decide to use Yes/No or other multiple choice-type questions, it might be useful to do a preliminary investigation using open-ended questions to help you to decide how to phrase the closed-ended questions and which possible responses should be included in the multiple choices.

If you are going to ask lots of questions, try to avoid building in a *response bias* which might cause incorrect answers from a careless participant. Response biases can occur when a series of questions have all been answered in the same way, for instance, a series of questions such as 'Have you suffered from smallpox?' and 'Have you ever mugged an old lady?' would all be answered 'No' by most people: if this series is immediately followed by a question such as 'Do you smoke cigarettes?' many smokers, especially those in a rush to finish, will answer 'No' to this question as well. Careful preparation of the list of questions can avoid the build-up of these habitual responses.

Field Studies

Too many psychological studies are done in the laboratory and don't reflect real life. This is a criticism that is often raised about psychology. There is a danger that we simply find out about what people do in laboratories when they know they are being studied; perhaps their behaviour is different than normal. When Psychologists do their experiments or observations in the real world they are using *field studies* (either field experiments or field observations). The big advantage of field studies is that they are more likely to have ecological validity (i.e. they are telling you about behaviour in the real world).

Field studies can, however, be difficult to organize because it is not so easy to control variables as it is in the laboratory where you have much more control of the situation.

When conducting a field study you should apply the same thought to the design of the experiment or observation that you would in the laboratory. Additional concerns that you may have include:

1 *The sample*. It will be more difficult to choose your sample of people to make sure they are representative. Allocating people to different conditions will not be as easy as saying you go here, you go there. You must judge how representative the people are and of what population. For example, if you do your study in a local shopping precinct you need to consider whether this precinct attracts a full range of shoppers (or is it up-market or down market). It is likely that it attracts different people at different times of day – does this matter to your study or not?

2 *Control of extraneous variables*. This is much more difficult.

3 *Permission*. Consider who you need to ask for permission to do the study. Does the area you are working in belong to anyone?

4 *Ethical problems*. How are you going to ensure informed consent or provide debriefing for those studied? Consent is not needed if you are simply observing natural behaviour in a public place (naturalistic observation), but do consider the ethical implications of any study that manipulates the situation that people are in and therefore may affect their behaviour.

Milgram deliberately chose the laboratory for his study of obedience (see p. 118) because this was the only way that he felt he could manipulate the range of variables that he wanted to. Hofling *et al.* (1966) followed Milgram's work with a field study of nurses on duty in hospital and showed that high levels of obedience when asked to do something unusual was not simply a laboratory effect. Hofling's study has been very influential in changing work in hospitals precisely because it was performed as a field study and could not be criticized for its lack of ecological validity.

Writing up a Report

Your report should be detailed enough for a reader to repeat your experiment without coming to ask you for extra information, so it must show exactly what you did and what you found.

TITLE
This is the first thing that the reader sees, so make sure it gives a reasonable idea of what the experiment was about, but don't expand it to more than a couple of lines.

ABSTRACT
The abstract should help readers decide whether they want to read the detail contained in the rest of the report. It should be a short synopsis or thumb-nail sketch of the practical, and should only rarely exceed one average paragraph in length. It should contain enough detail to let readers know what you did, with whom and to what effect. It lets them know if your study is of interest to them and whether it is worth their while reading on. State briefly who were used as participants, how the independent and dependent variables were measured, and what the experimental task was, what the outcome of the study was and what conclusion may be drawn from the study. Do remember to keep this section concise: this is not the place for elaboration.

INTRODUCTION
State what the aim of the study was and what hypothesis or hypotheses were being tested. Then outline the background to your study by describing the general area of psychology in which it is located and giving a brief review of relevant studies. Finally, you should explain how your study differs from the ones described, and how and what it adds to our understanding of this area of psychology.

METHOD
In this section you need to explain *exactly* how your study was carried out. This is the part between the planning and the analysis of results which in many people's minds *is* the practical. There are many ways to present this,

but it is customary for the section to be sub-divided. The following categories are those most frequently used:

> *Design*
> *Participants*
> *Apparatus*
> *Procedure*

Design. This refers to the 'technical' specifications of the study. What is its methodology? Is it a laboratory experiment, a field experiment, a survey, an observational study or what? If participants were allocated to conditions, how was this done: by repeated measures, matched pairs or independent pairs? If there are independent or dependent variables, what are they? How many conditions were used? How many trials did participants perform? What control procedures were used? Do not write at length here about exactly how the study was carried out, such detail belongs in the Procedure sub-section. This section should be concerned only with the overall 'shape' of the study.

Participants. Tell your reader how many participants were used and give any *relevant* details about them. It is unnecessary to list such things as their names and what they were wearing, unless these are an integral part of the study. Consider what characteristics may have influenced the results. Age, sex, intelligence, motivation and naivety/previous experience are usually relevant, although factors will vary according to the specific study. For example, in an experimental study of eye–hand co-ordination, whether the subjects were left- or right-handed would be relevant.

Apparatus. Give a full list of the specialist apparatus that you have used, and, if necessary, explain how it was used. If the apparatus used was unusual or complex, a diagram is often helpful. Be sure to include only technical or specialist apparatus – for example, a reaction-timer would be appropriate, but a table or a pencil would not.

Procedure. This sub-section may be considered to be of particular importance since it gives you the opportunity to tell the interested reader *exactly* what you did, and what the participants were required to do. Thus, it should constitute a clear statement of how your study was carried out, and you should say how any difficulties were dealt with. Reference should be made to all instructions that were given and *all* matters of procedure should be detailed. Tell the readers exactly what happened and provide them with sufficient information that they should be able to carry out a precise replication of your study.

RESULTS

A *summary* of your results should be presented in this section (e.g. totals, means). Raw data (e.g. participants' individual results) should not be included – these should be given in the appendices at the end of the report so that the readers may inspect them, should they so wish. Present the results as clearly and concisely as you can, so that the reader is easily able to appreciate them. It is up to you to do the hard work for them at this stage. Visual displays (e.g. summary tables, graphs, histograms) should be used whenever appropriate and they should always be clearly and exactly identified and labelled. The over-riding concern here should be that of clarity.

TREATMENT OF RESULTS*

If it is included, this section should present and justify the use of analyses (e.g. significance tests) that you have applied to your data, but do not include statistical calculations, which should be presented in the appendices. State why a particular statistic was used, and *briefly* what it tells us. This section should be particularly exact and precise. You might, for example, state what the obtained statistical value was, what the degrees of freedom or number of subjects was, what level of significance was employed, whether one or two-tailed tables were used, and what the resulting probability value was. Do not attempt to interpret your results at any length – this should be carried out in the next section – but make it clear exactly what the result was by stating whether the null or experimental hypothesis was accepted (write down the relevant hypothesis so that your reader does not need to search back to the introduction to check what it was).

DISCUSSION

In this section you are required to examine and critically evaluate the findings of your study. You should say how your findings relate to the hypothesis/ hypotheses you put forward at the beginning, and discuss the relationship of your findings to generally accepted psychological theory and results from other relevant empirical studies. In this way, you should evaluate your findings in the light of existing psychological knowledge. If your hypotheses have to be unexpectedly rejected, or if your results are in clear disagreement with previous research and/or theory, you should make a comprehensive attempt to explain the discrepancy. For example, was your study poorly designed? If so, discuss the problems, offer constructive im-

---

* The NEA GCSE syllabus does not require students to use statistical tests, and so some readers may miss this section from their report and simply provide a clear statement of their results.

provements and suggest ideas for further study which might clarify the issue. Be careful, however, to be sensible and realistic. Psychology experiments are rarely, if ever, carried out under perfect conditions, so don't write paragraphs telling the reader that there were slight fluctuations in the background noise levels, that the sun flitted in and out behind clouds on several occasions, that 'the *Sun*' was not published that morning, etc. – unless these factors are really relevant to the outcome of the study. In other words, you should be able to demonstrate an awareness of the limitations and weaknesses of your study, and be able to suggest logical modifications and improvements. This section should therefore be viewed as a *considered critique* of your study.

CONCLUSION
This should be a brief statement of the outcome of the study.

REFERENCES
In the main body of your report you should refer to books or papers by identifying the author(s) and the year of publication. In this section, you should list alphabetically (by author) all the works you have referred to, giving full details of each one. For example:

Heyes, S., Hardy, M., Humphreys, P. and Rookes, P. *Starting Statistics in Psychology and Education* (1993, Oxford University Press).

APPENDICES
It is customary that materials used in studies (e.g. standardized instruction sheets, progress sheets, raw data, statistical calculations) should be included in reports, so that they are available both for scrutiny and re-usage by others. However, it is inappropriate to include such reference items in the main body of the report, and consequently they are given as appendices at the end of each report. Include them as numbered sheets and refer to them whenever necessary in the main text.

When writing up your study in a format such as the one outlined above, try to bear in mind the aim of the exercise, namely, that of communicating your ideas with others – as we have said earlier, science is a social enterprise. So do not aim to be flash, just be accurate, honest and helpful.

Presenting your Results

When you have done an experiment, you may end up with masses of numbers; every subject will have at least one score. These results may appear confusing to you, so imagine what they would be like to the person who is simply reading your report. Your job is to summarize the results in a clear and understandable fashion. In this section we will show a number of ways in which this can be done.

Table of Results

Draw up a table showing each participant's score. If individuals have only one score this is easy but if they all have a few scores it is best to put an 'average' score for the participant in each condition.

Make sure that the table is clearly labelled, so that a reader can immediately see what it is about. If the numbers refer to seconds or minutes, or some other unit of measurement, say what it is rather than leaving the reader to guess. Table 19.2 shows one way of presenting a table of results.

When the table is presented on its own like this, the reader has to inspect it closely to see in which condition the subjects proved faster, and so it is important to give some sort of summary statistic that gives an overall idea of what happened in each condition. An 'average' for each condition would do this.

Table 19.2. To Show the Results of an Experiment to Test the Hypothesis that Participants will take Longer to Climb a Set of Stairs after Drinking Three Pints of Beer than when Completely Sober

Participant	Time taken to climb the stairs when sober (in seconds)	Time taken to climb the stairs after drinking (in seconds)
1	30	35
2	32	34
3	35	37
4	29	29
5	27	30
6	33	38
7	40	49
8	42	43

'Averages'

Work out the average of the following numbers:

$$2, 2, 3, 5, 8$$

You probably came up with an answer of 4 by adding up all the numbers and dividing by the number of numbers. This average is the *mean* average but the average for the above figures could also be 2 or 3. That really does sound like juggling the figures! The problem with the term 'average' is that it includes a number of different sorts of measures; as well as the mean it includes the *mode* (the most common number) and the *median* (the number in the middle when the group of scores are placed in ascending order).

Mean. The arithmetic average. (Add up all scores and divide by the number of scores.) For example:

$$5, 7, 4, 8, 6 \quad Mean = 30/5 = 6$$

Median. The middle score of a group of scores. This value has as many scores above as below it. Place the scores in order of size and find the middle number. For example:

$$3, 5, 6, \underline{7}, 9, 11, 13 \quad Median = 7$$

$$2, 2, 3, \_ 4, 7, 8 \quad Median \text{ lies between 3 and 4} = 3.5$$

Mode. The score which occurs most frequently. For example:

$$2, 3, 3, 4, 6, 7, 2, 3, 3 \quad Mode = 3$$

$$4, 7, 6, 3, 4, 9, 4, 4, 1 \quad Mode = 4$$

Sometimes the mean, median and mode of a group of scores are exactly the same, but this is not always the case, so you should say which one you are using. The most common one is the mean but there may be times when you decide you want to use one of the others: it is largely up to you to decide, but the following points may affect your decision.

ADVANTAGES (+) AND DISADVANTAGES (−) OF MEAN, MEDIAN AND MODE
Mean
(+) Takes into account the total and the individual values of all scores.
(−) Laborious to calculate for a large number of scores.
(−) Less representative than the median when the group of scores contains a few cases that are markedly higher or lower than the rest. For example:

$$2, 3, 4, 5, 6, 7, 57 \quad Mean = 12 \quad Median = 5$$

(Note: without the 'different' score of 57 the mean would be only 4.5.)

Median
(+) More representative than the mean when there are a few scores which are markedly higher or lower than the rest.
(+) Usually easier to calculate than the mean.
(−) It extracts less information than the mean, since it does not use the precise numerical values of the scores.

Mode
(+) Easy to find.
(–) Very crude, especially if there is not much difference in the frequencies of the scores.

The Range
A mean, median or mode gives a one-figure summary of a set of scores; hence it is much easier to make comparisons between the results of different conditions. It can, however, be useful to have information about the *spread* of scores.

These two sets of scores have the same mean:

$$21, 30, 45, 50, 60, 70, 80, 95 \quad Mean = 57$$

$$54, 55, 56, 57, 57, 58, 59, 60 \quad Mean = 57$$

Although these two groups of scores have the same mean, you can see that the first group is more widely spread out (dispersed) than the second. The mean cannot show the difference between these groups of scores. Some measure is needed to describe the variation in the data. There are a number of measures which do this, but we shall limit ourselves to the simplest which is known as the *range*. (Others are discussed in *Starting Statistics*, Heyes, Hardy *et al.*, 1993.)

The *range* of a group of scores is the difference between the lowest number and the highest.

$$21, 30, 45, 50, 60, 70, 85, 95 \quad Mean = 57 \quad Range = 74$$

$$54, 55, 56, 57, 57, 58, 59, 60 \quad Mean = 57 \quad Range = 6$$

When given the range the reader can immediately get an idea of the variation in the scores.

Problem with the range. Since it only takes into account the two extreme scores it cannot give a good description of a group which has an odd score which is markedly higher or lower than the rest. For example the following scores have a range of 71, which is not very representative of the group as a whole:

$$2, 4, 4, 5, 7, 9, 10, 73$$

Make sure that you don't use the range when the scores are arranged like this.

Graphs and Charts
As with tables of results, the important thing is that these are clear and easily understood; always label the axes and give an explanatory title.

If we were to draw a graph showing the relationship between the time of day and the temperature, the temperature would go on the vertical axis. The temperature is called a dependent variable because its value depends on what time of day it is. If it is possible to identify a dependent variable when drawing a graph it is customary to put it on the vertical axis.

Never use line graphs in situations where other visual forms are more appropriate. A common mistake that we have seen students make is to present the scores of individual participants as a line graph, but as you can see in the diagram below, the shape of the graph simply depends on which order to decide for the individuals. If you want to present this data visually, try using a *bar chart* which shows the individual score without linking it to its neighbour.

Figure 19.2.

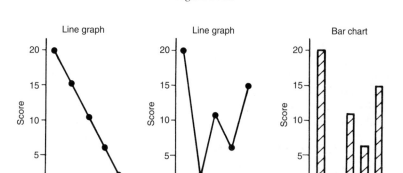

Frequency Distribution Curves

It is often useful to plot a graph which shows how frequently particular scores occur in your results. For example, if you wanted to show how intelligence is distributed in the population at large you would choose a lot of people at random and ask them to do an IQ test. You would probably present your results in the form of a frequency distribution graph. Since the subjects were chosen at random and there are many chance factors which may increase or decrease an individual's IQ, the graph you obtain would probably look like this:

Figure 19.3.

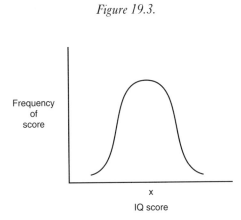

Mean, Median and Mode all have the same value (at point X).

A graph which looks like this is called a Normal Distribution. It has the following three properties:

1 Mean, median and mode occur at the same value.
2 It is bell-shaped and has the same shape either side of the mean.
3 The curve falls away relatively slowly at first on either side of the mean (i.e. many scores occur a little above or below the mean). Fewer and fewer scores are found with increasing distance from the mean.

A normal distribution is found when the following criteria are met:

(a) The data is continuous (like measures of height and weight which can vary by small amounts all the way along a scale, rather than separate or discrete measures like male/female or pass/fail in an exam where a person falls into one category or another).

(b) Each score is the result of a number of randomly distributed effects, some of which tend to increase the score whilst others decrease it, (e.g. your height is the result of a combination of many genes passed on from your parents, some of which tend to increase it, some to decrease it, and environmental variables such as the amount and type of food you eat which may also increase or decrease height).

(c) There are a large number of scores drawn randomly from the population.

Normal distributions are not always found when frequency graphs are plotted. The *skewed distribution* takes two forms, the median may have a higher or lower value than the mode.

Figure 19.4.

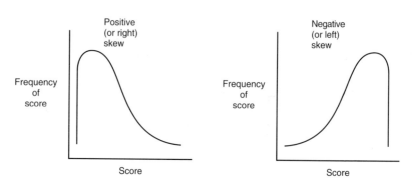

The characteristic of skewed distribution is that the mean, median and mode have difference values.

A skewed distribution is found when:

1 A small number of scores are taken.
2 A biased sample is taken of a population that may be normally distributed, for example: plot the frequencies of the heights of males in the room in which you are sitting. Plot the distribution of university students' IQs.
3 One end of the measuring scale has an attainable cut-off point, for example, with reaction time (the time taken to react to a stimulus): there is no definite cut-off point for slow times, since people can take as long as they like, but at the fast end of the scale it is not possible to better 0 seconds, a reaction time which is quite attainable (usually produced when the subject has anticipated the stimulus).

Correlation
We often want to find the relationship between two sets of variables. For example, we might want to know whether there was a relationship between

the amount of television that people watch and their intelligence. To do this we could ask people to record the amount of TV they watched over a particular period and also give them an IQ test. The results could be shown as in figures 19.5 and 19.6 in the form of a scattergram, where each point represents one person's score on the two variables (IQ and amount of TV watched).

Figure 19.5(a) shows a strong relationship between the two variables. Those people with the highest IQ watch the most TV. This type of relationship, where people who score highly on one variable tend also to do well on the other, is known as a *positive correlation*.

Figure 19.5.(a) Positive Correlation   Figure 19.5.(b) Negative Correlation

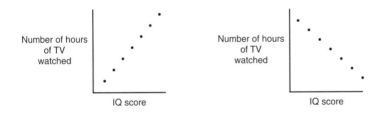

Figure 19.5(b) is another possible result which also shows a strong relationship between the two variables, but this time people with higher IQs tend to watch least TV. This type of relationship, where people who score highly on one variable tend to have a low score on the other, is known as a *negative correlation*.

In practice it is unlikely that we should find a very strong relationship between these two variables. The relationship shown in the scattergram in figure 19.6 is near zero.

Producing a scattergram from your data will give a quick visual impression of the relationship, but a correlation coefficient can tell you the extent to which two variables correlate. Correlation coefficients may be anything between +1 and −1. The closer the coefficient to +1 or −1, the more perfect the relationship; the closer it is to 0, the weaker is the relationship.

For a correlation of +1, every rise in variable A is reflected by a rise in variable B.

For a correlation of 0, there is no relationship between A and B.

Figure 19.6. Zero Correlation

For a correlation of −1, every rise in variable A is reflected by a fall in variable B.

Those readers who wish to work out a correlation coefficient from their own data should consult *Starting Statistics* (Heyes, Hardy *et al.*, 1993).

A very common mistake is to assume that because two variables correlate, one causes the other. It is vital that you do not make this assumption, because:

CORRELATION DOES NOT IMPLY CAUSATION.

There is a correlation of +0.95 between the length of railway line in a country and the incidence of certain types of cancer. This does not mean that railways cause cancer – there may be some underlying cause which affects both factors, such as industrialization. If two variables correlate, one *may* cause the other, but the correlation technique cannot confirm this.

Only the experimental method can study cause and effect. This is because it manipulates independent variables whilst controlling other variables in order to discover the effect on dependent variables (see p. 000).

Further Reading

Heyes, S., Hardy, M., Humphreys, P. and Rookes, P., *Starting Statistics in Psychology and Education* (2nd edn, 1993, Oxford University Press).

STOP PRESS

Rumbaugh, in a *Sunday Times* article on 25 July 1999, reported that Panbanisha, a 14-year-old pygmy chimpanzee could (using the methods outlined on p. 286):

- generate new sentences without prompting
- write words in English with chalk
- teach her one-year-old son Nyota to recognize words for his favourite foods.

An ethical debate now seems likely to begin. If (as nativists believe) language is unique to humans and some primates can be shown to have language, does this mean that some primates are human, with human rights?

References

Adorno, T. W., Frenkel-Brunswik, E., Levinson, D. J. and Sanford, R. N. (1950) *The Authoritarian Personality*, Harper.

Ainsworth, M. D. (1973) 'The development of infant–mother attachment', in Caldwell, B. B. and Ricciuti, H. N. (eds), *Review of Child Development Research*, vol. 3, University of Chicago Press.

Allport, F. H. (1924) *Social Psychology*, Houghton Mifflin.

Allport, G. W. (1954) *The Nature of Prejudice*, Addison-Wesley.

Altman, I. (1975) *The Environment and Social Behaviour*. Brookews/Cole, Monterey, California.

Anderson, R. C. and Myrow, D. L. (1971) 'Retroactive inhibition of meaningful discourse', *Journal of Educational Psychology*, 62, pp. 81–94.

Ardis, J. A. and Fraser, E. (1957) 'Personality and perception: the constancy effect and introversion', *Brit. J. Psychol.*, 48, pp. 48–54.

Argyle, M. (1967) *The Psychology of Interpersonal Behaviour*, Penguin.

Argyle, M. (ed.) (1973) *Social Encounters*, Penguin.

Arnold, M. (1960) *Emotion and Personality: Vol. 1. Psychological Aspects.* Columbia University Press, New York.

Asch, S. (1946) 'Forming impressions of personality', *J. Abnorm. & Soc. Psy.*, 41, pp. 258–90.

Asch, S. E. (1951) 'Effects of group pressure upon the modification and distortion of judgements', in Guetzkow, H. (ed.), *Groups, Leadership and Men*, Carnegie Press.

Ausubel, D., Joseph, D. and Hanesian, H. (1978) *Educational Psychology: Cognitive View*, Holt, Rinehart and Winston.

Averill, J. R. (1976) 'Emotion and anxiety: sociocultural, biological and psychological determinants', in Zuckerman, M. and Spielberger, C. D. (eds), *Emotions and Anxiety: New Concepts, Methods and Applications*, Lawrence Erlbaum.

Ax, A. F. (1953) 'The physiological differentiation between fear and anger in humans', *Psychosomatic Medicine*, 15, pp. 433–42.

Baddeley, A. D. (1980) *Human Memory* in Dodwell, P. C. (ed.), *New Horizons in Psychology 2*, Penguin.

Baddeley, A. D. (1983) *Your Memory: A User's Guide*, Penguin.

Bandura, A. (1965) 'Influence of a model's reinforcement contingencies on the acquisition of imitative responses', *Journal of Pers. Soc. Psychol.*, 1, pp. 589–95.

Bandura, A., Ross, D. and Ross, S. A. (1961) 'Transmission of aggression through imitation of aggressive models', *Journal of Abnormal and Social Psychology*, 63, pp. 575–82.

Bandura, A., Ross, D. and Ross, S. A. (1963) 'Imitation of film mediated aggressive models', *Journal of Abnormal and Social Psychology*, 66, pp. 3–11.

Bandura. A. and Walters, R. H. (1963) *Social Learning and Personality Development*, Holt, Rinehart and Winston.

Bard, B. and Sachs, J. (1977) 'Language acquisition in two normal children of deaf parents', *2nd Annual Boston University Conference on Language acquisition*, October 1977.

Barthel, C. E. and Crowne, D. P. (1962) 'The need for approval, task categorization and perceptual defense', *J. Consult. Psychol.*, 26, p. 547.

Bartlett, F. C. (1932) *Remembering*, Cambridge University Press.

Bateson, P. P. G. (1966) 'The characteristics and context of imprinting', *Biological Revue*, 41, pp. 177–200.

Baum, A. and Valins, S. (1977), *Architecture and social behaviour: Psychological studies of social density*, Erlbaum, Hillsdale, NJ.

Bee, H. (1989) *The Developing Child*, Harper & Row.

Bee, H. and Mitchell, S.K. (1980) '*The Developing Person, A Life-Span Approach*', Harper & Row, New York.

Belbin, E. and Belbin, R. M. (1963) *Training the Older Worker*, HMSO.

Benewick, R. and Holton, R. (1987) 'The peaceful crowd: crowd solidarity and the Pope's visit to Britain', in Gaskell, G. and Benewick, R. (eds), *The crowd in contemporary Britain*, Sage, London.

Berko, J. (1958) 'The child's learning of English morphology', *Word*, 14, pp. 150–77.

Bernstein, I. and Gordon, T. (1977) 'The function of aggression in primate societies' in Janis, I.L. (ed.), *Current Trends in Psychology*, W. Kaufmann Inc.

Biller, H. B. (1971) *Father, Child and Sex role: Paternal Determinants of Personality Development*, D. C. Heath.

Birch, H. G. (1945) 'The relation of previous experience to insightful problem-solving', *J. Comp. Psychol.*, 38, pp. 367–83.

Birney, R. C. and Teevan, R. C. (1961), *Instinct*, Van Nostrand.

Blakemore, C. and Cooper, J. F. (1970) 'Development of the brain depends on the visual environment', *Nature*, 241, pp. 467–8.

Block, L. K. and Stokes, G. S. (1989) 'Performance and satisfaction in private versus non-private work settings', *Environment and Behaviour*, 21, pp. 277–97.

Boker, J. (1974) 'Immediate and delayed retention effects of interspersing questions in written instructional passages', *Journal of Educational Psychology*, 66, pp. 96–8.

Bousfield, W. A. (1961) 'The problem of meaning in verbal behaviour', in Cofer, C. N. (ed.), *Verbal Learning and Verbal Behaviour*, McGraw-Hill.

Bower, G. H. (1970) 'Organizational factors in memory', *J. Cog. Psychol.*, 1, pp. 18–46.

Bower, G. H., Clark, M. C., Lesgold, A. M. and Winzenz, D. (1969) 'Hierarchical retrieval schemes in recall of categorised word lists', *Journal of Verbal Learning and Verbal Behaviour*, 8, pp. 323–43.

Bower, T. G. R. (1967) 'The visual world of infants', *Sci. Amer.*, offprint no. 502, pp. 80–91.

Bowlby, J. (1951) *Maternal Care and Mental Health*, World Health Organisation, Geneva.

Brady, J. P. (1958) 'Ulcers in 'executive' monkeys', *Scientific American*, 199, pp. 95–100.

Brand, C. (1982), cited in Cohen, D. and Shelley, D., 'High IQ as high speed thinking', *New Scientist*, 95, pp. 773–5.

Bransford, J. and Johnson, M. (1973) 'Consideration of some problems of comprehension', in Chase, W. D. (ed.), *Visual and Information Processing*, Academic Press.

Broadhurst, P. L. (1960) 'Experiments in psychogenics: applications of biometrical genetics to the inheritance of behaviour', in Eysenck, H. J. (ed.), *Experiments in Personality*, vol. 1, Routledge and Kegan Paul.

Brown, H. (1985) *People, Groups and Society*, Open University Press.

Brown, R. (1973) *A first Language*, Allen and Unwin, London.

Brown, R. (1986) *Social Psychology*, (2nd edn) Free Press.

Bruner, J. (1975) 'the ontogenesis of speech acts', *Journal of Child Language*, 3, pp. 255–87.

Bruner, J. S. and Goodman, C. C. (1947) 'Value and need as organizaing factors in perception', *J. Abnor. Soc. Psychol.*, 42, p. 33.

Bruner, J. S. and Kenney, H. (1966) 'The development of the concepts of order and proportion in children', *Studies in Cognitive Growth*, Wiley.

Bruner, J. S. and Minturn, A. L. (1955) 'Perceptual identification and perceptual organizaion', *J. Gen. Psychol.*, 53, p. 21.

Bruner, J. S. and Postman, L. (1947) 'Emotional selectivity in perceptual reaction', *J. Pers.*, 16, p. 69.

Bruner, J. S. and Postman, L. (1949) 'On the perception of incongruity', *J. Pers.*, 18, p. 206.

Bruner, J. S., Goodnow, J. J. and Austin, G. A. (1956) *A Study of Thinking*, Wiley.

Buck, R. (1975) 'Nonverbal communication of affect in children', *Journal of Personality and Social Psychology*, 31, pp. 664–673.

Buckhout, R. (1974) 'Eyewitness testimony', *Scientific American*, 231, pp. 23–31.

Bullinger, M. (1989) 'Psychological effects of air pollution on health residents – a time-series approach', *Journal of Environmental Psychology*, 9, pp. 103–18.

Burt, C. (1969), quoted in Jensen, A. R., 'How much can we boost IQ and scholastic achievement?', *Harvard Educational Review*, 39, pp. 1–123.

Bushnell, I. W. R., Sai, F. and Mullin, T. (1989) 'Neonatal recognition of the mother's face', *British Journal of Experimental Psychology*, 7, pp. 3–15.

Buss, D. M. and Schmitt (1993) 'Sexual strategies theory: an evolutionary perspective on human mating', *Psychological Review*, 100, 2, pp. 204–32.

Calhoun, J. B. (1962) 'Population density and social pathology', *Scientific American*, 206, pp. 139–48.

Cannon, W. B. (1932) *The Wisdom of the Body*, Norton.

Carpenter, B., Weiner, M. and Carpenter, J. T. (1956) 'Predictability of perceptual defense behaviour', *J. Abnor. Soc. Psychol.*, 52, p. 380.

Cattell, R. B. (1965) *The Scientific Analysis of Personality*, Penguin.

Chomsky, N. (1968) *Language and mind*, Harcourt Brace.

Cohen, D. and Shelley, D. (1982) 'High IQ as high speed thinking', *New Scientist*, 95, p. 773.

Cohen, G., Kiss, G. and Le Voi, M. (1993) *Memory: Current Issues* (2nd edn) Oxford University Press.

Conrad, R. (1964) 'Accoustic confusions in immediate memory', *British Journal of Psychology*, 55, pp. 75–84.

Cook, S. W. (1978) 'Interpersonal and attitudinal outcomes in cooperating interracial groups', *Journal of Research and Development in Education*, 12, p. 533.

Costa, P. T. and McCrae, R. R. (1992) 'Trait Psychology comes of age', in Soderegger T.B. (ed.), *Nebraska Symposium on Motivation: Psychology and Ageing*, pp. 169–203, University of Nebraska Press.

Cox, T. (1975) 'The nature and management of stress', *New Behaviour*, 25 (September), pp. 493–5.

Craig, M. M. and Glick, S. J. (1965) *A Manual of Procedures for Application of the Glueck Prediction Table*, University of London Press.

Craik, F. and Lockhart, R. (1972) 'Levels of processing: a framework for memory research', *Journal of Verbal Learning and Verbal Behaviour*, 11, pp. 671–84.

Craik, F. and Tulving, E. (1975) 'Depth processing and the retention of words in episodic memory', *Journal of Verbal Learning and Verbal Behaviour*, 12, pp. 268–94.

Craik, F. and Watkins, M. (1973) 'The role of rehearsal in short term memory', *Journal of Verbal Learning and Verbal Behaviour*, 12, pp. 599–607.

Cravioto, J. and De Licardie, E. R. (1968), in Scrimshaw, N. S. and Gordon, J. E. (eds), *Malnutrition, Learning and Behaviour*, MIT Press.

Crutchfield, R. S. (1954) 'A new technique for measuring individual differences in conformity to group judgement', *Proc. Invitational Conference on Testing Problems*, pp. 69–74.

De Longis, A., Coyne, J. C., Dakof, G., Folkman, S., and Lazarus, R. S. (19??) Relationship of daily hassles, uplifts and major life events to health status, *Health Psychology*, 1, pp. 119–36.

Deary, I. and Matthews, G. (1993) 'Personality traits are alive and well', *The Psychologist*, July 1993, pp. 299–311.

Dennis, W. (1960) 'Causes of retardation among institutional children: Iran', *Journal of Genet. Psychol.*, 96, pp. 47–59.

Dent, H. and Gray, F. (1975) 'Identification on parade', *New Behaviour*, 4.9.75, pp. 366–9.

Dixon, N. F. (1958) 'The effect of subliminal stimulation upon autonomic and verbal behaviour', *J. Abn. Soc. Psychol.*, 57, p. 29.

Dollard, J., Doob, L. W., Miller, N. E., Mowner, O. H. and Sears, R. R. (1939) *Frustration and Aggression*, Yale University Press.

Douglas, J. W. B. (1970) 'Broken families and child behaviour', *Journal of Royal College of Physicians*, 4, pp. 203–10.

Douglas, J. W. B. and Turner, R. K. (1970) 'The association of anxiety-provoking events in early childhood and enuresis', *Proc. Fifth International Scientific Meeting of International Epidemiological Associations*, Savremena Adinstracija, Belgrade.

Duncker, K. (1945) 'On Problem Solving', *Psychological Monographs*, 58, No. 270.

Ebbinghaus, H. (1885) *Memory*, Teacher's College.

Eibl-Eibesfeldt, I. (1975) *Ethology: The Biology of Behaviour* (2nd edn), Holt, Rinehart and Winston.

Eibl-Eibesfeldt, I. (1975) *Ethology: The Biology of Behaviour* (2nd edn), Holt, Rinehart and Winston.

Eich, J., Weingatner, H., Stillman, R. and Gillian, J. (1975) 'State dependent accessibility of retrieval cues in the retention of a categorised list', *Journal of Verbal Learning and Verbal Behaviour*, 14, pp. 408–17.

Ekman, P. (1982) *Emotion in the Human Face* (2nd edn), Cambridge University Press.

Ekman, P. and Friesen, W. (1967) 'Non-verbal leakage and clues to deception', in Argyle, M. (ed.) (1973) *Social Encounters*, Penguin.

Elder, G. H. Jr (1963) 'Parental power legitimation and its effect on the adolescent', *Sociometry*, 26, pp. 50–65.

Equal Opportunities Commission (1984) *Formal Investigation Report*, Ebbw Vale College of Further Education.

Eriksen, C. W. (1951) 'Some implications for TAT interpretation arising from need and perception experiments', *J. Person.*, 19, p. 282.

Eriksen, C. W. and Brown, C. T. (1956) 'An experimental and theoretical analysis of perceptual defense' *J. Abn. Soc. Psychol.*, 52, p. 224.

Eysenck, H. (1975) 'What is wrong with Psychology?', *New Behaviour*, May 1st, pp. 62–6.

Eysenck, H. J. (1977) *Psychology is About People*, Penguin.

Fantz, R. (1961) 'The origins of form perception', *Scientific American*, 204, pp. 66–72.

Felipe, N. J., and Sommer, R. (1966) 'Invasions of personal space', *Social problems*, 14, pp. 206–14.

Festinger, L., Pepitone, A., and Newcombe, T. (1952) 'Some consequences of deindividuation in a group', *Journal of Abnormal and Social Psychology*, 58, pp. 203–10.

Flynn, J. (1984) 'Race, IQ and grandparents', *New Scientist*, April 5th, pp. 29–31.

Forrest, D. W. and Lee, S. G. (1962) 'Mechanisms of defense and readiness in perception and recall', *Psychol. Monog.*, 76, no. 4.

Freedman, J. L. (1975) *Crowding and behaviour*, Viking, New York.

Freeman, N., Lloyd, S. and Sinha, C. (1980) 'Learning tests on babies', *New Scientist*, 88, pp. 304–7.

Frenkel, Brunswick E. (1949) 'Intolerance of ambiguity as an emotional and perceptual personalty variable', *J. Person.*, 18, p. 108.

Freud, A. and Dann, S. (1951) 'An experiment in group upbringing', *Psychoanalytic Study of the Child*, 6, pp. 127–68.

Friedman, M. and Rosenman, R. H. (1974) *Type A behaviour and your heart*, Knopf, New York.

Galton, F. (1869) *Hereditary Genius*, Fontana, 1962.

Garcia, J. and Koelling, R. (1966) 'Relation of cue to consequence in avoidance learning', *Psychonometric Science*, 4, pp. 123–4.

Gardner, A. R. and Gardner, B. (1969) 'Teaching sign language to a chimpanzee', *Science*, 165, pp. 664–72.

Garvin, J. B. and Sacks, L. S. (1963) 'Growth potential of pre-school-aged children in institutional care: a positive appraoch to a negative condition', *American Journal of Orthopsychiatry*, 33, pp. 399–408.

Geen, R. G. and O'Neal, E. C. (1969) 'Activation of cue-elicited aggression by general arousal', *Journal of Personality and Social Psychology*, 11, pp. 289–92.

Gergen, K. J., Gergen, M. M., and Bartron, W. H. (1973) 'Deviance in the dark', *Psychology Today*, October 1973, pp. 129–30.

Gibson, E. J. and Walk, R. D. (1960) 'The visual cliff', in Greenough, W. T. (ed.), *The Nature and Nurture of Behaviour, Developmental Psychology*, Freeman and Co.

Gilchrist, J. C. and Nesberg, L. S. (1952) 'Need and perceptual change in need-related objects', *J. Exper. Psychol.*, 44, p. 369.

Gill, J. J., Price, V. A., Friedman, M., and others (1985) 'Reduction in Type A behaviour in healthy middle aged American military officers', *American Heart Journal*, 110, pp. 503–14.

Gilligan, C. (1982) *In a different voice*, Harvard University Press, Cambridge Mass.

Glanzer, M. and Cunitz, A. R. (1966) 'Two storage mechanisms in free recall', *Journal of Verbal Behaviour and Verbal Learning*, 5, pp. 351–60.

Goldberg, P. (1968) 'Are women prejudiced against women?', *Transaction*, 5, pp. 28–30.

Goldfarb, W. (1943) 'Effects of institutional care on adolescent personality', *Journal of Experimental Education*, 12, pp. 106–29.

Gregory, R. L. (1977) *Eye and Brain* (3rd edn), Weidenfeld and Nicolson.

Gudjonsson, G. H. (1992) *The Psychology of Interrogation, Confessions and Testimony*, J. Wiley & Sons.

Guildford, J. P. (1967) *The Nature of Human Intelligence*, McGraw-Hill.

Guilford, J. P. (1967), *The nature of human intelligence*, McGraw-Hill, New York.

Guiton, P. (1959) 'Socialization and imprinting in Brown Leghorn chicks', *Animal Behaviour*, 7, pp. 26–34.

Hall, E. T. (1966) *The Hidden Dimension*, Doubleday, New York.

Hamer, D. *et al.* (1993) 'A Linkage Between DNA Markers on the X Chromosome and Male Sexual Orientation', *Science*, 261, pp. 321–7.

Harlow, H. F. (1949) 'The formation of learning sets', *Psychol. Rev.*, 56, pp. 51–65. Also in *Scientific American*, 181(2), pp. 36–9.

Harlow, H. F. (1959) 'Love in infant monkeys', *Scientific American*, 200, pp. 68–74.

Harries, K. D. and Stadler, S. J. (1988) 'Heat and violence: new findings from the Dallas field data 1980–1981', *Journal of Applied Social Psychology*, 18, pp. 129–38.

Hartley, E. L. (1946) *Problems in Prejudice*, King's Crown Press, New York.

Hartshorne, H. and May, M. A. (1928) *Studies in the Nature of Character, 1: Studies in Deceit*, Macmillan, New York.

Hebb, D. (1949) *The Organisation of Behaviour*, Wiley.

Hebb, D. (1958) *A Textbook of Psychology*, Saunders.

Heim, A. W. (1954) *The Appraisal of Intelligence*, Methuen.

Held, R. (1965) 'Plasticity in sensory-motor systems', *Scientific American*, 213(5).

Hendrickson, A. and E. (1980) 'IQ and brainwaves', *New Scientist*, 85, pp. 308–11.

Hess, E. H. (1956) 'Space perception in the chick', *Scientific American*, 195, pp. 71–80.

Hess, E. H. (1959) 'Imprinting', *Science*, 130, pp. 133–41.

Hess, E. H. (1965) 'Attitude and pupil size', *Scientific American*, 212, pp. 46–54.

Heyes, S., Hardy, M., Humphreys, P. and Rookes, P. (1986) *Starting Statistics*, Weidenfeld and Nicolson.

Hill, W. (1980) *Learning* (3rd edn), Methuen.

Hinde, R. A. (1970) *Animal Behaviour: A Synthesis of Ethology and Comparative Psychology* (2nd edn), McGraw-Hill.

Hinde, R.A. (1970), *Animal Behaviour: a Synthesis of Ethology and Comparative Psychology* (2nd edn), McGraw-Hill.

Hoffling, K, Brontzman, E., Dalyrimple, S., Graves, N. and Pierce, C. (1966) 'An experimental study in nurse–physician relationship', *Journal of Nervous and Mental Distress*, 143, pp. 171–80.

Hohmann, G. W. (1962) 'Some effects of spinal cord lesions on experienced emotional feelings', *Psychophysiology*, 3, pp. 143–56.

Holmes, T. H., and Rahé, R. H. (1967) 'The social readjustment rating scale', *Journal of Psychosomatic Research*, 11, pp. 213–18.

Howes, D. H., and Solomon, R. L. (1952) 'Visual duration of threshold as a function of word probability', *Journal of Experimental and Social Psychology*, 41, pp. 401–10.

Hubel, D. H. and Wiesel, T. N. (1962) 'Perceptive fields, binocular interactive and functional architecture in the cats' visual cortex', *J. Physiol. Psychol.*, 160, pp. 106–54.

James, W. (1980) *The Principles of Psychology*, Holt.

Jemmott, J. B., and Locke, S. E. (1985) 'Psychosocial factors, immunologic mediation and human susceptibility to infectious diseases: How much do we know?', *Psychological Bulletin*, 95, 78–198.

Jemmott, J. B., Bonisentio, M., *et al.* 'Academic stress, power motivation and decreases in salivatory secretory immunoglobin: A secretion rate.' *Lancet*, 1, pp. 1400–2.

Jensen, A. R. (1969) 'How much can we boost IQ and scholastic achievement?', *Harvard Educational Review*, 39, pp. 1–123.

Johnson, R. D., and Downing, L. L. (1979) 'Deindividuation and valence of cues. Effects on prosocial and antisocial behaviour', *Journal of Personality and Social Psychology*, 37, 1532–8.

Jolly, H. (1969) 'Play is work: The role of play for sick and healthy children', *Lancet*, 2, pp. 487–8.

Jones, W., Chernovertz, M. E., and Hanson, R. O. (1978) 'The enigma of androgyny', *Journal of Consulting and Clinical Psychology*, 46, pp. 298–313.

Jourard, S. M. (1966) 'An exploratory study of body accessibility', *British Journal of Social and Clinical Psychology*, 5, pp. 221–31.

Kagan, J. (1979) 'Overview: Perspectives on human infancy', in Osofsky, J. D. (ed.), *Handbook of Infant Development*, Wiley-Interscience.

Kamin, L. J. (1974) *The Science of Politics of IQ*, Halstead.

Karlins, M., Coffman, T. L. and Walters, C. (1969) 'On the fading of social sterotypes: Studies in three generations of college students', *J. Pers. and Soc. Psy.*, 13, pp. 1–16.

Kasl, S. V. and Mahl, G. F. (1965) 'The relationship of disturbances and hesitations in spontaneous speech to anxiety', *Journal of Personality and Social Psychology*, 1, pp. 425–33.

Katz, D. and Brady, K. W. (1933) 'Racial stereotypes of one hundred college students', *J. Abn. and Soc. Psy.*, 28, pp. 280–90.

Kelly, G. A. (1955) *A Theory of Personality – The Psychology of Personal Constructs*, Norton, New York.

Kelman, H. C. (1958) 'Compliance, identification and Internalization', *Journal of Conflict Resolution*, 2, pp. 51–60.

Kendon, A. (1967) 'Some functions of gaze direction in social interaction', in Argyle, M. (ed.) (1973) *Social Encounters*, Penguin.

Kobasa, S. C. (1986) 'How much stress can you survive?' in Walraven M. G. and Fitzgerald, H. E. (eds), *Annual Editions: Human Development*, 86/87, Dushkin, New York.

Kohlberg, L. (1981) *Essays on Moral development* (Vol. 1), Harper and Row.

Kohler, I. (1962) 'Experiments with goggles', *Scientific American*, offprint no. 465.

Kohler, W. (1925) *The Mentality of Apes* (trans. by E. Winter), Harcourt Brace.

Kuhlman, C. (1960), in Turner, J. (ed.), *Cognitive Development*, Methuen.

Lambert, W. W., Solomon, R. L. and Watson, P. D. (1949) 'Reinforcement and extinction as factors in size estimation', *Journal of Exper. Psychol.*, 39, pp. 6–37.

Langois, J. H. and Downs, A. C. (1980) 'Mothers, fathers and peers as socialization agents of sex-typed play behaviour in young children', *Child Development*, 51, pp. 1237–47.

Lashley, K. S. (1920) 'Studies of cerebral functioning in learning', *Psychobiology*, 2, pp. 55–135.

Latané, B. and Darley, J. (1977) 'Bystander apathy', in Janis, I. L. (ed.), *Current Trends in Psychology: Readings from American Scientist*, William Kaufmann Inc., Los Altos, California.

Lazarus, R. S. and McCleary, R. A. (1951) 'Autonomic discrimination without awareness', *Psychol. Rev.*, 58, p. 113.

Lazarus, R. S., Yousen, H. and Arenberg, D. (1953) 'Hunger and perception', *J. Person.*, 21, p. 312.

Lazarus, R. S., and Folkman, S. (1984) *Stress, Apprisal and Coping*, Springer, New York.

Levine, S. (1962) 'Psychophysiological effects of infantile stimulation', in Bliss, E. L. (ed.), *Roots of Behaviour*, Harper and Bros.

Lewin, K., Lippit, R. and White, R. K. (1939) 'Patterns of aggressive behaviour in experimentally created "social climates"', *Journal of Social Psychology*, 10, pp. 271–99.

Loftus, E. F. (1980) *Eyewitness Testimony*, Harvard University Press.

Loftus, E. F. and Palmer, J. (1974) *Journal of Verbal Learning and Verbal Behaviour*.

Loo, C. M. (1972) 'The effects of spatial density on the social behaviour of children', *Journal of Applied Social Psychology*, 2, pp. 372–81.

Lorenz, K. (1952) *King Solomon's Ring*, Methuen.

Lorenz, K. (1966) *On Aggression*, Methuen.

Lorenz, K. Z. (1966) *On Aggression*, Methuen.

Luchins, A. S. (1942) 'Mechanisation in Problem solving', *Psychological Monographs*, 54, No. 248.

Luchins, A. S. (1945) 'Social influences on perception on complex drawings', *J. Soc. Psychol.*, 21, p. 257.

Luchins, A. S. (1957) 'Primary-recency in impression formation', in C. Hovland (ed.), *The Order of Presentation of Persuasion*, Yale University Press.

MacKinnon, D. W. (1938) 'Volition and prohibitions', in Murray, H. A. (ed.), *Explorations in personality*, Oxford University Press, New York.

MacKinnon, D. W. (1962) 'The Personality Correlates of Creativity: A Study of American Architects' in Vernon, P. E. (ed.) *Creativity*, Penguin.

Mandler, G. (1967) 'Organization and memory', in Spence, K. W. and Spence, J. T. (eds.), *The Psychology of Learning and Motivation*, vol. 1, Academic Press.

Mandler, G. (1980) 'The generation of emotion: A psychological theory', in Plutchick, R. and Kellerman, H. (eds), *Theories of Emotion*, New York, Academic Press.

Manning, A. (1979) *An Introduction to Animal Behaviour*, (3rd edn), Arnold.

McClelland, D. C. (ed.) (1955) *Studies in Motivation*, Appleton Century Crofts.

McGarrigle, J. and Donaldson, M. (1974) 'Conservation accidents', *Cognition*, 3, pp. 341–50.

McGinnies, E. (1949) 'Emotionality and perceptual defense', *Psychol. Rev.*, 56, p. 244.

Mead, M. (1939) *Male and Female*, Morrow.

Mehrabian, A. (1968) 'Inference of attitudes from the posture, orientation and distance of a communicator', in Argyle, M. (ed.) (1973) *Social Encounters*, Penguin.

Meltzoff, A. N. and Moore, M. K. (1977) 'Imitation of facial and manual gestures', *Science*, 198, pp. 75–80.

Meyer-Bahlburg, H. (1984) 'Psychoendocrine Research on Sexual Orientation: Current Status and Future Option' *Progress in Brain Research*, 171, pp. 375–97.

Michaels, J. W., Blommel, J. M., Brocato, R. M., Linkous, R. A. and Rowe, J. S. (1982) 'Social facilitation and inhibition in a natural setting', *Replications in Social Psychology*, 2, pp. 21–4.

Milgram, S. (1961) 'Nationality and conformity', *Scientific American*, 205, December, pp. 45–51.

Milgram, S. (1974) *Obedience to Authority*, Tavistock.

Miller, G. A. (1969) 'Decision units in the perception of speech', *I R E Transaction on Information Theory*, 8, pp. 81–3.

Miller, N. E. and DiCara, L. V. (1968) 'Instrumental learning of stystolic blood pressure responses by curarized rats', *Psychosomatic Medicine*, 39, pp. 489–94.

Milner, B., Corkin, S. and Tueber, H. L. (1968) 'Further analysis of the hippocampal amnesia syndrome: 14-year follow-up study of H.M.', *Neuropsychologia*, 6, pp. 215–334.

Mischel, W. (1976) *Introduction to Personality* (2nd edn), Holt, Rinehart and Winston.

Mischel, W. (1986) *Introduction to Personality* (4th edn), Holt, Rinehart and Winston.

Moser, G. (1988) 'Urban stress and helping behaviour: Effects of environmental overload and noise on behaviour', *Journal of Environmental Psychology*, 8, pp. 287–98.

Murdoch, B. (1962) 'The serial position effect in free recall', *Journal of Experimental Psychology*, 64, pp. 482–8.

Newell, A. and Simon, H. A. (1932) *Human Problem Solving*, Prentice-Hall, Eaglewood Cliffs, New Jersey.

Newman, O. (1976) *Design Guidelines for Creating Defensible Space*, National Institute of Law Enforcement and Criminal Justice, US Department of Justice, Washington DC.

Newson, J. and E. (1965) *Patterns of Infant Care in an Urban Community*, Pelican.

Oborne, D. J. (1983) 'Cognitive effects of passive smoking', *Ergonomics*, 26, pp. 1163–71.

Olds, J. and Milner, P. (1954) 'Positive reinforcement produced by electrical stimulation of the septal area and other regions of the rat brain', *J. Comp. Physiol Psychol.*, 47, pp. 419–27.

Patterson, F. (1979) 'Conversation with a gorilla', *National Geographic*, 154(4), pp. 438–65.

Patterson, G. R., Littman, R. A. and Bricker, W. A. (1967) 'Assertive behaviour in children: A step towards a theory of aggression', *Monographs of the Society for Research in Child Development*, serial no. 113.

Patton, R. G. and Garner, L. I. (1963) *Growth Failure and Maternal Deprivation*, C. C. Thomas.

Pavlov, I. P. (1927) *Conditioned Reflexes*, Oxford University Press.

Pennington, D. (1986) *Essential Social Psychology*, Arnold.

Perrin, S. and Spencer, C. (1980) 'The Asch Effect – A child of its time?', *Bulletin of The British Psychological Society*, 33, pp. 405–6.

Peterson, L. and Peterson, M. (1959) 'Short term retention of individual items', *Journal of Experimental Psychology*, 58, pp. 193–8.

Pettigrew, T. (1958) 'Regional differences in anti-negro prejudice', *J. Abn. and Soc. Psy.*, 59, pp. 28–56.

Pettigrew, T. F., Allport, G. W. and Barnett, E. O. (1958) 'Binocular resolution and perception of race in South Africa', *Brit J. Psychol.*, 49, p. 265.

Piaget, J. (1954) *The Origins of Intelligence*, Routledge and Kegan Paul.

Piaget, J. and Inhelder, B. (1956) *The Child's Conception of Space*, Routledge and Kegan Paul.

Piaget, J. and Inhelder, B. (1956) *The Child's Conception of Space*, Routledge and Kegan Paul.

Piaget, J. and Inhelder, B. (1972) *Memory and Intelligence*, Basic Books.

Postman, L. and Brown, D. R. (1952) 'The perceptual consequences of success and failure', *J. Abn. Soc. Psychol.*, 47, p. 213.

Postman, L. and Bruner, J. S. (1948) 'Perception under stress', *Psychol. Rev.*, 55, p. 314.

Postman, L. and Crutchfield, R. S. (1952) 'The interaction of need, set and stimulus – structure in a cognitive first', *Amer. J. Psychol.*, 65, p. 196.

Postman, L., Bruner, J. S. and McGuiness, E. (1948) 'Personal values in selective factors in perception', *J. Abn. Soc. Psychol.*, 43, p. 142.

Riesen, A. N. (1950) 'Arrested vision', *Sci. Amer.*, offprint no. 408.

Robertson, J. and Robertson, J. (1967) *Young Children in Brief Separation: I, Kate Aged Two Years Five Months in Fostercare for 27 Days*. Tavistock Child Development Research Unit.

Robertson, J. and Robertson, J. (1967) *Young Children in Brief Separation: II, Jane Aged Seventeen Months in Fostercare for Ten Days*, Tavistock Child Development Research Unit.

Roe, A. (1952) 'A Psychologist Examines sixty-four Eminent Scientists' in Vernon, P. E. (ed.) *Creativity*, Penguin.

Rogers, C. R. (1961) *On Becoming a Person*, Houghton Mifflin, Boston.

Rokeach, M. (1960) *The Open and Closed Mind*, Basic Books.

Rose, S. (1976) *The Conscious Brain*, Pelican.

Rose, S., Lewontin, R. C, and Kamin L. J. (1984) *Not in Our Genes*, Penguin.

Rosen, B. C. and D'Andrade, R. G. (1959) 'The psychosocial origin of achievement motivation', *Sociometry*, 22, pp. 185–218.

Rosenman, R. H., Brand, R. J and others (1975) 'Coronary heart disease in the Western Collaborative Group Study: Final follow up experience of 8½ years', *JAMA*, 233, pp. 872–7.

Rosenthal, R. (1966) *Experimenter Effects in Behavioural Research*, Appleton.

Rosenthal, R. and Jacobson, L. (1968) *Pygmalion in the Classroom: Teacher Expectations and Pupils' Intellectual Development*, Holt, Rinehart and Winston.

Rosenzweig, M. R., Love, W. and Bennett, E. L. (1965) *Physiology and Behaviour*, vol. 3, pp. 819–25.

Rothbart, M. K. and Maccoby, E. E. (1966) 'Parents' differential reactions to sons and daughters', *Journal of Personality and Social Psychology*, 3, pp. 237–43.

Russell, W. R. and Nathan, P. W. (1946) 'Traumatic amnesia', *Brain*, 69, pp. 280–300.

Rutter, M. (1972) *Maternal Deprivation Reassessed*, Penguin.

Saario, T. N., Jacklin, C. N. and Tittle, C. K. (1973) 'Sex-role stereotyping in the public schools', *Harvard Educational Review*, 43, pp. 386–416.

Salame and Baddeley, A. D. (1982) 'Disruption of short term memory by unattended speech: Implications for the structure of working memory', *Journal of Verbal Learning and Verbal Behaviour*, 21, pp. 156–64.

Sander, L. W. (1969) 'Regulation and organisation in the early infant-caretaker system', in Robinson, R. (ed.), *Brain and Early Behaviour*, Academic Press.

Schachter, S. and Singer, J. E. (1962) 'Cognitive, social and physiological determinants of emotional state', *Psychological Review*, 69, pp. 379–99.

Schafer, R. and Murphy, G. (1943) 'The role of autism in a visual figure/ground relationship', *J. Exper. Psychol.*, 32, p. 335.

Schaffer, H. R. and Emerson, P. E. (1964) 'The development of social attachments in infancy', *Monograph of the Society for Research in Child Development*, 29.

Schaffer, R. (1977) *Mothering*, Fontana/Open Books.

Schiller, P. H. (1952) 'Innate constituents of complex responses in primates', in Riopelle, A. J. (ed) (1967) *Animal Problem Solving*, Penguin.

Schlosberg, A. (1952) 'The description of facial expressions in terms of two dimensions', *Journal of Experimental Psychology*, 44, pp. 229–37.

Schneider, D. J., Hastorf, A. M. and Ellsworth, P. C., *Person Perception*, Addison Wesley.

Sears, R. R., Maccoby, E. E. and Levin, H. (1957) *Patterns of Child Rearing*, Evanston: Row, Peterson.

Seeleman, V. (1940) 'The Influence of attitude upon the remembering of visual material', *Arch. Psychol.*, no. 258.

Segall, M. H., Campbell, D. T. and Herskovitz, M. J. (1963) 'Cultural differences in the perception of geometric illusions', *Science*, 139, pp. 769–71.

Seligman, M. (1975) *Helplessness*, San Francisco, Freeman.

Selye, H. (1979) *The Stress of Life*, Van Nostrand Reinhold, New York.

Sherif, M. (1966) *The Psychology of Social Norms*, Harper and Row.

Sherif, M. and Shefir, C. W. (1956) *An Outline of Social Psychology* (2nd edn), Harper and Row.

Sherrington, C. (1906) *The Integrative Action of the Nervous System*, Yale University Press.

Skeels, H. M. (1966) 'Adult status of children with contrasting early life experiences', *Monograph Social Research into Child Development*, 46.

Skinner, B. F. (1938) *Science of Human Behaviour*, Macmillan.

Slater, A., Mattock, A., and Brown, E. (1990) 'Size constancy at birth: Newborn infant's responses to retinal and real size', *Journal of Experimental Child Psychology*.

Sluckin, W. (1972) *Imprinting and Early Learning*, Methuen.

Smith, C. and Lloyd, B. B. (1978) 'Maternal behaviour and perceived sex of infant: Revisited', *Child Development*, 49, pp. 1263–5.

Smith, P. K., and Cowie, H. (1988) *Understanding Childrens' Development*, Basil Blackwell.

Spearman, C. (1904) 'General intelligence objectively determined and measured', *Am. J. Psychol.*, 15, pp. 201–93.

Spitz, R. A. (1945) 'Hospitalism: an inquiry into the genesis of psychiatric conditions in early childhood', *Psychoanal. Stud. Child*, 1, pp. 53–74.

Stern, D. N. (1977) *The First Relationship: Infant and Mother*, Fontana/Open Books.

Stratton, G. M. (1897), described in Gregory, R. L. (1977) *Eye and Brain* (3rd edn), Weidenfeld and Nicolson.

Stumpf, H. and Jackson, N. (1994) *Personality and Individual Differences*, 17.

Taylor, H. (1970) 'Experiments in intergroup discrimination', *Sci. Amer.*, 223, pp. 96–102.

Thorndike, E. L. (1911) *The Fundamentals of Learning*, College Bureau of Publications, 1932.

Thouless, R. H. (1932) 'Individual differences in phenomenal regression', *British Journal of Psychology*, 22, pp. 216–41.

Thurstone, L. L. (1938) 'Primary mental abilities', *Psychometric Monographs*, no. 1, University of Chicago Press.

Tinbergen, N. (1952) 'The curious behaviour of the stickleback', *Scientific American*, 187(no. 6, Dec.), pp. 22–6.

Tolman, E. C. (1948) 'Principles of purposive behaviour', in S. Koch (ed.), *Psychology: A Study of a Science*, McGraw-Hill.

Trevarthen, C. (1974) 'Conversations with a two-month old', *New Scientist*, 2 May.

Vernon, M. D. (1962) *The Psychology of Perception*, Penguin.

Vernon, P. E. (1972) *Intelligence and Cultural Environment*, Methuen.

Walker, S. (1984) *Learning Theory and Behaviour Modification*, Methuen.

Waters, E., Wippman, J. and Sroufe, L. A. (1979) 'Attachment, positive affect, and competence in the peer group: Two studies in construct validation', *Child Development*, 50, pp. 821–9.

Watson, J. B. (1925) *Behaviourism*, Norton.

Weinreich-Haste, H. (1984) 'A multiplicity of intelligence', *New Scientist*, June, p. 19.

Whiting, J. W. M. and Child, I. L. (1957) *Child Training and Personality*, Yale University Press.

Winterbottom, M. R. (1953) *The Relation of Childhood Training in Independence to Achievement Motivation*, University of Michigan, 5113.

Witkin, H. A., Dyk, R. B., Faterson, H. F., Goodenough, D. K. and Karp, S. A. (1962) *Psychological Differentiaton*, Wiley.

Wittrock, M. and Carter, J. (1975) 'Generative processing of Hierarchically organised words', *American Journal of Psychology*, 88, pp. 489–502.

Zajonc, R. B. (1965) 'Social facilitation', *Science*, 149, pp. 269–74.

Zimbardo, P. G. (1970) 'The human choice: Individuation, reason and order versus deindividuation, impulse and chaos', in Arnold, W. J. and Levien, D. (eds), *Nebraska Symposium on Motivation (1969)*, University of Nebraska Press.

Zimbardo, P. G. (1979) *Psychology and Life* (10th edn), Scott, Foresman & Co.

Index